Teaching Social Communication to Children with Autism

A Practitioner's Guide to Parent Training

Brooke Ingersoll
Anna Dvortcsak

THE GUILFORD PRESS
New York   London

© 2010 The Guilford Press
A Division of Guilford Publications, Inc.
72 Spring Street, New York, NY 10012
www.guilford.com

All rights reserved

Except as indicated, no part of this book may be reproduced, translated, stored in a retrieval system, or
transmitted, in any form or by any means, electronic, mechanical, photocopying, microfilming, recording,
or otherwise, without written permission from the publisher.

Printed in the United States of America

This book is printed on acid-free paper.

Last digit is print number: 9   8   7   6   5   4   3   2   1

LIMITED PHOTOCOPY LICENSE

These materials are intended for use only by qualified professionals.

The publisher grants to individual purchasers of this book nonassignable permission to reproduce
materials in Appendix A. This license is limited to you, the individual purchaser, for personal use
or use with individual clients. This license does not grant the right to reproduce these materials
for resale, redistribution, electronic display, or any other purposes (including but not limited to
books, pamphlets, articles, video- or audiotapes, blogs, file-sharing sites, Internet or intranet sites,
and handouts or slides for lectures, workshops, webinars, or therapy groups, whether or not a fee is
charged). Permission to reproduce these materials for these and any other purposes must be obtained
in writing from the Permissions Department of Guilford Publications.

Library of Congress Cataloging-in-Publication Data

Ingersoll, Brooke.
    Teaching social communication to children with autism : a practitioner's guide to parent training /
Brooke Ingersoll and Anna Dvortcsak.
        p.   cm.
    Part of a packaged 2-book set, which includes the manual for parents, plus DVD.
    Includes bibliographical references and index.
    ISBN 978-1-60623-441-9 (pbk. : alk. paper)
    1. Developmentally disabled children—Language.   2. Autistic children.   3. Autistic children—
Language.   4. Social skills in children—Study and teaching.   I. Dvortcsak, Anna.   II. Title.
    HV891.I485 2010
    649′.152—dc22

                                                                                    2009032678

This manual and DVD are available only as part of a package (ISBN 978-1-60623-442-6) comprising one
Practitioner's Guide to Parent Training with DVD and one *Manual for Parents* (ISBN 978-1-60623-440-2).

About the Authors

Brooke Ingersoll, PhD, is a psychologist and board-certified behavior analyst with a doctoral degree in experimental psychology from the University of California, San Diego. She completed a postdoctoral fellowship in clinical child psychology at the Child Development and Rehabilitation Center at Oregon Health and Science University, Portland, during which time she served as codirector of the Autism Treatment and Research Program at the Hearing and Speech Institute (now known as the Artz Center) in Portland, Oregon. Dr. Ingersoll is currently Assistant Professor of Psychology at Michigan State University, East Lansing. She has conducted training for practitioners on early intervention strategies for children with autism spectrum disorders both nationally and internationally. Dr. Ingersoll has published extensively on early intervention for children with autism spectrum disorders and presented her work at professional conferences.

Anna Dvortcsak, MS, CCC-SLP, is a speech–language pathologist in private practice in Portland, Oregon. She received her master's degree from the University of Redlands, California. Mrs. Dvortcsak provides training to families with children with autism and individualized speech and language services. She specializes in training professionals in conducting parent training for young children with autism spectrum disorders. Prior to starting her own practice, Mrs. Dvortcsak was codirector of the Autism Treatment and Research Program at the Hearing and Speech Institute (now known as the Artz Center) in Portland. She has experience conducting research on the efficacy of interventions for children with autism and has presented her findings at the annual conventions of the American Speech–Language–Hearing Association and the Oregon Speech and Hearing Association, as well as in peer-reviewed articles and chapters.

Preface

This book and its companion materials provide a comprehensive parent training curriculum developed specifically for families of young children with autism spectrum disorder (ASD). It is designed for use with children at the time of their earliest diagnosis to about age 6, and has also been used with older children with significant language delays (up to age 12). The curriculum provides practitioners with a step-by-step guide for teaching families to use naturalistic intervention strategies to enhance their child's social engagement, language, imitation, and play skills within meaningful activities and daily caretaking routines. The content may also be appropriate for children with other diagnoses who exhibit primary difficulties with social communication. The curriculum is designed to be taught by professionals working with families who have children with ASD, including special educators, speech–language pathologists, occupational therapists, social workers, psychologists, and behavioral specialists. As described in more detail in Part I of this volume, the parent training program offered here is a unique integration of intervention techniques drawn from the developmental and behavioral literature and placed within a parent training model. It has been shown to be effective for increasing social-communication skills in young children with ASD and related disorders (see Ingersoll & Dvortcsak, 2006).

This parent training program is the result of 5 years of development and implementation with over 200 families and schools across Oregon and Michigan. This program was originally designed to be conducted by clinicians in a one-to-one setting with the child and parent at the Artz Center (formally Hearing and Speech Institute) in Portland, Oregon. Through our collaborations with the Statewide Regional Program Autism Training Sites (RPATS), sponsored by Portland State University and the Oregon Department of Education, a group training component was added that allows the program to be conducted in early childhood special education classrooms. This group program is currently being used by model early intervention program sites throughout Oregon and Michigan. Detailed guidelines for conducting parent training in both individual and group formats are contained in this volume.

This comprehensive parent training program includes the following:

- A trainer manual, which covers how to conduct the program in individual and group modalities, provides all necessary forms and materials, and includes a guide to the accompanying DVD.

- An accompanying DVD, which contains PowerPoint slides for group presentation and video clips of parents using techniques with their children, also primarily for use in training groups.
- A parent manual, which is appropriate for either the individual or group program.

Trainer Manual

This book provides practitioners with necessary background information and detailed procedures for conducting the program with parents of young children with ASD. Part I presents the rationale and research support and describes the overall program, including the core social-communication skills targeted, the strategies used to teach children these skills, and the strategies used to train parents. The practicalities of planning and implementing a parent training program are also covered. Part II provides a step-by-step guide to conducting an individual parent training program. Organized into 24 sessions, it trains parents in 14 intervention techniques that build sequentially on each other. The program is designed for practitioners working with families one-to-one in a home or clinic setting. Part III provides a step-by-step guide to conducting parent training in a group format. This version of the program teaches parents the same 14 techniques but is organized into six group sessions alternating with six individual sessions for one-to-one coaching. This format is appropriate for practitioners who serve children primarily in a classroom or other group setting. Group sessions are taught with the visual aids of PowerPoint slides and video clips showing parents using techniques with their children. Part III includes thumbnail images of each slide and provides a suggested script of the important points for trainers to cover during group presentations. Both slides and video clips are contained on the accompanying DVD (see more below). Appendix A of the book contains copies of all supporting forms used in both individual and group versions of the program, including assessment and other data collection materials. Program purchasers are granted permission to reproduce the forms for use with families.

DVD and DVD Guide

The DVD at the back of this book includes the PowerPoint slide programs for the six group sessions detailed in Part III. Because parents attend group sessions without their children, the DVD also provides video examples of parents using the teaching techniques with their children. Appendix B explains the DVD's contents and how to use it in more detail.

Parent Manual

The accompanying parent manual is designed for use by parents in either the individual or group program. Briefly and clearly, it describes the purpose and procedures for each of the 14 intervention techniques. The manual includes illustrations and homework practice sheets. Additional copies of the parent manual may be purchased separately.

Throughout this book and the parent manual, we use the term *parent* to refer to all adults who are involved in the care of a child with ASD. However, we recognize that there are other caregivers who participate in parent training programs for children with autism, including step-parents, grandparents, other extended family members, as well as foster parents. Except for the trainer scripts in Part III, we use the pronoun "she" to refer to the parent and practitioner and "he" to refer to the child with ASD. This convention is used to maintain clarity and consistency throughout the text rather than to indicate a specific gender.

Acknowledgments

The parent training program presented in this manual has been influenced by the work of a number of pioneers in the field of parent training for children with ASD and other developmental disabilities, including Laura Schreibman, Robert Koegel, Ann Kaiser, Gerald Mahoney, and James MacDonald, as well as the Hanen Centre, Toronto, Ontario.

This program is the result of 5 years of development and implementation with over 200 families and multiple early intervention sites across Oregon and Michigan. Development of this program would not have been possible without the support of the many families who participated in the parent training program; the Hearing and Speech Institute in Portland, Oregon; Portland State University; and the Oregon Department of Education. We would especially like to thank the families who participated in the development of the DVD and who provided feedback to improve the quality of the parent training program. We would also like to thank Donald Rushmer, Executive Director at the Hearing and Speech Institute (now the Artz Center), for his continued support of the development of the parent training program; Claudia Meyer and Erica Steele, speech and language pathologists, who provided feedback throughout the development of the program and helped pilot the individual parent training program; Joel Arick, professor at Portland State University, for his support and feedback in the development of the group parent training program and help with dissemination; and Corey Hiskey for the DVD. We are also grateful to the staff at Northwest Regional Education Service District, Oregon, for piloting the group parent training program. A special thanks to Nancy Ford, program director; Sheila Magee, program coordinator; Karen Shepard, autism specialist; Debbie Sullivan, speech and language pathologist; Donna Hamilton, occupational therapist; and Krista Branson and Laura Lindley, classroom teachers. Finally, we would like to thank our editors at The Guilford Press, Rochelle Serwator and Barbara Watkins, for their insightful comments on the presentation of these materials.

Brooke Ingersoll: I am especially grateful for the training and support I received from Laura Schreibman throughout my graduate training. Much of this program would not have been possible without it. Thanks to my husband, Mark Becker, for his continued support, both personal and professional, throughout the development of this program. I would also like to thank my parents, Sheila Most and Warren Ingersoll, for their guidance and encouragement, and my beautiful daughter, Annabel, for inspiration.

Anna Dvortcsak: I would like to thank my wonderful family and friends for their support and patience during the writing of this manual. Special thanks to my husband, Alexey, for his continued encouragement, patience, and editing skills—I couldn't have done this without you; to my mother, Suzanne Kuerschner, for being a role model, encouraging me to work with children with autism, and taking time to read draft materials and provide feedback; and to my sisters, Vivian Kuerschner and Carrie MacLaren, and my father, Erich Kuerschner, for helping me maintain my sanity during the writing process.

Contents

PART III

Group Parent Training Program Session Guidelines

APPENDIX A

Reproducible Materials for the Individual and Group Training Formats

APPENDIX B

DVD Guide

PART I

An Introduction to Parent Training

Chapter 1

Training Parents
of Young Children with ASD

AN OVERVIEW

Autism spectrum disorders (ASD) are lifelong developmental disabilities that appear during the first 3 years of life. Individuals with ASD have pervasive deficits in social interaction and communication skills, and they exhibit inflexible and repetitive behaviors that interfere with learning and disrupt family life (American Psychiatric Association, 2000). Children with ASD may exhibit unusual sensory responses to the environment and behavioral difficulties, such as tantrums and aggression. The majority of children with ASD also exhibit delays in cognitive and adaptive functioning (Schreibman, 1988). Because ASD exist along a spectrum, the number of behaviors exhibited and the severity of the behaviors vary considerably among children.

The prognosis for individuals with ASD has historically been very poor, with the majority of adults unable to live independently or participate fully in the community (Howlin, Goode, Hutton, & Rutter, 2004). However, treatment advances in the past 30 years have improved the prognosis of individuals with ASD considerably, especially when they are identified at a young age and intensive treatment is begun early in life (Turner, Stone, Pozdol, & Coonrod, 2006). In the meantime, the past 15–20 years have seen a dramatic increase in the number of children diagnosed with ASD. Part of this increase is due to increased awareness, along with the development of more sophisticated diagnostic instruments and screening tools. The improvement in diagnostic practices for ASD has reduced the average age at first diagnosis from school age to 3 years of age (Mandell, Novak, & Zubritsky, 2005). Even children as young as 2 years old can be reliably diagnosed with ASD (Charman & Baird, 2002). Almost 6 in 1,000 preschool-age children are affected by some form of ASD (Chakrabarti & Fombonne, 2005). The increase in early diagnosis has left many intervention providers with the question of how best to treat the youngest children with ASD.

The Rationale for Parent Training

At the request of the U.S. Department of Education, a National Research Council (NRC) panel completed a thorough review of scientific, theoretical, and policy literature regarding the education of young children with ASD. The NRC (2001) recommended interventions for young children with ASD that focus on functional and spontaneous communication, deliver social instruction throughout the day, use specific and effective methods for teaching new skills, and support generalization and maintenance of skills in natural contexts. Experts agree that curricula for children with ASD should be designed to address deficits in communication, language, and social interactions.

Because the educational needs of children with ASD are significant, the NRC (2001) further recommended that "educational services should include a minimum of 25 hours a week, 12 months a year, in which the child is engaged in systematically planned, developmentally appropriate educational activity aimed toward identified objectives" (p. 220). These educational requirements make it a challenge to provide effective intervention for children with ASD within a cost-effective public program. At the same time, growing numbers of children are qualifying for special education services under the ASD eligibility criterion, and school districts are hard-pressed to provide the level of intensity required to educate these toddlers and preschool-age students. The majority of publicly funded early intervention (EI) or early childhood special education (ECSE) programs have difficulty meeting the recommended number of hours (Hume, Bellini, & Pratt, 2005). In response, many families seek additional private services at a substantial financial burden. However, private services are also limited in the number of hours of intervention that they typically provide for an individual child per week. For example, private speech–language, occupational therapy, and mental health services are rarely conducted more than twice a week for an hour. Even more intensive private programs, such as home-based early intensive behavioral intervention models, are limited in the number of children they can serve, leaving many children on waiting lists for services for a significant amount of time. Thus, even with the addition of private therapy, two-thirds of families report receiving fewer than 25 hours per week of intervention for their children with ASD (Hume et al., 2005). Many other families wish to pursue private services but are unable to do so, due to the expense or to a lack of services in their community.

Parent training is a way to increase the intervention hours a child with ASD receives and improve long-term outcomes. Experts agree that parent training is an important component in the treatment of children with ASD (NRC, 2001). The importance of teaching parents to serve as intervention agents for their children with ASD was first highlighted by Lovaas, Koegel, Simmons, and Long (1973). They noted that children with ASD who received intensive early intervention—and returned to homes where parents were prepared to support their learning—maintained their treatment gains better than children who were returned to institutionalized settings that did not carry over the treatment methods.

Defining Effective Parent Training

In working with young children with ASD, most practitioners are called upon to help parents teach and interact with their children. Thus most practitioners have already provided parent training in some manner. In our experience, most parent training that occurs within school programs and in the private sector is informal. Informal parent training typically involves providing information and suggestions to a family in the course of a conversation about a child, referring the family to books or handouts written for parents on the topic, and/or encouraging a parent to observe while the practitioner works with the child. Although all of these strategies are appropriate in certain situations, they have not, by themselves, been shown to produce significant changes in parent behavior.

Even workshops are limited in their ability to improve parent–child interactions, if they do not also include a formal coaching component. For example, Kaiser, Hemmeter, Ostrosky, Alpert, and Hancock (1995) examined the effectiveness of a group instruction model for teaching parents to use Milieu Teaching, a naturalistic behavioral intervention, to increase language skills in their preschool-age children with disabilities. The study found that after eight group instruction sessions, parents showed modest gains but did not reach criterion-level performance in their use of the intervention techniques. However, after receiving intensive feedback and coaching in the home, most parents achieved criterion-level performance, and their children learned the target language skills. This study suggests that although providing information about intervention techniques to parents may provide some benefit, hands-on coaching with feedback is necessary to achieve significant parent learning and gains in child skills. The research also indicates that for parent training to be effective, it should involve parent-selected goals or targets for the child (Brookman-Frazee, 2004), systematic instruction in intervention strategies for the parent (Mahoney et al., 1999), practice with coaching and feedback (Kaiser, Hemmeter, et al., 1995), and ongoing support and problem solving (NRC, 2001). The parent training program described in this book uses all of these research-tested formal parent training procedures. To provide this level and quality of parent training requires a significant amount of work on the part of the practitioner; however, the results are worth the effort.

Research on Parent Training in ASD

A growing body of literature demonstrates that parent training is an effective intervention model for young children with ASD (McConachie & Diggle, 2007; for a list of its benefits, see Table 1.1). Research indicates that parents can learn to use developmental (Aldred, Green, & Adams, 2004; Mahoney & Perales, 2003) and behavioral (Kaiser, Hancock, & Nietfeld, 2000; Koegel, Bimbela, & Schreibman, 1996) intervention strategies with their children with ASD, with a high degree of fidelity. Parents' use of these strategies results in children's increased frequency of verbalizations and spontaneous speech (Gillett & LeBlanc, 2007; Laski, Charlop, & Schreibman, 1988), increased use of target utterances (Kaiser et al., 2000), and better language development (Drew et al., 2002). It also results in improved social interaction (Aldred et al., 2004; Mahoney & Perales, 2003), joint attention (Rocha, Schreibman, & Stahmer, 2007), imitation (Ingersoll & Gergans, 2007), and play skills (Gillett & LeBlanc, 2007) in the children with ASD.

Table 1.1. Benefits of Parent Training in ASD

- Parents can learn to implement strategies with a high degree of fidelity.
- Results include better generalization and maintenance of skills.
- Parent training increases parents' leisure/recreation time.
- It increases parents' optimism about their children's future.
- It decreases parents' stress levels.
- It is cost-effective.
- Parents perceive it as the most effective practice contributing to development of their children.

Research has indicated that parent training is time- and cost-effective, and that it leads to better generalization and maintenance than therapist-implemented intervention models do (Koegel, Schreibman, Britten, Burke, & O'Neill, 1982). For example, one early study compared the effects of training parents to implement behavior therapy with their children to the effects of therapist-implemented intervention (Koegel et al., 1982). Parents in the parent training group received 5 hours a week of training with their children until they mastered the intervention, which took between 25 and 50 hours. The clinic treatment group received 4½ hours of treatment per week for a year, totaling roughly 225 hours.

Treatment gains were assessed as the numbers of appropriate behaviors (play, speech, and social behavior) and inappropriate behaviors (tantrums, self-stimulation, noncooperation) each child exhibited during a structured play observation with the therapist and a parent. Results indicated that although children in both groups made similar gains when observed with the treatment provider (therapist or parent), the children in the parent training group made considerably more gains with their parents—the people with whom the children spent the majority of their time. In addition, unstructured home observations indicated that the children in the parent training group were more likely to respond appropriately to parent questions and directions.

Another randomized study examined the effects of a developmental parent training program that focused on increasing joint attention and joint action routines in young children with ASD, compared to local services only (Drew et al., 2002). Results indicated that children in the parent training group exhibited better language comprehension as measured by the MacArthur Communication Development Index (Fenson et al., 1993), a parent report language assessment, and better overall language as measured by the *Autism Diagnostic Inventory—Revised* (Lord, Rutter, & Le Couteur, 1994), a diagnostic parent interview, than the children in the local-services-only group—despite the fact that the local-services-only group received more hours of formal intervention.

Parent training also improves the quality of life for a family by reducing parental stress (Moes, 1995; Smith, Buch, & Gamby, 2000; Tonge et al., 2006) and increasing parental leisure and recreation time (Koegel et al., 1982). This is particularly important, as research suggests that the stress of having a child with ASD affects most aspects of family life (DeMyer & Goldberg, 1983) and is greater than the stress of having a child with other developmental disabilities or chronic illnesses (Bouma & Schweitzer, 1990; Dumas, Wolf, Fisman, & Culligan, 1991; Koegel et al., 1992). Furthermore, parents who participate in parent training programs report more optimism about their own ability to influence their children's development (Koegel et al., 1982), which may help parents maintain their efforts with their children over time (NRC, 2001).

Given these benefits, all of the model ASD programs reviewed by the NRC include a formal parent training component, regardless of their intervention philosophy. This fact led the NRC to recommend:

> As part of local educational programs and intervention programs for children from birth to age 3, families of children with autistic spectrum disorders should be provided the opportunity to learn techniques for teaching their child new skills and reducing problem behaviors. These opportunities should include not only didactic sessions, but also ongoing consultation in which individualized problem-solving, including in-home observations or training, occur for a family, as needed, to support improvements at home as well as at school. (2001, p. 216)

These benefits are also recognized by parents, who report parent training to be the most effective practice in contributing to the development of their children with ASD (Hume et al., 2005).

Taken together, the research suggests that parent training is an effective and efficient method of providing early intervention for young children with ASD. The use of parent training for children with ASD allows for an increase in the number of hours of intervention a child receives per week, without an increase in the number of hours of direct intervention provided by professionals. Providing high-quality, intensive parent training, and asking parents to provide 10 hours a week of intervention to their children (as is typically done in many of the lab schools and model private programs reviewed by the NRC), may help parents and practitioners to work together to provide a greater number of hours of intervention to children with ASD. In addition, parent training may provide a "jump start" for families who are on waiting lists for more intensive services. More importantly, teaching parents to use these techniques maximizes children's learning by increasing generalization and maintenance of skills over time. Thus parent training can and should be considered a primary intervention strategy (Mahoney et al., 1999). However, it should not be considered an *alternative* to intensive services.

Obstacles to Parent Training

Despite the fact that parent training is now considered an essential component of successful intervention programs for children with ASD (NRC, 2001), formal parent training programs are still the exception in community-based treatment programs for young children with ASD (Hume et al., 2005). One obstacle is logistics. For example, most empirically based parent training models are conducted individually with a parent, child, and parent educator once or twice a week over many months (e.g., Aldred et al., 2004; Kaiser et al., 2000; Mahoney & Perales, 2003; Wetherby & Woods, 2006). However, early childhood special education for children with ASD over 3 years of age is typically provided in a classroom setting, which allows very little time for teachers to meet individually with the parent and child. It is difficult for most administrators and/ or practitioners serving children with ASD in a classroom setting to envision using parent training within their programs. We have included in this volume guidelines for both individual and group parent training formats, to help facilitate parent training in a variety of service delivery models. In Chapter 3, we also describe how to adapt our parent training program for classroom-based toddler groups.

A second obstacle to parent training is a philosophy that professionals should be solely responsible for providing intervention to children with ASD. This position may stem from the belief that specialists have a unique set of skills that allow them to serve children with ASD better than their parents can, or that parent training creates a role conflict for parents. It may also stem from concerns about placing any further burden on the parents or implicitly blaming parents for their children's difficulties. None of these views has been supported by the research (Mahoney et al., 1999). Rather, the research indicates that parents can learn to provide intervention to their children with a high degree of procedural fidelity (e.g., Kaiser et al., 2000), and that in most cases, parent training leads to a decrease rather than an increase in parental stress (Moes, 1995; Smith et al., 2000; Tonge et al., 2006). Thus some program administrators and professionals may need to reconsider their philosophies in light of the research. In some cases, parents may also hold these views, although most research suggests that parents report a strong desire to receive training in techniques for working with their children (Hume et al., 2005; Whitaker, 2002). When professionals offer to work with parents to meet the parents' own goals for their children, parents often become more receptive (Brookman-Frazee, 2004).

A final obstacle is that specialists working with children with ASD are rarely trained how to teach parents. Most practitioners who provide ASD services have been trained to work with children, not adults, and lack knowledge about how to teach parents specific skills (Mahoney et al., 1999; McCollum, 1999). To address this obstacle, this program includes a detailed description of strategies for teaching parents to use intervention techniques with their children.

Overview of Project ImPACT

The Project ImPACT (Improving Parents as Communication Teachers) parent training curriculum teaches families of young children with ASD (up to about age 6) how to use a combination of developmental and behavioral strategies to increase their children's social-communication skills during daily activities and routines. In this section, we first discuss the theoretical and empirical foundations of Project ImPACT, and describe how it compares with other training programs for parents of young children with ASD. Next, we describe the four core social-communication skills addressed by the program and the importance of teaching them to children with ASD. These skills are social engagement, language, social imitation, and play. Then we highlight the specific intervention techniques that parents are trained to use with their children. This curriculum provides trainers with the option of teaching these techniques to parents in either an individual or a group format. Finally, we provide a more detailed description of these formats.

Theoretical and Empirical Foundations

Most current parent training models for children with ASD are either developmental or behavioral in philosophy and approach. Project ImPACT offers a unique integration of these two approaches, based on research indicating the importance of early affective relationships (Stern, 1985) as well as of environmental contingencies in the development of social communication (Skinner, 1957). Project ImPACT is based on the following guiding principles: Intervention is naturalistic; typical development is used to guide selection of treatment targets; social communication develops through affect-laden interactions with responsive caregivers; and techniques are based on applied behavior analysis. These principles are listed in Table 1.2. We discuss each of them in more detail below.

Table 1.2. Guiding Principles of Project ImPACT

- Intervention is naturalistic (i.e., parents should be able to implement intervention within daily routines and activities).
- Typical development is used to guide selection of treatment targets.
- Children learn social communication through affect-laden interactions with responsive caregivers.
- Techniques are based on applied behavior analysis.

Intervention Is Naturalistic

A *naturalistic* approach means that a parent should be able to implement intervention with a child within the context of daily routines and activities. Research indicates that naturalistic teaching strategies often lead to better generalization and maintenance of skills than more structured teaching approaches do (Charlop-Christy & Carpenter, 2000; Delprato, 2001; McGee, Krantz, & McClannahan, 1985; Miranda-Linné & Melin, 1992). Naturalistic approaches also appear to be superior for teaching spontaneous social-communication skills (Schwartz, Anderson, & Halle, 1989). Although more highly structured teaching approaches are effective for children with ASD (NRC, 2001), they require a distraction-free teaching environment, the use of specific adult-selected teaching materials, repeated teaching drills, and often the use of artificial reinforcers (Schreibman & Ingersoll, 2005). Naturalistic teaching approaches, in contrast, are designed to be implemented within regular caregiving routines. This means that parents can use them throughout the day with their children with ASD without having to set aside significant time to conduct teaching drills. This aspect greatly increases the likelihood that parents will use the intervention (Schreibman & Ingersoll, 2005).

In addition, these approaches are similar to natural adult–child interactions, which makes them more acceptable to parents (Schreibman, Kaneko, & Koegel, 1991). Indeed, studies have found that parents who have been trained to implement these techniques exhibit more positive affect while teaching their children (Schreibman et al., 1991), and that both the parents and children exhibit more happiness and interest and less stress during family interactions (Koegel et al., 1996) than families in which the parents have been trained to implement highly structured behavioral techniques. These findings suggest that a naturalistic approach is easier for parents to implement, is more enjoyable for parents and children, and leads to a more positive family interaction style than structured approaches. For this reason, Project ImPACT utilizes naturalistic teaching procedures and teaches parents how to use these techniques within the context of their daily routines.

Typical Development Is Used to Guide Selection of Treatment Targets

Research indicates that social-communication skills are usually learned in a similar developmental sequence by all children, regardless of their ability (Gerber, 2003). In most areas, children with ASD exhibit delayed rather than deviant skills, and their developmental trajectories follow slower yet similar patterns (Morgan, Cutrer, Coplin, & Rodrigue, 1989; Snow, Hertzig, & Shapiro, 1987). Therefore, typical development is used to guide the selection of child goals. For example, typically developing infants begin using gestures and other nonverbal communicative behaviors prior to using words. Thus, for children with ASD who are nonverbal, parents are encouraged to target gesture use prior to language.

This approach to goal development has significant advantages. First, research suggests that children with ASD are able to learn skills that are appropriate for their developmental age more quickly than skills that are above their developmental age (Lifter, Sulzer-Azaroff, Anderson, & Cowdery, 1993). Second, research indicates that teaching early social-communication skills can lead to increased development of later-emerging behaviors in ASD (Ingersoll & Schreibman, 2006; Whalen, Schreibman, & Ingersoll, 2006). For example, Kasari, Paparella, Freeman, and Jahromi (2008) found that children with autism who received focused teaching in either joint attention or symbolic play had greater gains in expressive language 12 months after the intervention than children in a control group did. These findings suggest that teaching skills within a developmental framework leads to wider-ranging improvement in social communication. For this reason, Project ImPACT teaches early, nonverbal social-communication skills, including gestures, social imitation, and play, in addition to verbal skills.

Social Communication Develops within Affect-Laden Interactions with Responsive Caregivers

Research on typical development indicates a relationship between caregivers' responsiveness and their children's level of social-communication development (Bornstein, Tamis-LeMonda, & Haynes, 1999; Hoff-Ginsburg & Shatz, 1982; Mahoney & Perales, 2003; Prizant, Wetherby, & Rydell, 2000; Siller & Sigman, 2002). Responsiveness is a complex behavior that involves a variety of interactive components, including reciprocity, contingency, affect, and matching the child's developmental level, interests, and behavioral style (Mahoney, 1988; Mahoney, Finger, & Powell, 1985; Mahoney & Powell, 1988). Thus Project ImPACT includes a variety of interactive techniques to increase the parent's responsiveness to the child's behavior. First, the parent follows the child's lead or interest and joins him in his play. Second, the parent uses heightened animation to emphasize emotional expressions and affect sharing. Third, the parent responds to all of the child's communicative attempts as if they were purposeful, including unconventional (e.g., jargon, echolalia, hand leading, nonverbal protests) and preintentional (e.g., reaching and grabbing, eye gaze, crying, facial expressions, body postures) communication. Fourth, the parent adjusts her language to match her child's language abilities (Prizant et al., 2000).

These teaching components are shared by a variety of developmental social-pragmatic and relationship-based interventions, including the developmental, individual-difference, relationship-based (DIR)/floor time (Greenspan & Wieder, 1999); the Denver model (Rogers & DiLalla, 1991; Rogers & Lewis, 1989); responsive teaching (Mahoney & Perales, 2003); the Hanen Centre model (Manolsen, 1992; Sussman, 1999); and the social communication, emotional regulation, and transactional support (SCERTS) model (Prizant, Wetherby, Rubin, Laurent, & Rydell, 2006). Research indicates that these approaches are effective at promoting social engagement (Aldred et al., 2004; Mahoney & Perales, 2003) and language (e.g., Ingersoll, Dvortcsak, Whalen, & Sikora, 2005; McConachie, Randle, Hammel, & Le Couteur, 2005) in children with ASD and other developmental disorders. Project ImPACT teaches parents to use developmental strategies to increase their responsiveness to their children's behavior and to promote social engagement.

Techniques Are Based on Applied Behavior Analysis

Social-communication skills should be taught by using techniques that are firmly grounded in the science of learning; thus Project ImPACT includes teaching techniques that are consistent with applied behavior analysis. Learning theory posits that social-communication skills, like all voluntary behaviors, are developed and maintained by observable environmental events that come before them (antecedents) and after them (consequences). Behavioral teaching involves the manipulation of antecedent events and the systematic application of reinforcement (any consequence that increases the likelihood of the behavior). In addition, it uses such specific teaching tools as prompting (presenting a cue that increases the likelihood of specific response), chaining (linking two or more behaviors together), and fading (gradually decreasing prompts over time to encourage spontaneous responding) (Cooper, Heron, & Heward, 1987).

Behavioral interventions vary considerably in their level of adult-directedness and structure. The behavioral approach used in this program is naturalistic, as noted above. The naturalistic behavioral teaching approach includes the following basic components. First, teaching occurs in the natural environment during ongoing interactions between the child and the parent, such as play and daily routines. Second, the child initiates a teaching episode by indicating interest in an item or activity, at which point the parent provides a teaching trial focused on the child's expressed interest. Third, the parent explicitly prompts the child to produce a target behavior. Fourth, the parent reinforces the child's production of the target behavior with the item or activity of interest (natural reinforcement). Finally, the parent loosely shapes the child's behavior into a more complex response by providing reinforcement for attempts to respond (Delprato, 2001; Kaiser, Yoder, & Keetz, 1992).

These teaching components are shared by a number of other naturalistic behavioral interventions, including incidental teaching (Hart & Risley, 1968; McGee, Krantz, & McClannahan, 1985), milieu teaching (Alpert & Kaiser, 1992), and pivotal response treatment (Koegel & Koegel, 2006). There is strong empirical support for these approaches to teaching social-communication skills—including language (Koegel, O'Dell, & Koegel, 1987), imitation (Ingersoll & Gergans, 2007; Ingersoll, Lewis, & Kroman, 2007; Ingersoll & Schreibman, 2006), and play (Stahmer, 1995; Thorp, Stahmer, & Schreibman, 1995)—to children with ASD and other developmental delays. Therefore, Project ImPACT teaches parents to use naturalistic behavioral teaching techniques to teach their children new language, social imitation, and play skills within ongoing interactions.

Rationale for a Combined Approach

In many ways, the developmental and behavioral approaches are similar in their implementation. They can both be naturalistic and thus conducted within the context of meaningful activities, such as play and daily routines. Teaching follows the child's lead or interest in both approaches, which means that teaching materials and activities are selected by the child. Both approaches also use strategies to elicit initiations from the child, and the reinforcement for the child's communication is natural to the interaction.

At the same time, some critical differences between the approaches may have an impact on their effectiveness for children with ASD. For example, the developmental approach is focused on strategies that increase parent responsiveness and promote social engagement (e.g., Mahoney & Perales, 2003). However, it relies almost exclusively on child initiations to begin a teaching episode. This reliance on child initiations—particularly for children with ASD, who tend to have difficulty initiating—may prevent an adequate number of learning opportunities (Fey, 1986; Warren, Yoder, Gazdag, Kim, & Jones, 1993). Furthermore, without the use of explicit prompts, certain skills that are not presently within a child's repertoire may be very difficult to teach (Quill, 1995). The naturalistic behavioral approach, with its use of direct prompting and systematic reinforcement, is highly effective at teaching novel language, imitation, and play behaviors (e.g., Schreibman & Ingersoll, 2005). However, it does not focus on building social reciprocity with others (Ingersoll, 2009). Thus neither approach is sufficient for addressing the wide-ranging social-communication deficits found in ASD. However, a combined approach that includes the "best of both worlds" is likely to have more success (Ingersoll, 2009; Smith, Rogers, & Dawson, 2007). Given their many similarities, the approaches can be easily integrated with each other within a parent training model, yielding a potentially more powerful social-communication intervention for children with ASD. Unlike other parent training programs, Project ImPACT combines techniques from both developmental and behavioral interventions to promote social engagement and teach children with ASD novel skills in a step-by-step approach. We turn next to the specific social-communication skills the program addresses.

Core Skills to Increase

Social Engagement

One of the defining features of ASD is impairment in social engagement (American Psychiatric Association, 2000). *Social engagement* involves the ability to maintain interactions by responding to and initiating social bids with others. Children with ASD have significant difficulty maintaining interactions with adults and peers (Schreibman, 1988). A key aspect of social engagement is the use of joint attention. *Joint attention* is the ability to coordinate attention between an object and another person for social purposes; it includes showing, sharing, and pointing. Joint attention is a particularly important skill because it is believed to be involved in the development of language skills (Bates, Benigni, Bretherton, Camaioni, & Volterra, 1979). Children with ASD have difficulty both initiating and responding to joint attention bids from others, and it is thought that these deficits may lead to impaired language learning (Loveland & Landry, 1986).

The starting point of this program is to teach the parent to increase her child's social engagement, as it underlies all other social-communication skills. Furthermore, all children are more likely to learn when they are actively engaged. In addition, increasing joint attention in particular and social engagement in general has been shown to improve other social-communication skills, including language, play, and imitation in children with ASD (Kasari, Freeman, & Paparella, 2006; Kasari et al., 2008; Siller & Sigman, 2002; Whalen et al., 2006).

Language

Another defining feature of ASD is a deficit in language (American Psychiatric Association, 2000). Children with ASD have difficulty with all three of the major components of language: content, form, and use (Bloom & Lahey, 1978). Each of these components includes both receptive and expressive abilities. *Content* refers to vocabulary or the understanding of words and their meanings. *Form* includes the grammar and sounds of language, as well as *syntax* (i.e., the rules that govern how we put words in order to make a sentence). *Use* or *pragmatics* refers to reasons why we communicate (e.g., to protest, request, gain attention, maintain attention, label, describe, respond to a question, greet, give a direction, solve a problem, share experiences, and express feelings and interests). Use also involves the social rules that surround our communication (e.g., turn taking, maintaining a topic, the ability to read and use nonverbal cues, physical proximity, and ability to vary aspects of language according to the situation as well as the listener's response and needs).

Children with ASD have particular difficulty with pragmatics or use of language (Rogers & Pennington, 1991), as this is the most abstract component. In addition, their language is often characterized by unusual features, such as echolalia (the nonfunctional repetition of previously heard speech), pronominal reversal, jargon, and idiosyncratic speech (American Psychiatric Association, 2000). Language deficits extend to nonverbal skills, including the use of gestures (Bartak, Rutter, & Cox, 1975).

This program places a heavy emphasis on teaching expressive language skills, including nonverbal language (gestures), and, to a lesser extent, receptive language. It teaches parents strategies to improve *how* their children communicate (content and form) and *why* their children communicate (use). It is focused on teaching *spontaneous* language skills; thus it teaches parents how to adjust the support they provide, in order to avoid dependence on prompts.

Social Imitation

Children with ASD also demonstrate difficulty with imitation skills on a variety of tasks, including object, gesture, vocal, and facial imitation (Smith & Bryson, 1994; Williams, Whiten, & Singh, 2004). Imitation is an early-emerging social-communication strategy (Meltzoff & Moore, 1977) and plays a critical role in the development of other more complex social-communication skills, including language (e.g., Bates et al., 1988), play (Fiese, 1990; Uzgiris, 1991), and joint attention (Carpenter, Nagell, & Tomasello, 1998). Studies have found imitation ability to be strongly correlated with other social-communication behaviors in children with ASD (Curcio, 1978; Dawson & Adams, 1984; Stone, Ousley, & Littleford, 1997; Stone & Yoder, 2001), and suggest that children with ASD may rely even more heavily on imitation as a means to learn language than typically developing children do (Carpenter et al., 1998). These findings suggest that targeting imitation in young children with ASD is important for teaching new skills and may assist in the development of other social-communication behaviors, such as language and joint attention (Carpenter, Pennington, & Rogers, 2002; Rogers, 1999; Rogers & Bennetto, 2000). Indeed, most teaching approaches used with young children rely on imitation to teach new behaviors.

Imitation serves two functions: a learning function, through which infants acquire new skills and knowledge, and a social function, through which infants engage in social and emotional exchanges with others (Uzgiris, 1981). Although children with ASD have significant difficulty with imitation in general (Smith & Bryson, 1994; Rogers, 1999), research suggests that the social function of imitation may be particularly impaired in ASD (Ingersoll, 2008). Thus Project ImPACT focuses on teaching the social use of imitation during play interactions as a means of promoting overall social-communication development (Ingersoll & Schreibman, 2006).

Play

Children with ASD also have significant play deficits (American Psychiatric Association, 2000). As other behavioral characteristics of children with ASD do, degree of impairment in play skills varies significantly among children. Some children with ASD engage in nonfunctional (e.g., lining up toys, spinning wheels) and repetitive play (Lewis & Boucher, 1988). Other children with ASD do not express interest in toys. Many children with ASD have significant difficulty engaging in symbolic or pretend play (Jarrold, Boucher, & Smith, 1993); although some children with ASD are able to engage in symbolic and functional play in highly structured environments, it is clear from the research that their spontaneous play is quite restricted (Lewis & Boucher, 1988).

Play is an important social-communication skill for several reasons. Play skills are closely related to language skills, in that symbolic thinking (i.e., understanding that one thing can represent another) is necessary for both pretend play and language (Piaget, 1962). Therefore, teaching pretend play skills can help children with ASD develop more sophisticated language skills (Kasari et al., 2006; Stahmer, 1995). In addition, play is an excellent way to work on problem-solving skills (Sylva, Bruner, & Genova, 1976), conceptual and imaginative abilities (Saltz, Dixon, & Johnson, 1977), perspective taking (Berk, 2002), and fine and gross motor skills. Play also serves an important role in social development (Pelligrini & Smith, 1998): Since early peer interactions revolve around play activities (Piaget, 1962), children with ASD who possess better play skills are more likely to engage appropriately with their peers.

Project ImPACT teaches the use of play skills in a natural environment, with a focus on building flexible, spontaneous object and social play.

Intervention Techniques for Increasing a Child's Skills

To teach the above-described skills, Project ImPACT trains parents to use intervention strategies drawn from the developmental and behavioral literatures, as discussed earlier. Those strategies derived from developmental research, called *interactive teaching techniques*, are taught in the first part of the program as a way of increasing the parent's responsiveness to the child's behavior and the child's social reciprocity. Naturalistic behavioral techniques, called *direct teaching techniques*, are taught next as a way of teaching specific language, social imitation, and play skills. In the final part of the program, parents are taught to use both kinds of techniques together. Prior to introduction of these techniques, the parent is taught how to set up the family home environment so that the child has more meaningful opportunities to learn and the child is more likely to engage with the parent.

- *Set Up Your Home for Success.* The parent is taught strategies for arranging her home to increase the likelihood of positive parent–child interactions. These strategies include scheduling predictable routines, having a well-defined play space, limiting distractions, and rotating toys (Davis & Fox, 1999).

Interactive Teaching Techniques

The interactive teaching techniques are designed to increase child engagement, provide opportunities for the child to initiate communication, and increase the parent's responsiveness to her child's behavior. The parent is taught to use a variety of interactive strategies to engage her child within the context of naturally occurring situations (such as play) or daily routines (such as bathtime or snacks). The parent responds to all of her child's communicative attempts as if they were purposeful, and she adjusts her language to her child's language level (Prizant et al., 2000). Here are the specific interactive teaching techniques, in the sequence in which they are taught:

- *Follow Your Child's Lead.* In order to increase the child's motivation, the parent is taught to follow her child's focus of attention and to provide teaching opportunities around the activities her child chooses. The parent is taught to provide a limited variety of highly motivating materials (e.g., toys, games, snacks), to respond to her child's changing interests, and to assist her child in his play. This technique is used in all naturalistic interventions and has been shown to increase parent responsiveness and child motivation (e.g., Kaiser et al., 1992).

- *Imitate Your Child.* The parent is taught to imitate her child's vocalizations, actions with objects, and gestures. This strategy has been show to increase child responsiveness (Klinger & Dawson, 1992) and coordinated joint attention (Ingersoll & Schreibman, 2006), and is used to increase social engagement.

- *Animation.* The parent is taught to exaggerate her gestures, facial expressions, and vocal qualities, in order to increase her child's interest and to model appropriate nonverbal communication (Mahoney & MacDonald, 2007).

- *Modeling and Expanding Language.* The parent is taught to use a variety of indirect language stimulation techniques (e.g., descriptive talk, conversational recast) to talk about her child's focus of interest. These techniques have been shown to be effective at increasing the rate of children's speech (Ingersoll et al., 2005) and complexity of children's language skills (e.g., Camarata, Nelson, & Camarata, 1994; Kaiser et al., 1996).

- *Playful Obstruction.* The parent is taught to gain her child's attention during an interaction by playfully interrupting her child's activity. This technique is used to increase the child's spontaneous engagement and communication (Greenspan, Wieder, & Simons, 1998).

- *Balanced Turns.* The parent is taught to take turns with her child, to increase his reciprocity and to provide opportunities for her child to initiate communication (Mahoney & MacDonald, 2007).

- *Communicative Temptations.* The parent is taught to use a variety of strategies (in sight and out of reach; control of access; assistance; inadequate portions; sabotage; protest; silly situations) to encourage her child to initiate communication (e.g., Kaiser, Ostrosky, & Alpert, 1993).

Direct Teaching Techniques

The direct teaching techniques are derived from the naturalistic behavioral literature (e.g., Kaiser et al., 1992). They are designed to elicit specific communication acts, language structures, imitation, and play behaviors by using prompting, shaping, and reinforcement in natural contexts. The direct teaching techniques use the child's interest to elicit his response to the adult's requests to respond. The direct techniques build upon the interactive techniques. For example, the parent uses *Follow Your Child's Lead* and arranges the environment to provide opportunities for him to communicate. Usually this involves the child's wanting something that requires the parent's involvement. The parent then uses a series of prompts and natural reinforcement to increase the complexity of the child's social-communication behavior. The parent is first taught the basics of how to use prompting effectively, including providing clear and appropriate prompts, monitoring the child's motivation, providing wait time, and moving from less to more supportive prompts to help the child respond correctly (e.g., Kaiser et al., 1993). The parent is also taught to use immediate reinforcement that is contingent on appropriate behavior, to provide praise, and to expand her child's response (e.g., Kaiser et al., 1992; Koegel et al., 1987). Specific techniques involving prompting and reinforcement are then taught to parents for increasing expressive and receptive language, social imitation, and play skills. Here are the specific direct teaching techniques, in the sequence in which they are taught:

- *Teaching Your Child Expressive Language.* The parent is taught to use a variety of prompts (e.g., physical prompt, gestural prompt, verbal model, verbal routines, choices, cloze procedure, questions, and time delay) and reinforcement to teach her child new expressive language forms (e.g., Kaiser et al., 1993).
- *Teaching Your Child Receptive Language.* To teach her child to understand and follow directions, and thus to increase his receptive language, the parent is trained to use clear and direct verbal instructions, to use a variety of prompts (e.g., physical prompts, visual prompts, verbal instruction), and to use reinforcement (e.g., Kaiser et al., 1992).
- *Teaching Your Child Social Imitation.* The parent is taught to use a number of strategies to encourage her child to imitate her play with toys and gestures in a reciprocal fashion (Ingersoll & Gergans, 2007).
- *Teaching Your Child Play.* The parent is taught to use a variety of prompts (e.g., physical prompts, gestural prompts, modeling, instruction, leading questions, leading comments) to teach her child more complex play skills (Stahmer, 1995).

Putting It All Together

The parent is taught how to use the interactive and direct teaching techniques together. In particular, the parent is taught when to emphasize the interactive techniques, when to emphasize the direct techniques, and how to move back and forth between the two types during an interaction. For example, interactive teaching techniques are best when the parent cannot control access to desired items or activities and/or when the child is less motivated by the activity. Direct teaching techniques are best when the parent is able to control access to the desired item or activity and when the child is highly motivated.

Training Formats

The Project ImPACT parent training program can be implemented in either an individual or a group format. Both formats can be modified to fit a variety of service delivery models.

Individual Format

In the individual format, the trainer meets with a parent and child twice a week for 12 weeks. Training sessions are designed to be conducted for 90 minutes, but may also be effectively implemented in 60 minutes. At the end of the 24-session program, monthly follow-up sessions for support and coaching are recommended. The length of the program can be modified if needed. Ways to modify the program to meet a family's individual needs are discussed in Chapter 3.

The trainer spends the first one to two sessions describing the program, assessing the child's social-communication skills, and developing individualized social-communication goals for the child. Assessment includes recording a parent–child interaction on video. The trainer spends one to two sessions on each intervention technique. The parent is asked to read about the technique in the parent manual prior to the trainer's presentation. Every technique is then taught according to the following procedure: a description and discussion of the technique, tying it to the child's goals; trainer demonstration of the technique with the child; parent practice of the technique with trainer feedback; and homework practice of the technique. Homework practice is a crucial part of the program, and it is developed at the end of each session. The trainer helps the parent brainstorm how and when to use the technique in the home to target her child's goals. During this discussion, the parent trainer writes down the child's goals, the home activities selected as practice opportunities, and the specific techniques the parent should use. The parent is also instructed to write down how the child responds to the techniques. Homework sheets for recording the child's responses are included in the parent manual.

Progress reviews are conducted after all the interactive techniques have been taught, and again after the direct techniques have been taught. A parent–child interaction is again recorded on video, and then the trainer and parent review the video together. The parent is encouraged to assess both her and her child's interactions. At the end of the program, the trainer helps the parent update her child's goals. Detailed guidelines and session-by-session instructions for the individual format are presented in Part II of this book.

Group Format

The group format is designed to be conducted over 12 weeks in six 2-hour group sessions and six 45-minute individual coaching sessions. Groups consist of 6–10 parents without children. For coaching sessions, each parent and child meet individually with the trainer. The group format is accelerated; more than one intervention technique is presented in each group session.

In the first group session, the trainer reviews the research on parent training for children with ASD, describes the parent training program, overviews the intervention techniques, and discusses strategies for setting up the home for successful interactions. Subsequent sessions begin with a 20-minute discussion of the parents' use of the different intervention techniques in the home. The parent trainer then introduces a new intervention technique through a lecture accompanied with Microsoft® PowerPoint slides (see the DVD), video clips of parents using the techniques with their children (see the DVD), group discussion, and problem solving. At the end of each group session, each parent is instructed to write down one or two of her child's goals, home activities she typically completes with her child, and the intervention techniques she would use during those activities to target the child's goals. Each parent is then instructed to go home and practice the techniques over the next week, and to write down how her child responds. Group homework sheets for recording child's responses can be found in Appendix A (Forms 22–27) of this manual, copied and distributed to parents. Reading in the parent manual is also assigned as homework.

The individual coaching sessions are similar to sessions in the individual format, with the trainer helping the parent select individual goals in the first coaching session, followed by parent practice and feedback in the following coaching sessions. However, the trainer only briefly reviews the intervention techniques rather than discussing them in depth. The session moves quickly to having the parent work with her child and receive trainer feedback. The parent is also asked to practice more than one intervention technique at each coaching session. Detailed guidelines and session-by-session instructions for the group format are presented in Part III of this manual.

The next chapter of this manual describes important considerations for planning and implementing a parent training program, including the key strategies used to train parents.

Chapter 2

Planning and Implementing Project ImPACT

Trainers have two sets of issues to consider when planning and implementing a parent training program. The first set concerns setting the stage for a program. These issues include what skills and qualifications are needed to be a parent trainer, which children and parents are most likely to benefit, which training format to use, what setting is best for individual coaching sessions, and how to integrate the program into the existing curriculum. The second set of issues concerns the practical steps used to train parents effectively. Both sets of issues are discussed in this chapter.

Planning for Parent Training

Parent Trainers' Qualifications and Skills

Prospective parent trainers should have a background in child development and have professional experience working with young children who have ASD. Special educators, speech–language pathologists, occupational therapists, social workers, psychologists, psychiatrists, developmental pediatricians, and behavioral specialists may all become effective parent trainers.

Trainers should be fluent in their ability to implement the program's intervention techniques with children (Kaiser & Hancock, 2003). Because many of these techniques are also used in other developmental and naturalistic behavioral interventions, it is likely that most practitioners who work with young children with ASD will already be familiar with some or all of the techniques. However, familiarity is not the same as fluency. If practitioners do not regularly use *all* of the program's intervention strategies, they should strongly consider using the full curriculum with their own students, prior to teaching parents.

Fidelity of implementation for a trainer includes the ability to model for the parent each technique in isolation, as well as in combination with other techniques (Kaiser, Hester, Alpert, & Whiteman, 1995). Furthermore, because the number and severity of ASD characteristics can range from mild to severe, the trainer should have an understanding of how to adapt each technique for use with different children.

Prospective trainers should meet the fidelity-of-implementation standard in using the intervention themselves with a child prior to training parents. We have included an intervention fidelity form in Appendix A (Form 28) that can be completed by a supervisor or colleague during an observation of a prospective trainer. This form is designed to assess the trainer's ability to implement several related techniques together as they are presented in the coaching sessions of the group training format, as well as the entire intervention as a whole. In scoring the form, it is important to note that several different techniques can often be used to accomplish the same child outcome. For example, both *Playful Obstruction* and *Balanced Turns* are good techniques for encouraging a child to communicate when other techniques (e.g., *Imitate Your Child, Animation*) have been ineffective. Thus it is not important for a trainer to use each technique with each child in order to achieve fidelity of implementation, as long as the techniques she uses are successful at meeting a particular child's goals.

In addition to fluently implementing the techniques, the trainer should clearly understand the following information and be able to present it fluently to parents: the empirical and conceptual basis of the intervention techniques; the reason why each technique is important; the designed function of each technique; and the goals for which it may be most effective (Kaiser & Hancock, 2003). When parents have this knowledge, they are better able to use the intervention techniques to target new goals. It also increases their motivation to use the techniques throughout the day.

The trainer should also be familiar with basic behavior modification principles. The intervention techniques presented in this program are not specifically designed to reduce behavior problems; however, a significant number of young children with ASD exhibit such problems, including tantrums and aggression (Kaiser & Hancock, 2003). Trainers may find it necessary to teach the parents of such children basic strategies to manage the children's behavior. These strategies include functional assessment, antecedent strategies, reinforcement, extinction, and punishment procedures. In fact, it may be beneficial to incorporate specific instruction in behavior management into the social-communication curriculum. For an excellent parent-friendly manual on behavior management, see *Steps to Independence: Teaching Everyday Skills to Children with Special Needs*, fourth edition (Baker et al., 2004).

Furthermore, the trainer should have a responsive interaction style with parents (Kaiser & Hancock, 2003). The trainer should be able to listen to and respond sensitively to questions and concerns that parents might have. In addition, she should feel comfortable engaging a parent as fully as possible in decisions about the intervention and target behaviors for a child (Brookman-Frazee, 2004). Later in this chapter, we discuss a variety of rapport-building strategies that can be used to develop positive interactions with parents.

One of the most important aspects of adult learning—and of this program—is receiving feedback. A trainer must be able to effectively analyze a parent's behavior in practicing the techniques and then provide constructive feedback (Kaiser & Hancock, 2003). Most practitioners that we have worked with find this skill to be the most challenging. Although they may intuitively know how to use the intervention techniques with children, they struggle when trying to convey this information to parents. If trainers are not used to providing feedback to adults about their use of intervention strategies, we recommend that they practice analyzing and giving feedback before doing so with parents. One approach for improving these skills is having colleagues take turns giving feedback as each works with a child. Analyzing and giving feedback can also be practiced while watching videos of parents or other adults working with children with ASD. We have found not only that these strategies are beneficial for building parent training skills, but that they also typically improve a practitioner's ability to work with children herself. Methods for providing feedback are discussed in more detail later in this chapter.

Finally, it is important for a parent trainer to be able to adapt the program as needed to meet the individual needs of each child and parent (Kaiser & Hancock, 2003). In every case, the trainer must attend to the child's skill level and communication style, the parent's communication and learning styles, and the family's dynamics and culture when designing the program.

Who Can Benefit from Parent Training?

In the majority of research on parent training in ASD, mothers have been trained to be the intervention providers (e.g., Mahoney & Perales, 2003). However, recent research suggests that fathers can also be successfully taught to use naturalistic intervention strategies with their children with ASD (Elder, Valcante, Yarandi, White, & Elder, 2005; Winter, 2006). All parents are capable of learning effective strategies for promoting their children's development, but not all parents are ready or willing to implement them regularly. Parent training is most likely to be successful when a parent and a child exhibit the characteristics described below.

Parent Characteristics

It is important that a parent *choose* to participate in the program (Kaiser & Hancock, 2003). A willing parent is much more likely to make a commitment to learning and implementing the intervention techniques. This suggests that parent training should always be an intervention option, rather than the sole service offered. Parents who believe that their efforts will lead to improvements in their children's development are much more likely to learn and implement the intervention strategies. This is also true for parents who consider it a priority to be involved in the intervention for their children (Kaiser & Hancock, 2003). Moreover, a parent is most likely to be successful if she has adequate time and energy to devote to parent training, and if she has sufficient family support. For example, can she clear her schedule, take time off work, and arrange child care? If the parent is unable to attend the entire program, it may not be a good time for her to begin parent training; it may be better to wait until she has the interest and/or ability to participate in the entire program.

Parents from minority ethnic, racial, or cultural groups may be less likely to participate in parent training services in general (Harachi, Catalano, & Hawkins, 1997), but those who do are likely to benefit from programs such as this one (Kumpfer, Aldorado, Smith, & Bellamy, 2002). Consideration of the cultural issues discussed in Chapter 3 can make it more likely for minority parents to access the program and complete it.

Parents who exhibit serious mental health issues may not be good candidates for parent training. Although research on ASD suggests that parent training can lower family stress, parents with already excessive stress levels may not benefit as much from participation (Schreibman & Ingersoll, 2005). In these cases, it may be more beneficial if the children first receive direct services while the parents receive support to lower their stress; participation in parent training may then follow. Also, parents who have cognitive impairments themselves (Feldman, 1994) or maladaptive family interaction patterns (Griest & Forehand, 1982) may be more difficult to train, and the parent trainer will need to adapt the intervention to meet such parents' needs. We discuss parent mental health issues in more detail in Chapter 3.

It is important to remember that even if a parent does not seem an ideal candidate, it does not mean that she will not benefit from parent training. Indeed, a parent trainer can employ a number of strategies to help parents who might not otherwise be good candidates for parent training benefit from such a program. These strategies are also discussed in more detail in Chapter 3.

Child Characteristics

Project ImPACT was designed for children with ASD from earliest diagnosis to about 6 years of age who exhibit difficulty with social engagement and have significant language delays. Children with less severe symptoms and higher cognitive levels are likely to make more gains with their parents, as are children with fewer behavior problems (e.g., Kaiser, Hester, et al., 1995). Kaiser and Hancock (2003) suggest that children who are already responsive to their parents are most likely to benefit from participation in a parent training program. Although this is true, the children who are *not* responsive to their parents are often the ones most in need of strategies for improving parent–child interactions.

This program has also been used successfully with children with other developmental disabilities, older children (up to age 12), and children with relatively sophisticated language skills. The key to such successful use is a parent trainer's ability to adapt the techniques to target more complex behaviors. Older children with ASD who exhibit significant language and/or cognitive delays may benefit from the program without much adaptation. However, older children with more skills are likely to benefit from a program that also addresses peer or sibling interaction skills. This program can be used to train siblings and peers, with some adaptations. For more discussion on this issue, see the section on training siblings in Chapter 3. In addition, a child with better language skills may benefit from increasing speech intelligibility or learning more complex linguistic relations (e.g., past tense, prepositions, conversation skills). In such a case, the parent trainer may wish to work with a speech–language pathologist to develop specific speech and language goals and to determine techniques to address those goals, prior to teaching the parent to use the techniques.

When Should Parent Training Begin?

After a child receives a diagnosis of ASD, how soon should parent training be offered? There is no clear-cut answer. One approach is to offer parent training as soon as possible after diagnosis. There are several advantages to this approach. First, teaching a parent effective strategies for promoting social communication as early as possible is likely to have an important impact on the child's development (Vismara, Colombi, & Rogers, 2009; Wetherby & Woods, 2006). Second, many parents express significant frustration at the amount of time they must wait between their children's diagnosis and enrollment in services (Renty & Roeyers, 2006). Offering parent training services within several weeks of receiving a diagnosis provides the parent with a low-intensity treatment option as the child is placed on a waiting list for more intensive services. This approach may alleviate some parental stress by giving information about ASD, initiating treatment in a timely manner, and teaching the parent effective strategies for successfully engaging the child. If the training is being conducted in a group, a parent who is new to the diagnosis will have the opportunity to meet other parents of children with ASD and receive social support.

On the other hand, some parents of newly diagnosed children may not yet be emotionally ready to process information and apply it to their children (Whitaker, 2002). These parents may need a period of grieving before they can fully benefit from a parent training program. For such a parent, an individual program in a one-to-one setting may be appropriate. The parent can slowly come to terms with the diagnosis through the guidance of the parent trainer. Much less appropriate would be a program administered in a group context, where the parent is required to interact with multiple people.

Given these conflicting positions, it is difficult to know when to offer the program to parents. Perhaps the best strategy is to provide parents with the opportunity to participate in the program as soon as possible after they receive a diagnosis for their children. The program can then be offered again at a later point. Indeed, it may be necessary to revisit techniques taught in the initial parent training program as a child develops more skills (NRC, 2001; Whitaker, 2002). Many of the ECSE classrooms we have worked with provide the group training program twice a year (once in the fall and once in the spring), and families are invited to participate at either time. When the program is being offered in an individual format, it may be most effective to provide parent training, followed by a period of direct service, and then to return to parent training when the parent is more ready or when the child has gained a number of skills.

What Training Format Should Be Used?

The choice of the individual or group training format is usually limited by the setting. Early childhood educators working with children from birth to age 3 may find it easiest to implement individual parent training, because many individualized family service plans (IFSPs) are set up for services to be conducted in the home with a parent and child. This is also true for specialists who work in a clinic setting, as individual sessions are the typical model for private services. A group format is usually more feasible for educators who serve children in a classroom setting, and for specialists who do not see children individually for at least an hour at a time. In these settings, it can be very difficult to schedule individual sessions for each child, and the information may need to be presented in a group format with fewer individual coaching sessions. Finally, some parents may not be able to afford the higher cost of individual treatment, and group training may be the only option.

If trainers are not limited to a particular format and are considering the best format to use, they may wish to consider the various benefits and limitations of the two training formats (see Table 2.1). The most obvious benefit of an individual format is that a trainer can tailor the intervention to best meet the needs of each family, by focusing specifically on the strengths and weaknesses of each child and parent. This format allows significantly more time for the parent to practice with her child while being coached. This is likely to lead to better parent learning. Parents also report greater satisfaction and behavioral improvements in their children and have

Table 2.1. Benefits of Individual versus Group Training Formats

Individual	Group
• Trainer can tailor program to individual needs of child and family.	• Trainer can serve larger number of families.
• Parents receive more coaching.	• Groups are more cost-effective for parents.
• Parents report greater satisfaction with individual programs.	• Parents receive social support from other families.

better attendance in individualized parent training programs (Chadwick, Momcilovic, Rossiter, Stumbles, & Taylor, 2001). However, individual training programs can serve fewer families, and training is considerably more expensive and labor-intensive for trainers.

The main benefits of a group training format are that it is less time-intensive for the trainer and more cost-effective for the parent. These aspects make the program more accessible to a wider range of families. In addition, each parent gets the opportunity to meet and share with other families and to receive social support, which has been shown to have a positive impact on parent learning and mastery of intervention techniques (Stahmer & Gist, 2001). However, it is much more difficult to tailor the program to meet the needs of parents who have different learning styles, who begin training with different levels of competence, or whose children differ significantly in their abilities. A final limitation is often the added need for child care, since a parent is not attending the group sessions with her child.

At this point, there are no conclusive data to suggest that one format is better than another. However, research suggests that parents need intensive individual coaching sessions with their children to master techniques presented in a group training format (Kaiser, Hemmeter, et al., 1995). Therefore, regardless of the training format chosen, all families should receive some individual coaching sessions to practice the skills with their children while receiving trainer feedback.

Where Should Training Take Place?

Individual coaching sessions can be conducted in a family home, a classroom, or a clinic setting. There are benefits to providing individual training with the parent and child in the family home. When the training is presented in the natural environment, it is likely to lead to better generalization and maintenance of parent skills. This format also allows the trainer to teach the parent to use the intervention within routines that do not typically occur in a classroom or clinic setting, such as bathtime, dressing, and community outings. Moreover, it allows the trainer to teach skills within meaningful routines that are unique to the family. Finally, it provides the opportunity to involve more family members, such as siblings, who are less likely to come to a training session held elsewhere.

One of the limitations to training in the home is that it may be very difficult to get a parent's undivided attention. Siblings, telephone calls, visitors, and the demands of daily life may draw the parent away from the training session. The child may also be harder to work with, because he may exhibit more inappropriate behavior without the structure that a clinic or classroom can bring. Thus the parent may have more difficulty learning to use the intervention if training is conducted in the home.

The benefits and limitations of conducting training in a clinic or classroom are the opposite of those in the home. Typically, these specialized treatment settings are designed to minimize distractions and promote engagement. They include highly motivating toys and activities that a parent may not have in the home. In addition, if the child is already familiar with the setting, he is likely to associate the setting with work and may be more cooperative. Finally, when the session is conducted outside the home, the parent can avoid the hassles and disruptions of daily life that arise in the home, and she may thus be able to devote more attention to the training. For these reasons, the child may respond more favorably, and the parent may be more successful at implementing the techniques. This benefit may be particularly important in the beginning of training, when the parent is first learning how to use new intervention techniques. However, as training progresses, the parent may find that she is unable to generalize her use of the strategies to home because of the above-described distractions.

The trainer can use several techniques to try to minimize problems with generalization when training is conducted outside the home. These include having the parent bring in toys from home or having the parent work on several family routines, such as snacktime, in the treatment setting (see "Increasing Independence," later in this chapter). The trainer may also consider conducting the majority of the training in a treatment setting to build the parent's skills and confidence, and then conducting the final sessions in the home to facilitate generalization.

Fitting Parent Training into the Existing Curriculum

One question that frequently arises with parent training is how to integrate it into the existing intervention program. Given that the Project ImPACT parent training curriculum includes elements from both the developmental and behavioral treatment literatures, it is compatible with most intervention approaches used with young children with ASD and can greatly enhance a child's response to direct services.

If the existing curriculum is provided in a one-to-one setting, as in a clinic- or home-based program, the individual parent training program can be relatively easily implemented within the existing treatment model. Depending on the constraints of the existing program, parent training may be implemented in addition to or in lieu of direct service. We have found that if the existing program allows for only 1 or 2 hours of one-to-one intervention per week, children tend to make significantly more progress if this time is used for parent training rather than therapist-led intervention. In this case, the practitioner may consider suspending therapist-led service for several months in order to provide parent training, and returning to therapist-led service once the training is completed. However, use of both models simultaneously is clearly preferable.

It may be more difficult to integrate parent training into a classroom-based intervention program. The group format is likely to be the most compatible; however, even in a classroom, there may be an opportunity to use the individual treatment format. Issues to consider include when to schedule the group and individual coaching sessions. Most ECSE programs are designed to run several hours per day, several days per week; this often leaves little time to schedule sessions during the school day. In addition, many working parents may have difficulty attending multiple sessions during working hours. This means that classroom teachers may need to offer this program to parents in the evenings or on weekends. However, if the program is offered outside a trainer's typical work schedule, it may be difficult to maintain the program without additional trainer compensation. Regardless of when the group sessions are offered, it is important to offer the individual coaching during the day, since young children are often less alert in the evenings.

We have found that offering the group sessions in the evening and the coaching sessions during the day has been the most effective solution for the majority of classroom-based programs with which we have worked. If coaching is to be conducted in the classroom, we typically suggest that the trainer schedule the coaching sessions for all families on the same day, in 1-hour increments to facilitate planning. This schedule allows the trainer 15 minutes between families to take notes and prepare for the next family. The coaching days can be scheduled during teacher planning days when the children would not typically be present. If enough staff members are available, it is also possible to conduct coaching and/or group sessions during the typical school day in a separate space. Another approach is to offer coaching and/or group sessions in lieu of a portion of direct services for the duration of the parent program. Although many programs are concerned about the ramifications of "canceling intervention services," we emphasize that parent training *is* intervention. In our implementation of this group intervention model across the state of Oregon, we have had no parent complaints when programs have chosen to offer the coaching sessions in lieu of direct services, since parents so greatly value receiving the information.

It is recommended that if this program is being offered as part of a public EI/ECSE program, parent training services should be written into a child's IFSP or individualized education program (IEP). Including these services in the IFSP or IEP can help the parent appreciate parent training as an important component of the child's education program and may help increase parent participation.

Procedures for Training Parents

Training a parent begins with two crucial steps: building rapport and developing goals for the child. The trainer then teaches each intervention technique to the parent, using the following series of steps: presenting information on the technique and tying it to the child's goals; demonstrating the technique; parent practice of the technique with trainer feedback; assigning and reviewing parent homework; increasing the parent's independence; and collecting data (Kaiser & Hancock, 2003). Each of these steps is discussed in detail below. As explained briefly below and in Parts II and III, these steps differ somewhat, depending upon whether the training is conducted in the individual or group format. The coaching session fidelity form (Form 30) and the group session fidelity form (Form 29) in Appendix A can be completed by a supervisor or colleague during observation of the parent training sessions, to ensure that the trainer implements the training procedures with fidelity.

Building Rapport

The trainer begins the program by building rapport with the parent. A good working relationship with the parent should be developed and maintained throughout the training sessions. There are several strategies the trainer can use to do this. The first is to use a responsive interaction style, including taking time to listen and respond to the parent's questions and concerns, and using balanced turns (Kaiser & Hancock, 2003). The trainer should also engage the parent as much as possible in decisions about the intervention and target behaviors for her child (Brookman-Frazee, 2004), and should frequently invite both formal and informal feedback from the parent (Kaiser & Hancock, 2003).

Once instruction in the techniques begins, the trainer needs to be competent and confident while working with the child, but should be careful *not* to interact significantly better with the child than the parent does. This is especially important at the beginning of training. The parent will not yet have learned techniques for engaging the child, and she may experience distress when her child does not enjoy playing with her The trainer, meanwhile, has probably developed expertise in engaging difficult-to-engage children. When the disparity is too great between the parent's and the trainer's abilities to engage the child, the parent may feel ashamed and discouraged that she will never be able to master these skills. She may give up, preferring that the professional work with her child. This sentiment defeats the purpose of a parent training program. This is also why it is important for the trainer to demonstrate each technique in isolation: Doing so ensures that the trainer can coach the parent to have the same success she observes while watching the trainer. One exception to this rule is when the trainer demonstrates what the techniques look like together at the beginning of the individual training format. This demonstration is brief and is meant to provide the parent with an overview of what the techniques look like when they are used together. This overview is intended to increase the parent's understanding of the purpose of each technique as it is introduced in isolation. It should not adversely affect the parent's motivation, because the demonstration is brief and the parent is not required to interact with her child after the demonstration. Once the techniques are introduced, the trainer should be careful only to demonstrate what she will be able to coach the parent to do successfully.

For the same reasons, the trainer's feedback and coaching should be primarily positive, especially at the beginning. She should mostly point out things that the parent is doing correctly. During the first few coaching sessions, the parent may struggle considerably in her ability to engage her child and may feel defeated. Providing a high rate of positive feedback and encouragement at the beginning can help the parent develop confidence in working with her child. All of us like to hear good things about ourselves; thus providing positive feedback, as long as it is sincere, is a good way to develop a positive working relationship with the parent.

The trainer will have a significant amount of information to cover; however, she should take time to listen to the parent's concerns. The parent may need to express her feelings of guilt, sadness, or frustration, and there may be child behavioral issues that are causing the parent significant stress. Although it is important to remain on track, sometimes the best thing the trainer can do for the parent is to listen, acknowledge the parent's feelings, and offer suggestions when appropriate. If the trainer is not competent to address issues raised by the parent, such as marital/couple difficulties, medical or mental health issues, or severe behavior problems, the trainer should provide an appropriate referral to the parent. If the trainer is unsure whether or not a referral is appropriate, she should provide the referral anyway and let the parent decide whether to pursue additional services.

Pitfalls to Avoid

Although rapport is important, it is just as important to remain professional. The trainer interacts with the parent to a far greater extent than if she provided direct service to the child. The parent may begin to perceive the trainer as a friend, confidant, or therapist and to discuss inappropriate personal issues. If the parent attempts to share such personal issues, the trainer should remind the parent of the trainer's role. The trainer should also refrain from sharing her own personal issues.

It is wonderful when both parents can participate in training, and both should be supported. For this reason, it is important that a trainer avoid being pulled into a couple's disagreements. For example, when parents experience marital/couple stress or when there is a disagreement over how to parent, one parent may attempt to "recruit" the trainer into an alliance against the other parent. The trainer should avoid this, even if she secretly feels that one parent is right. The trainer may also need to structure the parents' interactions with each other. For example, to avoid parents' constant critiques of each other, the trainer can create a policy in which only the trainer can give feedback. To prevent one parent from dominating the parent–child interaction, the trainer can have each parent work with the child independently for a set amount of time.

Rapport in Parent Training Groups

In a group format, the trainer also needs to facilitate the development of rapport among the participating families. The parents will feel more comfortable discussing their children when they feel comfortable with the other parents. For this reason, the trainer should begin the first group session by having each parent introduce herself, identify a strength and a weakness about her child, and report what she hopes to gain from the program. This introduction should take about 10–20 minutes and helps parents begin to form relationships with each other. The trainer should also take a 15- to 20-minute break halfway through each group session; this gives parents an opportunity to talk to one another. Providing snacks during the break often increases parents' sociability. Once the parents feel comfortable with each other, usually about halfway through the program, the trainer should pass around a contact sheet so that parents can exchange contact information. As in any group, the trainer should review her confidentiality policy in the first group session. This policy should include, at a minimum, the agreement that personal information that parents discuss during group sessions should not leave the group.

Developing Goals for the Child

Appropriate treatment goals should be developed for each child. Goals need to be specific and measurable. They should also be based on the child's age and current skills, on the parent's goals for her child, and on what will have the greatest positive impact on the child's functioning in the family. Goals are important because they enable the trainer to track the child's progress to ensure that the program is effective. They also help the parent understand what skills to target when working with her child. A first step in goal development is information gathering.

Information Gathering

Goals are developed based on a review of the completed Child History Form (Appendix A, Form 2) and an initial assessment of the child's current social-communication skills. Ideally, both initial assessment and later progress monitoring will include video recording of parent–child interaction; however, some parents are uncomfortable having themselves or their children recorded, for fear of how the information may be used. If a parent is uncomfortable, the trainer may suggest that the parent keep the video or that it be destroyed as soon as it is reviewed. As with any recording, the trainer should review her confidentiality policies regarding video with the parent and obtain her written consent before taping.

The assessment process consists of parent report, interaction with the child, and observation of a parent–child interaction. Information from the parent is collected with the Social-Communication Checklist (Appendix A, Form 3). The trainer also uses the Social-Communication Checklist to identify the child's skills during her interaction with the child, and to collect data on the child's skills while the parent interacts with the child. The trainer should also take notes on any intervention techniques the parent is currently using and the effects they have on her child's behavior. If the information on the parent's checklist is significantly different from that in the trainer's observation, the trainer can address this difference by asking the parent open-ended and probing questions to clarify the discrepancies. The child's current skill level in the four core areas are then considered when the parent and trainer are developing goals. For example, a nonverbal child with very little babbling and no vocal imitation may have pointing to request as a language goal. A nonverbal child who makes a variety of babbling sounds and can imitate some words may have use of words to request as a goal.

The parent's goals for her child should also influence the treatment goals that the trainer selects. Parents report more satisfaction when trainers work collaboratively with them to develop treatment goals for their children that the parents value (Brookman-Frazee, 2004). If a parent does not see a goal as necessary for her child, she will not be motivated to target the skill at home.

Information on the parent's goals for her child can be collected via parent report, interaction with the child, and observation of the parent–child interaction. The Child History Form (Appendix A, Form 2) can provide the trainer with background on the parent's goals for her child, as well as on the child's early development and current and previous intervention programs.

Goal Selection Criteria

It is important that the child's goals can be reasonably met within the duration of the parent training program, so that the parent will experience success. For this reason, the trainer should limit the number of goals to no more than two goals per core skill area (eight goals total). In some cases, particularly in the group format, the trainer may need to select fewer goals in order to ensure that each parent is able to be successful in helping her child meet his goals.

As noted above, goals should be specific and measurable, and should follow developmentally from the child's current skill level. A parent often has global goals for her child, such as "I want my child to talk," rather than specific goals that can be measured. In this case, the trainer should restate the parent's global goal as a specific goal that is measurable, such as "The child will use single words to request desired items without a verbal prompt." For preverbal children, we typically recommend teaching natural gestures, such as tapping, reaching, and pointing, as opposed to signs or pictures. We take this position for several reasons. First, from a developmental perspective, young typically developing children begin using these natural gestures prior to developing spoken words, and research suggests that these gestures support the use of spoken language (Özçalişkan & Goldin-Meadow, 2005). Second, because most people in the community do not know sign language, teaching a child to use signs limits the number of people he can communicate with successfully. Similarly, although pictures are understandable to most people, they are not always available; thus teaching the child to point to pictures limits the environments in which the child can communicate. Natural gestures, however, are always available and understandable to all potential communication partners. However, signs and picture communication systems can also be successfully targeted in this program. Table 2.2 summarizes the above-described guidelines for selecting treatment goals. Tables 2.3 through 2.6 provide examples of specific, measurable goals for each of the core areas. These range across a number of developmental levels.

A parent may also have unrealistic expectations for her child, such as wanting a nonverbal child to use phrase speech. In this case, the trainer should emphasize that although the parent's

Table 2.2. Guidelines for Developing Treatment Goals

Gathering and reviewing information

    Child History Form (parent-completed)

    Social-Communication Checklist (trainer- and parent-completed)

    Brief trainer interaction with the child

    Observation of parent–child interactions

    Parent's goals for the child

Goal selection criteria

    Must be specific and measurable

    No more than two goals per core skill area

    Must follow developmentally from the child's current skill level

    Can be met within duration of the program

    Fit with parent's goals for the child

goal may be a great long-term goal, the trainer would like to help her select a goal that can be achieved within the length of the parent training program. When having this discussion, the trainer may need to emphasize how different skills develop and help the parent select an earlier-emerging skill to target (e.g., pointing) that is more appropriate for the child's ability. Once the trainer has identified appropriate goals, she should confirm them with the parent, to ensure that the parent is motivated to help her child achieve them.

Presenting Information on Techniques

The first step in teaching parents a technique is to present information on it. The techniques are explained both through the trainer's in-session description and through assigned reading in the parent manual. Use of these two modalities can increase parent learning and address different learning styles. In-session explanation begins with the rationale behind each technique. Simply telling a parent what to do will not help her understand why it is important. For example, when a parent says that her goal is for her child to talk, she may not want to use techniques that promote play development. As professionals, we know the importance of play skills in developing language skills; however, parents often do not understand the association, and teaching play may not seem important. Therefore, when teaching the parent, the trainer must explain the rationale of each technique and how skills are interrelated. Understanding the rationale behind each technique will also help the parent with generalization to new situations.

Next, the trainer should discuss the technique's key points, giving real-world examples that use the specific child's behaviors. The descriptions of the techniques in the parent manual can assist parents who have a hard time processing oral information; these give them something to refer to after the session and after the training is over. Some parents may have difficulty with both written and oral information; in this case, demonstration of techniques, as described below, is particularly important.

Trainers need to help parents think about each technique. People tend to learn best when given the opportunity to reflect on information and apply it to their own situation. For this

Table 2.3. Examples of Social Engagement Goals

Maintain interaction

- The child will demonstrate engagement with adults during functional play (e.g., pushing cars, putting dolls on the bus) through eye contact, active watching of adult's actions, or use of an intentional, reciprocal, response to adult's overtures (e.g., smile, frown, and vocalization).
- The child will allow others to play next to him for at least 5 minutes.
- The child will increase the amount of time he is engaged with a play partner, during functional play activities. Engagement is demonstrated by eye contact, smiles toward the play partner, or watching the play partner's turn.

Respond to adult

- The child will respond to an adult's attempt to draw his attention to something or someone with 80% accuracy.
- The child will use an intentional behavior (eye contact, gesture, word, or vocalization) to respond to an adults' request for attention at least 75% of the time.
- The child will increase his responsiveness to an adult during play, as evidenced by responding to the adult's initiation 80% of the time in a 5-minute segment.

Initiation

- The child will initiate his turn during play activities, using words or gestures.
- The child will initiate play with others, using words, gestures, or actions.
- The child will reference his communication partner when initiating a request at least 50% of the time.
- The child will initiate preferred activities that require adult participation, using specific gestures, vocalizations, or objects (10 initiations, or attempts to involve the adult in the interaction, per 75-minute session).
- The child will initiate play activities with an adult at three out of four opportunities.
- The child will point or show objects to an adult for the purpose of sharing.
- The child will seek attention appropriately by using a single word, gesture, or sign at least 75% of the time.

Turn taking

- The child will maintain engagement during social games (peek-a-boo) for at least three turns.
- The child will allow an adult a turn three or four times during an interaction.
- The child will engage in an interaction for three or four turns.
- The child will turn take during play with toys as initiator and recipient for at least three turns.
- The child will increase his turn-taking abilities to include trading toys with adults, allowing the play partner a turn, and watching the play partner's turn in 80% of opportunities presented.

reason, it is important that a trainer periodically ask questions to help a parent think about how she would apply the information to her own child. Parts II and III include ways to facilitate this dialogue. When posing questions to a parent, the trainer should allow adequate time for a response. This is particularly important during early group sessions, when parents may be hesitant to answer. In group sessions, the trainer should ensure also that all participants have an opportunity to respond, so that even shyer parents feel able to share with the group.

If a parent is having particular difficulty understanding a technique, the trainer can try

Table 2.4. Examples of Language Goals

Preverbal

- The child will use a single word or point to request objects and actions at four out of eight opportunities.

- The child will use vocalizations to request or respond to an adult 10 times during a 5-minute segment.

Emerging language

- The child will use vocalizations/words to initiate requests for actions or objects at four out of eight opportunities.

- The child will spontaneously use gesture and eye contact to initiate requests for actions or objects.

- The child will expand communicative functions to include appropriate protesting behaviors (e.g., "All done," "No," "Stop it").

- The child will appropriately request a change in activity by producing the words "All done," or using a gesture.

- The child will improve his ability to communicate basic needs to his family (e.g., pain by saying, "owie"), given a verbal prompt.

- The child will make a choice between two objects, using an appropriate gesture (pointing) or vocalization (single word or word approximation), with 80% accuracy.

- The child will communicate a choice through pointing, eye contact, or an appropriate verbalization, when given a choice of two objects.

Single words to simple phrases

- The child will increase expressive vocabulary to include spontaneous single words for the purposes of requesting, commenting, labeling, and greeting.

- The child will use two- and three-word phrases (e.g., "Pour milk") for a variety of pragmatic functions (e.g., requesting, protesting, responding, labeling, and commenting).

- The child will learn to answer "yes–no" questions positively (saying the word "yes" or nodding his head) as appropriate.

- The child will respond to simple "what" and "where" questions with 75% accuracy.

- The child will communicate his needs in times of stress through the use of pictures to support verbal language (e.g., identifying when he needs a "safe place").

Complex phrase speech

- The child will use words to describe play.

- The child will expand communicative functions to include commenting, sharing of ideas, greeting, and projecting feelings.

- The child will improve use of pronouns (e.g., "him," "her," "she," "he"), utilizing the appropriate pronoun in a known context.

- The child will expand use of specific labels for items/places during play, given an adult model.

- The child will increase spontaneous language, as evidenced by responding to "wh-" and "yes–no" questions rather than repeating the questions.

- The child will use language to request, protest, seek help, and seek attention.

- The child will make choices between two objects/actions.

- The child will use descriptive language to clarify comments and requests.

- The child will ask questions to gain information.

(cont.)

Table 2.4 (*cont.*)

- The child will retell past events.
- The child will respond to "why" questions.

Receptive language
- The child will follow one-step directions.
- The child will follow single-step directions with gestural cue.
- The child will follow directions containing age-appropriate quantity concepts (list targeted concepts).
- The child will demonstrate understanding of inferences, as evidenced by following directions containing inferential language at three out of six opportunities.

role-playing the technique with her. A role play can begin with having the parent pretend to be her child while the trainer in the parent role demonstrates the technique; the parent and trainer then switch roles. This is also an effective strategy if the parent is having difficulty implementing the technique with her child.

Demonstrating the Techniques

After explaining a technique, the trainer asks the parent to observe a demonstration, looking for the technique's specific elements and their effect on the child's behavior. The trainer then either demonstrates the technique with the child or, if in a group, shows a video clip demonstration (Kaiser & Hancock, 2003). These video clips can also be used with parents participating in the individual format as an additional way of presenting information.

In the individual training format or in the coaching sessions of the group format, the tech-

Table 2.5. Examples of Social Imitation Goals

Imitation of play
- The child will imitate pretend play with one or two objects.
- The child will spontaneously imitate complex play actions (requiring two or more steps) with toys.
- The child will imitate 8–10 pretend play actions with toys per session.
- The child will spontaneously imitate novel functional (e.g., figures sitting, figures eating, figures sleeping with props) and symbolic (e.g., hot food, yucky food, yummy food, pouring pretend juice, spilling pretend food) play sequences, given an adult model.
- The child will imitate novel symbolic play actions (e.g., pretending to eat hot food, pouring pretend liquid from a teapot) with prompting (e.g., verbal, gestural cues).
- The child will spontaneously imitate familiar play actions, given an adult model, at 8 out of 10 opportunities.

Imitation of conventional gestures
- The child will imitate conventional gestures (e.g., waving, pointing, clapping, blowing kisses, etc.) at three out of six opportunities.
- The child will imitate a wave bye-bye at the end of each session.
- The child will imitate a wave hello at the beginning of each session.

Table 2.6. Examples of Play Goals

Exploratory play

- The child will explore (touch, smell, taste) two new toys per session.

Combinational play

- The child will put toys in boxes or other containers when provided with an adult model.

Functional play

- The child will increase spontaneous use of functional play sequences (e.g., putting people in cars, push a car) when an adult is present.
- The child will engage in functional play with at least five new toys over a 2-month period.
- The child will use toys for their intended purpose at least 50% of the time when provided with an adult model.

Pretend play

- The child will combine two or three sequences in pretend play.
- The child will engage in spontaneous pretend play involving an adult as play partner.
- The child will increase his spontaneous pretend and symbolic play skills to include multistep functional play, and beginning symbolic use of objects (e.g., hot food).
- The child will increase his use of functional play skills; demonstrating linked play actions (e.g., pretending to cook food, then feed it to a puppet).

Symbolic play

- The child will allow more flexibility in play, as evidenced by decreasing the number of protests during play (e.g., protesting the adult's ideas/changes for his play schemes).
- The child will use three to five different schemes with nonfunctional play materials.
- The child will increase use of symbolic play skills, given prompting and modeling from an adult play partner.
- The child will increase his spontaneous pretend and symbolic play to include pretend play with characters, use of symbolic objects, and sequencing of events.

niques are demonstrated live with the child. During a live demonstration, the trainer initially helps the parent identify the techniques as she uses them and the child's response. As the program progresses, the parent begins to take the leading role in identifying the techniques that are used and the child's response. In the group training format, the trainer should ask open-ended questions after each video clip, such as "What did you observe?" If a parent is unable to identify the key points with an open-ended question, the trainer can then ask more specific questions. If the parent is still having difficulty noticing key elements, the trainer should lead her through a review of the technique and show the clip again. Specific questions or comments are included for each technique in the session guidelines for both the individual (Part II) and the group (Part III) formats.

Providing Feedback on Parent Practice

The most important step in training the parent is providing specific feedback while she practices the techniques with her child (Kaiser & Hancock, 2003). Feedback involves reminding the parent about the elements of a technique, helping her notice the child's response, and giving tips for changing her behavior to improve her child's response.

Live Feedback versus Video Review

Feedback can be given during live, in-session parent practice, or the practice can be recorded and feedback given while reviewing the video. The benefit of live feedback is its immediacy: The parent can correct her behavior immediately and does not practice the techniques incorrectly. The trainer can also jump in and model correct use of a technique at any time. However, live feedback may distract the parent while she is trying to work with her child. The parent may also be concerned about her child's hearing the trainer's suggestions.

A benefit of providing feedback while watching a video is that the parent is not distracted and can focus better on the interaction. The trainer also has more time to discuss the parent's and child's behavior. The parent can also video-record herself using the interventions in different settings and can receive feedback on that. A video allows the parent to see her own behavior, which is often a powerful behavior change tool in itself. To help the parent critically evaluate her own behavior, the trainer can have the parent complete a video review form after watching the video. Two video review forms are available in Appendix A: one for the interactive teaching techniques (Form 7) and one for the direct teaching techniques (Form 12). These forms are used to help the parent identify the techniques she used and her child's response. The trainer then discusses this information with the parent to help her identify the techniques that are most effective in working with her child. This helps increase the parent's independence and skill generalization. One final benefit is that a video can be reviewed when the child is not present. However, when feedback is provided from a video, the parent does not have the opportunity to correct her behavior immediately. In addition, as mentioned earlier, some parents are very uncomfortable being video-recorded and/or viewing themselves on video.

The individual parent training format mainly uses live feedback, with periodic progress reviews using video recording. However, additional video feedback can be used, depending on a parent's learning style. For example, we have found that video feedback can be especially helpful for parents who have learning difficulties or who speak English as a second language, because both the recorded interaction and the rate of verbal feedback can be slowed down. Due to time constraints, the coaching sessions in the group format use only live feedback. However, it is possible to use video feedback during group sessions instead. A parent may be asked to bring a video-recorded example of herself using the techniques at home with her child; feedback can then be provided within the group.

Being Succinct and Specific

When giving live feedback, it is important for the trainer to be succinct and specific. Trainer comments should not remove the parent from the interaction with her child for more than a few seconds. Although it is acceptable to take a few minutes to discuss what the parent is doing, the more the trainer talks, the less chance the parent has to practice. If the parent requests details about application of the technique in other environments, the trainer can provide time at the end of the session to discuss specific concerns.

Giving Much Feedback on Only a Few Techniques

Feedback should be given on a limited number of techniques per session; however, the trainer should comment on almost everything the parent does relevant to those techniques. The trainer should make at least one comment per minute. This strategy of offering a great deal of feedback on a small number of techniques will help the parent learn more effectively. As the parent moves through training, it is appropriate to give "review" feedback on techniques the parent has already learned, to keep her memory of them fresh.

Giving Positive Feedback

Training should always involve more positive than corrective feedback, but the trainer should use both. Positive feedback builds a parent's confidence in her ability, but it involves more than simply telling a parent that she has done a good job. It points out specific strategies that the parent is using correctly so that she can use them again. Even though a parent uses a strategy successfully, she may not realize what she is doing or why, or be aware of the positive effect it has on the child's behavior. Therefore, the trainer should keep pointing out things the parent is doing correctly, even if it seems that the parent has already mastered several techniques. It is especially important to focus on positive feedback early in training and with parents who are anxious and unsure of their ability to work with their children. There are several different ways for a trainer to give meaningful positive feedback:

- Point out specifically what the parent did correctly: "That was great how you got Jimmy's attention, *before* asking him what he wanted."
- Point out how the child responds to what the parent is doing: "Lucy is so engaged with you when you imitate what she is doing."
- Explain why the child is responding a certain way: "Peter is making beautiful eye contact, because you are holding the toy in your line of sight."

Giving Corrective Feedback

Parents differ in their ability to make good use of corrective feedback. Some parents take direction very well and welcome suggestions for improvement. Other parents may lose confidence in their ability or become defensive. The best ratio of positive to corrective feedback will depend on each parent's learning style. For parents who are highly resistant to getting corrective feedback, the trainer may need to focus far more on positive feedback. Corrective feedback should always be followed with positive feedback, especially when a parent has followed a suggestion.

There are several ways for the trainer to give meaningful corrective feedback. Some of these strategies are directive, such as telling or showing the parent what to do. Other strategies are less directive, such as describing the situation. Less directive strategies require the parent to infer what she should do differently. They may be more difficult for the parent to follow, but they also allow her to become a better problem solver. It is usually a good idea to be more directive in the beginning of training and become less directive as the parent increases her skills. If the parent is having a difficult time responding to the less directive strategies, the trainer can be more directive. Strategies for corrective feedback include the following:

- Suggest a strategy for the next opportunity: "Next time Scott reaches for the ball, wait a few seconds before you ask him what he wants."
- Remind the parent of a technique: "Remember to describe what you are doing."
- Tell the parent what to do: "Hold the car back so Carly can't grab it from you."
- Model a technique and have the parent imitate it immediately.
- Describe the situation to prompt the parent to change her behavior: "Jason is playing with the car now."
- Explain why the child is responding in a certain way: "Carson is not paying attention to you, because he is busy playing with the car."
- Point out how the child responds to what the parent is doing: "Mark imitates fewer words when you use longer sentences."
- Ask a question to prompt the parent to change her behavior: "Why do you think Mandy is not paying attention to you?"

Both positive and corrective feedback should include an explanation of why and how the child is responding to the parent's behavior. This strategy not only helps the parent understand the reasons for using the techniques, but increases her ability to generalize the use of the techniques to new situations.

There will be times when a parent is not comfortable implementing a technique that the trainer feels is crucial. For example, the parent may be very uncomfortable simply playing with her child. In this case, it may be helpful for the trainer to reiterate the rationale behind the technique and to explain how it is used to address one of the child's goals. The trainer can also have the parent practice the technique for short periods with the trainer present to build up confidence before being asked to implement the technique at home (and possibly failing miserably).

Assigning and Discussing Homework

Homework is a critical element of parent training. Assigning specific homework helps the parent apply the techniques during daily activities at home, increases her independence in using the techniques, and increases the likelihood that she will practice at home. In both the individual and group formats, homework is assigned at the end of each session and reviewed at the beginning of the following session. The parent manual includes homework sheets for each session in the individual training format. These homework sheets may also be used for the group format. Alternatively, group homework sheets that include more than one technique per session can be found in Appendix A of this manual; these can be copied and distributed at group sessions. All the homework sheets summarize the key points of the techniques covered in the session. They also provide places for writing down specific goals and practice opportunities, and include questions for parents to answer after practicing at home with their children.

Homework is introduced at the end of each session. Using that session's homework sheet, the trainer first reviews the key elements of the technique(s) taught during that session and helps the parent select at least one specific goal to target at home. The goal is written on the sheet. The parent and trainer then identify at least one home activity (during play or a daily routine) in which to use the technique to address the goal. This information is also written on the session's homework sheet. The trainer should take time to review the questions on the homework, to ensure that the parent understands the expectations and to increase the likelihood that the parent will be successful at home. Homework almost always includes reading in the parent manual about the techniques to be taught in the next session.

The next session then begins with a discussion of the homework from the previous week. When the parent knows there will be a discussion on homework, it increases the likelihood that she will have practiced over the week. The discussion allows the parent to share successes and challenges, and it allows the trainer to determine whether the parent needs additional support in using the technique. If the parent has forgotten or has not completed her homework, the trainer should still ask the parent to respond to the questions on the homework sheet. Parents will be less likely to practice if they are not able to receive feedback on activities at home. Over the course of the program, the amount of help the trainer gives the parent in selecting homework goals and practice opportunities should decrease significantly

Increasing Independence

The goal of parent training is for the parent to implement the intervention successfully without the trainer's presence or feedback. Therefore, the trainer needs to facilitate the parent's ability to use the techniques independently and to generalize their use to new situations. Building independence needs to be planned throughout training. If the trainer does not build in opportunities for the parent's independent use of the techniques from the beginning, she may find that the parent is unable to work with her child without the trainer present.

The key to building independence in all parent training programs is to allow time for the parent to practice the techniques and receive feedback. Even in a group training format, the trainer should allow time to work individually with each family. This is why individual coaching sessions are an integral part of the group format. Each parent in a group should have an opportunity to work on these skills in a meaningful and supported way. The more practice and feedback a parent gets, the quicker she will become independent in her ability to implement the techniques. By the end of training, the parent should be providing most if not all of the intervention, while the trainer provides only feedback in gradually decreasing amounts. The trainer's physical proximity to the parent and child should also be slowly decreased over the course of the training. For example, at the beginning the trainer may sit near the parent and child while providing feedback, and may be actively involved in the parent–child interaction by helping the parent select and arrange materials. By the end of training, the trainer should be across the room from the parent, mainly observing. If the trainer has an observation room or window, she can leave the room and observe while making periodic suggestions over a room microphone, "bug-in-the-ear" microphone, or at the end of the session. This distance between the parent and the trainer will help the parent feel more independent, as it will more closely mimic her situation at home when the trainer is not present. It will also help the child see his parent as the primary intervention provider, and he will be more likely to respond to her.

It is not uncommon for a parent to be excellent at working with her child in one situation (usually wherever the training is conducted), and to have difficulty using the techniques with her child in a different activity or setting. The best way to overcome this problem is to have the parent practice using the techniques across settings and activities. This is easiest when the training is conducted in the home, more difficult when training is conducted in a clinic or school, and very difficult when training is conducted in a group. In a home training situation, the training sessions can be scheduled at different times during the day, so that the trainer's time in the home will coincide with different household routines (snacktime, naptime, playtime with a sibling, bathtime, etc.). If this is not possible, the trainer can arrange to have the parent conduct a familiar routine outside of its normal time while she is there. She could also schedule some training in community settings that the family attends regularly (parks, preschool, play group, grocery store, etc.). If the trainer is conducting training in a clinic or school, she may wish to have the parent bring in some toys from home and plan to do a household routine (dressing, snack, etc.) at the training site.

It is important for the parent trainer to allow time during training to discuss using the techniques in other settings and activities. At the beginning, the trainer may wish to provide the parent with specific suggestions for when and how to use the techniques at home. However, over time, the trainer should encourage the parent to problem-solve and decide for herself how to apply the techniques at home.

Collecting Data

It is important for the trainer to collect data on the child's progress toward meeting his goals. This documents the child's successes, identifies areas in which the child is struggling, and allows the trainer to modify the child's program to best meet his needs. Most practitioners are used to collecting data, either on a session-by-session basis, or periodically throughout a child's program. If the trainer already has a data collection strategy that she uses for assessing a child's progress toward social-communication goals, she may choose to use the same strategy for tracking child behavior in this program. We have included a Session Data Sheet (Appendix A, Form 14) for data collection on the child's goals, behavior, and the techniques used to elicit the specific behavior.

It is also important to collect data on the parent's mastery of the intervention techniques. This information will allow the trainer to tailor the pace of the program to maximize parent learning. We have included forms that can be used to track parent behavior during coaching for both the individual program (Appendix A, Form 8) and the group program (Appendix A, Form 18). When conducting the individual program, the trainer should take notes on the parent's behavior in each session since the parent will be learning only one technique at a time. The Individual Format Coaching Form (Appendix A, Form 8) can then be used during the three review sessions (*Review of the Interactive Teaching Techniques*, *Review of the Direct Teaching Techniques*, and the second *Putting It All Together* session) to monitor the parent's ability to use the techniques together. Since the group format covers a number of different techniques in each coaching session, the Group Format Coaching Form (Appendix A, Form 18) can be used during each session to monitor the parent's ability to use the techniques together.

As mentioned earlier, several different techniques can often be used to accomplish the same child outcome. Thus it is not important for the parent to use each technique when interacting with her child, as long as the ones she uses are successful at achieving the child's goals. For example, the parent may find that certain *Communicative Temptations* work better than others for eliciting child initiations, or that *Playful Obstruction* is more successful at producing child communication than *Balanced Turns*.

Live, in-session data collection is very important, but it is sometimes difficult to collect good data with naturalistic interventions. The targeted behaviors are varied based on the child's initiations, and both child and parent behavior change need to be tracked. In these circumstances, data collection can be overwhelming. This is why we recommend periodically making video recordings of sessions. These videos can be scored at a later time for a more in-depth analysis of the child's and parent's behavior change. The Individual Format Coaching Form (Appendix A, Form 8) can be used to track parent behavior, and the Session Data Sheet (Appendix A, Form 14) can be used to track child behavior. When the trainer reviews the video with the parent and has the parent identify use of the technique and the child's response to the technique, the video review forms described earlier (Appendix A, Forms 7 and 12) should be used.

Chapter 3

Program Challenges, Solutions,
and Modifications

A number of issues may interfere with the effectiveness of a parent training program. These include the language and culture of the family, whether the family has any mental health or cognitive difficulties, the consistency of the parent's attendance at the training sessions, compliance with homework, and child behavior problems. We discuss these issues below and suggest strategies that can be used to deal with them. We then turn to ways that the Project ImPACT program can be modified for different situations.

Challenges and Solutions

Cultural Issues

The social-communication intervention presented in this program, as in the majority of other parent training programs, is derived from studies of parent–child interactions in mainly middle-class European American families (Forehand & Kotchick, 1996, 2002). Yet parenting practices are influenced by cultural values, ethnicity, and socioeconomic status (Forehand & Kotchick, 1996). Thus the Project ImPACT intervention techniques may be less compatible with parenting practices used by families from minority cultures. For example, African American culture places a strong value on child obedience to authority figures (Forehand & Kotchick, 1996); this may be at odds with intervention techniques based on the premise of "following the child's lead." In many Asian American cultures, it is common for parents to view themselves as educators of their children, but not as play partners (Forehand & Kotchick, 1996); thus some Asian American parents may feel uncomfortable playing with their children. In Latino/Latina culture, a significant amount of parenting responsibility is placed on extended family members, particularly grandparents (Forehand & Kotchick, 1996); therefore, including only parents in a parent training program may neglect important family members. It is important to be sensitive to particular ethnic or cultural groups, while also being aware that there is often more variability within a group than between groups (Forehand & Kotchick, 2002). Trainers should avoid stereotyping families on the basis of their ethnic or cultural background.

There is little research on cultural differences in client response to parent training programs that teach social-communication strategies for children with ASD. There is, however, an emerging field of research examining cultural differences in clients' responses to parent training programs that teach behavior management strategies for children exhibiting a wide range of behavior problems. This research suggests that minority families are less likely to access intervention and more likely to terminate intervention prematurely than families from the cultural majority are (Harachi et al., 1997). However, the research also suggests that, among families who complete the intervention as originally designed, the outcomes are similar for majority and minority clients (Kumpfer et al., 2002). These findings indicate that effective cultural adaptations should be focused on developing strategies to decrease attrition rates among minorities, rather than on altering the intervention content (Kumpfer et al., 2002). Many of the strategies discussed below under "Failure to Attend Sessions" may be effective for increasing minority clients' participation and completion of the parent training program.

Another important cultural issue is the language of the family. In many cases, the parents or grandparents may not be fluent in English. This can be a significant barrier to participation (Harachi et al., 1997). The ideal situation is to have a bilingual parent trainer who conducts training in the family's native language (Harachi et al., 1997); however, in many cases, this may not be feasible. An alternative is for the trainer to use an interpreter. Another option is a parent-to-parent training model: One bilingual parent who has received training teaches a non-English-speaking parent, with the help of the trainer. We have found that for non-English-speaking families, individual training with an interpreter can be very effective, especially when the interpreter has received an overview of the program prior to working with the family.

One additional consideration for bilingual families is which language the parents should use when working with their children with ASD. Many bilingual families are told to use only English with their children when the children receive a diagnosis of ASD. This recommendation is based on the concern that the use of two languages with these children could further delay their language development (Thordardottir, 2006). However, the research suggests that instruction in both languages does not impair language acquisition for children with language delays such as ASD (Bruck, 1982). In addition, many non-native English speakers place great value on having their children learn their native language, so that the children can communicate with family members who do not speak English. Many parents also feel more comfortable interacting with their children in their native language. Thus, while parent training may need to be conducted in English for logistical reasons, every parent should be encouraged to use the language she feels most comfortable with at home with her child.

Failure to Attend Sessions

One of the most often cited impediments to a successful parent training program is low attendance at training sessions (e.g., Kazdin & Wassell, 1998). Attendance is typically more of a problem when training is conducted in a group, because when a parent misses a group session, she misses a significant portion of the information. When training is conducted individually, the trainer can cover the missed material in the next session. However, we have found that a high number of absences has a negative impact on parent learning even in individual training when all sessions are made up. Parents who miss multiple sessions may be less committed to the program, or they may be experiencing other life stressors that affect their ability to use the intervention strategies. Many issues can affect a parent's attendance at training sessions, including lack of child care, low commitment to the program, conflicting work schedules, transportation difficulties, and other family responsibilities (Harachi et al., 1997). As discussed below, the key to overcoming these obstacles is to be flexible and resourceful.

The biggest obstacle to parent attendance is usually the lack of child care, particularly during group sessions. Securing child care can be particularly difficult for parents of children with ASD. Even parents who have the ability to pay may have difficulty finding babysitters or respite providers willing to watch their children with ASD. It may be necessary for the training program to arrange for child care providers capable of supervising children with ASD. Indeed, we have worked with a number of ECSE programs that used the group training model, some of which provided child care and some of which did not. The programs with child care had higher attendance rates by far. The child care was provided by classroom assistants, either on a volunteer basis or for extra-duty pay. One possibility in planning group programs is to provide parents with the option of paying for low-cost child care provided by classroom assistants (e.g., $5 per child). Since the classroom assistants will already know the children, most parents will be comfortable leaving their children in the assistants' capable hands.

Conflicting work schedules can pose another obstacle to parent attendance. Flexible scheduling (including offering sessions during the evenings and on weekends) can greatly enhance parent participation, especially among fathers, who are more likely to work outside of the home (Winter, 2006).

A third obstacle is transportation difficulties. For some families, arranging reliable transportation to sessions may be difficult, particularly for those who must use public transit and have difficulty handling their children in public. For these families, providing training in the home or in a community location close to the family, such as a church or day care center, may improve attendance (Harachi et al., 1997). Other families may live so far from the treatment site that transportation on a weekly basis is impractical. For these families, the intensity or length of the training may need to be adjusted. This may mean scheduling the training sessions less often over more weeks or condensing training into a shorter period of time. For example, Koegel, Symon, and Koegel (2002) developed an effective parent training model for families who lived in locations geographically distant from the training center. In this model, individual training in naturalistic teaching techniques was conducted several hours per day over the course of a week. Parents were able to master the intervention techniques during this week, and generalized their use with their children when they returned home. These types of accommodations may be more effective in an individual than in a group program.

Attendance may also be affected by a parent's discomfort with the demands of the program or by lack of commitment. If a parent is uneasy with the intervention techniques being presented, she may be less inclined to make it to sessions. Research suggests that the quality of the relationship between the trainer and the parent has a significant impact on parent satisfaction, and ultimately on attendance (Alexander, Barton, Schiaro, & Parsons, 1976). The parent trainer can work to build a positive relationship with the parent by using a facilitative style, as discussed in Chapter 2 under "Building Rapport." Working with the parent to set child goals together can also increase the parent's commitment to the program.

For families whose attendance is compromised by the multiple competing demands of life, the trainer may wish to use reinforcement to increase parents' motivation to attend training sessions. We have found that providing a low-cost dinner during evening parent groups is an effective reinforcer for many families. Another possibility is to offer incentives or rewards (e.g., gift certificates for a toy store), for attendance and progress in the program (Forehand & Kotchick, 2002). Another approach is to ask each parent to pay a refundable deposit to register for the program, and then return a portion of the deposit for each session the parent attends (Forehand & Kotchick, 2002).

Parent Mental Health Issues and Cognitive Limitations

Some parents may suffer from mental health issues or cognitive limitations that can impair their ability to benefit from the program (Forehand & Kotchick, 2002). Depression is the most common mental health issue that a practitioner is likely to encounter in working with families of children with ASD (Bitsika & Sharpley, 2004). These parents are often struggling with the process of accepting their children's diagnosis, and it can be helpful to combine the parent training program with a parent support group. Stahmer and Gist (2001) found that parents of children with ASD who received individual parent training and who also attended a support group learned the intervention techniques more effectively than the parents who only received the parent training. Another possibility is to combine parent training on intervention techniques with stress management training (Egan, 1983; Hastings & Beck, 2004).

It is not trainer's responsibility to provide therapy to parent. However, it is useful for the trainer to develop some knowledge of common mental health concerns, in order to identify needs and provide referral to appropriate services. In all of these cases, it is important for the parent to receive help to address any mental health issues prior to beginning parent training. If, at any point, a trainer is concerned that a parent is abusive or unable to care effectively for her child, the trainer should contact the appropriate authorities. This policy should be made clear to parents when they consent to treatment.

In some cases, the parent may struggle to learn the intervention techniques because of her own cognitive limitations. Indeed, we have worked with a number of children whose parents had learning disabilities or were on the autism spectrum themselves. When a parent has cognitive limitations, it may be best to provide training in an individual format that allows the parent to move through the techniques at a slower pace. In addition, the use of pictures (perhaps displayed in the home) may be more effective than a written manual for helping the parent understand and remember to use the intervention techniques (Feldman, Ducharme, & Case, 1999). We have worked with some parents who benefited from an increased use of video for presenting the intervention techniques and for providing feedback, as well as from extended role play with the trainer. Since many individuals with cognitive limitations experience difficulty with generalization, training sessions in the home may be more successful than at a clinic or school (Tymchuk & Andron, 1992).

Child Behavior Problems

Most young children with ASD also exhibit behavioral issues, such as noncompliance, tantrums, aggression, property destruction, sleeping or eating problems, or elopement, that can affect their families' quality of life and disrupt the children's learning (Schreibman, 1988). In most cases, these behaviors are mild and can be addressed while teaching the parents to use the social-communication intervention. However, in some cases, these behaviors may be extreme, requiring additional intervention. A child may exhibit significant behavioral difficulties during coaching sessions that interfere with a parent's ability to learn the social-communication strategies. Even when the child's behavior is under control during coaching sessions, it can be so disruptive at other times that the parent is unable to focus on homework practice of the intervention until the child's behaviors are under control. If the parent trainer is well versed in behavior management strategies, she may choose to continue with parent training, but focus instead on behavior management until the child's behavior is under control. Otherwise, the trainer should work with a behavioral specialist to develop an effective behavior plan for the child that can be implemented across settings.

Modifications to the Program

The Project ImPACT program can be modified for different situations. We encourage the trainer to make adaptations to the information outlined in Parts II and III to best meet her own and each family's needs. In this section, we describe how to modify the program for use in fewer sessions, in a toddler group, and with siblings.

Fewer Sessions

The individual format is designed to be conducted in 24 sessions, meeting twice a week for 12 weeks. However, in some cases, service providers may be only able to see clients once a week. Although we emphasize that the original format is optimal for parent learning, we have found that many parents have been able to learn the intervention techniques effectively in fewer than the recommended sessions. When the curriculum needs to be covered in fewer sessions, we recommend devoting a single session to techniques that are covered in more than one session, occasionally covering more than one technique a session, and eliminating the video review. Table 3.1 provides a recommended schedule for an individual format conducted in 12 weekly sessions.

It is also possible to modify either the group or the individual format to be conducted intensively with a single or multiple families over the course of a week. This modification has been used successfully with families who need to travel long distances to receive training (Koegel et al., 2002).

Toddler Groups

An additional intervention format that is available within some school districts and in the private sector is the toddler group. Toddler groups are designed to provide parent education while also preparing the children for participation in a classroom setting. These groups usually involve a small number of students, their parents, and two intervention providers; sessions last 60–90 minutes each and are provided once or twice a week. Groups are usually run like a preschool ESCE classroom, with a number of developmentally appropriate classroom-based activities (e.g., greeting, sensory–motor activity, gross motor activity, music, free play, snack, tabletop activities, and closing circle). Activities are usually run by the intervention providers, with each parent serving as her child's assistant.

The individual format can be modified for use during these groups by having one teacher provide individual coaching to one family while a second teacher leads the other families in

Table 3.1. Suggested Schedule for 12-Session, 12-Week Individual Training Format

Session	Content
1	*Overview of the Program* and *Goal Development*
2	*Review Goals* and *Set Up Your Home for Success*
3	*Follow Your Child's Lead; Imitate Your Child; Animation*
4	*Modeling and Expanding Language*
5	*Playful Obstruction*
6	*Balanced Turns*
7	*Communicative Temptations*
8	*Overview of the Direct Teaching Techniques*
9	*Teaching Your Child Expressive Language; Teaching Your Child Receptive Language*
10	*Teaching Your Child Social Imitation; Teaching Your Child Play*
11	*Putting It All Together; Update Goals*
12	*Moving Forward* and follow-up plan

group activities. The classroom schedule should consist of a number of short activities (e.g., 15 minutes) that families rotate through, so that each parent has the opportunity to support her child during small-group activities targeting the child's developmental goals, as well as to receive individual coaching. Given that each parent coaching session is significantly shorter than in the other formats, it is likely that the trainer will need to spend more than one session on each technique in order for the parent to master it.

An example of how to divide time and rotations during a toddler group to include parent training is outlined in Table 3.2. This format is used during 90-minute toddler groups with two staff members and five children and their parents. To use this format, it is necessary to have two clearly defined spaces. During the coaching rotation, one teacher provides coaching to each parent as she works with her child. During the small-group activity rotations, one teacher takes the leading role while the parents observe and assist their children. During the full-group activities, one teacher leads the activity while the other teacher and the parents assist the children.

The above-described modification allows families who enter the program at different times to begin parent training at the time of their enrollment. With this format, it is expected that

Table 3.2. Sample Schedule for 90-Minute Toddler Group

Time	Teacher 1	Teacher 2
8:30–8:35	Full group—greeting (lead)	Full group—greeting (assist)
8:35–8:50	Small group—sensory–motor activity	Coaching—free play (Family 1)
8:50–9:05	Coaching—free play (Family 2)	Small group—music
9:05–9:15	Small group—snack	Coaching—snack (Family 3)
9:15–9:30	Coaching—free play (Family 4)	Small group—art activity
9:30–9:40	Full group—gross motor activity (assist)	Full group—gross motor activity (lead)
9:40–10:55	Small group—tabletop activity	Coaching—free play (Family 5)
9:55–10:00	Full group—closing circle (lead)	Full group—closing circle (assist)

different families may be at different points in the program, depending on when their children start the group. If all children begin the group at the same time, it may be more practical to present the information to the parents in the group presentations, without the children present. The toddler group time can then be used as a place to provide the individual coaching.

Children may become distracted when more than one activity is occurring, due to the increase in auditory and visual stimuli; this creates a challenge in providing coaching in a group setting. In order to address this concern, it is important to have clear visual and physical boundaries and to limit the stimuli in the environment. The structure of the physical environment or the layout of the room should follow the same principles that are outlined in the discussion of *Set Up Your Home for Success* (see Part II, Session 2).

Training Siblings

Children with ASD exhibit significant difficulty interacting socially with other children, including their siblings (Schreibman, 1988). Most typically developing siblings are interested in playing with their siblings with ASD, but they often do not know effective strategies for interacting (El-Gououry & Romanczyk, 1999). Promoting positive interactions between a child with ASD and a typically developing sibling is often a goal for parents, and sibling training can be an effective method for reaching this goal (Schreibman, O'Neill, & Koegel, 1983; Sullivan, 1999; Strain & Danko, 1995; Tsao & Odom, 2006). It may be an excellent choice when a sibling has expressed interest in training or needs to attend with the parent. We have found that many typically developing children welcome the opportunity to be involved in their siblings' therapy, and that they respond very positively to the additional adult attention provided in a sibling training program.

Typically developing siblings often provide better language and play models than their parents, since they are closer in age to the children with ASD. Furthermore, research has shown that children with ASD are more likely to initiate play episodes with their siblings than with their parents (El-Ghoroury & Romanczyk, 1999) and may imitate the behavior of siblings and peers more than that of adults (Jones & Schwartz, 2004). Below, we discuss how to determine whether a child with ASD and a sibling would benefit from such a program, as well as specific strategies for training the sibling.

Characteristics of the Child with ASD

Research suggests that naturalistic peer-mediated interventions can be effective for children with ASD with varying levels of ability (e.g., McGee, Almeida, Sulzer-Azaroff, & Feldman, 1992; Pierce & Schreibman, 1995a, 1995b, 1997; Tsao & Odom, 2006). However, we have found that children who have some verbal abilities (e.g., single words or word approximations) are generally more successful. Typically developing children may be more motivated to interact with their siblings with ASD when they are able to respond. A child with ASD should not exhibit behavior that could place a sibling in any potential danger.

Sibling Characteristics

Research has shown that typically developing children as young as 4 years of age can be trained to use naturalistic prompting strategies with their peers with ASD (McGee et al., 1992). Two-year-olds can be taught to imitate the play of peers with ASD (Ingersoll & Stahmer, 2002). Although these studies indicate that even very young typically developing children can be successfully taught to use some social-communication strategies with their peers with ASD, the younger the children, the more support they will need to learn the intervention strategies. Older children (age 8 and above) are usually able to use a larger number of strategies independently after they have been taught (Pierce & Schreibman, 1997).

A sibling should have a number of prosocial behaviors and should be motivated to participate in a training program. If the sibling feels resentment because of the amount of time spent helping the child with ASD, then giving the sibling one more activity may not help either child. If the sibling is a good candidate, the trainer should work with the parent to determine appropriate timing for incorporating the sibling into the parent training program.

Training Strategies

The strategies for training siblings are very similar to the strategies used to train parents; however, children often need additional support and practice, and training sessions may need to be shorter (10–15 minutes) to keep the siblings' interest. Depending on the siblings' age and ability, the trainer may teach all of the intervention techniques in the parent program or choose a limited number of techniques that are likely to have the greatest impact on increasing sibling interactions. Table 3.3 lists the techniques and strategies that we have found to be most effective for training siblings, in child-friendly language.

The number of sessions required for the typical sibling to master the intervention techniques will vary, depending on the number and type of techniques; the sibling's age, motivation, and social skills; and the responsiveness of the child with ASD. Most successful sibling/peer training programs range from 10 to 20 sessions (e.g., McGee et al., 1992; Pierce & Schreibman, 1995a, 1995b, 1997; Tsao & Odom, 2006).

Explaining the Program. The trainer should explain to the sibling that the sibling will be learning strategies to help the child with ASD learn how to play. The trainer should then explain the intervention techniques that she will be teaching the sibling to use.

Presenting Techniques. The trainer should describe the techniques in child-friendly language (see Table 3.3). It is also helpful for the sibling to receive a manual that describes the techniques

Table 3.3. Effective Techniques and Strategies for Training Siblings

Project ImPACT intervention technique/strategy	Child-friendly description
Follow Your Child's Lead	*Join and Help Your Brother/Sister*
Imitate Your Child	*Copy Your Brother/Sister*
Modeling and Expanding Language	*Talk about Play to Your Brother/Sister*
Balanced Turns	*Take Turns with Your Brother/Sister*
Teach Your Child Expressive Language	*Ask Your Brother/Sister to Talk*
Teach Your Child Social Imitation	*Get Your Brother/Sister to Copy You*
Reinforcement (part of all direct teaching techniques)	*Praise your brother/sister for good trying*

with simple words and pictures (Pierce & Schreibman, 1995a, 1995b), so that he or she can follow along as the trainer presents the techniques. Pictures provide great cues while the sibling is working with the child with ASD. Alternatively, the trainer can write and read the sibling a short story that describes a child using the techniques with a sibling with ASD (Tsao & Odom, 2006).

Role Playing. After providing a verbal description of the techniques, the trainer should role-play use of the techniques for the sibling to observe. Pierce and Schreibman (1995a, 1995b) recommend using two adults, one acting as the child with ASD and one as the sibling. It's best to use toys and activities that both siblings are likely to use during play at home. The adult acting as the sibling should provide *both* good and poor examples of implementing the intervention techniques. After each example, the trainer should ask the sibling questions about the interaction, to help him or her understand the key points of each technique. The trainer can use the parent as the second adult, or can record the role play on video so that she can conduct the training without the parent. The sibling can then watch the video with the trainer and discuss the implementation of the techniques after each example.

After observing a number of examples, the sibling should engage in role play, with the trainer pretending to be the child with ASD. The trainer should ask the sibling to demonstrate each intervention technique (e.g., "Show me how you would copy your brother"). The trainer should respond positively to the techniques sometimes and not respond at other times, to reflect the likely interaction with the child with ASD. After each example, the trainer should ask the sibling questions to help him or her understand the key points, and should provide the sibling with feedback on his or her implementation.

Choosing Play Activities. The trainer should begin training with structured activities that have well-defined spaces, materials, and rules, such as hide and seek, hot potato, Simon says, and catch. These are typically more successful than open-ended activities. Once the sibling is successful at engaging the child with ASD in more structured activities, the trainer can introduce activities that are less structured. If the typically developing sibling is particularly focused on the toys and has difficulty taking turns with the child with ASD (this often occurs with younger sibling trainers), the trainer may allow the typical child a short period of time with toys before interacting with the child with ASD.

Providing Feedback. After the sibling has shown the ability to carry out the techniques during role play, the trainer should tell him or her to use them with the child with ASD. The trainer should provide the sibling with both positive and corrective feedback during the sibling interaction. Once the typical sibling is able to use the intervention strategies effectively with the child with ASD, the trainer should begin to fade the amount of feedback she provides, with the goal of having the children play together without adult support. Particularly with younger children, it may be necessary to continue to have an adult present (this could be the parent), to encourage the sibling to maintain his or her efforts with the child with ASD over time.

Reinforcing the Sibling. When working with a younger typically developing sibling, the trainer may wish to include a reinforcement system to keep the child's motivation high. This system should be simple and contingent on the child's active effort to play with his or her sibling with

ASD. For example, the trainer may suggest that the parent provide her typically developing child with a special outing or playtime with just her, as reinforcement for successful periods of play with the child with ASD. If the child with ASD is particularly unresponsive, the trainer may need to keep this system in place over the course of the intervention, because the sibling's motivation may wane over time. However, the sibling is often naturally reinforced when the child with ASD begins to respond to him or her; thus the reinforcement system can often be faded over time. An effective strategy for encouraging typical siblings to maintain their use of the intervention in the absence of adult attention is to teach them to self-monitor their use of the techniques with the children with ASD and to self-reinforce (Sainato, Goldstein, & Strain, 1992).

Maintaining the Program. To ensure the success of a sibling training program, it is important for the parent to be involved. The trainer should teach the parent to set up appropriate activities, and to provide feedback and reinforcement to her typically developing child (Strain & Danko, 1995; Tsao & Odom, 2006).

The above-described training protocol may also be used to teach typically developing peers how to support the communication and play of their friends with ASD. Research suggests that training typical peers to use naturalistic intervention techniques with their peers with ASD leads to improvements in social interaction skills, as well as increased peer acceptance (Rogers, 2000). Furthermore, the program may be used to train other adults who provide care to children with ASD, such as day care providers and professionals (Jocelyn, Casiro, Beattie, Bow, & Kneisz, 1998).

In sum, several program modifications can be made to increase the success of Project ImPACT for individual families, as well as to expand its use to a broader range of intervention settings and providers. The key to a successful program is to be flexible and creative, and to have a strong philosophical commitment to training those individuals who interact with children with ASD outside a traditional intervention environment.

Individual Parent Training Program Session Guidelines

Part II of this manual provides a step-by-step guide to conducting an individual parent training program. Practitioners working with families on a one-to-one basis in a home or clinic setting will use this model for Project ImPACT (Improving Parents As Communication Teachers).

The individual parent training program is designed to be conducted in 24 sessions, ideally held twice a week over a 12-week period. Sessions are designed to run for 90 minutes (1 hour and 15 minutes of direct treatment, and 15 minutes for indirect activities such as note taking, preparation, and cleanup). We recognize that each family's needs are different; therefore, the program can be adapted to fit shorter sessions or fewer sessions per week as appropriate (see Part I, Chapter 3). Upon completion of the 24-session program, we recommend follow-up sessions with the family once a month for up to a year, or as long as the child continues to require services to address social-communication goals. These sessions encourage the parent to maintain her use of the intervention, help her to address any new concerns, and help her understand how the techniques can address new goals.

Because the parent (or other primary caregiver) is the primary provider, and the techniques build upon each other, it is essential that the same parent be present for all sessions. This requirement does not preclude additional family members from attending sessions with the primary parent as their schedules permit. However, attendance without the primary parent is not recommended, because other family members will not have learned previously taught techniques. The primary parent should be encouraged to give information to the other family members by sharing written materials, describing the techniques, and sharing videos of sessions.

Sequence of Sessions

Because the techniques in this program build upon each other, it is important to follow the specific sequence in which techniques are presented in the following pages. This sequence should remain essentially the same for all families. However, the pacing of the sessions can be tailored to each family. The amount of time spent on each step and each technique can vary, depending on the parent's style, previous training, and educational background. Table II.1 lists the techniques and their sequence, along with a rough guide to the number of sessions each technique might take; however, you should feel comfortable adjusting the number of sessions spent on each technique.

Table II.1. Sequence of Sessions for Individual Parent Training Format

Session 1:	*Overview of the Program and Goal Development*
Session 2:	*Review Goals and Set Up Your Home for Success*
Session 3:	*Follow Your Child's Lead*
Session 4:	*Imitate Your Child*
Session 5:	*Animation*
Sessions 6–7:	*Modeling and Expanding Language*
Session 8:	*Playful Obstruction*
Sessions 9–10:	*Balanced Turns*
Session 11:	*Communicative Temptations*
Session 12:	*Review of the Interactive Teaching Techniques*
Sessions 13–14:	*Overview of the Direct Teaching Techniques*
Sessions 15–16:	*Teaching Your Child Expressive Language*
Session 17:	*Teaching Your Child Receptive Language*
Session 18:	*Teaching Your Child Social Imitation*
Session 19:	*Teaching Your Child Play*
Session 20:	*Review of the Direct Teaching Techniques*
Sessions 21–22:	*Putting It All Together*
Sessions 23:	*Update Goals*
Session 24:	*Moving Forward (Final Session)*

The techniques presented in this program can be used with children at different levels of functioning. Therefore, the first step (completed in Session 1) is to determine the child's current levels of performance and to develop individualized goals. The child's functioning is assessed via the Child History Form (Appendix A, Form 2), the parent-completed Social-Communication Checklist (Appendix A, Form 3), your interaction with the child, and observation of the parent–child interaction.

Individualized goals for the child are then developed with the parent and need to reflect the parent's priorities. You will refer to these goals throughout the program when you explain the rationale for each technique.

Session Format

Each session in this section of the manual provides a brief outline of the main trainer tasks of the session, followed by an explanation of how to carry out those steps. Each session ends with a section on "Troubleshooting Tips" for implementing that session.

Most sessions follow a standard format as follows with approximate time allotments:

1. Review homework from previous session (10–15 minutes).
2. Introduce the rationale for the new technique (explain how the technique is used to address the child's individual goals) (5 minutes).
3. Explain how the technique relates to previously taught techniques (5 minutes).
4. Describe the technique's key points (5–10 minutes).
5. Demonstrate use of the technique with the child (5–15 minutes). The amount of time spent demonstrating decreases as you progress through the program.
6. Have the parent practice the technique while you provide feedback (10–25 minutes). The amount of time the parent spends practicing should increase as she progresses through the program.
7. Discuss and assign homework (10–15 minutes).

It is important to follow this format in teaching each technique, to ensure that the parent is able to implement the entire program at the end of the 24 sessions. At times it can be tempting to skim over or omit a technique, particularly at the beginning of the program. This can occur for a variety of reasons. First, the parent may have been using the technique appropriately prior to the implementation of this program. Second, the parent may not feel that the technique elicits change in her child's behavior and may urge you to move at a rapid pace. Last, some parents want to move through the program as quickly as possible to be able to use all the techniques together. It is important to resist the temptation to do this. Moving too quickly through the techniques can cause a parent to have difficulties implementing and integrating the techniques.

Steps to Complete Prior to the First Session

Prior to the first session, mail an introduction letter (Form 1) to the family. Families enrolling should then receive the Child History Form (Form 2). These forms can be found in Appendix A. Request that the parent bring the completed Child History Form to the first session. The purposes of this form are (1) to determine the parent's perception of how and why her child communicates; (2) to find out which interventions the child has been involved in; (3) to find out the parent's perspective on these interventions; and (4) to provide information on the parent's goals for her child and for herself. This knowledge will help you as the parent trainer to explain the program in language familiar to the parent.

The Child History Form should be reviewed with the parent during the first session. It lays the groundwork for the two main tasks of Session 1: giving the parent an overview of the program and developing goals for the child. This history form does not have questions regarding prenatal, perinatal, medical, or developmental history. To obtain this information, you may choose to use a different history form from your clinic or school. But if you choose this option, it is important that you also obtain information regarding the four purposes listed above for the Child History Form, because this information is referred to during the parent training program.

Overview of the Program
and Goal Development

Session Goals

1. Help the parent understand the rationale for parent training.
2. Provide an overview of the goals of this program and the training format.
3. Give an overview of the intervention techniques used in this program.
4. Develop goals for the child.

Materials

1. Parent manual
2. Child History Form (Appendix A, Form 2), in case the parent does not return it
3. Two copies of Social-Communication Checklist (Appendix A, Form 3)
4. Goal Development Form (Appendix A, Form 4)
5. Toys to keep child occupied
6. Parent consent forms for video recording, if not already signed

Outline of Session

- Introduce session agenda (5 minutes).
- Review Child History Form (10 minutes).
- Describe the program (10 minutes):

    Rationale for parent training
    Program goals
    Core skill areas: Social engagement, language, social imitation, play
    Parent and trainer roles
    Format for training parents in the techniques

- Develop goals for the child (30–40 minutes):

    Have parent complete Social-Communication Checklist
    Interact with child yourself.
    Observe and video-record a 10-minute parent–child interaction; complete
        Social-Communication Checklist based on observation.
    Write goals for the child with the parent.

- Provide overview of intervention techniques (20–30 minutes):

    Interactive teaching techniques—explain and demonstrate.
    Direct teaching techniques—explain and demonstrate.
    The pyramid of techniques—explain.

- Discuss and assign homework (5 minutes):
    1. Give the parent the parent manual and have her read *Overview of the Program* and *Set Up Your Home for Success* (Chapters 1 and 2) before the next session.
    2. Have the parent complete the Daily Activity Schedule in the parent manual at home and bring it to the next session.

About This Session

Parents can be hesitant to participate in parent training programs. They may feel that being referred for such programs means they are not good parents, and they may blame themselves for their children's social-communication delays. They may also feel that they would not able to provide an intervention as well as a professional could. Both reasons are unfounded. It is important to address these possible misconceptions during the initial description of the program. Explain to the parent that Project ImPACT (Improving Parents As Communication Teachers) does not teach parenting skills. Rather, it trains parents to use special techniques to teach better social-communication skills to their children. Research shows that parents can learn to use these techniques just as well and can be just as effective as professionals, if not more so. Research also reveals that teaching parents to use these techniques improves outcomes for their children.

As you explain the program, adapt the amount of detail to each parent's individual needs. Some parents enjoy reading research articles that provide additional information, while other parents may prefer a brief description accompanied by live or video-based demonstrations. The amount of time spent on each section will vary, depending on individual needs.

Introduce Session Agenda

Introduce yourself and describe the purposes of the session:

- To present an overview of the parent training program.
- To develop goals for the child.

Explain that it takes one to two sessions to accomplish these tasks.

Goals are developed on the basis of the Child History Form, the Social-Communication Checklist, your own (the trainer's) interaction with the child, and observation of the parent–child interaction. Explain that the parent–child interaction is video-recorded now to collect baseline data, and later in the program to assess progress and to provide feedback. Be sure to obtain the parent's written consent before making the video, in accord with your own or your clinic's confidentiality policies. If the parent is hesitant, suggest that she keep the video or that it be destroyed as soon as it is reviewed.

Review Child History Form

The parent-reported Child History Form (Appendix A, Form 2) should have been completed by the parent and brought to the first session. It is used as a starting point to obtain information about the child's skill level and the goals the parent has for the child and herself. It also provides information on the child's current and previous therapies. Take time to clarify any answers that are not specific or may be difficult to interpret. If the parent did not complete the form, have her respond orally to the questions while you take notes.

Describe the Program

Parents are more likely to implement an intervention at home if they understand the program rationale, the goals, and the steps used to address the goals. Use the information from the Child History Form to individualize this explanation for the parent. For example, if the parent indicates that her child has been enrolled in a developmental intervention (e.g., responsive teaching or DIR), explain that like other developmental programs, Project ImPACT focuses on increasing parent responsiveness and utilizing child-directed activities in order to teach new skills. However, unlike other developmental programs, this program also uses techniques and strategies derived from the naturalistic behavioral literature (e.g., prompting and shaping) to teach specific skills. Conversely, if the child has been enrolled in an applied behavior analysis program, explain that, like other behavior programs, Project ImPACT utilizes prompting and reinforcement to teach specific skills. However, unlike other behavior programs, this program also uses interactive teaching techniques to promote engagement and social interaction, and to target different functions of language.

Rationale for Parent Training

Explain to the parent that children with ASD have difficulty engaging with other people, have trouble initiating social interactions with others, and do not learn language in the typical way. However, with intervention, children with ASD can learn to improve their social-communication skills. Teaching parents to use specific techniques when interacting with their children improves outcomes for the children.

Explain that you have learned to use these techniques in your professional training. But research shows that parents can learn to use these techniques successfully. This is much better for the children than if only a professional uses them. Parents are their children's first teachers. They know the children best and spend the most time with them. When a parent learns to use the techniques in this program, the child benefits in at least three ways: (1) The child gets many more hours of teaching than he could at school or on a one-to-one basis with a professional; (2) the child can be taught skills at home during natural interactions and daily routines, such as bathtime, mealtime, and bedtime; and (3) the child is more likely to apply the skills to new situations and to keep using the skills over the long term. For the child, all of this means better language development, better social interaction, and fewer behavior problems. It also means less parent stress and a better parent–child relationship.

Parents who would like to read more about the benefits of parent training should be referred to the "Further Reading" list at the back of the parent manual.

Program Goals

Explain that this program's primary goal is to teach the parent to use strategies to improve her child's social-communication skills. This program helps the parent build the child's skills in four core areas: social engagement, language, social imitation, and play.

This session will be spent developing individual goals for the child in each of the four core areas. In future sessions, you and the parent will discuss how to use the techniques to address the goals, as well as to track progress toward goals.

Now describe each core skill area in turn to the parent.

Core Skill Area: Social Engagement

The term *social engagement* refers to the ability to take turns, initiate language or play with others, respond to others, gain another's attention, and maintain interactions over a period of time. The ways that children engage others are eye contact, body language, gestures, and/or words. Children with ASD usually have difficulty engaging with others, which impedes their ability to learn from others. The starting point of this program is to help the parent improve her child's ability to engage with her. When a child can engage with others, and can give others his attention, he is more likely to learn. Each technique in this program will focus on social engagement, since this skill provides the foundation for developing social-communication skills.

Explain that later in this session, you and the parent will identify the skills the child already has for social engagement, and what skills he may need to learn. From this assessment, goals can be developed for initiating and responding, as well as for increasing the length of the child's engagement with others.

Core Skill Area: Language

A very important core skill area involves the ability to use and understand verbal and nonverbal language for a variety of purposes. *Verbal language* includes the words or word combinations the child uses. *Nonverbal language* includes the use of gestures, signs, eye contact, body posture, and facial expressions. The purposes of communication include requesting, protesting, gaining others' attention, commenting, sharing, and responding. Explain to the parent that once the child's skills are identified, goals will be developed for both verbal and nonverbal language and for specific language functions. This program also focuses on helping the child use language spontaneously. Explain to the parent that this means goals will focus on helping the child communicate on his own, without any help from the parent.

Core Skill Area: Social Imitation

Social imitation is important because children use it to learn new information (i.e., observational learning) and to communicate interest in others (i.e., reciprocal imitation). Teaching children with ASD to observe others in new environments and to imitate their behavior can help them to participate more successfully in social situations. This program shows the parent how to teach imitation skills in the natural environment and how to use imitation to enhance the child's development in other areas.

Core Skill Area: Play

Play skills are closely related to language skills, since both require symbolic thinking (i.e., understanding that one thing can represent another). Teaching pretend play skills can help children develop more sophisticated language skills. In addition, play is an excellent way to work on problem-solving skills, conceptual and imaginative abilities, and fine and gross motor skills. Play is also the most natural way to teach language, because children learn how to interact with others through play. Goals are developed in this area to increase the variety and complexity of the child's play skills.

Parent and Trainer Roles

Emphasize to the parent that she will take the lead role in this program. Explain to the parent that her interactions with her child are important because she spends the most time with her child. In this program, she will be the primary intervention provider; this means that she helps select goals, practices techniques, and implements the intervention in the home and community. Your role as trainer will be to act as the parent's coach by providing her with feedback in each of these areas.

Format for Training Parents in the Techniques

Explain to the parent that one to three sessions will be spent on each technique. This ensures that she has time to practice and that she has the necessary tools to implement the technique at home. Let the parent know that the two of you will work as a team to determine the pace of each session.

Explain that you will introduce new techniques to the parent one at a time. Each technique will be taught in the same way, following these steps:

1. *Description of the technique.* The parent will read about each new technique prior to the session in which you present it. Then in the session, you will describe the technique and discuss with the parent when and how to use it with her child.

2. *Demonstration of the new technique.* You will first demonstrate the technique with the child.

3. *Parent practice.* The parent will then practice the technique with her child while you provide her with feedback.

4. *Homework.* At the end of the session, you will help the parent select goals and activities in which to practice the technique at home with the child. After practicing, she should answer the questions in the parent manual. At the beginning of the next session, you will then review her answers and discuss any questions or challenges she may have.

Develop Goals for the Child

The goals for the child are developed on the basis of the parent's report, your own interaction with the child, and your observation of a parent–child interaction. It is important to develop specific and measurable goals within the first few sessions for two reasons. First, they enable you to track progress to make sure the program is effective. Second, they enable you to explain how each technique can be used to address the child's goals.

Have Parent Complete Social-Communication Checklist

Explain to the parent that the Social-Communication Checklist (Appendix A, Form 3) is used to determine her understanding of her child's social engagement, language, social imitation, and play skills at home, and thus to help in the development of goals. While the parent completes the checklist, be available to respond to any questions that may arise and to obtain clarification of any responses that may be vague or difficult to interpret. When two parents attend the training, ask them whether they want to complete a checklist together or independently. Acknowledge that sometimes children interact differently with different adults and in different situations.

Interact with the Child Yourself

While the parent completes the Social-Communication Checklist, interact with the child to gain a brief understanding of his social engagement, language, social imitation, and play skills. Take this time to determine which techniques are most effective with the child. This knowledge is helpful when you demonstrate use of the techniques at the end of this session.

Observe and Record a 10-Minute Parent–Child Interaction

Instruct the parent to play with her child as she would at home. Explain to the parent that this interaction will be used to collect baseline data. While she interacts with her child, use another Social-Communication Checklist to record information on the child's use of skills in each of the four core areas with you and with the parent. It is also beneficial to note any techniques the parent is using and their effect on the child's behavior. This information will be useful when you are describing the treatment techniques in subsequent sessions. If the parent has allowed you to record the session on video, it is often helpful to go back and review the video to collect additional data.

When two parents are present, allow each one to interact individually with the child for 5 minutes. Clearly announce transitions between your interaction with the child and each parent's interaction. For example, with two parents present, you might say: "Molly, you can begin the interaction with your son. Jim, you can come stand with me and observe the interaction. ... Thank you, Molly. Jim, now it is your turn to play with your son as you would at home. Molly, come stand with me to watch them play." A clear transition statement sets the precedent for separating parents throughout the program while they practice and receive feedback. This ensures that each parent has time to practice and receive feedback.

Write Goals for the Child with the Parent

Goals are developed with the Goal Development Form (Appendix A, Form 4). The first step is to determine one to two global goals the parent would like to address in each of the four core areas. To determine the parent's goals, review the Child History Form and ask the parent about her goals for her child. If the parent does not have a goal for each of the four areas, ask probing questions, suggest a goal, and then ask the parent whether she agrees. Here are some sample questions:

1. "I notice that Brian often leaves the interaction when you join in his play. Is this something you would like to address? How would you feel about a goal to increase the length of time he plays with others?"

2. "As we discussed earlier, Sam does not use phrase speech on his own. Rather, he reaches toward an object and waits for you to say the phrase and repeats what you said. How would you feel about adding a goal to increase his spontaneous use of two- to three-word phrases?"

3. "Sam appears to have difficulty playing with toys in a pretend manner. Do you find this to be true at home? How would you feel about adding a goal to increase his pretend play?"

Write these goals on the Goal Development Form under "Global Goals."

The next step is to help the parent understand her child's current level of functioning in each area. The current level of functioning is determined by comparing the two completed Social-Communication Checklists (covering the parent's report, your interaction with the child, and your observation of the parent–child interaction) and by reviewing previous evaluations. Many times you will find consistency across these two checklists and previous evaluations, which will make identifying the child's skill level relatively easy. However, sometimes there are differences that need to be reconciled before goals can be developed. Differences in reports and observations usually occur when (1) the child has difficulty engaging and communicating in a new environment, and therefore does not display his typical skills; (2) the parent has a different interaction style when being watched and recorded on video; and/or (3) the parent is unaware of the child's level of functioning and the amount of support she provides. If the information on the parent's checklist is significantly different from your observation, this difference can be explored by asking open-ended and probing questions. Questions can help clarify the parent's responses and inform you whether the observation is typical of the child's performance. Here are some sample questions:

1. "Did this seem to be typical of play at home with your child? If not, how was it different?"

2. "I noticed you reported that your child uses two to three words to communicate at home. He seemed to be fairly quiet today. Can you give me some examples of his language at home?"

3. "Today your child appeared to repeat language he heard. I did not hear him say anything without you saying it first. Do you find this to be true?"

4. "Your child seems to ask questions even when he knows the answer. Do you find this to be true?"

Once you and the parent agree on the child's current level of functioning, it should be written on the Goal Development Form under "Current Skills."

The last step is to translate the targeted behaviors into specific goals that are measurable and appropriate for the child's skill level. You should write these specific goals to be consistent with your current method of data collection, so that you can document the child's progress. The specific goals should be written under "Measurable Goals" on the Goal Development Form. Be sure to check in with the parent to confirm that she is in agreement with these goals. In some cases, it may take five or six sessions to determine the child's level of functioning and develop measurable goals in all areas.

The following case studies illustrate how goals are developed during a first parent training session for Brian, a child who is not yet using language, and Sam, a child who is using single words spontaneously and imitating phrase speech. Chapter 2 in Part I of this manual contains additional information regarding goal setting and includes sample goals for the four core areas targeted in this program.

Case Study 1: Brian

Brian is a 3-year-old boy who has recently been diagnosed with an ASD. Brian and his mother have come to the clinic for their first parent training session. Brian enters the room and sits on the floor holding two squishy balls while the trainer and his mother discuss the program. Brian does not attempt to interact with his mother or the trainer while they are talking.

During the parent–child interaction, Brian is observed to play next to his mother for 1 minute before leaving and moving to a new activity. He does not attempt to communicate with her unless he is unable to access a toy on his own. When this occurs, Brian takes his mother's hand and leads her to the toy. Some of the time he is noted to sign "more," although it is not always clear what he wants more of. Once Brian has the toys, he typically lines them up or drops them on the floor.

Brian's mom indicates on the Social-Communication Checklist that Brian likes to play near her some of the time, and that he communicates primarily by taking her hand and leading her to what he wants. She reports that he sometimes makes sounds, but that he does not use words. In regard to his imitation skills, she indicates that he sometimes imitates a wave for bye-bye, but that he does not imitate other gestures or play. She reports that his play skills are primarily limited to exploratory play, adding that Brian usually explores toys by touching, smelling, or tasting them, and that he does not play with toys correctly.

When the trainer interacts with Brian, she notices that he is beginning to reach toward objects that he likes. She also notices that when Brian is shown how to use a toy, he imitates the play action when he is engaged. This occurs infrequently, because Brian does not stay engaged very long; he usually leaves an activity after about a minute. In terms of effective techniques, she notes that Brian responds well to *Playful Obstruction* and *Animation* to gain his attention. He does not seem to respond to verbal or gesture prompts, but allows the clinician to help him point. He also appears to make some sounds when he wants an object.

After gathering the initial information on Brian's current levels of performance, the trainer begins goal development by reviewing the Child History Form and asking the mother about her goals for Brian. Brian's mother indicates that she would like Brian to be able to have a conversation and play with her; she also wishes that Brian would say hello and good-bye when people come over. The trainer tells the mother that these are excellent long-term goals for Brian. The trainer then explains that the next few minutes will be spent developing goals for improving Brian's ability to talk with others and play with others. She explains that in order for Brian to communicate with others, the first step is to improve his engagement with others. The trainer then asks Brian's mother questions to determine her perception of Brian's engagement, as well as her goals for him in this area. The trainer says: "I notice that Brian plays near you for about a minute before he moves to another activity. Is this something you would like to address?" His mother indicates that she would like him to be able to play with her longer, but that he doesn't seem to like to play. The trainer explains that both goals can be addressed in this program, and that both skills will lead to her overarching goals of improving Brian's ability to talk and play with her. The first goal will be to increase the length of his interactions with her, and the second goal will be to increase his functional play skills. Once the parent agrees to the goals, the trainer writes them on the Goal Development Form under "Global Goals," as shown in Figure S1.1. The trainer then proceeds to ask probing questions; she determines that Brian's mother would also like Brian to be able to use language to request and to imitate a wave for hello and good-bye. These goals are also written on the Goal Development Form. Notice that all goals are related to

Child's name: Brian

Date: 2/9/09

Global Goals	Current Skills	Measurable Goals
Social Engagement		
Increase length of interactions	Brian allows his parent to play near him for 1–2 minutes.	Brian will increase the amount of time he is engaged with a play partner to at least 5 minutes.
Language		
Increase expressive language to request	Brian requests using primarily gestures (reaching and signing "more"). He uses vocalizations sporadically to request.	Brian will use a point, vocalizations, or single word to initiate requests for actions or objects at 5 out of 10 opportunities.
Social Imitation		
Increase gesture imitation	Brian was not observed to imitate gestures. His mother reports that he sometimes imitates a wave.	Brian will imitate conventional gestures (e.g., wave, point, clap) at 3 out of 6 opportunities.
Play		
Increase functional play	Brian plays with toys mainly by exploring them (lining up, dropping, holding).	Brian will use toys for their intended purpose at least 50% of the time when provided with a model.

Figure S1.1. Example of completed Goal Development Form (Appendix A, Form 4) for Brian (Case Study 1).

Brian's mother's initial statement that she would like Brian to be able to talk and play with her. Using the parent's goals in this way motivates her and increases the likelihood that she will practice the techniques at home.

Case Study 2: Sam

Sam is a 4-year-old boy with a diagnosis of an ASD. He and his mother have come to the clinic for their first parent training session. Sam comes into the room and begins to play with a set of cars while the trainer discusses the program with his mother. Sam mumbles to himself while he is playing. His mother identifies what he is saying as lines from the movie *Cars*, which she reports is his favorite movie.

The parent trainer begins the process of setting goals. Sam's mom indicates on the Social-Communication Checklist that Sam initiates activities with her some of the time, and shows her objects some of the time. She reports that he does not yet take turns with her. She reports that Sam uses words to describe objects, actions, and attributes, and that he uses sentences to communicate sometimes. In regard to Sam's imitation skills, she indicates that he sometimes imitates novel play with toys, but not consistently. She also reports that Sam's play skills mainly involve functional play with objects.

Throughout the parent–child interaction, Sam plays next to his mother. His play consists mainly of holding and ordering the cars, although he occasionally pushes a car around the floor in a circle. He periodically holds up one of the cars to his mother and labels it by name (all the names are from the *Cars* movie). Although it appears that these communications are directed toward his mother, he does not make eye contact with her. On several occasions, Sam's mother attempts to take a turn with one of the cars he is playing with; each time, Sam screams and pushes his mother's hands away. He does, however, respond to her questions to label the color of each car and to count the cars. Sam's mother reports that this interaction is typical of their play at home, with Sam using language (labeling colors, naming character, and counting) centered around specific routines (involving cars).

When the trainer interacts with Sam, she notices that he spontaneously uses single words to request items that interest him (cars, bubbles); however, she does not observe him using phrase speech spontaneously. She also notices that Sam engages in highly repetitive play with cars, but is able to imitate some familiar pretend play actions with a stuffed bear when the cars are removed. In terms of effective techniques, she notes that Sam responds well to being imitated with *Animation*, by using eye contact and smiling. He also responds well to several *Communicative Temptations* to gain his attention. However, he gets very frustrated when she tries to use *Balanced Turns* with him. He is able to answer direct questions with single words, and to imitate two- to three-word phrases. Again, however, he does not use phrase speech spontaneously.

After reviewing the Child History Form and gathering the initial information on Sam's current levels of performance, the trainer begins goal development by asking Sam's mother about her goals for him. Sam's mother indicates that she would like Sam to be able to play with his younger brother. Currently, he pushes or hits his brother whenever his brother tries to play with his toys. The trainer suggests that one way to improve Sam's play with his sibling is to increase his ability to take turns with others. Since he has problems taking turns with adults, the first goal will be to increase his ability to take turns with his mother—starting with trading toys, and moving toward giving her a turn. The trainer then asks Sam's mother what language goals she would like to work on. Sam's mother says that she would like to see Sam use longer sentences. The trainer mentions that although she has observed Sam imitating phrase speech, she has not seen him use any phrase speech spontaneously. The trainer asks whether this would be a good goal to work on. Sam's mother agrees, and the trainer writes this goal on Sam's Goal Development Form, as shown in Figure S1.2. The trainer asks additional probing questions and determines that Sam's mother would also like Sam to become more creative in his play. Based on his current play skills, the parent and trainer decide to add both an imitation and a play goal devoted to improving Sam's ability to use pretend play.

Child's name: Sam

Date: 7/21/09

Global Goals	Current Skills	Measurable Goals
Social Engagement		
Increase turn taking	Sam does not currently allow his parent to take a turn (becomes upset or leaves activity).	Sam will increase his turn-taking abilities to include trading toys with adults, allowing the play partner a turn, and watching the play partner's turn at 80% of opportunities presented.
Language		
Increase expressive language	Sam uses two- to three-word phrases to request and comment when given a verbal model. He primarily uses single words spontaneously.	Sam will use two- and three-word phrases (e.g., "pour milk") spontaneously for a variety of pragmatic functions (e.g., requesting, protesting, responding, labeling, and commenting).
Social Imitation		
Increase object imitation	Sam was observed to imitate some basic pretend actions with a stuffed animal.	Sam will imitate pretend and symbolic actions with toys at 50% of opportunities.
Play		
Increase pretend play	Sam was not observed to use toys in a pretend manner without a model.	Sam will use toys in a pretend manner when given choices (e.g., "Should we fill the car with gas or wash the car?").

Figure S1.2. Example of Completed Goal Development Form (Appendix A, Form 4) for Sam (Case Study 2).

In the sessions that follow, we will return to Brian, Sam, and their mothers to show how the trainer explains the intervention techniques in terms of the individual goals for each boy.

Provide Overview of Intervention Techniques

Explain to the parent that the techniques used in Project ImPACT were chosen because they are easy to incorporate into daily routines and because research shows that they are effective; children learn from them. Teaching during daily activities has been found to be more effective, receives higher satisfaction ratings from parents, and is easier to use in the home than highly structured approaches.

The techniques in this program are child-centered. This means that they are used with toys, objects, and activities chosen by the child. Because the child chooses the activity or toy, everyone can be sure that he is interested, engaged, and motivated. These are the best conditions for the parent to teach and for the child to learn. These techniques were also chosen because they lead to fewer behavior problems and more positive parent–child interactions. Depending on the parent's knowledge of and/or experience with other interventions, you can relate the techniques in this program to other treatment approaches.

Explain to the parent that over the course of the program, she will be learning two sets of techniques: *interactive teaching techniques* and *direct teaching techniques*.

Interactive Teaching Techniques

Interactive teaching techniques are taught in the first half of this program. They promote the child's engagement and his initiating of communication through child-chosen activities. These techniques are based on developmental research indicating a relationship between parents' degree of responsiveness and their children's social-communication development. When the interactive teaching techniques are used together, they follow the sequence outlined below.

1. Use the technique called *Follow Your Child's Lead* (i.e., the child chooses the activity; the parent sits face to face with the child and joins the play).
2. Create an opportunity for the child to engage or communicate (most interactive teaching techniques provide ways to create these opportunities).
3. Wait for the child to engage or communicate. The child should acknowledge the parent in some way, such as eye contact, gestures, body posture change, facial expressions, affect, play, or verbal language.
4. Respond to the child's behavior as meaningful, comply with it, and demonstrate a more complex response. Give the parent an example, using goals developed for her child. For example, in the first case presented above, Brian is using a reach to request items; when he reaches, the parent will comply with the request while modeling a point and a single word (i.e., a more complex response).

Emphasize to the parent that the interactive teaching techniques focus on increasing the child's engagement and initiating of communication. Therefore, it is important to create an opportunity for the child to engage or communicate and then to *wait*, giving the child an opportunity to show engagement or communicate. Once the child shows *any* sign of engagement or communication, the parent should respond to the child's behaviors as if they were meaningful.

Demonstrate the interactive teaching techniques sequence with the child, explaining how these techniques are used to address one of the child's goals. For example, if a goal is to "increase expressive language to request," and the child's current skill level is to reach, explain to the parent that she will begin by following the child's lead and then creating an opportunity for the child to communicate. Once the child gestures to request (i.e., communicates), the parent will respond by giving him the object he wants while saying the object's name and pointing to the object. Naming a wanted object and pointing to the desired object are more complex responses than reaching for it. As you demonstrate the techniques, explain to the parent how you are following the child's lead; creating an opportunity for the child to engage or communicate; waiting for the child to engage or communicate; and responding to the child's behavior as meaningful while modeling a more complex response. For example, you might say: "Here I am modeling pointing, a more complex response, when your child reaches towards the toy."

The demonstration of the interactive teaching techniques and the direct teaching techniques is the one time this session that you show the parent skills that the parent is not yet able to use. Explain to the parent that by the end of the program, she will be able to use the techniques together to address her child's goals.

Direct Teaching Techniques

Direct teaching techniques are taught in the second half of the program. They all build on the interactive teaching techniques by adding two sets of strategies called *prompting* and *reinforcement* to teach specific skills to the child. The direct teaching techniques are drawn from behavioral research and focus on teaching language, social imitation, and play skills. When the direct teaching techniques are used together, they follow the sequence below.

1. Use *Follow Your Child's Lead* (i.e., the child chooses the activity; the parent sits face to face with the child and joins the play).
2. Create an opportunity for the child to communicate (i.e., use an interactive teaching technique from the middle of the pyramid [see below] to create an opportunity for communication).
3. Wait for the child to communicate. The child should initiate communication with the parent in some way, such as eye contact, gestures, body posture change, facial expressions, affect, play, or verbal language.
4. Prompt the child to use more complex language, imitation, or play (the direct teaching techniques concern how to elicit a more complex skill).
5. Provide a more supportive (helpful) prompt as necessary, to help the child use the new skill.
6. Reinforce and expand on the child's response (i.e., give the child what he wants and demonstrate a more complex skill).

Emphasize that the first three steps in the direct teaching techniques sequence are identical to the first three steps in the interactive teaching techniques. This is why it is important to start with the interactive teaching techniques. What is different is that the parent prompts the child and the child uses a more complex response *before* the parent acts on the child's communication.

After describing a few examples of the direct techniques, demonstrate their use with the child to address one of the child's global goals (see Appendix A, Form 4). As before, explain to the parent how you are carrying out each of the six steps. At the end of the demonstration, the parent should be able to identify the similarities and differences between the two approaches.

The Pyramid of Techniques

Show the parent the pyramid that illustrates how the techniques build on each other in Project ImPACT (see Figure S1.3). Explain to the parent that the pyramid's base contains four sets of interactive teaching techniques that are almost always used: *Follow Your Child's Lead*, *Animation*, *Imitate Your Child*, and *Modeling and Expanding Language*. These techniques are used to increase the child's motivation and engagement, and to map language onto the child's actions. The parent will learn to use these first, in order to successfully implement the techniques in the middle layer of the pyramid.

The middle layer of the pyramid contains three more sets of interactive teaching techniques: *Playful Obstruction*, *Balanced Turns*, and *Communicative Temptations*. These techniques are added to those on the bottom level to encourage the child to communicate. The parent must learn to use these prior to learning the direct teaching techniques, at the top level of the pyramid.

As described above, the direct teaching techniques use prompting and reinforcement to

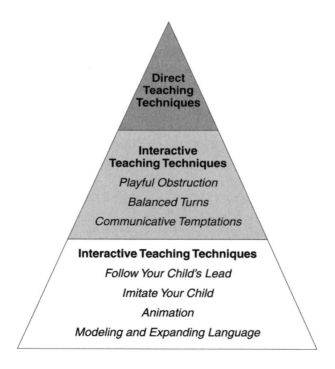

Figure S1.3. The pyramid of Project ImPACT intervention techniques.

teach specific language, social imitation, and play skills. These techniques are taught last, because they build on the interactive teaching techniques on the two lower levels of the pyramid. Direct teaching techniques challenge the child, which can be good, but can also be frustrating if used too often. They are used about a third of the time in interactions with the child.

Discuss and Assign Homework

1. Give the parent the parent manual and have her read *Overview of the Program* **and** *Set Up Your Home for Success* (Chapters 1 and 2) before the next session. Chapter 1 of the parent manual reviews the information that was covered in today's session; tell the parent to read this chapter and come with any questions she may have about either the interactive or the direct teaching techniques. Explain to the parent that Chapter 2 of the parent manual will be reviewed during the next treatment session. The parent does not need to complete the *Set Up Your Home for Success* homework until after the next treatment session.

2. Have the parent complete the Daily Activity Schedule at home and bring it to the next session. Review the Daily Activity Schedule in the Parent Manual (also Appendix A, Form 5) with the parent and instruct her to complete it prior to the next session. Explain that the Daily Activity Schedule is used to gain information about the child's daily routine. This information will be used throughout the program to help the parent identify times she can use the social-communication intervention within already occurring daily activities. The completed Daily Activity Schedule will be reviewed during the next treatment session.

Session 2

Review Goals and Set Up Your Home for Success

Session Goals
1. Finalize the child's goals.
2. Teach the parent why it is important to structure the home environment and create predictable routines.
3. Teach the parent how to structure the home environment.
4. Help the parent identify routines in which to teach the child.

Materials
1. Parent manual
2. Completed Goal Development Form (Appendix A, Form 4)

3. Toys to keep child occupied
4. Completed Daily Activity Schedule (Appendix A, Form 5)

Outline of Session

- Review homework from Session 1 (10–15 minutes):
    Review the Daily Activity Schedule (or have parent complete it).
- Ask the parent whether she read *Set Up Your Home for Success* (Chapter 2 of the parent manual).
- Review the child's goals from Session 1 (10–25 minutes).
- Introduce the rationale for *Set Up Your Home for Success* (5 minutes):
    It increases meaningful learning opportunities.
    It increases the child's engagement.
- Discuss the key points of *Set Up Your Home for Success* (10–15 minutes):
    Schedule predictable routines.
    Set up a defined play space.
    Limit distractions.
    Rotate toys.
- Review the Daily Activity Schedule (10–25 minutes):
    Have the parent identify routines in which to teach.
    Have the parent identify a space to use at home.
- Discuss and assign homework (10–15 minutes):
    1. Have the parent complete homework for *Set Up Your Home for Success.*
    2. Have the parent read *Follow Your Child's Lead* (Chapter 3 of the parent manual).

Review Homework from Session 1

Ask the parent whether she completed the Daily Activity Schedule. If she has, praise her and say that you will look at it together later in the session. If she has not, have the parent take time to complete the Daily Activity Schedule. If you do not think the parent is able to read or write, ask the parent the questions and write the answers down for her.

Now ask the parent whether she has read the chapter in the parent manual on setting up the home for success. If she has, reward her with a positive comment, like, "Wonderful!" or "You're off to a great start." If she hasn't, and she is able to read, have her read this chapter before you introduce the technique. Emphasize that reading about each technique prior to the session is important, because it decreases the amount of time required for the explanation. While the parent reads the chapter, interact with the child. If the parent is unable to read, the program will need to be modified in order for you to spend extra time on the description.

Review the Child's Goals from Session 1

Review the global goals for the child (listed in the left column of the Goal Development Form) that were developed in each of the core areas (i.e., social engagement, language, social imitation, and play) in Session 1. If you have not yet developed measurable goals, explain to the parent that measurable goals will be developed during the next few treatment sessions.

Introduce the Rationale for *Set Up Your Home for Success*

Today's session teaches the parent how to set up the family home environment so that the child has more meaningful opportunities to learn and the child is more likely to engage with the parent. Relate the technique's purpose to the parent's goals for her child. Learning and using the technique will have the following benefits for the child.

It Increases Meaningful Learning Opportunities

As explained in the parent manual, children learn best when an activity is meaningful. For young children, the most meaningful activities are everyday routines, such as playtime, mealtime, bathtime, and getting dressed. The techniques taught in this program are designed to be used during these daily routines. Emphasize to the parent that by adding 5–10 minutes to a routine such as mealtime or bathtime, she can significantly increase the number of meaningful learning opportunities the child has throughout the day. This also increases the child's ability to use the skills in new settings (generalization).

It Increases the Child's Engagement

Children with ASD often have difficulty engaging with others for long periods of time. The timing of daily routines and the physical arrangement of the home will both have a significant impact on the child's ability to engage with the parent and others. Thus, before she learns to use the other intervention techniques, it is helpful for the parent to set up the home to maximize her child's engagement.

Explain to the parent how this technique will address her child's individual goals. For example, when explaining the rationale to Brian's mother (see Case Study 1 in Session 1), the trainer you might say: "Brian has a goal of increasing the length of time he will interact with you during play. Arranging the environment and limiting distractions will help Brian increase the amount of time he can engage with you."

Discuss the Key Points of *Set Up Your Home for Success*

There are four strategies, outlined below, for creating an environment conducive to learning. These strategies are particularly effective for children who are easily upset by changes in routine, who are distracted by auditory and visual stimuli, and who prefer to move rapidly from activity to activity or place to place.

Schedule Predictable Routines

Children with ASD often have difficulty when things are unpredictable. By scheduling major household routines at about the same time each day and conducting them the same way each time, the parent can help the child begin to anticipate what is coming next. This can lower the child's frustration level, which can improve his engagement with his parent. Emphasize to the parent that the consistency of her routines at home can have a significant impact on her child's behavior.

Consistency in routines means this: (1) The same routines happen at about the same times each day, and (2) the parts of each routine are performed in the same sequence. For example, getting up, meals, naps, bath, and bedtime should all happen at about the same times each day. A routine like bedtime might consist of this sequence: Help the child get into pajamas, have him brush his teeth, read him a book, and put him to bed.

Since children with ASD often have poor play skills and may be resistant to having their parents play with them, many parents do not have a consistent play routine with their children. Play is an important skill for a child to learn, as well as the best way for the parent to practice some of the intervention techniques. Thus it is important for the parent to schedule 15–20 minutes of playtime with her child each day. Explain to the parent that creating a predictable play routine (e.g., play before bedtime or after mealtime) increases the success of the interaction because it allows the child to anticipate it. This is particularly helpful for a child who may initially become frustrated when a parent tries to interact with him. Let the parent know that if her child is initially unable to engage for a full 15–20 minutes at a time, she can schedule several shorter periods throughout the day.

Set Up a Defined Play Space

A defined play space—one that has visual and physical boundaries—limits distractions and creates physical proximity between the parent and child. This leads to an increase in child engagement. The type of space will vary, depending on the child. Children who run when others attempt to interact with them benefit from physical boundaries with no clear runways. Other children may benefit from having a defined place to sit, such as a bean bag chair or a chair and table. Discuss with the parent the type of space that would benefit her child. Often a family finds it helpful to use the child's bedroom or another room in the home when playing with the child. Or the family may wish to rearrange the furniture in the living room to create an enclosed space.

Limit Distractions

Any stimulus in the environment other than the parent is a potential competitor for the child's attention. This includes visual stimuli, such as art on the wall, toys, lights, television, books, and clutter; auditory stimuli, such as music, people talking, or toys that make noise; and olfactory stimuli, such as perfumes, lotions, cooking, and scented candles. Discuss all of the stimuli that may be present in the environment and how these stimuli can decrease the child's engagement with people. Ask the parent whether she has noticed if any particular type of stimulus affects her child's behavior. The effect a stimulus has on different children may vary; for example, soft music in the background helps some children with regulation, while for others it can be distracting. Work with the parent to identify the type of environment that will be most conducive to learning for her child.

Rotate Toys

Explain how rotating the toys that are freely available to the child in the home can help maintain the child's interest in toys and increase engagement. Help the parent determine how she will organize and rotate toys at home. As described in the parent manual, toys can be organized into groups with only one group made available to the child for a period of time (e.g., 2–3 weeks). Favorite toys should be evenly distributed among the rotating toy groups.

Favorite toys can also be used to increase the child's motivation to interact with the parent. If you feel that this would help the child, have the parent identify one to two of the most highly motivating toys for her child, and explain how use of these toys during times she is interacting with her child can increase motivation. Be sure that the parent limits access to these special toys when her child is not interacting with her.

Review the Daily Activity Schedule

Review the Daily Activity Schedule with the parent to determine activities that are part of the family's daily routine. Ask probing questions about these activities, to determine how they are structured and whether the family's schedule is predictable. For example, if the parent indicates that the family sits down for dinner and that the child enjoys this activity, you might ask the parent one or more of the following questions:

1. "Who sets the table for dinner?"
2. "Do you serve the food before the plates are brought to the table?"
3. "Who cleans the table once the meal is finished?"
4. "Do you talk about particular topics during dinner, such as what everyone did that day?"

These questions will help you determine whether the child can become more of an active participant in the routine, particularly if this is something he enjoys. If the family does not have a consistent routine, try to determine from the parent whether this is adversely affecting the child's behavior. If so, help the parent decide how to make her child's day more consistent. This review should also provide you with more information about the child's skills in different environments, which can be used to develop additional goals.

Have the Parent Identify Routines in Which to Teach

While you are reviewing the Daily Activity Schedule, help the parent identify several daily routines that she does with her child in which she can practice using the intervention techniques. Routines that the parent has marked as "Enjoys" are good to begin with, since the child is already motivated by these activities. For example, if the child enjoys bathtime, the parent may choose to use this activity to target her child's social-communication skills. However, if the child resists bathtime, this activity should not be chosen. Remind the parent that she will need to add 5–10 minutes to the current routine to provide enough time to use the intervention techniques. In addition, help the parent schedule a 15- to 20-minute play session at some time during her day, if she does not already do this with her child. If the child is likely to have difficulty engaging for that length of time, help the parent select several shorter periods of time distributed throughout the day in which to play.

Have the Parent Identify a Space to Use at Home

With the parent, brainstorm ways to set up the home environment to help promote her child's engagement. In particular, help her select a defined space and determine how she can limit distractions in that environment. Have the parent take the leading role in identifying a space at home. If the parent is unable to identify a space, you may offer choices or describe spaces that other families have used. (See also "Troubleshooting Tips," below.)

Next, discuss ways in which the parent can reduce distractions in that environment. For some spaces, the distractions may already be reduced. However, if the parent is using a larger space or a space with multiple purposes, she may need to remove or cover some distractions in that environment. For example, if the room the parent selects has a computer or television that is very distracting for her child, suggest ways that she can limit the child's access to it (e.g., unplug it, cover it, put it in a locked cabinet, place something else in front of it, turn it around). When conducting the intervention in the home, take this time to help the parent create an environment for her child.

Discuss and Assign Homework

1. Have the parent complete homework for *Set Up Your Home for Success*. Review the rationale and key points that are outlined on the homework sheet for *Set Up Your Home for Success*. Take time to read over the questions with that the parent. This ensures the parent understands the questions and that she will be able to respond to the questions at home. If applicable, write notes next to the key points to remind the parent of what she will try at home. For example, if the parent has decided that she will limit distractions by organizing toys and turning off the TV, write a reminder next to "Limit distractions." Instruct the parent to answer the questions at home and to write down how her child responds to the techniques encompassed in *Set Up Your Home for Success*.

2. Have the parent read *Follow Your Child's Lead* (Chapter 3 of the parent manual). Explain to the parent that the next intervention topic, *Follow Your Child's Lead*, will be introduced during the next session. This technique focuses on increasing the child's engagement and motivation. The parent should read the chapter and come back with any questions. The parent does not complete the homework for this topic until after the next treatment session.

Troubleshooting Tips

Sometimes it becomes apparent that a parent has no consistent schedule. This can be an issue, because it affects the child's ability to make sense of his day and because it is hard to identify routines in which the parent can practice the intervention techniques. The parent may have an unpredictable schedule due to either external pressures (e.g., swing shift at work, inconsistent child care) or her own personality style. In either case, it is often difficult to get the parent to schedule a predictable routine. If the parent is unable or unwilling to do so, suggest that she select a single activity that she and her child enjoy, and make sure that the activity occurs every day.

A parent may sometimes also have difficulty identifying a space with reduced distractions in which to work with her child. This is usually the case when the family has limited space and/ or a large number of family members. If this issue arises, let the parent know that it is not necessary for the family to have an entire room for the child, and that there may be a number of ways to create a space. For example, we have worked with families who created a space by using the bathroom (bathtub), a walk-in closet, the kitchen table (under the table with a tablecloth and flashlights), or a tent within a room. Help the parent think creatively about how to arrange a space in the home.

Session 3

Follow Your Child's Lead

Session Goals
1. Help the parent understand why she may need to use different interaction strategies to interact successfully with her child.
2. Teach the parent strategies that can improve her interactions with her child.
3. Help the parent identify how and why her child communicates on his own (without support/prompts).

Materials
1. Parent manual
2. Completed Goal Development Form (Appendix A, Form 4)
3. A number of highly preferred toys

Outline of Session
- Review homework from *Set Up Your Home for Success* (10–15 minutes).
- Explain why play can be difficult (5 minutes).
- Introduce the rationale for *Follow Your Child's Lead* (5–10 minutes):

    It increases social engagement and motivation during play.
    It increases opportunities for initiations.
    It lays the foundation for the entire program.
    It shows how and why the child communicates without support.

- Discuss the key points of *Follow Your Child's Lead* (5–10 minutes):

    Let your child choose the activity.
    Stay face to face with your child.

Join in your child's play.

Comment on play, but don't ask questions or give commands.

Wait for your child to engage or communicate with you.

Be sensitive, but persistent.

Control the situation.

- Help the parent identify the behaviors her child uses to communicate and learn how to respond to these behaviors (5 minutes).
- Demonstrate use of *Follow Your Child's Lead* (10–15 minutes).
- Have the parent practice *Follow Your Child's Lead* while you provide feedback (15–20 minutes).
- Discuss and assign homework (10–15 minutes).
    1. Have the parent complete homework for *Follow Your Child's Lead*.
    2. Have the parent read *Imitate Your Child* (Chapter 4 of the parent manual).

Review Homework from *Set Up Your Home for Success*

Review the questions from the homework sheet for *Set Up Your Home for Success*. If the parent has had difficulty creating a space at home, take time to help her identify possible solutions. If there is still a problem, it may be necessary to make a home visit to assist in creation of an appropriate environment in the home setting.

Other challenges frequently arise for a parent. She may have difficulty trying to interact with the child while siblings are present. To address this concern, ask the parent to describe the sibling interaction and see whether the sibling could be involved in play. If this is not feasible for either or both children, review the parent's schedule to see whether she can identify a 10-minute period in which to play with each child separately.

A parent also frequently has trouble fitting playtime into an already demanding schedule. To address this concern, review the Daily Activity Schedule to determine whether play can be scheduled within already existing daily activities. Help the parent identify activities with which her child may be able to help—for example, cooking, washing the dishes, or separating the laundry. Explain how the child can become involved in the activity even if he is not yet able to help. For example, during dishwashing the child may enjoy putting his hands in the water or holding the towel, even if he is unable to assist in the actual washing process. When you are helping the parent identify an activity, it is important to take into consideration the individual needs and skills of her child. If the child's involvement in daily chores would not work because the parent needs to accomplish the task quickly, then identify an activity the child likes (e.g., balloons, bubbles, etc.) and ask if the parent can engage in one of these activities with the child for 5 minutes after mealtime before she cleans up.

Explain Why Play Can Be Difficult

Ask the parent whether it is difficult to play with her child. Discuss the following reasons why play can be so difficult for a child with ASD:

- Such a child often has difficulty playing appropriately with toys.
- The child may stay with an activity longer than the parent wants to stay with it, or leave an activity before the parent is finished with it.
- The child also may move slowly and be repetitive, causing the parent to become bored.
- A child with ASD also has difficulty staying in an interaction with another person for any length of time.
- The child has difficulty taking his turn during interactions and may become frustrated when the parent tries to play.

If the child leaves the interaction quickly or objects to the parent's joining his play, the parent may begin to feel that her child does not love her or want to be with her. These emotions may make her less inclined to try to play with her child. Acknowledge that difficulty engaging a child in play can lead to feelings of guilt and frustration, while informing the parent that the difficulty is not due to poor parenting; rather, it is due to the fact that her child learns in a different way.

Explain that this session focuses on teaching the parent how to make small changes in the way she interacts with her child to improve his social engagement during play.

Introduce the Rationale for *Follow Your Child's Lead*

This session teaches the parent to observe and become part of her child's play. This allows the child's interests to lead the interaction and increases motivation and engagement. As you explain the rationale, relate the technique's purpose to the parent's goals for her child. Learning and using the technique will have the following benefits for the child.

It Increases Social Engagement and Motivation during Play

The child with ASD may have difficulty engaging in and maintaining social interactions around activities because he is not interested in the activities. Following the child's lead to an activity is one way to make sure that he is interested and motivated by it. This increases the opportunity for learning to take place and can also increase the length of the interaction.

It Increases Opportunities for Initiations

A parent often ends up directing a child's play, which places the child in a responder role. Allowing the child to choose the activity and the way to play at it provides the child with an opportunity to initiate with the parent. The more often the child initiates communication, the more opportunities there are for the parent to teach.

It Lays the Foundation for the Entire Program

This program is based on using the child's interests to create opportunities for learning. Using the child's interests to teach increases generalization and spontaneous language. This technique is used throughout the Project ImPACT program to increase engagement and motivation.

It Shows How and Why the Child Communicates without Support

The parent knows her child better than anyone and is often quite good at anticipating the child's needs. This is something the parent should continue to do some of the time to decrease frustration. However, it is important that the child learn to communicate so that others can understand as well. Using this technique in isolation allows the parent to understand the child's independent communication and play skills.

More specifically, the purpose of using this technique in isolation is to identify:

- The child's interests.
- The number of times the child initiates communication without support.
- The reasons the child communicates.
- The behaviors (e.g., eye contact, gestures, words, etc.) the child uses to communicate.

Explain to the parent that the strategies encompassed within *Follow Your Child's Lead* are the least supportive ones in the program; therefore, changes in the child's behavior may not be observed.

Remember to tell the parent how this technique will address her child's individual goals. For example, in the case of Brian from Session 1, the trainer might tell Brian's mother: "Brian has a goal of increasing the length of time he will interact with you during play. This technique directly addresses that goal by joining him in something he likes to do."

In the case of Sam, also from Session 1, the trainer might say: "Sam has a goal of increasing spontaneous language; this technique allows us to observe the language Sam can use on his own without prompts. It also allows him time to initiate, as we will wait and follow his lead rather than provide him with a behavior to imitate."

Discuss the Key Points of *Follow Your Child's Lead*

There are seven key points encompassed in *Follow Your Child's Lead*. These are outlined in the parent manual and should be reviewed with the parent. Let the parent know that this technique can be difficult to implement in isolation, and that this session is the *only* time this technique is used in isolation.

Let Your Child Choose the Activity

The purpose of this step is to determine the child's interests. Children without social-communication difficulties are often interested in any activity an adult initiates, because they are interested in the social aspect of the interaction. Children with ASD, however, are often not interested in adult-led activities and may be interested in activities that adults find unusual.

Instruct the parent to observe how her child plays, even if it is unusual. Explain to the parent that the goal is to determine the child's interest, not to increase his attention to a task; therefore, the parent should follow the child as he moves between activities. If the home environment is set up well, the number of activities to which a child can move will be limited.

Once the child has chosen an activity, the parent should wait and see how her child plays with the toy or activity. This can be challenging, because adults often have their own ideas about how to play with a toy.

Stay Face to Face with Your Child

Throughout this program, the parent is encouraged to remain within her child's visual field. This ensures that the child can see what the parent is doing. It also sets up opportunities for the child to use eye contact with the parent, to watch the parent's behavior, and eventually to imitate the parent's behavior. For some families, this may already be occurring and may come naturally to the parents. Other parents may interact more often with their children on their laps, next to their children, or behind their children. Different physical proximity patterns occur because a child has indicated to a parent over the years that this is his preference. One child with ASD may move away from the parent when she comes too close to his visual field. Another child may sit on the parent's lap to have more control over the parent's actions and more control over the activity. Regardless of the reason for the child's behavior, the parent should be encouraged to move within her child's visual field. Let the parent know that the child may move away, but that she should continue to move into her child's visual field and try to make it into a game. Depending on the child, the proximity of the parent to the child may vary; initially it may be easier if the parent is a little further away during the interaction. Another option may be to interact while parent and child are both looking in a mirror. Use your clinical judgment and provide the parent with concrete information on proximity during these first interactions. For example, if the child seems to back away because the parent moves too close, tell the parent to allow an arm's length of space between her and her child.

Join in Your Child's Play

Once the child has chosen an activity, and the parent has observed how he is playing, she should join him in his play. This might mean helping the child or contributing to his activity; for example, the parent might hand the child a block if he is stacking them, or add a block to his stack. This could also mean joining the child in physical or sensory play. If the child likes to climb, the parent could engage in rough-and-tumble play; if he likes to spin, she could spin him in a chair; if he likes to touch textures, she could give him a lotion rub; if he likes to stare at lights, they could play with flashlights together. Provide the parent with other concrete examples of how she can join in her child's play. Remind the parent that the child is the leader and that her role is to join in the play, not to "correct" the child's play.

If the child protests with a change in behavior (e.g., eye contact, body posture change, words, etc.), the parent should respond by complying appropriately, remembering that the child is the leader. For example, if the child protests when the parent puts a block on his stack, the parent should respond by removing the block and then attempting to join his play in another way.

Comment on Play, but Don't Ask Questions or Give Commands

One of the purposes of this technique is to increase the child's initiations. By asking the child questions and giving directions, the parent creates an opportunity for the child to respond rather than initiate. By commenting on the child's play, the parent can indicate interest and acceptance of her child's choices and allow him to initiate—for example, "You've picked a red block. I like red. That tower is really getting tall."

Wait for Your Child to Engage or Communicate with You

Instruct the parent to wait and observe how her child engages or communicates with her. You should discuss the possibility that the child may not acknowledge the parent, because techniques to make play interactive have not yet been introduced. In this event, the parent should be encouraged to use this time to observe and track how the child initiates on his own without her support.

Be Sensitive, but Persistent

Some children may prefer to play alone and may initially be resistant to their parents' attempts to join them in their play. Acknowledge that this technique may be difficult, but emphasize that the parent should be persistent in order to begin the process of enhancing social communication.

Control the Situation

Explain that the parent is in control of the situation. Although she wants to follow her child's lead, it is equally important to be consistent with rules and consequences. Let the parent know that she needs to determine what behaviors are permitted and what behaviors should be eliminated. One essential rule is not to allow any behaviors that destroy property or may injure the child or another person. With this exception, allowable behaviors may vary, depending on the family. The parent should know that she is in control of the situation, and she should inform you of any behaviors that are not allowed at home.

Help the Parent Identify the Behaviors Her Child Uses to Communicate and Learn How to Respond to These Behaviors

After the parent implements any of the steps described above, the child may attempt to communicate with the parent. The behavior the child uses to communicate with the parent may be subtle or obvious. Examples of behaviors may include moving to a new activity, changing body posture, changing facial expressions, making eye contact, using gestures, or using verbalizations. Ask probing questions to help the parent identify how her child communicates *without* support. Here are some sample questions:

1. "What does your child do when you sit face to face with him?"
2. "What does your child do when you join in his play?"

Explain to the parent that she should respond to her child's communication by complying with his apparent desire. For example, if her child looks at her when she moves into his line of sight, she should respond by saying, "Hello." Conversely, if her child moves away when she moves into his line of sight, she should respond by saying, "Move" or "Bye-bye." Discuss with the parent how she can respond to her child's behaviors.

Acknowledge that it will often be difficult for the parent to determine all of the subtleties of communication when she is involved in the interaction. As a team, you and she will work together to observe each other's interactions with the child to identify the types and purposes of the child's communication.

Demonstrate Use of *Follow Your Child's Lead*

Prepare for the demonstration by summarizing for the parent the key points of the technique, the communication behavior you will look for from the child, and the way you will comply with that response. Individualize this for each child and family, based on the child's interests and goals. Then briefly demonstrate how to use the different strategies to improve engagement and the length of the interaction, identifying each one as you use it and the child's communication. For example, the trainer in Brian's case (see Section 1) might say:

> "Brian is playing with the ball. I'm following him to that activity and moving into his line of sight (staying face to face). Next, I am waiting to see how he communicates. ... He looked at me. I will respond to his communication and make a comment on his play: 'Ball.' ... Now he's moved to another activity. I follow him again and move into his visual field again (staying face to face) to give him an opportunity to communicate. ... Remember, we want to be persistent, to increase the opportunities he has to communicate."

Once you have completed the demonstration, review the strategies you used and the child's response. If the child does not respond, explain to the parent that *Follow Your Child's Lead* is the least supportive technique and therefore may not elicit a response from the child. It is still important to practice this technique, however, because it lays the foundation for the entire program and reveals how the child communicates without supports.

Have the Parent Practice *Follow Your Child's Lead* While You Provide Feedback

Announce the transition between your interaction with the child and the parent's practice. Then suggest a specific behavior for the parent to practice. For example, the trainer in Brian's case might say: "Now I would like you to interact with Brian while I sit behind you and provide feedback. Remember to follow Brian's lead to the activity; if he is playing with the ball, move into his line of sight and attempt to join him in his play."

The parent should have at least 15 minutes to practice the *Follow Your Child's Lead* technique. Your role during the parent's practice is to be her assistant. Provide feedback in order to improve her ability to implement the technique. Since this is the first coaching session, give primarily positive feedback. (See Part I, Chapter 2, for ways to give feedback.) Be sure to provide feedback not only on use of the technique, but also on the child's behavior (e.g., how and why her child is communicating)—for example: "Great joining in Brian's play. He communicated by looking at you. This appeared to be to request to have you join his play again (the reason why he is communicating)."

This technique can be difficult for the parent to implement. When the activity is not functional or is repetitive, the parent may have trouble staying with the activity as long as the child does. Conversely, the child may flit from activity to activity. In these or other situations, acknowledge the difficulty while reminding the parent that following the child's lead will increase motivation and engagement. This is critical to the success of the program—and to achieving the parent's goals for the child.

Remind the parent to be persistent in her attempts. If the parent is having trouble with one aspect of the technique (e.g., letting the child's interests lead the activity), have the parent focus specifically on that aspect (e.g., "Once you follow your child to the activity, wait and see what he chooses to do with the toy").

If you are providing coaching in the home, have the parent practice in the controlled environment that was chosen during Session 2. If you are coaching in a clinic or school, have the parent practice with a limited number of toys available. A controlled and predictable environment helps to decrease the amount of the child's movement between activities.

Discuss and Assign Homework

1. Have the parent complete homework for *Follow Your Child's Lead.* Review the homework sheet in the parent manual with the parent. Go over the rationale and the key points of this technique, listed at the top of the homework sheet. As you complete the review, emphasize the strategies that seem most effective for the child. For example, if the child responds well to the parent's joining in his play, circle this strategy to remind the parent to use it as she interacts with her child at home.

The homework sheet provides spaces for filling in the particular goal or goals the technique addresses for the child, and the specific activity or activities during which the parent will practice the technique. Fill in these spaces. Examples of goals include increasing engagement, increasing initiations, increasing the length of the interaction, or identifying the child's skills when they are not given support. Ask the parent to think of times when she may be able to practice this technique. For now, the technique is practiced during play or another enjoyable activity. Once the parent learns additional techniques that incorporate *Follow Your Child's Lead,* the parent will use them during other daily activities. If the parent is unable to identify a time to use *Follow Your Child's Lead,* review the Daily Activity Schedule and identify an activity the child enjoys.

Read through the questions on the homework sheet and have the parent respond to them, based on her interaction with her child during this session. Inform the parent that she should practice using *Follow Your Child's Lead* daily, at home, before the next session and write down how her child responds to the technique. Explain that the homework will be reviewed at the start of each session.

2. Have the parent read *Imitate Your Child* (Chapter 4 of the parent manual). Explain to the parent that the second step of the program is to create opportunities for the child to engage or communicate. *Imitate Your Child* is one of four techniques she will learn to use to create such opportunities. This technique will be taught during the next individual coaching session. The parent does not need to complete the homework for the technique until it has been reviewed and practiced during the next session.

Troubleshooting Tips

Children with ASD are usually better at responding than at initiating, and can become dependent on prompts from their parents. Many parents have figured this out and become quite directive (e.g., asking questions, giving commands) when interacting with their children, in order to get a response. When a parent is no longer directing a child's play, it can initially be challenging for the child to interact with the parent. In some cases, the parent may express a concern that you are asking her to stop asking questions or giving directions, especially when the child has some language and can respond. If this occurs, explain to the parent that this is a challenge, while letting her know that *Follow Your Child's Lead* lays the foundation for the program. It also provides information on the child's skills in the absence of support. Assure the parent that she will eventually get back to asking questions and giving directions when you cover the direct teaching techniques.

Session 4

Imitate Your Child

Session Goals

1. Help the parent understand how *Imitate Your Child* can help her child interact more successfully with her.
2. Teach the parent strategies to improve her child's engagement, imitation skills, and spontaneous language.

Materials

1. Parent manual
2. Completed Goal Development Form (Appendix A, Form 4)
3. Pairs of highly preferred toys

Outline of Session

- Review homework from *Follow Your Child's Lead* (10–15 minutes).
- Introduce the rationale for *Imitate Your Child* (5 minutes):

  It increases engagement.
  It increases imitation skills.

It increases appropriate behaviors.

It increases spontaneous language and play.

- Explain how *Imitate Your Child* is used with previously taught techniques (5 minutes).
- Discuss the key points of *Imitate Your Child* (5–10 minutes):

    Imitate play with toys.

    Imitate gestures and body movements.

    Imitate vocalizations.

    Only imitate appropriate behavior.

- Demonstrate use of *Imitate Your Child* (10–15 minutes).
- Have the parent practice *Imitate Your Child* while you provide feedback (15–25 minutes).
- Discuss and assign homework (10–15 minutes):

    1. Have the parent complete homework for *Imitate Your Child*.
    2. Have the parent read *Animation* (Chapter 5 of the parent manual).

Review Homework from *Follow Your Child's Lead*

Review the questions from the homework for *Follow Your Child's Lead*. If the parent has had difficulty implementing this technique at home, take time to help her identify possible solutions. With a child who moves quickly from activity to activity, the parent may report that she was unable to interact because the child would not stay in one place. In this event, brainstorm ways the parent can create a smaller and more intimate space at home. Another frequently reported problem is that the parent became bored or did not know what to do because the child's play was so repetitive. In this case, empathize with the parent and explain that *Follow Your Child's Lead* begins to increase the length of time the child interacts with a particular activity; this can cause the parent to become bored. Then explain that subsequent sessions are spent making play more interactive and increasing the complexity of the child's language and play. If the parent indicates that her child would not communicate with her, take time to observe her using the strategies in *Follow Your Child's Lead,* and help her identify the way in which her child communicates.

Introduce the Rationale for *Imitate Your Child*

Explain the purpose and benefits of the technique to the parent. As in previous sessions, be sure to relate the technique's purpose to the parent's goals for her child. Learning and using the technique will have the following benefits for the child.

It Increases Social Engagement

Imitating the child's behavior increases the child's engagement with the parent and creates opportunities for learning to take place. It has also been shown to increase coordinated joint attention in children with ASD (shifting gaze between a parent and toys).

It Increases Imitation Skills

Children with ASD often have difficulty watching people and imitating their behaviors. When a child's engagement increases, he has an opportunity to observe a new skill and possibly to imitate it either immediately or later.

It Increases Appropriate Behaviors

Imitation of children's behaviors increases the occurrence of those behaviors. Discuss what child behaviors the parent would like to increase. These could include vocalizations, words, toy play, or gestures.

It Increases Spontaneous Language and Play

Some children with ASD already easily imitate their parents' sounds, words, and play. In such a case, when the parent imitates the child, it provides the child an opportunity to spontaneously generate his own language and play.

As before, explain to the parent how this technique will address her child's individual goals. For example, when explaining the rationale to Brian's mother (Case Study 1 from Session 1), the trainer might say: "This technique will help Brian increase the length of time he can interact with others during play (a social engagement goal). It will also help increase the number of functional play schemes that Brian uses (a play goal)."

For Sam (Case Study 2 from Session 1), the trainer might say to his mother: "Sam has a goal of increasing object imitation. By imitating Sam's play, we can increase the likelihood that he will later imitate our play."

Explain How *Imitate Your Child* Is Used with Previously Taught Techniques

Imitate Your Child builds on *Follow Your Child's Lead*. The parent begins by letting the child choose the toy or activity. Then the parent places herself face to face with the child. Once the parent is in the child's line of sight, she adds the technique of *Imitate Your Child* to create an opportunity for her child to engage or communicate. Imitation is another way to join with the child's play. After the parent imitates her child, she waits for her child to indicate engagement or initiate communication.

Discuss the Key Points of *Imitate Your Child*

There are four key points to the technique of *Imitate Your Child*. These are outlined in the parent manual and should be reviewed with the parent. *Imitate Your Child* can also help the parent follow her child's lead, because it provides her with a concrete way to become part of her child's play.

Imitate Play with Toys

Imitating how the child plays with a toy increases the child's engagement and spontaneous play skills. It is helpful to have two similar or identical toys. As in *Follow Your Child's Lead*, instruct the parent first to watch her child's play, then to get into a face-to-face position, and then to imitate his actions with an identical or similar toy. The child may change his behavior once he sees that the parent is imitating him, to determine whether she also will change her behavior. This is an example of a child initiation. The parent should respond by imitating the changed behavior. Or the child may look at the parent, which indicates that this technique is effective in gaining the child's attention. The parent should respond by continuing to imitate the child's behavior.

Imitate Gestures and Body Movements

The second strategy is used to increase the child's engagement, purposeful behavior, and gestures. Instruct the parent to place herself in the child's visual field and then to mirror her child's gestures and body movements. This can be a particularly useful strategy for children who do not engage well with toys or who tend to wander aimlessly. If the child is not actively engaged, suggest that the parent imitate and exaggerate all of the child's subtle body movements. Provide the parent with specific examples of gestures and body movements that she could imitate.

Imitate Vocalizations

Vocal imitation is used to increase the child's vocalizations and spontaneous language. The parent should imitate the child's vocalizations or appropriate language. The parent can do this to let her child know that she has received his message. Depending on the child's skill level, the type of vocalization imitated varies. Provide the parent with concrete examples of her child's vocalizations that she should imitate. This strategy is also used later with expansion of language.

Only Imitate Appropriate Behavior

Imitation of behaviors increases the likelihood that the child will do them again. Therefore, instruct the parent to imitate only those behaviors that she would like to increase. For an unwelcome behavior, explain how she can imitate the child's emotion as she slightly changes the behavior to make it appropriate. For example, if the child flaps his arms to indicate that he is excited, she can imitate the affect while clapping her hands. Again, the parent should dictate which behaviors are and are not appropriate within her family. The basic rule is not to imitate any behavior that may be self-injurious, may cause others injury, or may be environmentally destructive.

Demonstrate Use of *Imitate Your Child*

Prepare to demonstrate the technique by reviewing what you will imitate, the behavior you will look for from the child, and how you will respond to the child. Individualize this explanation for each child and parent based on the child's interests and the child's goals. For example, when explaining this to Brian's mother in terms of his goals, the trainer might say:

"Since Brian enjoys playing with the ball, I am going to imitate his ball play. I will look for any response that indicates he is engaged. This could include eye contact, body posture changes, a gesture or a sound. [Then the trainer briefly demonstrates each type of imitation, telling the parent as she uses it. For example:] Now I am going to imitate Brian's vocalizations and then wait to see how he responds. [Trainer imitates, followed by wait; child vocalizes, trainer imitates.] He vocalized again. I responded to his communication (the vocalization) by imitating him again."

Explain how this pattern encourages back-and-forth communication, turn taking, and engagement. If the child does not respond when his behaviors are imitated, tell the parent. For example, the trainer might say to Brian's mother: "I am imitating Brian's toy play and waiting to see how he responds. He is not responding to me, so I am going to continue to imitate his play, but I will also try to imitate his body movements to see how he responds."

Have the Parent Practice *Imitate Your Child* While You Provide Feedback

Announce the transition between your interaction with the child and the parent's practice. Then suggest a specific behavior for the parent to practice imitating. For example, the trainer might say to Brian's mother: "Now I would like you to interact with Brian while I sit behind you and provide feedback. Let's start with imitating Brian's toy play. Imitate everything Brian does with the toy, and see how he responds."

Have the parent practice *Imitate Your Child* for at least 15 minutes. Explain to the parent that she should use *Follow Your Child's Lead* and then imitate her child's behavior. Based on what the child is involved in, the parent may choose to imitate play, gestures, or vocalizations. Your role during this time is to assist and provide feedback to improve the parent's ability to implement the technique. For example, if the child is playing with a toy, try to find a similar toy and give it to the parent. Be sure to provide positive feedback on the parent's use of the technique, even if her child does not respond.

If you are providing coaching in the home, have the parent practice in the controlled environment that was chosen during Session 2. If you are coaching in a clinic or school, you should have the parent practice with a limited number of toys available. Limiting distractions helps decrease the child's moving among activities.

Discuss and Assign Homework

1. Have the parent complete homework for *Imitate Your Child*. Review the homework sheet in the parent manual with the parent. During this review, emphasize the rationale and the key points of *Imitate Your Child*. As you complete the review, emphasize the strategies that seem most effective for the child. For example, if the child responds well to imitation of gestures and body movements, circle this strategy to remind the parent to use it as she interacts with her child at home. Write down on the homework sheet any strategies from *Follow Your Child's Lead* that may increase the success of the parent–child interaction at home. Review the child's goals and ask the parent to identify the goals *Imitate Your Child* addresses for her child. For example, this technique can be used to increase the child's engagement, appropriate behaviors, imitation skills, and language skills. For children with limited vocalizations and play, this technique may increase the occurrence of these behaviors. For children who readily imitate, this technique often increases spontaneous skills. In Brian's case, use of this technique will address his mother's goals of increasing the amount of time he is engaged with her playing, increasing his gestures (such as imitation of waving good-bye), and increasing his vocalizations.

Once you and the parent identify the goals that will be addressed, write these goals on the homework sheet in the parent manual, to remind the parent of why she should practice them.

Ask the parent to think of times she could practice this technique and examples of activities she may complete with her child. Write down these activities for the parent. If needed, use the Daily Activity Schedule to help the parent identify at least two activities in which she could practice this technique. Explain to the parent that this technique can be used during a variety of daily activities, and provide her with concrete examples.

Read through the questions on the homework sheet and have the parent respond to the questions orally, based on her interaction with her child during this session. If the parent is unable to respond to the questions, ask probing questions or demonstrate the technique and have the parent identify the child's response. Instruct the parent to practice *Imitate Your Child* daily at home before the next session, and to write down how her child responds to the techniques. Explain that the homework will be reviewed at the beginning of the next session.

2. Have the parent read *Animation* (Chapter 5 of the parent manual). Instruct the parent to read *Animation* prior to the next session. *Animation* is another technique that can be used to create an opportunity for the child to engage or communicate. This technique is often paired with additional techniques in this program, such as *Imitate Your Child* and *Playful Obstruction*. *Animation* corresponds to the second and third steps in the sequence of interactive teaching techniques (i.e., create an opportunity for the child to engage or communicate, and wait for the child to engage or communicate). Remind the parent that she does not complete the homework for *Animation* until the technique has been reviewed and practiced during the next session.

Troubleshooting Tips

Three challenges can occur with *Imitate Your Child*. The first is that the child may not respond when the parent imitates him. Explain to the parent that *Imitate Your Child* may be more effective once her child increases his engagement with her, and that you can return to use of this technique at a later time.

The second challenge is that the parent may imitate one aspect of the child's behavior more than others (e.g., only vocalizations). In this case, you may want to demonstrate and provide feedback on use of each strategy in isolation. For example, describe imitating play with toys, demonstrate it, and have the parent practice while you provide feedback. Continue with this pattern until all of the strategies in *Imitate Your Child* are introduced.

A third challenge is that the parent may express concern regarding imitating the child's unusual or self-stimulatory behavior. If this is the case, emphasize that imitating behaviors that the child enjoys, even if they are unusual, communicates to the child that you value his interests. Assure the parent that although she may see an initial increase in his unusual behavior (i.e., imitating the child often increases the behavior being imitated), it can also lead to increased social engagement. And with increased social engagement, the child's play is likely to become more appropriate over time. One good rule of thumb regarding imitating usual or self-stimulatory behavior is that if it leads to engagement (e.g., eye contact, positive affect), the parent should continue to imitate the unusual behavior. However, if the child uses the behavior to "tune the parent out," the parent should only imitate the child when he engages in appropriate behavior, and instead attempt to join him in his play in another way.

Session 5

Animation

Session Goals

1. Teach the parent how to use additional strategies to interact successfully with her child.
2. Teach the parent to use strategies to improve her child's engagement, awareness of nonverbal communication, and initiations.
3. Teach the parent to use strategies to help her child remain regulated.

Materials

1. Parent manual
2. Completed Goal Development Form (Appendix A, Form 4)
3. Number of highly preferred toys

Outline of Session

- Review homework from *Imitate Your Child* (10–15 minutes).
- Introduce the rationale for *Animation* (5 minutes):

    It increases engagement.
    It increases awareness of nonverbal communication (e.g., facial expressions, vocal quality, gestures).
    It increases initiations.

- Explain how *Animation* is used with previously taught techniques (5 minutes).
- Discuss the key points of *Animation* (5–10 minutes).

    Be excited about the activity.
    Exaggerate gestures.
    Exaggerate facial expressions.
    Exaggerate vocal quality.

Use attention-getting devices.
Wait with anticipation.
Adjust your animation to help your child remain regulated.

- Demonstrate use of *Animation* (10–15 minutes).
- Have the parent practice *Animation* while you provide feedback (15–25 minutes).
- Discuss and assign homework (10–15 minutes):
    1. Have the parent complete homework for *Animation*.
    2. Have the parent read *Modeling and Expanding Language* (Chapter 6 of the parent manual).

Review Homework from *Imitate Your Child*

Review the questions from the homework for *Imitate Your Child*. If it was difficult for the parent to implement this technique at home, take time to help her identify solutions. One frequently reported challenge is that the child does not allow the parent to be in his line of sight; the child is then unaware when the parent imitates his behavior. In this case have the parent practice *Imitate Your Child* in front of a mirror rather than being face to face. A mirror works best when the parent and child can stand next to each other and look in the mirror. When reviewing the homework, ask the parent whether she attempted to use this technique in different environments and how her child responded.

Introduce the Rationale for *Animation*

Children with ASD often have difficulty engaging with others. They also have trouble interpreting and using nonverbal communication and initiating communication. *Animation*—being highly animated—is used to increase the child's skills in each of these areas. *Animation* is one of the techniques used to create an opportunity for the child to engage. This technique is used in conjunction with many other interactive teaching techniques, because it increases the effectiveness of the other techniques. As you explain the rationale, relate the technique's purpose to the parent's goals for her child.

It Increases Engagement

Being excited about the activity and exaggerating body movements and facial expressions can draw the child's attention. This increases his engagement and motivation within the activity.

It Increases Awareness of Nonverbal Communication

Nonverbal communication is often subtle and difficult to interpret. Emphasizing and exaggerating this aspect of communication can improve the child's awareness and comprehension of nonverbal language. This is particularly important for children with ASD, who have a difficult time understanding the meaning of facial expressions, gestures, and vocal tone.

It Increases Initiations

One of the elements of *Animation* is the use of wait time. Children with ASD often require additional time to initiate and respond to others. Allowing the child more time increases the number of opportunities he has to initiate.

> Explain to the parent how *Animation* is used to address her child's specific social engagement goals. For example, when explaining the rationale to Brian's mother (see Session 1, Case Study 1) in terms of his goals, the trainer might say: "*Animation* can be used to increase the length of time Brian interacts with you (a social engagement goal) and to increase his ability to initiate a request (a language goal)."
>
> The trainer might say to Sam's mother (see Session 1, Case Study 2): "Sam does not always look towards you when he is making a comment. *Animation* is one technique you can use to increase his engagement and eye contact with you during interactions."

Explain How *Animation* Is Used with Previously Taught Techniques

Animation is used in conjunction with *Follow Your Child's Lead* and *Imitate Your Child*. Using *Animation* can enhance the child's response to imitation. *Animation* is often paired with other intervention techniques (to be taught in later sessions), as it can also increase their effectiveness. *Animation* and *Imitate Your Child* are strategies that create an opportunity for the child to demonstrate engagement (the second step of the interactive teaching techniques).

Discuss the Key Points of *Animation*

There are seven key points in *Animation*. These elements are outlined in the parent manual and should be reviewed with the parent. Each element of *Animation* is usually performed in the context of an activity.

Be Excited about the Activity

A child with ASD often matches the parent's affect; the more excited the parent is about an activity, the more motivated the child may be to interact with her. Provide the parent with specific behaviors she can use to demonstrate that she is excited about the activity, such as maintaining eye contact with her child, smiling and laughing when appropriate, and joining her child in his activity of interest. Listed below are additional ways to indicate excitement.

Exaggerate Gestures

Provide the parent with concrete examples of how to make her gestures bigger within activities her child enjoys. Exaggerating gestures calls attention to aspects of nonverbal communication that are often subtle and difficult to interpret. Take time to help the parent identify gestures we use to highlight meaning, and discuss how these can be exaggerated. Some examples might include exaggerating a wave, exaggerating a gesture to indicate surprise (hand to mouth), exaggerating a point, exaggerating a gesture to indicate the size of an object (hands apart for "big"), exaggerating a clap of excitement. By exaggerating these movements, she can make them less subtle and easier to interpret.

Exaggerate Facial Expressions

It is often difficult for a child with ASD to interpret and respond to facial expressions. Instruct the parent to exaggerate her facial expressions. For example, she can use a big smile when she plays with her child to show enjoyment. Surprise can be exaggerated with raised eyebrows and an "O"-shaped mouth. If the child hurts himself, the parent can make a sad face with a down-turned mouth and a frown. Provide the parent with concrete examples that she could use with her child. Acknowledge that initially it may feel awkward to exaggerate facial expressions.

Exaggerate Vocal Quality

Vocal quality refers to the rate, tone, and volume of speech. Children with ASD sometimes have difficulty changing their vocal quality and interpreting the meaning of voice changes in others. This causes them to misinterpret many messages. Instruct the parent to exaggerate this aspect of language while pairing it with verbal or nonverbal language to increase the child's comprehension of her message. For example, she can use slow and soft speech along with a down-turned mouth to express sadness. Quickened speech and raised pitch, along with eye contact and a big smile, can be used to express excitement or enjoyment. The parent can change her intonation to indicate whether something is a question or a comment. Exaggerating vocal quality helps increase the child's awareness and comprehension of the meaning of changing vocal quality.

Use Attention-Getting Words or Devices

Attention-getting devices can be effective in gaining the child's attention. Examples of such words or devices include "Uh-oh," "Oh, no," "Wow," or an audible gasp (inhaling audibly). Some children respond to attention-getting words more than to a complete word or their name. It's helpful for parents to use an attention-getting device prior to exaggerating a gesture or facial expression.

Wait with Anticipation

Explain to the parent that presenting too much auditory information can cause her child to shut down or leave the interaction. Children with ASD often require additional time to initiate and respond. Waiting with a charged attitude of anticipation gives the child this time. The amount of wait time required varies considerably, depending on the child, and may range from 2 to 30 seconds. When possible, give the parent a specific amount of time to wait, based on your clinical judgment. Instruct the parent to pair the pause with an expectant look and an attention-getting device. Combining these strategies increases the likelihood that the child will respond. Waiting with anticipation is often difficult for parents to implement, as many are uncomfortable with long periods of silence. However, it is probably one of the most important strategies in this program. It is used in conjunction with the other key points discussed in *Animation*; it will also continue to be used with techniques that are taught in subsequent sessions, to increase the likelihood the child will engage or communicate.

Adjust Your Animation to Help Your Child Remain Regulated

In order to maximize learning, it is important for the child to be in a regulated state—neither withdrawn nor overly aroused. Some children become overaroused when an adult is highly animated. In this case, the parent should decrease her use of gestures, vocal volume, and facial expressions. Conversely, if the child is quiet and withdrawn, instruct the parent to exaggerate her gestures, facial expressions, and vocal quality to increase her child's alertness. Discuss the child's regulatory pattern with the parent, and identify how the parent should implement this strategy with her child. Once the parent implements this element, she should wait to see whether the child begins to match her affect. The child will often decrease his vocal volume if the parent begins to whisper, and will increase vocal volume and excitement to match the parent's affect if the parent demonstrates excitement. Once the child responds, the parent should continue to use this strategy to help regulate her child.

Demonstrate Use of *Animation*

Prepare to demonstrate the technique by reviewing what you will exaggerate, the behavior you will look for from the child, and how you will respond to the child. Explain to the parent that you will begin by following the child's lead to the activity, and then use *Animation* to create an opportunity for the child to communicate. Individualize this explanation for each family based on the child's interests and the child's goals. For example, when explaining this to Brian's mother in terms of his goals, the trainer might say:

> "Since Brian enjoys playing with the ball, I am going to follow his lead to this activity. Next, I am going to exaggerate excitement about ball play by using big gestures and catching the ball. I will then exaggerate facial expressions and vocal quality to indicate excitement about catching the ball. After that, I will wait with anticipation and hold the ball as though I am going to throw it. I will look for any sign of communication from Brian. This could include eye contact, body posture changes, a gesture, or a sound. Once he shows engagement or attempts to communicate with one of these behaviors, I will respond by giving him the ball. If he does not indicate engagement or attempt to communicate, I will exaggerate my excitement about play with the ball by bouncing it while making my gestures big. I will then stop my play and wait with anticipation to see if this elicits communication from him."

Once you have reviewed the technique, demonstrate how to use the different elements described in *Animation*, identifying each element, the child's response, and your response to the child. For example, the trainer might say to Sam's mother:

"After I blew up a little bit of the balloon, I exaggerated my facial expression by making a big smile and looking intently at Sam. I then waited with anticipation to see how Sam would respond. He said, 'Blow.' I responded to his communication by blowing more air into the balloon."

Explain how you continue to use the techniques that were introduced in previous sessions. For example, if the child uses a gesture to request a desired object, explain how you would respond to his communication by giving him the desired object and joining him in his play (i.e., *Follow Your Child's Lead*). You would then imitate his actions in play and make them bigger (*Imitate Your Child* and *Animation*), and then wait with anticipation (*Animation*) to see how the child responds. This aspect is particularly important if the parent has difficulty implementing a previous technique.

Have the Parent Practice *Animation* While You Provide Feedback

Announce the transition between your interaction with the child and the parent's practice. Then suggest a specific behavior for the parent to practice. For example, the trainer might say to Sam's mother:

"Remember to follow Sam's lead to the activity. If he is playing with the cars, exaggerate your gestures and facial expressions by having a big smile and moving your arms back and forth while saying, 'Drive he car.' Then wait to see how Sam responds" If he takes a long time to respond, use an audible gasp and see if this is effective in gaining Sam's attention (eliciting engagement)."

Have the parent practice the *Animation* techniques for at least 15 minutes while you provide feedback. Explain to the parent that she should use *Follow Your Child's Lead*, and then use one or more of the elements described above for *Animation*. Based on what the child is interested in, the parent may choose to exaggerate facial expressions, body language, or vocal quality, or to use attention-getting devices. Once the parent uses one of these elements, the parent should wait with anticipation to see how her child responds.

Remind the parent to respond to all of her child's appropriate communications. If the parent is unable to identify her child's communicative behaviors, describe them to her prior to the interaction. For example, the trainer might tell Sam's mother:

"Sam usually uses one word to request an item. When you see this behavior, respond to him by giving him the item he wants or repeating the action he enjoys. This teaches him that his communication carries meaning and will increase his spontaneous language."

Give the parent specific examples of how she can exaggerate her gestures, facial expressions, or vocal quality. Another feedback strategy is to provide the parent with an attention-getting device she should use or the amount of time she should wait for a response. Be sure to provide the parent with feedback on her use of the technique and the child's response.

Discuss and Assign Homework

1. Have the parent complete homework for *Animation*. Review the homework sheet in the parent manual with the parent. During this review, emphasize the rationale and key elements encompassed in *Animation*. As you complete the review, emphasize the strategies that were most effective for the child. For example, if the child responds well to exaggerated gestures or waiting with anticipation, circle these strategies to remind the parent to use them as she interacts with her child at home. Remind the parent to continue to use *Follow Your Child's Lead* to increase motivation, and *Imitate Your Child* to create an opportunity for her child to engage.

Review the child's goals and help the parent choose one to two goals that she would like to address at home over the next week. *Animation* addresses goals related to engagement, initiations, and understanding and use of nonverbal language. Once the parent has identified a goal or goals, this information should be written on the homework sheet in the parent manual, to remind the parent of why she should practice this technique at home.

For example, in Brian's case, this technique could be used to address his goals of increasing the length of the interaction (engagement) and/or increasing expressive language to request (initiations). The trainer would ask Brian's mother whether she would like to address one or both of the goals at home during the next week. If she answered that she would like to work on engagement, the trainer would write this next to Brian's goals on the homework sheet.

Ask the parent to think of times she may be able to practice *Animation* at home. If the parent is unable to identify an activity, review the Daily Activity Schedule and have her identify two activities her child enjoys. Having the parent practice in more than one activity will help her generalize use of the technique across settings. Write down the activities for the parent and provide her with concrete examples of how this technique can be used within the chosen activity.

Read through the questions on the homework sheet and have the parent respond to them, based on her interaction with her child during this session. If the parent is unable to respond, ask probing questions or demonstrate the technique and have the parent identify the child's response. Inform the parent that she should practice using this technique at home before the next session and write down how her child responds to the technique. Explain that the homework is reviewed at the beginning of the next session.

2. Have the parent read *Modeling and Expanding Language* (Chapter 6 of the parent manual). Instruct the parent to read *Modeling and Expanding Language*. This strategy is used to provide the child with a model of the language the parent would like him use. This technique expands on the fourth step of the interactive teaching techniques sequence, which is to respond to the child's behavior as meaningful and model a more complex response. Two sessions are spent on *Modeling and Expanding Language* because of the number of strategies encompassed in the topic.

Troubleshooting Tips

Animation can be one of the most difficult techniques to teach parents to use, because adults vary significantly in their interaction styles. Some parents are naturally animated and will find this technique easy to use. However, parents who are naturally reserved may have significant difficulty with *Animation*, even after coaching. In order to increase the likelihood that a very reserved parent will use this technique effectively, be sure to describe each component in a concrete manner. It may also help to tell the parent to pretend that she is trying to communicate to someone from across the street who cannot hear what she is saying. As in *Imitate Your Child*, it may be beneficial to demonstrate and provide feedback on each individual component. Another strategy is to have the parent verbalize how she will use the technique prior to practicing with her child. Finally, it may help simply to acknowledge that it may feel really funny to the parent to exaggerate her actions, and that she does not look as "silly" to others as she may feel.

Sessions 6–7

Modeling and Expanding Language

Session Goals

1. Teach the parent to respond to all of her child's actions as purposeful, to improve his functional language skills.
2. Teach the parent to change the way she speaks, to improve her child's understanding and use of language.

Materials

1. Parent manual
2. Completed Goal Development Form (Appendix A, Form 4)
3. Number of highly preferred toys

Outline of Sessions

- Explain the format of these sessions (2 minutes, Session 6).
- Review homework:

    Animation (10–15 minutes, Session 6)
    Modeling and Expanding Language (10–15 minutes, Session 7)

- Introduce the rationale for *Modeling and Expanding Language* (5 minutes, Session 6):

    It teaches the child that his actions carry meaning and elicit a response.
    Improves expressive and receptive language skills.

- Explain how *Modeling and Expanding Language* is used with previously taught techniques (5 minutes, Session 6).
- Discuss the key points of *Modeling and Expanding Language* (15–20 minutes, Session 6; 5–10 minutes, Session 7):

    Give meaning to your child's actions.
    Adjust your language: Simplify language, speak slowly, stress important words, be repetitive, and use visual/gestural cues.

Model language around your child's focus of interest: Use parallel talk, self-talk.

Expand on your child's language.

Provide focused stimulation.

Avoid questions.

- Demonstrate use of *Modeling and Expanding Language* (10–15 minutes each session).
- Have the parent practice *Modeling and Expanding Language* while you provide feedback (20 minutes, Session 6; 30–40 minutes, Session 7).
- Discuss and assign homework (10–15 minutes each session):
    1. Have the parent complete homework for *Modeling and Expanding Language*.
    2. Have the parent read *Playful Obstruction* (Chapter 7 of the parent manual) (Session 7 only).

Explain the Format of These Sessions

Explain to the parent that two sessions will be spent on this technique because of the number of elements within this intervention topic. The times on the outline reflect the approximate amounts of time that should be spent during Sessions 6 and 7. All elements of *Modeling and Expanding Language* should be discussed during Session 6 and briefly reviewed during Session 7. Session 7 is typically spent demonstrating the technique and coaching the parent.

Review Homework from *Animation* (Session 6)

Review the questions from the homework in the parent manual. If the parent was unable to implement the technique at home, or if it was not effective, take time to help her identify solutions. Challenges with *Animation* are usually related to difficulty identifying activities in which to use this technique, rather than with the understanding of the technique. In this event, help the parent identify different activities and the emotions that may be coupled with those activities. As discussed in Session 5, it is also beneficial to provide concrete examples of how to exaggerate nonverbal language.

Review Homework
from *Modeling and Expanding Language* (Session 7)

Read over the homework in the manual that was assigned during Session 6; ask the parent to answer the questions even if she did not fill out the homework. Discuss any aspects of the technique that presented a challenge at home. The responses to this homework inform Session 7. During Session 7, spend time on aspects that presented a challenge by defining the critical elements, demonstrating use, and providing feedback.

Introduce the Rationale
for *Modeling and Expanding Language*

As its name indicates, the *Modeling and Expanding Language* techniques provides the child with a model of a more complex language form or function in order to facilitate language development. This technique sets the stage for prompting language, because the child is provided with a "model" of what he will later be required to use. As you explain the rationale, relate the technique's purpose to the parent's goals for her child.

It Teaches the Child that His Actions Carry Meaning and Elicit a Response

It can be difficult to determine the meaning or function of behaviors for some children with ASD. Other children with ASD may exhibit behaviors that do not appear to be communicative. Giving a child's actions meaning is one way to increase the child's intentional language. Explain to the parent that this addresses her child's goals related to language use with others.

It Improves Expressive and Receptive Language Skills

Children with ASD often have delayed receptive and expressive language skills. Providing appropriate language models around a child's area of interest gives language to new concepts and increases vocabulary. *Modeling and Expanding Language* is also used to teach new language functions (e.g., requests, greetings, protests, comments).

Explain to the parent how *Modeling and Expanding Language* is used to address her child's specific social language goals. For example, when explaining the rationale to Brian's mother, the trainer might say: "Brian has a goal of using a point, vocalization, or single word to request actions or objects. When he requests items with a reach, we are going to show him another way he can request, to increase the likelihood that he will use the new skill."

The trainer might say to Sam's mother: "Sam has a goal of increasing his use of two- to three-word phrases to comment, request, and protest. When he uses one word on his own, we are going to expand on his language by adding words to create a phrase or a sentence. This strategy will increase the likelihood that he will use the new skill."

Explain How *Modeling and Expanding Language*
Is Used with Previously Taught Techniques

Explain to the parent that *Modeling and Expanding Language* is the fourth of the interactive teaching techniques. By this point, the parent should be doing these things:

1. Using *Follow Your Child's Lead*.
2. Creating an opportunity for her child to engage or communicate (*Imitate Your Child, Animation*). The parent will learn additional techniques for doing this (*Playful Obstruction* and *Balanced Turns*) in subsequent sessions.

3. Waiting for her child to engage or communicate. The child must acknowledge the parent in some way (e.g., eye contact, body posture change, facial expressions, gestures, or words). At this point, the parent should be aware of the form and function of her child's language.

4. Responding to the child's behavior as meaningful and complying with it. *Modeling and Expanding Language* elaborates on this step by teaching the parent how to show—that is, to model—a more complex response.

Discuss the Key Points of *Modeling and Expanding Language*

There are six key points described in *Modeling and Expanding Language*. Because of the number of elements encompassed in *Modeling and Expanding Language*, it is often beneficial to provide a brief demonstration of each element as you explain it.

Give Meaning to Your Child's Actions

In previous sessions, the parent has been provided with examples of how to respond to the child's behavior. This session elaborates on this concept. Explain to the parent that she should give meaning to the child's behavior even if it seems unintentional. She acts as the child's interpreter, responding and complying with the child's communication. If applicable, describe the child's behavior and the meaning it might carry. Help the parent attend to cues in the environment to interpret the meaning of her child's communication. Continue to provide the parent with concrete examples of how to respond to her child's behavior even if it seems unintentional. For children who have intentional communication, this strategy may be less important to emphasize.

Adjust Your Language

Review the five aspects of adjusting language: simplify language, speak slowly, stress important words, be repetitive, and use visual/gestural cues. Provide the parent with concrete examples of how to adjust her language to match her child's language level. Some children may use lengthy sentences but have errors within the structure of the sentence. Other children may delete words within a sentence, and some children may not yet be using language.

Simplify Language

Identify the child's language level, and provide the parent with examples of how she can simplify her language (e.g., one word, two words, emphasis on verbs, use of gestures, accurate syntax) to promote language development.

Speak Slowly

Emphasize the importance of decreasing the rate of the parent's speech. Children with ASD often require extra time to process information. If auditory information is presented too quickly, it may cause the child to tune out his parent's language.

Stress Important Words

Stressing important words is particularly useful for children who use sentences but delete words or do not use descriptors. Emphasizing an important word or a missing word improves the child's attention to the word and increases the likelihood that he will associate the word with the object or action.

Be Repetitive

The amount of repetition the parent uses is directly related to her child's skills. Children who are not yet verbal benefit from multiple repetitions of a single word. Through repetition, the parent can also develop verbal routines (e.g., "Ready, set, go"; "Here come tickles") for her child, which she can eventually use to prompt language with the direct teaching techniques. Repetition is also used when the parent is teaching a new concept (e.g., attributes), a new form (e.g., verbs), a new sentence structure (e.g., "is [verb]ing"), or a new function (e.g., greeting). Although repetition may feel awkward at first, it improves the child's ability to understand and to use the word later.

Use Visual/Gestural Cues

It is particularly important to use visual and gestural cues with children who are not yet verbal. This strategy provides the child with an alternative way to communicate, and provides the child with a model of the skill the parent will prompt with the direct teaching techniques. Brainstorm types of gestures to model. A point is a great gesture to teach for requesting, as it is communicative and easily understood by other people. Other gestures could include conventional sign language or gestures that are chosen by you and the parent to signify a certain object or action (e.g., a tap on an object for "Open" instead of the sign). When you and the parent are determining which gesture to use, it is important to take into account the family's cultural background, because that may affect the type of gestures you model. For example, many Native Americans consider pointing with the finger impolite, and gestures are given with the head or the lips.

Model Language around Your Child's Focus of Interest

Children are more likely to use a new word for an object or action if it is something they are interested in and attending to. When the parent is modeling language, it is important for her to provide language models around her child's area of interest. This can be accomplished by using *parallel talk* (describing everything the child is experiencing) or *self-talk* (describing what the parent is experiencing while the child is attending). Provide the parent with examples of times she might use parallel talk and times she might use self-talk.

Brainstorm with the parent the type of language she can use around her child's activities of interest. This is accomplished by thinking of all of the objects (i.e., labels), actions (i.e., verbs), and attributes (i.e., descriptive words) within an activity. For a child with more language, you may also want to discuss emotions that could be modeled within the activity. In addition, the parent can model language to increase her child's use of different language functions (e.g., protesting, requesting, labeling, commenting, gaining attention, seeking attention, and sharing information). Discuss with the parent the reasons for her child's communication. Give the parent examples of how she can provide models to expand the forms and functions of her child's communication. For example, some children may ask questions they already know the answers to in order to initiate (e.g., "What color is the car?"). If the parent knows the child knows the answer to a question, the parent will want to model a comment the child could use to initiate instead (e.g., "Look at my red car").

Expand on Your Child's Language

Expanding language involves adding more information to what the child has said, or modeling appropriate grammar or sentence structure. This strategy is used to expand or revise the child's communication without direct correction. To use this strategy, the parent restates what her child says, adding information or appropriate grammar and syntax. For example, if the child says, "Car," the parent could add information by saying, "Red car"; if the child says, "Baby cry," the parent could model appropriate grammar by saying, "The baby *is crying*." Help the parent identify specific ways to expand her child's language.

Provide *Focused Stimulation*

Providing focused stimulation involves choosing a specific word, phrase, or function to model frequently throughout the child's day. Like repetition, focused stimulation increases the likelihood that the child will learn a new form of communication. Work with the parent to identify new words, concepts, phrases, sentence structures, gestures, or functions of language that relate to the child's area of interest and that she can use frequently throughout the day.

Avoid Questions

The concept of avoiding questions has been explained during *Follow Your Child's Lead*. Remind the parent that she should provide comments and avoid questions, including rhetorical and "test" questions. Help the parent identify how she can turn rhetorical questions into comments and model new information, rather than "testing" her child's knowledge. Explain that while there is a place for questions, they do not promote reciprocal interactions. Imagine if every time you spoke to your partner, all he or she did was ask you test questions. The conversation would feel very one-sided. Thus it is important to avoid these types of questions, especially at the beginning. Ways to ask questions that get a response and promote reciprocal communication are covered in the direct teaching techniques.

Demonstrate Use of *Modeling and Expanding Language*

Prior to the demonstration, you should identify two to three aspects of the technique on which to focus. Base your choices on the parent's interaction style and the aspects you think will have the biggest positive effects on the interaction. For example, if the parent asks a lot of questions, you may focus on having her avoid questions (and make comments instead). Once you have determined which elements you will highlight, explain these to the parent. You should also provide the parent with specific examples regarding the types of language and gestures you will model.

After discussing these items with the parent, briefly demonstrate how to use the technique. Explain to the parent how you follow the child's lead and ensure that the child is engaged before using *Modeling and Expanding Language*. For example, the trainer might say to Brian's mother:

> "Brian was playing with the ball. I joined his play and used *Animation* to create an opportunity for him to engage and waited for a response. He looked at me. I responded to his communication (eye contact) by giving him the ball while modeling a point and the single word 'Ball' (a more complex response)."

At times the child may repeat the language or imitate the gesture; however, stress that you respond to the child's communication even when the child does not use the more complex language form. Use of the more complex language form is discussed during the second portion of this program. It is important for the child to learn that his communication carries meaning and elicits a response; learning this will increase his initiations. Constant correcting of language can cause a child to become reliant on the language model and can decrease his initiations. Explain to the parent how you also model language to describe what the child is doing, even if you have not created an opportunity for him to engage or communicate with you. This improves his language by putting new language forms to his actions.

Have the Parent Practice *Modeling and Expanding Language* While You Provide Feedback

The parent should practice this technique for at least 20 minutes in the session it is first presented (Session 6), and for at least 30–40 minutes in the following session (Session 7). These are longer than previous sessions' practice periods. This longer parent practice pattern continues throughout the remainder of the program, to increase the parent's independence.

Prepare the parent for practice by helping her identify the type of language to model and the specific techniques and strategies to use. For children who are not yet verbal, remind the parent to use gestures with the single word. For children who are highly verbal, help the parent identify forms and functions of language to model. It is also beneficial to remind the parent of the techniques and strategies she will use before she practices. For example, the trainer might say to Sam's mother:

> "Remember to follow Sam's lead to the activity. If he is playing with the cars, you could imitate his play and use *Animation*, and wait to see how he responds. Sam usually responds by simply labeling the item—in this case, 'Car.' Once he responds, expand on his language by adding a word or two to describe an action or attribute of the car. For example, you might say, 'Push car' (action) or 'Red car' (attribute)."

Provide feedback on the parent's use of the technique and the child's response. Remind the parent to respond to all types of her child's appropriate communication. The parent may also model language to describe what the child is doing, even if the child does not engage or communicate with the parent. You may also continue to coach the parent on use of the previously taught techniques; however, remember to coach on no more than two to three techniques at a time. Have the parent practice *Modeling and Expanding Language* with at least two activities to help the parent generalize use of the technique.

Discuss and Assign Homework

1. Have the parent complete homework for *Modeling and Expanding Language*. The homework sheet remains the same for both sessions *Modeling and Expanding Language*, because the parent is practicing the same technique. Make a photocopy of the homework sheet, in the manual, so that the parent has a clean copy to complete after Session 7.

Introduce the homework with a brief review of the homework sheet, including a brief review of the rationale and key points of *Modeling and Expanding Language*. Because you typically spend two sessions on this technique, it can be effective to choose a few elements for the parent to practice after each session. Circle the elements the parent should focus on after each session. Remind the parent to continue to use *Follow Your Child's Lead, Imitate Your Child,* and *Animation* to increase engagement and to create an opportunity for her child to engage.

Once you have identified the elements of the technique the parent should focus on, the next step is to review the child's goals and identify the goal(s) the parent will target at home. This technique addresses all of the child's goals that are related to expressive and receptive language. It also addresses goals related to the functions of language. Help the parent identify words or types of words to model, based on the child's individualized goals. For example, if the goal is single words, help the parent identify words that have a high rate of frequency in daily activities, such as "Open," as the repetition can help the child begin to use the words. If the child's goal is related to use of descriptors or comments, identify descriptors and comments the parent could use during specific activities. While you complete the goals, write down the activities in which the words occur. For example, if you identify the word "Open," brainstorm all activities in which this word could occur (e.g., opening the door, opening the fridge, opening the milk carton), and write these examples on the homework sheet. At this point, the parent should be able to identify multiple activities in which to use the technique; however, if she continues to have difficulty, refer to the Daily Activity Schedule.

Figure S6-7.1 illustrates part of the completed homework sheet for this technique. Notice how the trainer has included brief examples of when the target words could be highlighted throughout daily activities. The trainer has also included gestures to use to pair with the verbalization. Work with the parent to identify a gesture to pair with the word; this is particularly important for children who are nonverbal.

Review the questions on the homework sheet and have the parent respond orally to the questions, based on her interaction with her child during this session. Again, you may want to target half of the questions after Session 6 and half of the questions after Session 7. If the parent is unable to respond to the questions, ask probing questions or demonstrate the technique and have the parent identify the child's response. Inform the parent that she should practice using this technique at home before the next session and write down how her child responds to the technique. Remind her that the homework will be reviewed at the beginning of the next session.

2. Have the parent read *Playful Obstruction* (Chapter 7 of the parent manual). Instruct the parent to read *Playful Obstruction* prior to the next session. This is another technique the parent can use to create an opportunity for her child to communicate with her, thereby increas-

HOMEWORK	*Modeling and Expanding Language*

Rationale: This techniques teaches your child that his actions carry meaning and elicit a response from you, and it increases your child's receptive language (language understanding) and expressive language skills.

Key points to remember and carry out:

Give meaning to your child's actions.

Adjust your language: Simplify language, speak slowly, stress important words, be repetitive, and use gestures/visual cues.

Model language around your child's focus of interest: Use parallel talk and self-talk.

Expand on your child's language.

Provide focused stimulation: Use the same words, phrases, and gestures 15–20 times a day in a variety of situations.

Avoid questions.

A response by your child is not required. You are mapping language to what your child sees, hears, and does.

Goals of the Week

Child's goals: Increase single words. Use gestures with the words.

Activities: Open (opening the car door, opening a door, opening the refrigerator, opening a toy box or any container), help (any time he needs help), off and on (lights on and off, water on and off, the car on and off, toys on and off).

Language you will model: Target words: "open," "help," "off," "on." Use single words and pair a gesture with each word. Gestures could include a tap for open, a sign for help, and a point up for on and down for off.

Figure S6-7.1. Filled-in example of the *Modeling and Expanding Language* homework sheet, first part.

ing engagement. The parent should come to the next session with any questions she may have about the technique. The parent does not need to complete the homework for this technique until it has been reviewed and practiced during the next session.

Troubleshooting Tips

Several challenges may arise when you are teaching *Modeling and Expanding Language*. First, the parent may want her child to repeat her language before she gives the child the desired item. This can become particularly problematic if the child is not verbal and is unable to repeat the language. In addition, it can decrease the child's spontaneous language, because the parent is beginning to require something new each time the child initiates. In this case, reiterate to the parent that it is most important now for her child to learn that his communication carries meaning and elicits a response from her. She needs to help him increase his initiations before requiring a more complex response. Constant correcting of his language can cause the child to become reliant on the parent's language model and can decrease his initiations. Explain that strategies to prompt expressive language are discussed during Sessions 15 and 16 of this program.

A second common challenge is the parent's use of rhetorical questions when interacting with her child (e.g., "Is the boy going down the slide?"). The parent may do this to fill up space especially when the child is not responsive. Help the parent change the question into a comment (e.g., "The boy is going down the slide").

Another challenge occurs when the parent has difficulty learning to use all of the elements in this technique. When this occurs, coach her on one to two elements at a time. For example, if the parent is having trouble simplifying her language (e.g., the parent is asking questions or using too many words), have the parent focus specifically on that aspect of the technique—for example, "Let's use only one word when modeling language. In this activity, let's use the word 'ball.'" Continue with this pattern until all of the strategies in *Modeling and Expanding Language* are introduced.

One final challenge can occur when a parent is very quiet and rarely models language. If this is the case, have the parent practice providing a "play-by-play" narration of her child's play in isolation, without worrying about using other interactive teaching techniques or simplifying her language. Once she is comfortable with talking more, coach her to simplify what she says and to use *Modeling and Expanding Language* with *Imitate Your Child* and *Animation*.

Session 8

Playful Obstruction

Session Goal

1. Teach the parent strategies to increase the number of opportunities her child has to communicate with her and to increase engagement.

Materials

1. Parent manual
2. Completed Goal Development Form (Appendix A, Form 4)
3. Number of highly preferred toys

Outline of Session

- Review homework from *Modeling and Expanding Language* (10–15 minutes).
- Introduce the rationale for *Playful Obstruction* (5 minutes):

    It increases opportunities for communication.
    It increases engagement.

- Explain how *Playful Obstruction* is used with previously taught techniques (5 minutes).
- Discuss the key points of *Playful Obstruction* (5–10 minutes):

    Use an anticipatory phrase.
    Present a playful obstruction.
    Wait for your child to engage or communicate.
    Respond to the child's communication.

- Demonstrate use of *Playful Obstruction* (10–15 minutes).
- Have the parent practice *Playful Obstruction* while you provide feedback (15–25 minutes).
- Discuss and assign homework (10–15 minutes).

    1. Have the parent complete homework for *Playful Obstruction*.
    2. Have the parent read *Balanced Turns* (Chapter 8 of the parent manual).

Review Homework from *Modeling and Expanding Language*

Discuss the parent's responses to the questions on the homework. If it was difficult for the parent to implement this technique at home, take time to help her identify solutions. Challenges usually center around implementation or requesting a response from the child, as discussed in "Troubleshooting Tips" for Sessions 6–7. For example, the parent may report that it is hard to use only two to three words or not to use questions. In this case, acknowledge the challenge of changing her typical language patterns, and then provide the parent with suggestions on ways in which she can implement this technique. To address the second challenge, explain to the parent that teaching the use of language and gestures will be discussed in subsequent sessions, and that at this point she is providing a model of what she will prompt her child to use later. Reiterate the importance of responding to her child's initiations to increase his spontaneous skills.

Introduce the Rationale for *Playful Obstruction*

Explain the purpose and benefits of the technique to the parent. In *Playful Obstruction,* the parent playfully interrupts the child's play. This technique is used when *Imitate Your Child* and *Animation* are not effective in creating an opportunity for the child to communicate. Relate the technique's purpose to the parent's goals for her child. Learning and using the technique will have the following benefits for the child.

It Increases Opportunities for Communication

Children with ASD often have difficulty initiating interactions and communicating with others. *Playful Obstruction* is sure to elicit a response from a child every time, thus increasing the opportunities the child has to respond. This technique can be used to increase both requests and protests (child's language goals).

It Increases Engagement

Playful Obstruction can also be used to recruit the child's attention and increase engagement. Unlike *Imitate Your Child* and *Animation*, this technique is certain to elicit a response.

Explain to the parent how *Playful Obstruction* will address her child's individual goals. For example, when explaining the rationale to Brian's mother, the trainer might say:

> "Brian has a goal of increasing his expressive language to request. *Playful Obstruction* creates multiple opportunities for Brian to request an item or action from you. You are then able to model a more complex form of communication. This gives you more opportunities to show him the new word and gesture, which increases the likelihood that he will use it on his own (a language goal). Playful obstruction is also another way to increase the length of your interaction with Brian (a social engagement goal)."

The trainer might say to Sam's mother: "Sam has a goal of increasing spontaneous language. *Playful Obstruction* creates multiple opportunities for Sam to request from you or to protest your action."

Explain How *Playful Obstruction* Is Used with Previously Taught Techniques

Refer to the diagram of the Project ImPACT pyramid at the beginning of the parent manual (Figure 1.1 there; see also Figure S1.3 in Session 1, this manual) to help the parent visualize how the techniques are used together. *Playful Obstruction* is located in the middle layer of the pyramid. Remind the parent that the techniques on the middle level build on the techniques on the bottom level of the pyramid and are used to elicit communication from the child.

The parent continues to use *Follow Your Child's Lead* to determine what her child is interested in, and to position herself face to face with her child. She then joins the play by using *Imitate Your Child* or *Animation* and waits for the child to demonstrate engagement or communicate. If these techniques are not effective in eliciting an interaction from the child, the parent can use *Playful Obstruction* paired with *Animation* to create an opportunity for the child to engage or communicate. *Animation* is always coupled with *Playful Obstruction*, to decrease the child's frustration. The parent continues to use *Modeling and Expanding Language* around the child's attentional focus while using *Playful Obstruction*.

Discuss the Key Points of *Playful Obstruction*

Explain that there are four parts to *Playful Obstruction*: giving an anticipatory (warning) phrase, presenting the playful obstruction itself, waiting for the child to engage or communicate, and responding to the child's communication. This technique, especially the first step, is used in conjunction with *Animation*; combining these techniques decreases frustration. Ask the parent whether she has tried to interrupt her child's play in the past. If she has tried this technique, inquire about the child's response.

Use an Anticipatory Phrase

Spoken before play is interrupted, an anticipatory phrase allows the child to know that something is going to change. It also gives him an opportunity to communicate before the change takes place. Without this strategy, there is no warning or opportunity for the child to "protest" the change, and he may become frustrated. Brainstorm with the parent possible anticipatory phrases she could use, based on her child's interests. Examples include "I am going to catch you," "Here I come," or "Here comes the puppet."

Present a *Playful Obstruction*

Following the anticipatory phrase, the parent interrupts the child's play in some way to elicit a response from the child. Give the parent concrete examples. For example, if the child enjoys running around the room, the parent could become a "roadblock" or catch him. The parent might gain access to a toy the child has in a playful way, or block an action the child is trying to complete. It can often be effective and less frustrating for the child if the parent uses a puppet to obstruct the play.

Wait for Your Child to Engage or Communicate

Review with the parent how her child might engage or communicate: eye contact, shifts in body posture, gestures (pointing or leading by the hand), vocalizations, or words. These behaviors can indicate the child's awareness that the parent is interacting with him.

Respond to the Child's Communication

Explain to the parent that when she is obstructing the child's play, it is important to respond to all forms of the child's communication to decrease his frustration. This is particularly true for a child who is not yet verbal. If the child protests before the obstruction is presented, the parent should withdraw the obstruction. Remind the parent that the purpose of this technique is to elicit a response from the child, not to block her child or obtain a toy. Therefore, if the child protests prior to her obstruction, she should respond by stopping. If he reacts more positively, she should present the obstruction and then respond to his communication appropriately (giving him the item he wants, etc.).

Demonstrate Use of *Playful Obstruction*

Explain to the parent that you will now demonstrate *Playful Obstruction*, but will begin with *Follow Your Child's Lead* to increase motivation. Describe the response you will look for from the child, and how you will then respond to the child. Individualize this for each child and family, based on the child's interests and the child's goals. For example, when explaining this for the goals developed in Brian's case, the trainer might say:

> "Brian is holding the ball. I will use the frog puppet to gain access to the ball, which will elicit a response from Brian. I will use the anticipatory phrase 'Here I come,' and slowly move the puppet toward the ball to see how Brian responds. I will take the ball if he does not protest. If he does protest, I will not take the ball. Because the goal is to increase interaction and communication, I will look for any behavior that indicates he is engaged or attempting to communicate. This could include eye contact, body posture changes, a gesture, or a sound. I will comply with his communication and respond appropriately."

Demonstrate how to use the different elements of *Playful Obstruction*, identifying the technique as you use it and the child's response. For example, the trainer might say to Sam's mother: "Sam was running around the room. I said, 'I'll get you,' and caught him. Then I waited to see what he would do. He said, 'Go,' so I let him go."

As you demonstrate this technique, it is important to emphasize the child's communication, particularly if he protests with subtle behaviors. The parent needs to be able to spot and interpret the child's communication before she can respond to it. Reiterate to the parent that she should continue to use *Follow Your Child's Lead* to determine her child's interest, and that she should always pair *Animation* with *Playful Obstruction* to decrease frustration.

Have the Parent Practice *Playful Obstruction* While You Provide Feedback

Have the parent practice *Playful Obstruction* for at least 15 minutes. Provide the parent with specific techniques to use and behaviors she should look for. For example,

> "Sam often protests before his play is obstructed by saying, 'No puppet.' Remember that the purpose of this technique is to increase the opportunities for communication. Therefore, you want to respond to that protest by moving the puppet and then expanding on his language by saying, 'I don't want the puppet.'"

When coaching on this technique, provide the parent with specific examples of how she can use playful obstruction to create an opportunity for her child to respond. For example, the trainer might say to Brian's mother: "Brian is holding the ball. I wonder what would happen if you used *Playful Obstruction* to get the ball. Remember to use *Animation* and an anticipatory phrase to give him the opportunity to protest before you take the ball."

When providing feedback, determine which step the parent is having difficulty with and provide feedback around that element. Again, *Playful Obstruction* has four steps. First, always use an anticipatory phrase to warn the child that something is about to happen. Second, playfully interrupt the child's play. Third, wait for the child to engage or communicate in some way. And, fourth, respond to the child's communication. You want to make sure that the parent is successful with the first before coaching her on the second one, and with the second step before coaching her on the third and fourth ones. In addition, encompassed in the first step in particular are the *Animation* strategies; if the parent is not pairing these effectively with the anticipatory phrase, you may choose to coach her first on *Animation* before discussing ways to playfully obstruct the child's play.

Examples of feedback could include reminding the parent to use an anticipatory phrase, reminding her to pair *Animation* with the technique, giving her an idea of how to block the child (e.g., using her hand to interrupt his action with the toy), or providing her with a specific amount of time to wait. Be sure to provide the parent with feedback on both the technique and the child's response. Also assist the parent by giving her items (e.g., a puppet or toy to block play) or removing distracting items from the environment.

Discuss and Assign Homework

1. Have the parent complete homework for *Playful Obstruction*. Review the homework sheet in the parent manual with the parent. Emphasize the rationale and the key points of *Playful Obstruction*. As you complete the review, underline or circle the strategies that seem to be most effective for the child. For example, if the child responds well to the use of an anticipatory phrase, circle this strategy to remind the parent to use this strategy as she interacts with her child at home. You should also underscore any strategies that seem difficult for the parent to use and have her practice them before the next session.

Review the child's goals with the parent, and have her identify at least one goal related to initiations (e.g., requests, protests) or engagement (e.g., length of the interaction, turn taking). Write down the goal or goals on the homework sheet. For example, in Brian's case, his goals are related to increasing the length of his interaction and increasing use of language to request. The trainer would ask his parent if she would like to use the technique to address one or both of these goals, and write her response down next to the child's goals.

Ask the parent to think of times and activities she may be able to practice this technique with her child. At this point in the program, the parent should be able to identify at least one daily routine within which she will practice *Playful Obstruction*. However, if she has difficulty, refer her to the Daily Activity Schedule and have her identify at least one activity her child enjoys. Write down the activities for the parent, and give the parent concrete examples of how this technique is used within the chosen activity. Explain to the parent that this technique can be used throughout the day to gain her child's attention and to create opportunities for communication.

Once the child's goals and the activities have been identified, help the parent choose language she may model during the interaction. This helps the parent remember to model language appropriate to her child's developmental level. For example, in Brian's case, the trainer would help his mom choose single words and gestures that she could model with each activity.

Review the questions outlined on the homework sheet for *Playful Obstruction*, and have the parent respond orally to the questions, based on her interaction with her child during this session. If the parent is unable to respond to the questions, ask probing questions or demonstrate the technique and have the parent identify the child's response. Inform the parent that she should practice using this technique at home before the next session and write down how her child responds to the technique. Remind her that you will review the homework at the beginning of the next session.

2. Have the parent read *Balanced Turns* (Chapter 8 of the parent manual). Instruct the parent to read *Balanced Turns* prior to the next session. She should come to the next session with any questions she may have about the technique. She does not need to complete the homework for the technique until it has been reviewed and practiced during the next session. Inform the parent that two sessions will be spent on *Balanced Turns*. The first session will focus on turn-taking skills, and the second session will focus on modeling and expanding play.

Troubleshooting Tips

A parent may be hesitant to use *Playful Obstruction* because she does not want to upset her child. In this case, you should reiterate that the technique is used to create an opportunity for the child to communicate, not to obstruct the child. Therefore, if the child communicates protest in any form, the parent should respond by complying. Remind the parent that communication can take the form of body movement changes, gestures, fleeting eye contact, or words. Responding to subtle aspects of the child's behavior will teach him that his behavior carries meaning and elicits a response.

Another challenge occurs when the parent does not pair *Animation* and the anticipatory phrase with *Playful Obstruction*. In this case, provide the parent with a phrase to use, and explain how she should exaggerate gestures with a pause time. Explain that exaggerating gestures and moving slowly will allow the child time to process what is about to happen and give the child time to respond to the parent with either a protest (a desire to stop the action) or a request (a wish for more of the action). Take this time to identify specific gestures the parent could exaggerate during activities of interest with her child. Explain that without these strategies, the child may become frustrated because the change is sudden and abrupt, without warning.

Since this technique is usually very successful at eliciting child initiations, a parent may begin to rely heavily on it, obstructing her child's play during the majority of the interaction. When this happens, the child may become frustrated or resistant to playing with the parent. If this occurs, remind the parent of the pyramid diagram at the beginning of the parent manual. Emphasize that techniques in the middle layer, such as *Playful Obstruction*, should only be used during about two-thirds of the interactions. If they are used too often, the child is likely to get frustrated. Remind the parent to return to using a technique in the bottom layer of the pyramid, such as *Follow Your Child's Lead* or *Imitate Your Child*, after the parent has used *Playful Obstruction*.

Balanced Turns, Part 1

TURN TAKING

Session Goals

1. Teach the parent strategies to encourage turn taking with her child.
2. Teach the parent strategies to increase opportunities for her child to communicate.

Materials

1. Parent manual
2. Completed Goal Development Form (Appendix A, Form 4)
3. Number of highly preferred toys

Outline of Session

- Explain the format of this session and the next (2 minutes).
- Review homework from *Playful Obstruction* (10–15 minutes).
- Introduce the rationale for *Balanced Turns* (5 minutes):

    It increases turn taking.
    It increases opportunities or communication.
    It improves play skills.

- Explain how *Balanced Turns* is used with previously taught techniques (5 minutes).
- Discuss the key points of *Balanced Turns, Part 1: Turn Taking* (5–10 minutes).

    Help your child anticipate turns.
    Take short turns.
    Wait for your child to communicate for his turn.
    Always return materials.
    Trade toys (optional).

- Demonstrate use of *Balanced Turns, Part 1: Turn Taking* (10–15 minutes).
- Have the parent practice *Balanced Turns, Part 1: Turn Taking* while you provide feedback (15–25 minutes).
- Discuss and assign homework (10–15 minutes).

    1. Have the parent complete homework for *Balanced Turns, Part 1: Turn Taking*
    2. Have the parent review *Balanced Turns* (Chapter 8 of the parent manual).

About Sessions 9 and 10

Balanced Turns consists of two skill sets: (1) turn taking and (2) modeling and expanding play skills. Turn-taking strategies should be taught first (Session 9). Strategies for modeling and expanding play are then taught (Session 10), since the parent will model new play when it is her turn. As in all techniques, the amount of time spent on each component may vary among families. For some parents, both skill sets may be taught within one session, with the next session devoted to practice. It is your role to individualize the amount of time spent on each set, based on the parent's needs.

Explain the Format of This Session and the Next

Explain to the parent that this session and the next will be spent on the topic of *Balanced Turns*, with this session spent on turn-taking techniques and the next on modeling and expanding play.

Review Homework from *Playful Obstruction*

Read over the homework in the parent manual. Ask the parent to answer the questions even if she did not complete the homework. If it was difficult for the parent to implement this technique at home, take time to help her identify solutions. Common challenges at home are similar to those discussed in "Troubleshooting Tips" for Session 8. These challenges are often intensified during home practice, because the child may not be used to the parent's interrupting his play. If the parent sees an increase in her child's response to her, she may begin to use this technique too frequently at home, which may lead to frustration when the child hears the anticipatory phrase. Or the parent may not have practiced this technique at all, due to the fear that the child will get frustrated. In either case, take time to brainstorm solutions with the parent. One strategy is to help the parent identify how she can balance use of this technique with other strategies that create an opportunity for her child to engage (e.g., *Imitate Your Child* and *Animation*). If the parent was hesitant to use *Playful Obstruction*, but it is effective with her child, take time to reiterate the *Animation* strategies that are paired with this technique to increase its effectiveness. If necessary, take time to practice *Playful Obstruction* before you introduce *Balanced Turns*.

Introduce the Rationale for *Balanced Turns*

Explain the purpose and benefits of the technique to the parent. *Balanced Turns* involves the parent's taking the child's toy for a turn during play and then returning the toy to the child. Be sure to relate the technique's purpose to the parent's goals for her child. This technique is effective for children who have difficulty sharing toys and taking turns, initiating their turn, and requesting.

It Increases Turn Taking

Children with ASD often have difficulty sharing toys and taking turns with others. This technique is used to increase a child's understanding of and use of turns. This technique also facilitates back-and-forth interaction, which is important for both play (e.g., turn taking) and language (e.g., conversation). It also allows for more sophisticated social interactions with adults and peers, and it teaches early negotiation skills.

It Increases Opportunities for Communication

Children with ASD often have difficulty initiating requests or social interactions with others. Children who have difficulty initiating have fewer opportunities to develop good communication skills and may have difficulty getting their needs met. Even children with good language skills may have difficulty indicating what they want when they want it if they do not initiate well. Taking *Balanced Turns* with a child increases the number of opportunities the child has to communicate. It can also increase the child's engagement and the length of the interaction by increasing the back-and-forth communication. Thus you would explain to the parent that *Balanced Turns* addresses the child's goals related to engagement and communication.

It Improves Play Skills

Children with ASD often have delayed play skills and play with toys in an atypical manner. Helping them develop play skills is important for a variety of reasons. Play is an activity that children engage in with each other; enhancing a child's play skills can increase his ability to interact with peers during play. Play can also be an excellent way to target problem solving and reasoning skills.

Explain to the parent how *Balanced Turns* will address her child's individual goals. When explaining this, highlight the child's social engagement, language, and play goals. For example, the trainer might say to Brian's mother:

> "Teaching Brian to take turns will address a number of his goals. It will increase the length of time he is able to engage with another person during play. It will also address Brian's language goal (increasing his expressive language to request), because it increases the opportunities he has to communicate and the opportunities you have to model new language forms for him. This is also true for play, as you will have the opportunity to model functional play skills when it is your turn."

The trainer might say to Sam's mother: "Sam has a goal of increasing turn taking; this technique directly addresses this goal."

Explain How *Balanced Turns* Is Used with Previously Taught Techniques

Balanced Turns builds on *Follow Your Child's Lead, Imitate Your Child,* and *Animation.* It is another technique that can be used to create an opportunity for the child to communicate (the second step in the interactive teaching techniques). Taking turns with materials the child has chosen increases the likelihood that he will request a turn. *Balanced Turns* is similar to *Playful Obstruction* in that it is highly likely to elicit communication from the child. However, it differs from *Playful Obstruction* in that the parent follows through with a short turn even if the child protests.

Discuss the Key Points of *Balanced Turns, Part 1: Turn Taking*

Reiterate that there are two parts to *Balanced Turns*: taking turns and modeling/expanding play. This session will be spent discussing the key points of turn taking. Modeling and expanding play will be discussed during the next session. Ask the parent whether she has tried to take turns with her child. If she has tried this technique, inquire about the child's response.

Help Your Child Anticipate Turns

Explain that the parent should always use the same brief phrase to signal the child that she is about to take a turn. This is similar to the use of an anticipatory phrase in *Playful Obstruction*. Keeping this phrase consistent helps the child anticipate what will happen, thereby decreasing his frustration. Choose an anticipatory phrase based on the child's skill level. For example, a child may not understand pronouns, as in "my turn" and "your turn." In this case, names can be used to indicate turns (e.g., "Mom's turn," "Brian's turn"). Or the child may benefit from the pairing of gestures with the verbal statement (e.g., the parent's pointing to herself along with the words "My turn," or holding out her hand with the palm up to indicate her turn). Help the parent identify a phrase she should use to help her child anticipate turns.

Take Short Turns

The parent's turn should be kept short, to prevent the child from losing interest when he loses access to the toy. Help the parent identify the appropriate amount of time for her turn. In some instances the parent's turn may be fleeting, while on other occasions the parent may be able to model play (see Session 10). At this point, the parent can imitate the child's play during her turn; in the next session, you and she will discuss how to model and expand play during her turn.

Wait for Your Child to Communicate for His Turn

Waiting for the child to initiate is similar to the waiting with anticipation discussed in *Animation*. Explain to the parent that after she takes her turn, she should wait for her child to initiate his turn. Remind the parent that she needs to respond to all types of communication (e.g., body posture, eye contact, vocalizations). Review with the parent ways her child may communicate his turn, based on information from previous sessions.

Always Return Desired Materials

Emphasize to the parent that she must always end a turn-taking activity by returning the object to the child, even if the child seems to have lost interest (e.g., he walks away). Sometimes children do not initiate a turn because they believe that once they have lost access to the object, it is gone forever. Other children may lose interest once they lose access because they may not know how to gain access to the object again. Returning the object to the child teaches him that there is a way to get the object back.

Trade Toys (Optional)

For a child who becomes highly frustrated with turn taking, it can often be beneficial to trade identical objects rather than to take turns with one object. Once the child becomes familiar with the back-and-forth nature of the interaction, the parent can begin to take turns with one object. For a child who readily takes turns with one object but has difficulty sharing a favorite part of a toy (e.g., he always wants the blue train), the parent can teach early negotiation skills by trading different objects. When using this technique, the parent should make sure to keep her turn short, to use an anticipatory phrase, and to return the object to the child.

Demonstrate Use of *Balanced Turns, Part 1: Turn Taking*

Identify the *Balanced Turns* strategies that will be most beneficial for the child. For some children, you may begin by trading toys prior to taking turns with one object. Other children may readily allow the adult to take a turn, in which case you could focus on modeling new play (see Session 10). Explain to the parent what you will do, the response you will look for, and how you will respond to the child. Individualize the technique for each child and parent, based on the child's interests and goals. For example, the trainer might say to Brian's mother:

> "Brian is holding the ball. I will take a turn to gain access to the ball, which will elicit a response from Brian. I will use an anticipatory phrase, 'It's [clinician's name] turn,' and gesture toward myself. I will then take the ball for a quick turn. Unlike in *Playful Obstruction*, I will take a quick turn even if he protests. At this point, I will keep my turn short (about 1–2 seconds). I will then return the ball to Brian and say, "Brian's turn," while gesturing toward him. If he becomes frustrated, I will use another ball and begin by trading balls."

Demonstrate the turn-taking steps, identifying them as you use them, along with the child's responses. For example, the trainer might say to Sam's mother:

> "Sam is playing with the cars. I am going to say, 'My turn,' take the car, briefly imitate his play, and wait to see how he responds. [Trainer does this.] He looked at me. So I responded to his communication (eye contact) by giving him back the car. It is important to respond to Sam's communication, even if it is nonverbal."

Have the Parent Practice *Balanced Turns, Part 1: Turn Taking* While You Provide Feedback

Have the parent practice the *Turn Taking* part of *Balanced Turns* for at least 15 minutes. Remind the parent of the specific steps for the technique prior to her beginning the interaction—for example, "Remember to follow Brian's lead to the activity. If he is playing with the ball, gain access to the ball while using your anticipatory phrase, 'Mom's turn.' Next, take a turn and wait to see how he responds. Then give him back the ball."

Remind the parent to respond to all types of appropriate communication by giving her child a turn. At this point, the parent should be successful in gaining a response from the child; however, she should not yet prompt the child for a more complex response. As with previously discussed techniques, it is important to help the parent pay attention to how the child indicates that he wants something and to respond to that communicative behavior as purposeful. You also want to limit the number of items available, in order to increase the child's attention to the parent's turn.

Discuss and Assign Homework

1. Have the parent complete homework for *Balanced Turns, Part 1: Turn Taking*. Review the rationale and the key points of *Balanced Turns*. Emphasize the strategies that seem most effective for the child. For example, if the child responds well to trading toys, circle this technique to remind the parent to use this strategy as she interacts with her child at home. Discuss other strategies that have been effective in creating an opportunity for the child to engage or communicate, and write down strategies the parent might use if turn taking is not successful. Have the parent practice the strategies that were used in this session.

Identify at least one goal that the parent will target at home, and write this on the homework sheet for this session in the parent manual. *Balanced Turns* is used to encourage the child to initiate, to improve back-and-forth communication, and to improve his ability to share toys with others. Help the parent identify activities in which *Balanced Turns* may be most effective. For some children, this may need to be practiced during a structured activity. Identify at least two activities in which the parent could practice *Balanced Turns* with her child. Write the activities in which the parent will practice on the homework sheet.

Once the child's goal(s) and the activities have been identified, help the parent choose language she may model during the interaction. This helps the parent remember to model language appropriate to her child's developmental level. For example, in Brian's case, the trainer would help the mother choose single words and gestures that she could model with each activity. Write the language and/or gestures she should model on the homework sheet.

Review the questions on the homework sheet and have the parent respond orally, based on her interaction with her child during this session. Choose the questions based on the techniques that were used in this session. If the parent is unable to respond to the questions, ask probing questions or demonstrate the technique and have the parent identify the child's response. Inform the parent that she should practice using this technique at home before the next session and write down how her child responds. Explain that the homework will be reviewed at the beginning of the next session.

2. Have the parent review *Balanced Turns* (Chapter 8 of the parent manual). Instruct the parent to review *Balanced Turns* prior to the next session. She should come to the next session with any questions she may have about the technique. She does not need to complete the homework for *Balanced Turns, Part 2: Modeling and Expanding Play* until it has been reviewed and practiced during the next session.

Troubleshooting Tips

Initially, a child may have a difficult time taking turns even if the parent's turn is short. In this case, discuss trading toys before taking turns with one object. If the child loses interest in the toy as soon as the parent takes a turn, try having only one toy available at a time. Structured activities that lend themselves to turn taking, such as throwing a balloon or a ball back and forth, can also increase the child's success with turn taking. If frustration continues and *Playful Obstruction* was successful, have the parent use *Playful Obstruction* while saying, "My turn," and then quickly returning the object to the child. Another strategy is to have the parent balance the use of *Balanced Turns* with *Imitate Your Child*.

Session 10

Balanced Turns, Part 2
MODELING AND EXPANDING PLAY

Session Goals
1. Teach the parent strategies to encourage turn taking with her child.
2. Teach the parent strategies to increase opportunities for her child to communicate.
3. Teach the parent to model new play actions to promote play development.

Materials
1. Parent manual
2. Completed Goal Development Form (Appendix A, Form 4)
3. Number of highly preferred toys

Outline of Session
- Review homework from *Balanced Turns, Part 1: Turn Taking* (10–15 minutes).
- Review the rationale for *Balanced Turns* (5 minutes):

    It increases turn taking.
    It increases opportunities for communication.
    It improves play skills.

- Discuss the key points of *Balanced Turns, Part 2: Modeling and Expanding Play* (5–10 minutes):

    Help your child anticipate turns.
    Take short turns.
    Model play.
    Wait for your child to communicate for his turn.

Always return materials.
Trade toys (optional).

- Demonstrate use of *Balanced Turns, Part 2: Modeling and Expanding Play* (10–15 minutes).
- Have the parent practice *Balanced Turns, Part 2: Modeling and Expanding Play* while you provide feedback (15–25 minutes).
- Discuss and assign homework (10–15 minutes).
    1. Have the parent complete homework for *Balanced Turns, Part 2: Modeling and Expanding Play.*
    2. Have the parent read *Communicative Temptations* (Chapter 9 of the parent manual).

Review Homework from *Balanced Turns, Part 1: Turn Taking*

Read over the homework in the manual that was assigned during the previous session; ask the parent to answer the questions even if she did not fill out the homework. Discuss any aspect of the technique that presented a challenge at home. The response from this homework should inform this second session on *Balanced Turns*. During this session, spend time on techniques that presented a challenge or that were not introduced in Session 9.

Review the Rationale for *Balanced Turns*

As discussed in Session 9, *Balanced Turns* is effective for children who have difficulty sharing toys, taking turns, initiating their turn, and requesting, as well as for children who have delayed play skills. The purpose of this session is to teach the parent to model and expand play to enhance her child's play skills. Briefly review the rationale that was discussed in Session 9; in this session, emphasize the technique's role in enhancing the child's play skills. Modeling and expanding on the child's play will be used to enhance the type and complexity of the child's play. Development of play skills is important for a variety of reasons. In addition to the ones discussed in Section 9, it can improve joint attention skills, because the child has to shift his attention between the toy and the person.

Briefly review with the parent how this technique can be used to target the child's play goals. For example, the trainer might say to Brian's mother:

"We are going to continue to use *Balanced Turns* to increase the length of our interaction with Brian and to increase his opportunities to communicate. Today we will add modeling and expanding play when it is our turn. This element of *Balanced Turns* is used to improve play skills. By showing Brian different ways a toy can be used, we can expand his play skills."

The trainer might say to Sam's mother: "We are going to continue to use *Balanced Turns* to improve Sam's ability to take turns with others. Today we will add modeling and expanding play when it is our turn. This element of *Balanced Turns* will be used to improve Sam's pretend play with toys."

Discuss the Key Points of *Balanced Turns, Part 2: Modeling and Expanding Play*

Briefly review the key points of *Balancing Turns, Part 1: Turn Taking*. Then introduce *Part 2: Modeling and Expanding Play*. Individualize the explanation of this part of the technique for each parent, based on the child's interests and goals.

Help Your Child Anticipate Turns

Reiterate that the parent should always use the same brief phrase to signal the child that she is about to take a turn.

Take Short Turns

Help the parent continue to work on identifying the appropriate amount of time for her turn, if this is needed.

Model Play

Explain to the parent that when it is her turn, she should show the child a new way to play with the materials. The type of play the parent models should be directly related to her child's interests and at or slightly above the child's skill level. This gives the child an example of more complex play. The parent should model play for the amount of time the child can wait between turns. Help her to brainstorm different ways to play with her child's favorite toys that are at or slightly above his current play level. You may wish to refer her to the chart of play development stages and the chart of play skills to model in the parent manual (Figures 1.3 and 8.2 there). Once you and the parent have targeted a type of play, help the parent identify specific play actions she could model during her turn.

For example, Brian's play is at the exploratory level, and his play goal is to increase functional play. The trainer would explain to his mother that when it is her turn, she should play with the toys in the manner in which they were intended. The trainer would then provide specific examples of how she could do this with toys that are of interest to Brian. Since Brian enjoys playing with squishy balls, the examples would be related to ball play. Examples of functional play Brian's mother could model with the squishy ball could include bouncing, throwing, or kicking the ball. His mother could also create a basket for Brian to throw the ball into, or line up bowling pins and use the ball to knock them down.

Wait for Your Child to Communicate for His Turn

Remind the parent that after she takes her turn, she should wait with anticipation for her child to initiate his turn. Reiterate that she should respond to all types of communication (e.g., body posture, eye contact, vocalizations). Help her identify how her child will communicate his turn, based on information from previous sessions.

Always Return Materials

Emphasize again to the parent that she must always end a turn-taking activity by returning the object to the child, even if the child seems to have lost interest.

Trade Toys (Optional)

For children who become highly frustrated with turn taking, it can often be beneficial to trade identical objects rather than to take turns with one object, as noted in Session 9. If the parent has been using this strategy during turn taking, explain to the parent that she should now model new play with her toy. It is important to pair this with *Animation*, to call the child's attention to the new play that is modeled.

Demonstrate use of *Balanced Turns,*
Part 2: Modeling and Expanding Play

Identify the *Balanced Turns* strategies that will be most beneficial for the child, including the play skills to be modeled. Explain to the parent what you will do, the response you will look for, and how you will respond to the child. Individualize this for each child and family based on the child's interests and goals. For example, the trainer might say this to Brian's mother:

> "As I did last session, I am going to continue to follow Brian's lead before determining the toy we will use for turn taking. Once I identify his interest, I will take a turn to gain access to the toy, which will elicit a response from Brian. I will use the anticipatory phrase I used last time, 'It's [clinician's name] turn,' and gesture toward myself. I will then take the toy for a quick turn. This time during my turn, I am going to show him a new way to play with the toy. After I model the new play, I will return the toy to Brian and say, 'Brian's turn,' while gesturing toward him."

During your demonstration, explain to the parent the new play you are modeling and how the child responds to the new play model. In some cases the child may begin to imitate the play, while in other cases the child may continue to play with the toy in a preferred manner. Explain to the parent that either response is OK. Once the direct teaching techniques are introduced, there will be a discussion of how to help the child use the new play skill; at this point, the goal is to show the child a new way to play.

Have the Parent Practice *Balanced Turns, Part 2: Modeling*
and Expanding Play While You Provide Feedback

Have the parent practice all of the elements of *Balanced Turns* for at least 15 minutes. Explain to the parent that she should first follow her child's lead and determine his interest. She will then take turns with the toy he is interested in and will model a new play action when it is her turn.

Help her identify new play ideas for toys her child is interested in before she begins to practice. You should also review and highlight any turn-taking techniques that were difficult for the parent during the last session.

Feedback during this session should be primarily related to modeling and expanding play. Be sure to provide the parent with feedback even if the child does not respond. Again, remind the parent that the purpose of this technique is to show the child how to play with a new toy. The direct teaching techniques will discuss how to help the child play with the toy in a new way.

Discuss and Assign Homework

1. Have the parent complete homework for *Balanced Turns, Part 2: Modeling and Expanding Play*. Review the rationale and the key points of *Balanced Turns*, emphasizing the strategies that were most effective for the child. Discuss other techniques that have been effective in creating an opportunity for the child to engage (*Imitate Your Child* and *Animation*) or communicate (*Playful Obstruction*). Write down strategies the parent might use if turn taking or modeling play is not successful.

Identify the play goal that the parent will target at home (e.g., functional play, pretend play, symbolic play, etc.) with *Balanced Turns, Part II: Modeling and Expanding Play*. Write the play goal on this session's homework sheet in the parent manual. Then ask the parent what toys the child plays with at home. Provide her with concrete play she could model with these toys to address her child's goals. Write these examples on the homework sheet. For example, Sam's play goal is to improve pretend play skills, and Sam's mother reports that he likes to play with cars at home. The trainer would explain to his mom that she could pretend that the car is dirty and wash the car, put gas in the car, drive to a location such as the park or the store, or pretend that the car has a flat and fix the tire. You would then write these examples on the homework sheet.

Help the parent identify activities in which *Balanced Turns* may be most effective. For some children, this may need to be practiced during a structured activity. Identify at least two activities in which the parent could practice *Balanced Turns* with her child. Write the activities in which the parent will practice on the homework sheet.

Review the questions on the homework sheet and have the parent respond orally, based on her interaction with her child during this session. Choose the questions based on the techniques that were used in this session. If the parent is unable to respond, ask probing questions or demonstrate the technique and have the parent identify the child's response. Inform the parent that she should practice using this technique at home before the next session and write down how her child responds. Explain that the homework will be reviewed at the beginning of the next session.

2. Have the parent read *Communicative Temptations* (Chapter 9 of the parent manual). *Communicative Temptations* will provide another way to create opportunities for the child to communicate.

Troubleshooting Tips

See the "Troubleshooting Tips" for Session 9. In addition, sometimes a child may become frustrated when the parent plays with the toy in a new way. In this event, the parent should keep her turn short and model new play on only half of her turns. If this continues to cause frustration, instruct the parent to trade identical toys and to model a new play action each time before she trades the toy.

Session 11

Communicative Temptations

Session Goals

1. Teach the parent to set up the environment to encourage initiations from her child.

Materials

1. Parent manual
2. Completed Goal Development Form (Appendix A, Form 4)
3. Snacks that can be served in small pieces
4. Toys that the child has trouble using alone (e.g., bubbles, tops, wind-up toys)
5. Variety of clear storage containers (e.g., jars with screw lids, Ziploc bags, large bins, shelving) in which to place desired items

Outline of Session

- Review homework from *Balanced Turns, Part 2: Modeling and Expanding Play* (10–15 minutes).
- Introduce the rationale for *Communicative Temptations* (5 minutes):

    It gains the child's attention.
    It increases the child's initiations.
    It creates an opportunity to model or prompt language.

- Explain how *Communicative Temptations* is used with previously taught techniques (5 minutes).
- Discuss the key points of *Communicative Temptations* (5–10 minutes).

    In sight and out of reach
    Control access
    Assistance
    Inadequate portions
    Sabotage
    Protest
    Silly situations

- Demonstrate use of *Communicative Temptations* (5–15 minutes).
- Have the parent practice *Communicative Temptations* while you provide feedback (25–40 minutes).

- Discuss and assign homework:
  1. Have parent complete homework for *Communicative Temptations*.
  2. Have the parent read *Review of the Interactive Teaching Techniques* (Chapter 10 of the parent manual).

Review Homework from *Balanced Turns, Part 2: Modeling and Expanding Play*

Read over the parent's homework sheet from the parent manual; ask the parent to answer the questions now if she did not fill out the homework. Discuss any aspect of the technique that presented a challenge at home. The most common challenge is that the child does not allow the parent a turn. This occurs more often at home than in the clinic, because the child is used to having unrestricted access to his toys at home. One way to address this difficulty is to help the parent identify structured activities that lend themselves to turn taking (e.g., throwing a ball or balloon). Another possible solution would be to have two identical items with which to take turns. If the child responded well to *Playful Obstruction*, explain to the parent how she can use this strategy and pair it with the visual and verbal model used in *Balanced Turns*. Another challenge that may occur is that the child may not want the parent to play with the toy in a new way (i.e., to model new play). As discussed in the "Troubleshooting Tips" for Session 10, if this occurs, the parent should keep her turn short and model new play on only half of her turns. If this continues to cause frustration, the parent can trade identical toys and model a new play action each time before she trades the toy prior to taking turns with one toy. In some cases, it may be helpful to practice with the toys that caused this challenge. If you are conducting sessions in the clinic setting, have the parent bring the toys to the next session. If necessary, allow the parent time to practice *Balanced Turns* before introducing *Communicative Temptations*.

Introduce the Rationale for *Communicative Temptations*

The *Communicative Temptations* technique encourages the child to initiate communication by setting up a temptation and waiting to see how the child responds. These techniques are effective for children who initiate very little and for children who have difficulty attending and responding to others during play. As you explain the rationale, be sure to relate the technique's purpose to the parent's goals for her child.

It Gains the Child's Attention

Children with ASD often have difficulty attending to others and directing their communication toward others. The strategies of *Communicative Temptations* increase attention to others, because activities are set up so that a child needs to approach a parent to gain access to them.

It Increases the Child's Initiations

Children with ASD often have difficulty initiating requests or social interactions with others. Using *Communicative Temptations* creates opportunities for the child to initiate by setting up the environment to encourage the child to communicate with the parent.

It Creates an Opportunity to Model or Prompt Language

Like those of previously taught techniques, the strategies discussed here are used to ensure that the child is engaged and attending to the adult prior to providing a language model or prompt. When the child is attending to the parent, he is more likely to respond appropriately to his parent's language model or prompt.

Explain to the parent how *Communicative Temptations* can be used to address her child's specific goals. For example, when explaining the rationale to Brian's mother, the trainer might say:

"Brian has a goal of using a point, vocalization, or single word to initiate a request. By using *Communicative Temptations*, you increase the opportunities Brian has to initiate communication with you. You are also sure to have his attention when he does initiate, which creates an opportunity for you to model the language form that you would like him to be using."

You might say to Sam's mother: "Sam has a goal to use two- to three-word phrases spontaneously to request. *Communicative Temptations* will increase the opportunities that Sam has to initiate communication with you, which will improve his spontaneous language skills."

Explain How *Communicative Temptations* Is Used with Previously Taught Techniques

In *Playful Obstruction* and *Balanced Turns*, the parent interrupts the child's play in some way to elicit communication from the child. In *Communicative Temptations*, the environment is set up so that the child must seek out the parent (i.e., must initiate) to access items and activities that he enjoys. When the child initiates contact, the parent responds to the child's initiation as purposeful by complying, and models a more complex response. Once the child is involved in the interaction, the parent continues to use previously taught techniques (*Imitate Your Child, Animation, Balanced Turns*, etc.) to increase the length of the back-and-forth interaction and communication.

Discuss the Key Points of *Communicative Temptations*

There are seven *Communicative Temptations* strategies that can be used to create an opportunity for the child to initiate communication. These strategies are outlined in the parent manual and should be reviewed with the parent.

In Sight and Out of Reach

The first strategy consists of placing preferred items where the child can see them but cannot access them on his own. This strategy provides multiple opportunities throughout the day for the child to initiate with the parent. In addition, if free access to toys is limited, the child may be more likely to play longer with one toy, Thus increasing his engagement. Discuss toy storage systems or shelves that the parent can use at home to limit the child's free access to desired items.

Control Access

The second strategy differs from the first one because the parent has control of the object. This teaches the child to reference the parent with eye contact and to increase the number of his initiations. The parent holds the item so that the child can see it but cannot access it without referencing the parent. Encourage the parent to hold the object near her eyes to promote eye contact. If the child attempts to grab the item, the parent should stand up or hold the item so that the child cannot grab it away.

Assistance

The third strategy involves the use of toys or activities that the child needs assistance to activate or engage. Again, since the goal is for the child to initiate communication, the parent should place the item within the child's reach and wait for him to initiate with her. If the child does not initiate, the parent activates the toy (e.g., blows a balloon once and then lets it go, spins a top once), places it within the child's reach, and waits to see if he initiates. If the child does not initiate, the parent can be reasonably sure that the child is not interested. She should wait and follow the child's lead to a new activity.

Inadequate Portions

In the fourth strategy, the parent provides only a small portion or a part of a desired item, and then waits to see whether the child communicates for more. This strategy is particularly effective during mealtime and during play with toys that have multiple identical parts (e.g., puzzles, train tracks, etc.). This strategy should be used only with highly motivating activities or foods. The child will not request more if he does not like an activity or food. When using this strategy, the parent should remain present and within the child's line of sight.

Sabotage

When the child is familiar with multiple parts of an activity or toy, the parent may wish to withhold a part to encourage the child to request the missing item (e.g., provide paper but no crayons). This strategy is especially effective for teaching the child to ask questions (e.g., "Where is the _____?"). In order for sabotage to be effective, the child must be able to identify that a particular item is missing. For children who do not yet have a concept of all parts of an activity, inadequate portions should be used. Again, the parent should remain in the child's line of sight when using this strategy and should show the items to the child if he does not spontaneously initiate.

Protest

The sixth strategy involves doing an activity the "wrong way" in order to elicit a response from the child. For some children who are very routine-bound, using protest may encourage the child to initiate in order to rectify the situation. This can be very effective for teaching more appropriate protesting skills (e.g., saying the word "Stop" instead of screaming). The parent should be sure to overlay the appropriate response immediately in response to the child's initial behavior, before a tantrum occurs. For example, if the child likes to have toy animals in a specific order, the parent could move an animal; then as soon as the child begins to protest (fuss), the parent should model the correct target ("Stop") and respond to the child appropriately (e.g., put the toy back). This technique can be frustrating for some children and difficult for parents to use if they do not want their children to become upset. Thus, this technique should not be used too often.

Silly Situations

In the final strategy, a familiar activity is completed the wrong way to encourage the child to initiate the right way. For example, the parent may attempt to put the child's shoe on his hand instead of his foot. This strategy requires that the child have a concept of the right and the wrong ways to complete activities, and thus it may not be effective for younger or lower-functioning children. When using this approach, the parent should use *Animation* and emphasize that her behavior is "wrong." Many children find this strategy to be funny, and it can be used to develop affect sharing. If the child does not respond, the parent explains visually and verbally how the situation was "silly."

The *Communicative Temptations* strategies are eventually paired with prompting for an elaborated response. However, at this point the parent should continue to respond to all of the child's communications, while modeling a more complex response.

Demonstrate Use of *Communicative Temptations*

It is often beneficial to demonstrate, and then to have the parent practice, one strategy at a time. Prior to the demonstration, tell the parent which strategy you will use, the response you will look for, and how you will respond to the child. Individualize your explanation for each family, based on the child's interests and the child's goals. For example, when explaining this to Brian's mother, the trainer might say:

"Since Brian enjoys play with squishy balls, I am going to put the balls into a container that he cannot open without my help (in sight and out of reach). Then I am going to wait to see whether he seeks my assistance to open the container. I will look for any sign of communication from Brian. This could include giving the jar to me, eye contact, a gesture or a sound. Once he attempts to communicate with me using one of these behaviors, I will respond by opening the container and giving him the ball. I will also model a tap on the container (our chosen gesture for 'Open') and the single word 'Open.' If he does not attempt to communicate with me, I will open the container, take a ball out, and play with it while using *Animation*. I will then return the ball to the container, close the lid, and wait to see if he responds."

Next, briefly demonstrate, identifying the strategy as you use it and the child's response. For example, the trainer might say to Sam's mother: "Here I am using inadequate portions and waiting to see how Sam responds. He said, 'cracker.' I gave him more crackers and expanded his language by saying, 'Eat cracker.'"

Explain to the parent that she should continue with a strategy until the child loses interest. Maintaining the interaction can sometimes be difficult for the parent, as it is repetitive. Remind the parent that the child benefits from this repetition. As with previously discussed techniques, it is important to help the parent pay attention to how the child indicates that he wants something.

Have the Parent Practice *Communicative Temptations* While You Provide Feedback

The parent should have at least 25 minutes to practice using *Communicative Temptations* to increase her child's initiations. Again, it may be beneficial to coach her on each strategy in isolation, to decrease the amount of information the parent has to attend to while practicing. Prior to having the parent practice, provide her with specific strategies to use—for example, "Remember to place the item within Brian's line of sight but out of his reach, and wait for him to communicate with you."

Remind the parent to continue to respond to all types of appropriate communication by providing the object and then modeling a more complex response. If the parent is having trouble with a specific aspect of this technique (e.g., when she is attempting to control access to items, the child grabs the toy away from her), have the parent focus specifically on holding the item out of the child's reach. This can be accomplished by having the parent stand up or placing the item on a high shelf. Also, have the parent practice these strategies during a variety of routines. In the clinic setting, this practice could include play with toys, a snack (inadequate portions), or putting on the child's jacket and shoes (protest or silly situations) at the end of the session.

Discuss and Assign Homework

1. Have the parent complete homework for *Communicative Temptations*. Begin with a review of the rationale and critical elements. Emphasize the strategies that were most effective for the child. For example, if the child responds well to silly situations, circle this strategy on the homework sheet in the parent manual to remind the parent to use it as she interacts with her child at home. Circle any additional strategies the parent should continue to emphasize at home.

Review the child's goals and identify at least one goal the parent would like to target at home. The *Communicative Temptations* strategies address all goals related to initiations. Examples could include initiating a request for an item with eye contact, initiating with a single word, or initiating with eye contact and a verbalization. The *Communicative Temptations* strategies are also effective in increasing the length of the interaction. Once the parent has identified the goal or goals, this information should be written on the homework sheet to remind the parent of why she should practice this technique at home. For example, this technique could be used to address Brian's goal of increasing expressive language to request (initiations).

Ask the parent if she can think of a time she can practice this technique with her child. Identify at least three activities in which the parent can practice this technique, to increase her ability to use the different strategies across settings. Emphasize that *Communicative Temptations* can be easily applied throughout familiar routines, such as meals, dressing, and bathtime, to provide increased opportunities for initiations during meaningful activities. These strategies are only effective if the child enjoys an activity. Tell the parent to plan extra time during these daily child care routines to use these strategies to enhance the child's communication. If the parent is having trouble identifying routines, refer to the Daily Activity Sheet and help identify three activities the child enjoys in which she could use these strategies.

Once the child's goals and the activities have been identified, help the parent choose language she may model during the interaction. This helps the parent remember to model language appropriate to her child's developmental level. For example, in Brian's case, the trainer would help the mother choose single words and gestures that she could model with each activity. Write the language and/or gestures she should model on the homework sheet.

Review the questions on the homework sheet and have the parent respond to the questions, based on her interaction with her child during this session. If the parent is unable to respond to the questions, ask probing questions or demonstrate a strategy and have the parent identify the child's response. Inform the parent that she should practice using this technique at home before the next session and write down how her child responds. Remind her that the homework will be reviewed at the beginning of next session.

2. Have the parent read *Review of the Interactive Teaching Techniques* (Chapter 10 of the parent manual). Explain to the parent that now that she has learned to use all of the interactive teaching techniques, the next session will be spent using the techniques together to address her child's goals. The next session will include a verbal review of all the interactive teaching techniques, demonstration of the techniques to address the child's goals, parent practice of the techniques while receiving feedback, a video recording of the parent interacting with her child, and a review of the video. The parent should not complete the homework for the next topic until it has been reviewed and practiced during the next session.

Troubleshooting Tips

If a child is unable to initiate at all, the child may not request even his favorite items. In this case, the parent could "market" the item to the child, by handing the child the container holding the favorite item to increase the child's motivation. If the child is still not interested, the parent should follow his lead to another activity.

Another caution is that sometimes children are very creative and arrange furniture to access what they want rather than request help. In such a case, the parent should be encouraged to use clear containers that can be kept safely within the child's reach, but that the child is unable to open without the parent's assistance. The parent may also choose to use a lock and stay near the child, so that he learns that he can open the cupboard or door with assistance.

Lastly, waiting for a child to initiate can be difficult for a parent, especially when the child is able to respond to questions or to repeat lengthy sentences. In this case, it is important to stress to the parent that while it is wonderful that she can anticipate what her child wants and prompt an elaborated response, she wants to teach her child to *initiate* language, so that he can communicate with others when the parent is not present.

Session 12

Review of the Interactive Teaching Techniques

Session Goals

1. Improve the parent's ability to use the interactive teaching techniques.
2. Determine whether additional time should be spent on the interactive teaching techniques.

Materials

1. Parent manual
2. Completed Goal Development Form (Appendix A, Form 4)
3. A number of highly preferred toys
4. Interactive Techniques Review Sheet (Appendix A, Form 6)
5. Video-recording equipment
6. Interactive Teaching Techniques Video Review Form (Appendix A, Form 7)
7. Individual Format Coaching Form (Appendix A, Form 8)

Outline of Session

- Explain the format of the session (3 minutes).
- Review homework from *Communicative Temptations* (10–15 minutes).
- Discuss the interactive teaching techniques sequence, using Appendix A, Form 6 (10–15 minutes):

  1. Use *Follow Your Child's Lead.*
  2. Create an opportunity for your child to engage or communicate.
  3. Wait for your child to engage or communicate.
  4. Respond to your child's behavior as meaningful, comply with it, and model a more complex response.

- Demonstrate use of the interactive teaching techniques (5–10 minutes).
- Have the parent practice the interactive teaching techniques while you provide feedback (5–15 minutes).
- Record the parent–child interaction on video (5 minutes).
- Review the video with the parent (15 minutes).
- Discuss and assign homework (10–15 minutes):
  1. Have the parent complete homework for *Review of the Interactive Teaching Techniques*.
  2. Have the parent read *Overview of the Direct Teaching Techniques* (Chapter 11 of the parent manual).

About This Session

The purposes of this session are to improve the parent's ability to use the interactive teaching techniques together and to determine whether additional time should be spent on these techniques. Before you introduce the direct teaching techniques, the parent should be using *Follow Your Child's Lead*; using techniques to create an opportunity for her child to engage (*Imitate Your Child* and *Animation*) and communicate (*Playful Obstruction, Balanced Turns,* and *Communicative Temptations*); and responding to her child's behavior as meaningful, complying with it, and modeling a more complex response. These steps are outlined in the parent manual and are reviewed in this session with the parent.

Explain the Format of the Session

Explain that the format of this session is different from previous sessions: It will be spent reviewing the interactive teaching techniques. You will provide a brief recap of the techniques and demonstrate them. The parent will then practice the techniques with her child while you video-record the interaction. You and the parent will then review the video together. The video review helps the parent identify and assess her use of the techniques and her child's response. It may take two sessions to complete the steps outlined in this session, particularly if two parents attend or if the parent is having difficulty with one or more of the interactive teaching techniques.

Review Homework from *Communicative Temptations*

Discuss the homework for *Communicative Temptations* with the parent. Ask her whether she noticed an increase in her child's initiations with the use of this technique. Discuss any aspects of the technique that presented a challenge at home. Common challenges that occur at home are similar to those discussed in the "Troubleshooting Tips" for Session 11. If the parent reports that using in sight and out of reach created an unsafe environment, help the parent identify containers she could use rather than placing items up high. If the parent reports difficulty maintaining use of the technique because of the repetition that can occur with *Communicative Temptations* strategies, reiterate the importance of repetition and help the parent identify ways to vary the interaction. For example, with inadequate portions, she could model a new way to play with a toy prior to giving it to the child. If the parent reports that using *Communicative Temptations* during a daily routine made the routine take too long and was impractical, remind her to plan to add 5–10 minutes to the routine. If she is unable to do this (e.g., the child needs to finish breakfast quickly to catch the bus for school), help her select another routine that she can extend in which to use the techniques.

Discuss the Interactive Teaching Techniques, Using Form 6

Go through the Interactive Teaching Techniques Review Sheet (Form 6) with the parent. This form can be found in Appendix A of this manual, as well as in the parent manual (Form 10.1 there). Use the form to provide a brief overview of these techniques. Allow the parent ample time to ask questions before you demonstrate the techniques. If the parent has questions about a specific technique, take this time to review it, including demonstrating and having the parent practice it in isolation. It is important for the parent to understand how to use each technique before learning how to use them together.

Next, review the four steps of the interactive teaching techniques sequence:

1. Use *Follow Your Child's Lead.*
2. Create an opportunity for your child to engage or communicate.
3. Wait for your child to engage or communicate.
4. Respond to your child's behavior as meaningful, comply with it, and model a more complex response.

Demonstrate Use of the Interactive Teaching Techniques

Once the parent has an understanding of each technique in isolation, demonstrate use of the interactive teaching techniques together. Explain the goal (e.g., eye contact, maintaining the interaction, turn taking, gestures, words, play, imitation); ways to *Follow Your Child's Lead*; the techniques used to create an opportunity for the child to engage (*Imitate Your Child* or *Animation*) or communicate (*Playful Obstruction, Balanced Turns,* or *Communicative Temptations*); the child's communication (e.g., eye contact, gestures, words); and the type of communication you model (e.g., point, single word, descriptor). For example, the trainer might say to Brian's mother: "Brian is playing with the cars. I will move into his line of sight and hold up more cars to create an opportunity for him to respond. [Trainer does these things.] He looked at me. I responded by giving him the car, and I modeled the word 'Car.'"

Take time to demonstrate any technique that has been difficult for the parent to implement. Once you have demonstrated the techniques together two or three times, have the parent identify the techniques you used for each step. Because the interaction moves quickly, have the parent focus on one step at a time—for example, "Watch to see the technique I use to create an opportunity for Brian to communicate. What technique did I use? How did he communicate?" Doing this helps the parent begin to observe how specific techniques affect her child's social-communication skills.

Have the Parent Practice the Interactive Teaching Techniques While You Provide Feedback

Ask the parent to identify the technique she will use for each step—for example, "How will you create an opportunity for your child to communicate? How do you think he will communicate? What type of language will you model?" Then have the parent practice using the interactive teaching techniques for at least 5 minutes, or until she is successful at using the techniques together. If the parent is having difficulty with one or more of the techniques or their component strategies, provide feedback to improve accuracy of implementation.

Record the Parent–Child Interaction on Video

Video-record the parent–child interaction for 5 minutes. If two parents are present, record only one parent at a time. Provide a clear transition statement to the parent before you begin recording: Instruct her to use the interactive teaching techniques now to increase her child's engagement, initiations, language, imitation, and play skills. In lieu of providing live feedback, complete the Individual Format Coaching Form (Form 8) in Appendix A while you observe and tape the interaction. This form helps you identify any techniques that may require additional coaching. This form is for your reference and is not shared with the parent.

Review the Video with the Parent

The purpose of reviewing the video with the parent is to increase her ability to identify techniques she is using and her child's response to the techniques. This is accomplished by watching the tape together, having the parent complete the Interactive Teaching Techniques Video Review Form (Appendix A, Form 7), and asking the parent open-ended and probing questions.

Begin by giving the parent Form 7 from Appendix A. Explain that you will watch the video together; instruct her to look for examples of when she used techniques to create an opportunity for her child to communicate, and of how her child responded to the technique. Because the interactions happen so fast, you should pause the recording and watch the segment a number of times. Have the parent tell you whenever she would like you to stop the video to review or discuss the interaction. If the parent does not have you stop the video after 2 minutes, stop the video and ask the parent an open-ended question (e.g., "What did you observe?"). If she is unable to respond, provide her with a specific behavior to look for—for example, "Let's watch the video and pause it when you use a technique to create an opportunity for Sam to communicate."

It is also helpful to have the parent watch a clip of when she used all of the steps in the interactive teaching techniques sequence. In order to accomplish this, ask the parent the following questions and watch the same clip a number of times, to provide her with the opportunity to observe each step.

- "How did you use *Follow Your Child's Lead?*"
- "What techniques did you use to create an opportunity for your child to engage or communicate?"

- "How did your child engage or communicate with you?"
- "What type of language did you model for your child?"

Continue to watch the remainder of the video. Provide the parent with specific behaviors to look for as she watches, and pause the video when she notices those behaviors. The feedback during the review of the video should be primarily positive. However, if the parent has difficulty with a specific technique and you do not think she is aware of it, the video can be used to provide feedback. For example, if the parent asks a lot of questions and the child does not respond, pause the tape when the parent asks a question and ask her to identify her behavior (the question) and the child's reaction (no response). Have her compare this to a time she uses an interactive teaching technique (e.g., *Playful Obstruction*) and the child's response to that technique (e.g., vocalization).

Discuss and Assign Homework

1. Have the parent complete homework for *Review of the Interactive Teaching Techniques*. Begin by reviewing the rationale and steps involved in the interactive teaching techniques. Ask the parent to identify the technique(s) she feels may be most effective in creating an opportunity for her child to communicate (*Imitate Your Child, Animation, Playful Obstruction, Balanced Turns,* or *Communicative Temptations*). In many cases, it is effective when the parent combines two or three of the techniques. For example, *Animation* and *Playful Obstruction* can be used together to increase the likelihood that the child will initiate or respond. On the homework sheet for this session in the parent manual, circle the techniques the parent will use in Step 2: "Create an opportunity for your child to engage ... or communicate. ..." Continue this process and, next to each step, write down any technique or strategy on which the parent should focus. For example, if the child uses gestures to communicate, write on the homework sheet "Model single words and gestures" next to Step 4: "Respond to your child's behavior as meaningful, comply with it, and demonstrate a more developed response."

Next, review the child's goals and identify one to three goals the parent would like to address at home. Now that the interactive teaching techniques are used together, the parent should be able to target all of her child's individualized goals. Write the goals in the usual space on the homework sheet. The next step is to identify activities in which the parent can target the goal. Try to identify at least two activities for each goal, to help the parent generalize her use of the techniques. If necessary, refer to the Daily Activity Schedule to identify activities the child enjoys.

The next step is to determine the specific language the parent will model. Ask the parent questions to help her determine how she thinks her child will respond and the behavior she should model. Your role is to make sure the language modeled is developmentally appropriate for the child. Write down the language the parent will model on the homework sheet.

Instruct the parent to practice these techniques at home and to write down how her child responds. Remind the parent that at this point her child is not required to respond in a specific manner; rather, she should show (i.e., model for) her child the behavior she would like him to use. Explain that homework will be reviewed at the beginning of the next session.

2. Have the parent read *Overview of the Direct Teaching Techniques* (Chapter 11 of the parent manual). Explain to the parent that two sessions will be spent on the next topics because of the amount of information presented. Session 13 will focus on providing the parent with a general introduction to the direct teaching techniques. Session 14 will focus in somewhat more detail on prompting and reinforcement. The parent should not complete the homework for these techniques until they have been reviewed and practiced during these two sessions.

Troubleshooting Tips

As discussed earlier, some parents may not want video recordings to be used. In this case, have the parent complete the Interactive Teaching Techniques Video Review Form while observing you interacting with her child. Model a variety of examples to help the parent identify how the techniques affect her child's social communication. During parent practice, you should continue to provide feedback in the same manner as in previous sessions.

Another challenge is that some parents may change their interaction style while being recorded. In this case, pause the video, provide feedback, and then resume recording. It is important for the parent to have positive examples of herself using the techniques that she can view on video.

Sessions 13–14

Overview of the Direct Teaching Techniques

Session Goals

1. Provide a general introduction to the direct teaching techniques.
2. Teach the parent ways to increase the effectiveness of prompts.
3. Teach the parent ways to provide reinforcement to increase the likelihood that her child will use a specific behavior.

Materials

1. Parent manual
2. Completed Goal Development Form (Appendix A, Form 4)
3. A number of highly preferred toys
4. Variety of clear storage containers (e.g., jars with screw lids, Ziploc bags, large bins, shelving) in which to place desired items

Outline of Sessions

- Explain the format of these sessions (2 minutes, Session 13).
- Review homework:

    Review of the Interactive Teaching Techniques (10–15 minutes, Session 13).

    Overview of the Direct Teaching Techniques (10–15 minutes, Session 14)

- Introduce the rationale for the direct teaching techniques (5 minutes, Session 13):

  They increase the complexity of the child's language, imitation, and play skills.

- Explain how the direct teaching techniques build on the interactive teaching techniques (5 minutes, Session 13).
- Introduce the six steps of the direct teaching procedure (20–30 minutes—you may split this discussion between Sessions 13 and 14):

  1. Use *Follow Your Child's Lead.*
  2. Create an opportunity for your child to communicate (*Playful Obstruction, Balanced Turns,* or *Communicative Temptations*).
  3. Wait for your child to communicate.
  4. Prompt your child to use more complex language, imitation, or play.
  5. Provide a more supportive (helpful) prompt as necessary.
  6. Reinforce and expand on your child's response.

- Explain when and what to prompt, and how these apply to the particular child (5 minutes).
- Explain ways of making prompts effective (20–30 minutes):

  Monitor your child's motivation.
  Give clear prompts.
  Give relevant prompts.
  Give developmentally appropriate prompts.
  Follow the three-prompt rule.
  Use wait time.
  Require the prompted response.
  Change prompt levels over time.

- Explain ways of making reinforcement effective:

  Make it natural.
  Make it immediate.
  Require the prompted response.
  Reinforce only appropriate behavior.
  Provide praise.
  Expand on your child's response.

- Demonstrate use of the direct teaching procedure (10–15 minutes each session).
- Have the parent practice the direct teaching procedure while you provide feedback (20 minutes each session).
- Discuss and assign homework (10–15 minutes):

  1. Have the parent complete homework for *Overview of the Direct Teaching Techniques.*
  2. Have the parent read *Teaching Your Child Expressive Language* (Chapter 12 of the parent manual) (Session 14 only).

About These Two Sessions

The outline of these sessions reflects approximate times that should be spent on each component. One way to divide the information between sessions is to spend the first session providing the parent with a general introduction to the direct teaching techniques and helping the parent identify when and what to prompt, and to spend the second session reviewing the rules that make prompting and reinforcement effective. It is important to be sure that the parent is able to identify when and what to prompt, before introducing the specific types of prompts that are taught in subsequent sessions on the specific direct techniques (*Teaching Your Child Expressive Language, Teaching Your Child Receptive Language, Teaching Your Child Social Imitation,* and *Teaching Your Child Play*).

Explain the Format of These Sessions

Explain that two sessions will be spent on the *Overview of the Direct Teaching Techniques* because of the number of elements involved. There is typically more talking in these sessions than in previous sessions, because the rules of prompting and reinforcement need to be taught before prompts can be used effectively. These sessions provide the parent with an overview of what the direct teaching techniques look like when they are used together, help the parent identify good times to prompt, help the parent identify skills to prompt, and teach the parent the rules of prompting and reinforcement. Because you will not be teaching the parent the specific types of prompts, the parent will not practice using the prompts. Instead, the coaching sessions will be spent identifying good times to prompt and identifying skills the parent may like her child to use (i.e., skills to prompt).

Review Homework from *Review of the Interactive Teaching Techniques* (Session 13)

Begin the session by reviewing the homework from the previous session and discuss whether the parent had any difficulty using the interactive teaching techniques together. Parent-reported challenges are usually related to difficulty with creating opportunities for the child to engage or communicate during activities at home. If this occurs, help the parent identify alternative techniques she could use to create an opportunity for her child to engage or communicate. Explain that a part of this session will be spent identifying techniques to use to gain her child's attention (i.e., to create an opportunity for the child to communicate).

Review the Homework from *Overview of the Direct Teaching Techniques* (Session 14)

Review the homework from Session 13. Ask the parent to respond to the questions even if she did not fill out the homework. Challenges are rarely reported during the review of this homework, because the parent has not yet learned to use specific prompting techniques. However, if the parent was unable to respond to a question during the review, take time to help her identify the skills she would like to see her child use and times she might prompt the skill.

Introduce the Rationale for the *Direct Teaching Techniques*

Up to this point, the main focus of this program has been on increasing the child's engagement and initiations. The second half of the program focuses on increasing the complexity of the child's language, imitation, and play skills by using the direct teaching techniques, all of which involve the use of *prompting* and *reinforcement*. *Prompting* involves using cues (*prompts*) to help the child produce a more complex response. *Reinforcement* is any positive consequence the parent will provide after her child uses the more complex response. This increases the likelihood that he will use it again. As you explain the rationale, be sure to relate the techniques' purposes to the parent's goals for her child.

They Increase the Complexity of the Child's Language, Imitation, and Play Skills

Children with ASD often have delayed language, imitation, and play skills. The direct teaching techniques are the most effective ways to promote development in these areas. Providing prompting and reinforcement in the natural environment and in relation to the child's interests, rather than in a structured setting, increases the likelihood that the child will use these skills in new situations (generalization) and continue to use the skills over time (maintenance).

Explain to the parent that the direct teaching techniques will be used to address her child's specific social language, imitation, and play goals. For example, when explaining the rationale to Brian's mother, the trainer might say: "The direct teaching techniques will be used to improve Brian's ability to use a point or a word to request, to improve his imitation of gestures, and to improve his functional play with toys."

The trainer might say to Sam's mother: "The direct teaching techniques will be used to improve Sam's ability to use two to three words spontaneously for a variety of functions, to improve his imitation of pretend and symbolic actions with toys, and to improve his pretend play."

Explain How the *Direct Teaching Techniques* Build on the *Interactive Teaching Techniques*

Refer the parent to the pyramid diagram at the beginning of the parent manual (Figure 1.1 there; see also Figure S1.3 in Session 1, this manual) to help her visualize how the techniques are used together. Emphasize that the first three steps outlined in the procedure for the direct teaching techniques are identical to the first three steps in the sequence of the interactive teaching techniques: The parent will continue to use *Follow Your Child's Lead*, create an opportunity for the child to communicate, and wait for him to communicate (techniques in the pyramid's lower and middle levels). However, instead of responding to all of her child's behavior as meaningful, she will use a prompt to elicit a more complex response and then provide reinforcement (techniques in the top level of the pyramid). Inform the parent that she should use the direct teaching techniques for only about one-third of an interaction. If she prompts too often, her child is likely to get frustrated.

Introduce the Six Steps of the Direct Teaching Procedure

Introduce (or review) the six steps of the procedure for the direct teaching techniques.

1. Use *Follow Your Child's Lead*. When using the direct teaching techniques, the parent continues to use *Follow Your Child's Lead* prior to using another technique. This technique is always used first, because it increases the child's motivation and engagement, thereby increasing the likelihood he will learn and retain the prompted skills. For parents who are familiar with behavioral principles, you might explain that this is one of the key differences between naturalistic and structured behavioral teaching techniques.

2. Create an opportunity for your child to communicate. The parent continues to use *Playful Obstruction, Balanced Turns,* or *Communicative Temptations* to create an opportunity for her child to communicate. Use of these techniques ensures that the child is engaged and motivated by the activity before the parent provides a prompt to increase skills. The child is less likely to respond if he is not attending to the parent when she provides the prompt.

3. Wait for your child to communicate. Wait time is critical throughout the program, as it provides the child with extra time to retrieve and execute a response, thereby decreasing the amount of support he needs to communicate. This strategy also ensures that the parent is prompting an appropriate behavior.

4. Prompt your child to use more complex language, imitation, or play skills. During the next five to six sessions, the parent will learn to use specific prompts to increase the complexity of her child's language, imitation, and play skills. If the parent consistently uses prompts that are too supportive (e.g., the parent always has the child repeat her language rather than trying to get him to find a word on his own), it can make the child prompt-dependent. By choosing prompts that provide just enough support for the child to use the skill, the parent can increase the child's ability to use it spontaneously. Once the parent learns the different prompts to use, you and the parent will work together to determine the prompt level that is most appropriate for the child to prevent him from becoming prompt-dependent.

5. Provide a more supportive (helpful) prompt as necessary. On some occasions, the child will not be able to respond appropriately to the first prompt that is used. In order to help the child respond correctly, the parent will need to use prompts that are more supportive. This is important, because the child must learn there is a way he can access the desired object or action, or he may give up on the interaction. For parents who have an understanding of behavioral principles, you may explain that this step and the previous step constitute a method of prompt fading.

6. Reinforce and expand on your child's response. Once the child produces the desired response, it is important to reinforce it by giving him access to the desired item or activity and praising him. As the parent reinforces the child's response, she expands on it. For parents who have an understanding of behavioral principles, you might explain that the use of natural response–reinforcer relationships is another key difference between naturalistic and structured behavioral interventions.

Let the parent know that her child may become more frustrated at first, because she will now require him to use a more complex response prior to providing reinforcement. Assure her that with time, her child will get used to the higher expectations, and his frustration will decrease.

Explain When and What to Prompt, and How These Apply to the Particular Child

When to Prompt

The parent should only prompt her child when she has the child's attention. The best times are when he is highly engaged by the activity or interaction and has initiated a request. To gain the child's attention and engagement, and to elicit communication, she will continue to use these interactive teaching techniques: *Follow Your Child's Lead, Imitate Your Child, Animation, Playful Obstruction, Balanced Turns,* and *Communicative Temptations.* Review with the parent the techniques that have been most effective in creating opportunities for her child to communicate.

What to Prompt

Help the parent identify skills that she should prompt. The parent should prompt her child to use a skill that is slightly more complex than the skill he currently uses. These skills are the same skills that she has been modeling during use of the interactive techniques. For example, if she has been modeling single words, she will now prompt the use of single words. The same holds true for social imitation and play goals. If she has been modeling a point, she will now prompt a point. If she has been modeling functional play, she will now prompt functional play.

Once you have introduced the procedure for the direct teaching techniques and reviewed when and what to prompt, it may be appropriate to demonstrate and practice gaining the child's attention (i.e., creating an opportunity for the child to communicate), identifying times to prompt (i.e., times you have the child's attention), and identifying behaviors to prompt (i.e., behaviors you model for the child that you would like him to use). In this event, describe the elements of effective prompting and reinforcement during the next treatment session.

Explain Ways of Making Prompts Effective

Explain the qualities and procedures for effective prompts.

Monitor the Child's Motivation

The parent should attend to her child's motivation. Motivation drives the child's behaviors. This is particularly true for a child with ASD; the more motivated the child, the more likely he will be to stay with an activity even when he is pushed to work harder. Conversely, if the child is not very motivated by the activity, he may leave if the prompts get too hard. It is important for the parent to monitor her child's motivation. His motivation tells the parent when it is best to prompt, how difficult a response she can require, and how much support she will need to provide.

Give Clear Prompts

In order for the prompts to be effective, the parent should make sure that her prompts are clear. Inform the parent that for a prompt to be clear, she must have her child's attention and must be sure her child understands what is being asked of him. For example, if the parent would like her child to use a single word to request, she should provide him with a simple question ("What do you want?") rather than a complex prompt ("Tell me what it is that you want. Say that you want the block").

Give Relevant Prompts

The prompt should relate to what the child is doing. For example, if the child is playing with the blocks, the parent should prompt him to use language to communicate about the blocks. Examples could include "What do you want?", "How many blocks do you want?", "What color blocks do you want?", or "What will you do with the block?"

Give Developmentally Appropriate Prompts

The parent should attend to the child's developmental level when deciding which skills to prompt. As noted earlier, the skill the parent prompts for should be slightly more complex than the skill the child is currently using. For example, if the child is pointing but not yet using single words, the parent should prompt to increase the use of single words or word approximations. If the child is not yet playing functionally with a toy, she should prompt functional play before pretend play. Help the parent identify skills in each of the core areas that are developmentally appropriate for her child. These skills should directly correspond to the measurable goals that were developed during the first two sessions. For example, when helping Brian's mother identify developmentally appropriate goals, the trainer might say: "Brian has a goal of using a point, vocalization, or single word to request actions or objects. These are the skills that we will prompt when we begin to teach him expressive language."

Follow the Three-Prompt Rule

The three-prompt rule is a rough guideline to limit the number of prompts the parent gives before the child successfully responds and gains the desired object. This helps to decrease frustration and ensure that the child stays with the activity. If the child is unsuccessful after one or two prompts, the parent needs to add more support to the prompt to ensure a response. This helps the child understand that there is a way to obtain the desired object or action. That being said, the exact number of prompts used is dependent on the child's motivation. If the child appears to be extremely motivated for the activity, more than three prompts may be provided. Conversely, if the child is not motivated, it may be necessary to use fewer than three prompts. Explain to the parent that you will help her determine the number of prompts to use, based on her child's motivation and ability.

Use Wait Time

Reiterate to the parent the importance of wait time. This has been discussed at the beginning of the program and reiterated throughout the sessions on the interactive teaching techniques. It is often necessary to remind the parent to wait, so that she does not move through the prompts too quickly. If the child is bombarded with too much auditory information, he will be unable to respond and may begin to "tune out" the words. At times it may be necessary to provide the parent with a concrete amount of time to wait. The amount of time can vary substantially, from 2 seconds to 30 seconds. Work with the parent to determine the appropriate amount of time to wait for her child.

Require the Prompted Response

Prompting differs from the use of the interactive teaching techniques, because a specific response is required from the child before he is provided with what he wants. In order to teach the child to respond to questions and follow directions, the parent must withhold the desired object or action while providing support until the child is able to respond.

Change Prompt Levels over Time

Prompts range in level from most to least supportive (or helpful). Explain to the parent that she should begin with the least supportive prompt necessary to obtain a correct response. This decreases her child's reliance on prompts and can increase his spontaneous language. When the child is first starting to use a new skill, it is best to use a more supportive prompt. After the child has been able to respond successfully, she can start using a less supportive prompt. If the child is unable to respond to a less supportive prompt, the parent needs to increase the level of support. Explain to the parent that you will help her identify the most appropriate prompt level when specific prompts are introduced, and that you will discuss how to add support.

Explain Ways of Making Reinforcement Effective

Reinforcement is any consequence the child receives for a behavior that increases the likelihood of his using the new skill again. Explain to the parent that reinforcement can be anything that the child wants or enjoys, including tickles, toys, attention, praise, or food. The parent has been using reinforcement throughout the program by responding to her child's communication as meaningful and providing him with the desired object or action. To be most effective, reinforcement should be natural, immediate, and contingent on the child's appropriate response. Verbal praise should also be given at the same time the parent expands on the child's response.

Make It Natural

The reinforcement used in this program is natural. This means that the child is rewarded by the natural consequences of his behavior. If the child wants a toy car and says, "Car," he is handed the car. Getting the car because of saying the word "Car" is a natural consequence, as opposed to getting a piece of candy for the same behavior. The child's interest determines the type of reinforcement the parent provides. The parent follows the child's lead to his activity of choice, creates an opportunity for the child to communicate, and reinforces the child's communication.

Make It Immediate

Reinforcement should be provided immediately after the child responds. This helps the child make the connection between his behavior and the consequence (reinforcement). If the parent waits too long, the child may not make this connection.

Require the Prompted Response

It is important that the parent only provide reinforcement for the prompted response or an attempt at it. For example, if the child uses a single word to request a desired object, the parent should prompt him to say two words. The reinforcement (desired object) is delivered only when he attempts to respond to the prompt (i.e., he says two words or a word approximation paired with the single word). If the child does not respond to the prompt, the parent should provide an additional prompt or increase the support to help him be successful.

Remind the parent that this rule applies only when the child has been prompted to use a more complex response. The parent should also continue to use the interactive teaching techniques, which do not require a response from the child before giving him the desired object. Remind the parent that the direct teaching techniques are used only about one-third of the time.

Reinforce Only Appropriate Behavior

The parent should provide reinforcement only when the child exhibits an appropriate behavior. This is because reinforcement increases the likelihood that the child will use that behavior more frequently. Inappropriate behavior should not be reinforced, because it can increase its occurrence. If the child uses an appropriate behavior (e.g., he says the word "Car") and an inappropriate behavior (e.g., he hits the parent) simultaneously, the child should not receive reinforcement, because he may be unaware of which behavior (e.g., the word or the hitting) elicited the positive consequence.

Provide Praise

When delivering the desired object to the child, the parent should use praise to help him know that what he did was correct and to help him use the behavior in the future. Pairing praise with reinforcement may also teach the child to respond to praise as well as tangible reinforcement.

Expand on the Child's Response

The parent should expand on her child's response. This strategy is similar to expansion as used in the interactive teaching techniques (e.g., *Modeling and Expanding Language*). Instruct the parent to repeat the child's response adding one element to it while she provides him with the reinforcement. For example, if the child requests with a single word (e.g., "Car"), the parent expands his language by adding a word (e.g., "Red car") while giving him the reinforcement (e.g., the toy car).

Demonstrate Use of the Direct Teaching Procedure

It is important that the parent is able to gain her child's attention and that she is aware of the skill she should prompt (i.e., understands her child's developmental level).

Prior to the demonstration, explain to the parent the technique that you will use to gain the child's attention and the type of skill you might prompt. Individualize this explanation for each family, based on the child's interests and the child's goals. For example, when explaining this to Brian's mother, the trainer might say:

> "I am going to use *Playful Obstruction* and *Animation* to gain Brian's attention during play. I will wait for him to communicate with me. Times that he communicates with me would be good times to prompt. Because Brian is using a reach to request, I want to prompt a point or a single word (skill to prompt) prior to providing the toy (reinforcement)."

When explaining this to Sam's mother, the trainer might say:

> "Sam is using single words to request. I would like to increase that to two to three words. Sam is playing with the cars, so I will follow his lead and join his play with the cars. I am going to gain Sam's attention by using *Playful Obstruction*. I bumped his car. Sam looked at me and said, 'Car' (demonstrating attention), indicating that this would be a great time to prompt. So I modeled 'Red car.' This language is what he will be required to use once the expressive language prompts are introduced. At this point, I am just going to give him the car."

Have Parent Practice the Direct Teaching Procedure While You Provide Feedback

During the first session, the parent should continue to practice until she is able to identify good times to prompt (i.e., times she has her child's attention) and behaviors to prompt (i.e., skills she would like her child to use). Provide coaching on these aspects until the parent is successful. If the parent is unable to gain her child's attention or to identify what to prompt, she will not be able to use subsequent techniques.

Once the parent is able to identify times and behaviors to prompt, coaching should be provided on reinforcement. Again, the length of time spent on this coaching varies, depending on the parent's level of skill. Coaching should be related to providing reinforcement that is natural, immediate, and contingent on appropriate behavior.

The length of the demonstration and practice will vary, depending on the parent's skills. If the parent is able to gain her child's attention, identify skills to prompt, and provide immediate and contingent reinforcement, the demonstration and parent practice can be brief.

The second session can then be spent demonstrating the use of the reinforcement rules. It is important that the parent provide natural and immediate reinforcement and that it is provided contingent on an appropriate response. However, at this point the parent continues to reinforce the child's spontaneous communication, because she has not yet been taught specifically how to prompt new skills. Explain to the parent that before the specific types of prompts are introduced, it is important that reinforcement is provided correctly, as it increases the likelihood that the child will use this behavior again.

Discuss and Assign Homework

1. Have the parent complete homework for *Overview of the Direct Teaching Techniques*. The homework sheet remains the same for Sessions 13 and 14. Make a photocopy of the homework sheet in the parent manual, so the parent has a clean copy to complete after Session 14.

Introduce the homework with a brief review of the homework sheet, including a brief review of the rationale and the key points of *Overview of the Direct Teaching Techniques*. Because you typically spend two sessions on this topic, it can be effective to choose a few elements for the parent to practice after each session. Circle the elements the parent should focus on after each session. For example, if the parent does not always gain her child's attention, write down techniques she should use next to "Create an opportunity for your child to communicate."

Next, identify the goal the parent would like to target at home. This should correspond to "Prompt your child to use more complex language, imitation, or play." Help the parent make the goal appropriate for her child's developmental level, and remind the parent that at this point, she will model the skill but not require her child to use it. Ask the parent if she can think of a time she can practice the skill with her child. You may wish to refer back to the Daily Activity Schedule and review ways to practice this during daily activities.

At the end of Session 13, you will have the parent respond orally to questions 1–3 in on the homework sheet, and then instruct her to practice at home and to write down responses to these questions.

At the end of Session 14, have the parent respond orally to questions 4 and 5, based on her interaction with her child during the session, and then instruct her to respond to the questions after she interacts with her child at home. Explain that the homework will be reviewed at the beginning of the next session.

2. Have the parent read *Teaching Your Child Expressive Language* (Chapter 12 of the parent manual). Once you complete Session 14, instruct the parent to read *Teaching Your Child Expressive Language*. This technique is used to increase the complexity of the child's language skills. Two sessions will be spent on this intervention topic because of the number of strategies it encompasses. The parent should not complete the homework for this technique until it has been reviewed and practiced during the following session.

Troubleshooting Tips

Sometimes parents are anxious to move quickly through these sessions, because they do not feel that they provide a lot of new information. In this event, it may be beneficial to provide the parent with one prompt to use to change her child's behavior while she practices the prompt rules and reinforcement. In this case, introduce a prompt to which you know the child can respond successfully.

Teaching Your Child Expressive Language

Session Goals

1. Teach the parent strategies to increase the complexity of her child's language.
2. Teach the parent to use the least supportive prompt necessary to increase her child's spontaneous language skills.

Materials

1. Parent manual
2. Completed Goal Development Form (Appendix A, Form 4)
3. Number of highly preferred toys
4. Variety of storage containers (e.g., clear containers with screw lids, Ziploc bags, large bins, shelving) in which to place desired items.
5. Blank Flowchart for Prompting Expressive Language (Appendix A, Form 9)

Outline of Sessions

- Explain the format of these sessions (1–2 minutes, Session 15)
- Review homework:

   Overview of the Direct Teaching Techniques (10–15 minutes, Session 15)
   Teaching Your Child Expressive Language (10–15 minutes, Session 16)

- Introduce the rationale for *Teaching Your Child Expressive Language* (5 minutes, Session 15):

   It increases the child's expressive language skills.
   It increases the child's spontaneous language.

- Explain how *Teaching Your Child Expressive Language* is used with previously taught techniques (5 minutes, Session 15).
- Discuss the key points of *Teaching Your Child Expressive Language* (10–15 minutes, Session 15; 5-minute review, Session 16):

   Physical prompt
   Gesture prompt
   Verbal routine
   Verbal model
   Choice
   Cloze procedure
   Direct question
   Time delay

- Identify language skills to prompt (5–10 minutes each session).
- Demonstrate use of *Teaching Your Child Expressive Language* (15–20 minutes each session).

- Have the parent practice *Teaching Your Child Expressive Language* while you provide feedback (20–30 minutes, Session 15; 30–45 minutes, Session 16).
- Have the parent complete the Flowchart for Prompting Expressive Language (Appendix A, Form 9) (5–10 minutes, Session 15).
- Discuss and assign homework (10–15 minutes each session):

Session 15

1. Have the parent practice *Teaching Your Child Expressive Language* with the completed Appendix A, Form 9, as a guide.
2. *Optional:* If there is time to preview the homework sheet in the parent manual at the end of the session, have the parent complete it.

Session 16

1. Have parent complete homework for *Teaching Your Child Expressive Language*.
2. Have the parent read *Teaching Your Child Receptive Language* (Chapter 13 of the parent manual).

About These Sessions

All elements of this technique should be introduced during Session 15 and prior to demonstration and parent practice. Session 16 should be spent primarily on parent practice of the technique with feedback. The outline above indicates which activities are completed during each session and the approximate times.

Explain the Format of These Sessions

Explain to the parent that two or more sessions will be spent on *Teaching Your Child Expressive Language* because of the number of elements involved.

Review Homework from *Overview of the Direct Teaching Techniques* (Session 15)

Review the homework from the previous session. Ask the parent whether she had difficulty identifying times to prompt, behaviors to prompt, or use of reinforcement. Challenges are rarely reported at this point, because the parent has not yet learned to use a specific prompting technique. However, if the parent is unable to respond to a question during the review, help her identify the skills she would like to see her child use and times she might prompt the skill. It is particularly important that the parent be able to identify times to prompt (i.e., times she has her child's attention) before she uses the strategies in *Teaching Your Child Expressive Language*.

Review Homework from *Teaching Your Child Expressive Language* (Session 16)

Review the flowchart (Appendix A, Form 9) you completed with the parent during Session 15. Discuss the types of prompts the parent used and her child's response. A common problem involves difficulty eliciting a response from the child. This can be particularly challenging when the child is not yet verbal and the parent is hesitant to use a physical prompt. Take time to review any aspects of this technique that presented a challenge, and review those aspects during this session.

Introduce the Rationale for *Teaching Your Child Expressive Language*

Explain to the parent that she will learn to use different types of prompts to increase the complexity and spontaneity of her child's language. As you explain the rationale, relate the technique's purpose to the parent's goals for her child.

It Increases Expressive Language Skills

Children with ASD often have difficulty using language to communicate with others. One way to teach such a child to use new language forms and functions is to use prompting and reinforcement. These two sessions discuss prompts that are designed for eliciting expressive language.

It Increases Spontaneous Language

Children with ASD and other language disorders can become reliant on cues from their parents. This causes the children to have difficulty communicating when a prompt is not provided. These two sessions describe a set of prompts that vary in the amount of support they provide. When a parent adjusts the amount of support she provides, she can help her child use language more spontaneously.

Explain to the parent how the prompts discussed in *Teaching Your Child Expressive Language* are used to address her child's specific language goals. For example, when explaining the rationale to Brian's mother, the trainer might say: "Brian's language goal is to improve his ability to use a point, single word, or vocalization to initiate a request. Today you will learn specific prompts to help him use these new skills."

The trainer might say to Sam's mother: "Sam's language goal is to improve his use of two- to three-word phrases spontaneously for a variety of functions. Today you will learn specific prompts to help him learn these new skills."

Explain How *Teaching Your Child Expressive Language* Is Used with Previously Taught Techniques

Refer to the pyramid diagram at the beginning of the parent manual (Figure 1.1 there and Figure S1.3 in this manual) to help the parent visualize how *Teaching Your Child Expressive Language* is used with previously taught techniques. *Teaching Your Child Expressive Language* uses prompting and reinforcement. That makes it a direct teaching technique, located at the top level of the pyramid. Remind the parent that these techniques build on the interactive teaching techniques. Before presenting an expressive language prompt, the parent uses interactive teaching techniques to determine what her child is interested in (*Follow Your Child's Lead*), to gain her child's attention (create an opportunity for her child to communicate), and to wait for a communication. Instead of then complying with (reinforcing) the child's communication, the parent will use a prompt to increase the complexity of her child's language skills. When the child responds appropriately, she provides him with reinforcement. Remind the parent that she should be prompting her child for a more complex response only about one-third of the time during an interaction. If she prompts too often, her child is likely to get frustrated and/or will become dependent on prompts to communicate.

Discuss the Key Points of *Teaching Your Child Expressive Language*

There are eight kinds of prompts in *Teaching Your Child Expressive Language*. Each type is described below. The prompts are listed in order from the most to the least supportive. These are also described in the parent manual and should be reviewed with the parent.

Physical Prompt

A physical prompt is the most supportive type and is used to teach gestural communication to children who are unable to imitate verbal language or gestures. Explain to the parent that gestures can act as a bridge to speech. Show the parent how she can provide physical assistance to help her child use gestures. Explain that the amount of physical support can be decreased as the child begins to use the gesture. For example, when teaching a child to point, the parent may initially need to help the child lift his hand and form his finger into a point. After some time, the parent may be able to provide physical support to the child's elbow to cue him to point.

Gesture Prompt

Like physical prompts, gesture prompts are useful for children who are not yet verbal. They can also be used with children who are verbal but do not use gestures to communicate. This type of prompting is similar to the gesture cues the parent has learned to use in *Modeling and Expanding Language*. However, if the parent prompts by making a gesture and the child does not imitate the gesture, then the parent should provide a physical prompt to help the child make the gesture before providing the reinforcement. Work with the parent to identify gestures that can be used to signify certain objects, actions, or people.

Verbal Routine

Verbal routines are helpful for children who are not yet using language and children who are just beginning to use language, because they are repetitive and consistent. "Peek-a-boo" and "Ready, set, go" are examples of verbal routines. Instruct the parent to use such a routine repetitively and to leave off the last word, while using wait time and an expectant look. If the child is unable to complete the verbal routine, instruct the parent to provide a gesture prompt and then a physical prompt to elicit a response.

Verbal Model

A verbal model is the most successful prompt type for children who are beginning to imitate words or sounds and for children who have some verbal language. To use this technique, the parent models (i.e., says) the word she would like her child to use. Explain to the parent that this strategy differs from *Modeling and Expanding Language*, because the child is now required to respond. If the child does not imitate the word, the parent should add more support (i.e., gesture or physical prompt) until the child increases the complexity of his language. On the other hand, if the child readily imitates the verbal model, the parent should be cued to decrease the amount of support by using choice or the cloze procedure.

Choice

Choice is an effective prompt type for children who are imitating a variety of words but are having difficulty using words spontaneously. If a child has difficulty making choices, suggest that the parent use a highly preferred item and a nonpreferred item. If the child has the tendency to repeat the last word given, tell the parent to provide the desired choice first and the undesired choice second. For example, if the child wants a ball, the parent might say, "Ball or hat?" The parent should then reinforce her child by immediately giving him the item that he labels, even if it is the nonpreferred item. This technique increases the child's attention to the words he is using.

Cloze Procedure

Explain to the parent that a *cloze procedure* asks the child to fill in a blank. The parent gives the beginning of a message, and the child is required to complete the message. This type of prompt is effective for children who have difficulty retrieving words in response to questions, and for children who are able to imitate a verbal model but cannot use the word spontaneously. The cloze procedure differs from a verbal routine, in that there can be more than one correct answer and the answer may change, depending on the contextual cues. For example, with "I want _____," the child could respond with a variety of words. An example in which a child would need to use environmental cues would be "The baby is in the _____ [bed]" while pointing to a baby in the bed. The parent should be encouraged to use a visual cue (e.g., point to the item that completes a sentence) to help the child respond appropriately.

Direct Question

Direct questions cue the child to respond to the parent. When teaching the child to respond to questions, the parent should only use questions when she expects an answer and is able to add support to help the child answer. Questions can be used to help the child learn new words or sentence structures. Review the different types of questions with the parent (i.e., "who," "what," "where," open-ended) and identify the type of question she should use with her child. Unless it is a specific goal, tell the parent to avoid questions requiring only "yes–no" answers; they are less likely to expand the child's vocabulary.

Time Delay

Wait time has been used throughout the program to improve the child's ability to communicate without support. Time delay differs slightly from wait time. In strategies such as waiting with anticipation, the parent responds to any communication the child gives as meaningful. With time delay, the parent waits with an expectant look for the child to expand on his initial communication. To implement this strategy, the parent waits for the child to demonstrate interest in an object or activity, and then waits with an expectant look to see whether her child will expand his response without further support. Unlike the other types of prompts, a time delay does not provide the child with specific information about what his response should be. Thus it increases the child's spontaneous language skills.

The parent may need to add information to help the child increase the complexity of his response. One strategy is to pair a visual cue (e.g., point to the item she wants the child to name) with the expectant look to help the child retrieve the word on his own. Another strategy is to use a time delay after the child has been prompted to communicate in the same way several times in a row. For example, the parent might prompt her child to request crackers during snack by using a verbal model ("Crackers"). After the child has imitated "Crackers" several times, the parent can then use a time delay to encourage him to say the word on his own.

Explain to the parent that she will learn to move up and down the continuum of prompts as she is teaching a new skill. The type of prompt the parent uses is dependent on the child's goal and ability. For example, to increase spontaneous language skills, the parent should use a time delay. However, to teach new vocabulary, the parent may initially use a verbal model. Explain to the parent that you will help identify the type of prompt to use for each goal during demonstration of the technique.

Identify Language Skills to Prompt

As in *Modeling and Expanding Language*, the parent should prompt language skills that are slightly above the level of the skills the child now uses on his own. For example, if the child is leading the parent by the hand to what he wants, the parent should prompt a tap or a point; these are more conventional gestures. If the child is vocalizing, she should prompt single words. The parent should be encouraged to wait for her child to indicate that he wants something, and then prompt him to add one level of complexity to his communication.

Demonstrate Use of *Teaching Your Child Expressive Language*

First, review the child's goals with the parent and identify one language goal to address. Explain the type of prompt that you will use first to elicit this skill and how you will add support if the child does not respond—for example, "I am going to use questions to increase Sam's ability to use verbs. If he does not respond, I will use the cloze procedure and then choices."

It is also helpful to review the entire procedure with the parent, to call attention to the interactive teaching techniques you will use to increase the effectiveness of prompts—for example, "Prior to asking the question, I will wait to see what Sam is interested in, and then I will use *Balanced Turns* to create an opportunity for him to communicate. This should increase the likelihood that he will respond to my question."

During the demonstration, identify the technique you use, the child's response, and how you vary the amount of support to help the child respond. For example, the trainer might say to Sam's mother:

"Sam was playing with the ball. I used *Playful Obstruction* to gain access to the ball (create an opportunity for him to communicate) and waited to see how he would communicate. He said, 'Ball.' I asked a 'what' question: 'What should I do with the ball?' He responded by saying, 'Ball,' so I added support by using a choice: 'Throw ball (preferred) or hide ball (non-preferred)?' He said, 'Throw ball,' so I threw the ball to him and expanded on his response by saying, 'Throw the red ball.'"

Have the Parent Practice *Teaching Your Child Expressive Language* While You Provide Feedback

Immediately after your demonstration, have the parent practice using the types of prompts that are appropriate for each of her child's language goals. Explain to the parent that the type of prompt used will change, depending on the goal. For example, you might use the time delay to increase the child's use of spontaneous language to request, and use questions to increase his use of verbs. Before having the parent implement the technique, ask her if she has any questions and provide her with specific strategies to use. Remember to tell her how to add more support if the child does not respond—for example, "Remember to use questions to increase Sam's use of verbs. If he doesn't respond, use a cloze procedure and then provide him with a choice."

Provide feedback to help the parent use the appropriate prompt and to help the parent learn to move between prompts (i.e., to add or decrease support as indicated). For example, if the parent is struggling to get her child to respond, coach her to increase support. Likewise, after the parent has been successful in prompting at one level several times (e.g., verbal model), provide feedback to her to help her decrease the amount of support (e.g., cloze procedure to increase her child's independence).

Practice prompting during a range of activities, to help the parent understand how to use prompts in different situations. If you are coaching in the clinic, it is helpful to have the parent bring toys from her home to use during the session.

Have the Parent Complete the Flowchart for Prompting Expressive Language (Form 9)

The flowchart in Appendix A, Form 9, is used to help the parent visualize how the different types of prompts can be used together for her child. Help the parent fill out the flowchart, based on an activity that she will try at home. Have the parent identify the goal she would like to address, the activity within which she would like to address the goal, and the technique she will use to gain her child's attention. Write this information at the top of the chart. Next, have the parent identify the type of prompt she will start with and how she will add support to help her child use the target. Use probing questions to help her complete the flowchart, as in this example:

PARENT TRAINER: What goal would you like to address with your child?

PARENT: I would like him to use different words when he wants something. He often says, "I want," but does not use other verbs.

PARENT TRAINER: Great. Let's write that the goal is for him to add more verbs to his requests. When would you like to work on this?

PARENT: Maybe when he wants something to drink. He likes juice a lot.

PARENT TRAINER: Great idea. What technique will you use to gain his attention?

PARENT: I think having the juice in sight and out of reach.

PARENT TRAINER: Great. That *Communicative Temptations* strategy will let you know if he is interested in the juice, and it allows you to gain his attention. Once you have his attention, what type of prompt will you use first?

PARENT: Maybe I should wait and see what he says.

PARENT TRAINER: Great idea. Let's say that you will start with a time delay and wait to see what he says. If he says, "Pour the juice," you want to immediately pour the juice. What will you do if he just says, "I want juice?"

PARENT: I will say, "Mom, pour the juice."

PARENT TRAINER: I wonder if he could respond to the question "What should I do?" This strategy allows him another opportunity to generate his own language before you tell him what to say. If he says, "Pour the juice," immediately reinforce him and expand on his response. If he doesn't respond, what will you do?

PARENT: I should give him a choice.

PARENT TRAINER: Great. When thinking of choices, we want to have a choice he wants and a choice he doesn't want. One idea would be to say, "Mom, pour the juice," or "Mom, drink the juice." If he says, "Pour the juice," immediately reinforce his response by giving him the juice. If he says, "Drink the juice," you would drink the juice. Depend-ing on his frustration level, you may wish to provide him with the verbal model in order to ensure he gets the reinforcement—that is, the juice.

The parent trainer should write down the examples on the flowchart and have the parent practice this at home. Ask the parent to write down at home how the child responds to the use of these techniques.

Figure S15–16.1 illustrates how this information is written on the flowchart. Notice that "Time delay" is circled under "Parent chooses most appropriate prompt to get child to respond." Remember to identify the prompt with which the parent should start. You can either highlight or circle this prompt to call her attention to the appropriate prompt with which to start.

Figure S15–16.2 represents a flowchart for a child who has a goal of using single words. The goal for this child is to increase his use of single words during ball play. In this case, "Direct ques-tion" is circled, as that is the prompt the parent and the trainer have selected as the least sup-portive prompt. However, examples for other prompts are written, in the event that the parent would like to change the amount of support she provides during play at home.

Figure S15–16.3 represents a flowchart for a child who is preverbal. Again, notice that the prompt level that the parent should start with ("Verbal model") is circled, and that examples for several types of prompt are provided. Make sure to use this form to provide the parent with concrete examples of types of prompts she can use.

Discuss and Assign Homework

Session 15

1. Have parent practice teaching expressive language with the completed Form 9 (Appen-dix A) as a guide. Typically, there is not enough time to go over the homework sheet for *Teaching Your Child Expressive Language* in the first session. Explain to the parent that she does not need to complete this portion of the homework until after the next session. If you are able to complete this aspect of the homework during the first session, it should be reviewed during the following session.

Session 16

1. Have the parent complete homework for *Teaching Your Child Expressive Language*. Review the rationale and the key points of *Teaching Your Child Expressive Language*. While reviewing the key points, remind the parent of any prompt rules she should use, and write the rules on the homework sheet in the parent manual. As you complete the review, emphasize the types of prompts the parent should use to elicit a new skill.

Next, help the parent identify one to two goals she will address at home. This technique addresses all of the child's goals related to use of language. Examples could include using a single word to request, responding to "why" questions, using comments, or retelling past events. Choose from the language goals that were developed for the child during the first session. Write the child's goal(s) on the homework sheet in the parent manual.

Once you have identified goals, have the parent choose at least three activities in which to

Child's goal: Increase use of verbs to request

Activity: Snack time (when he wants a drink)

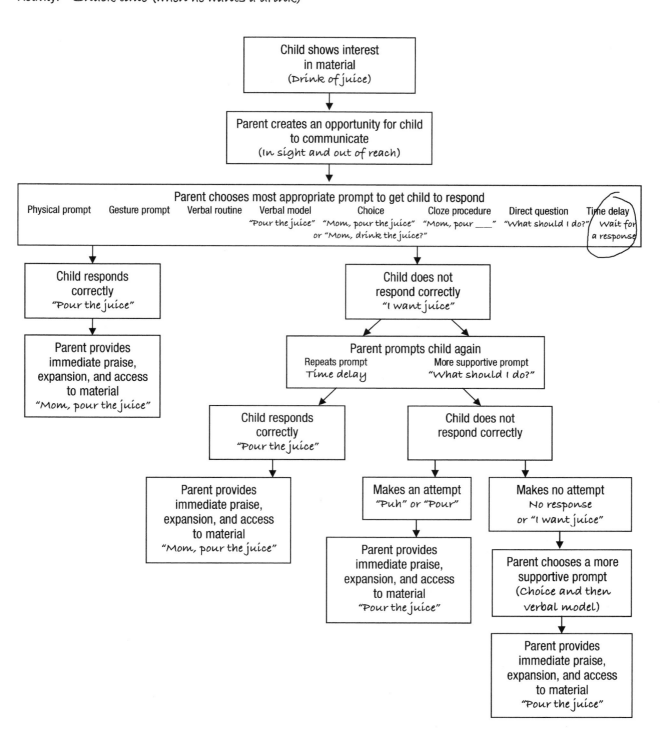

Figure S15–16.1. Example of completed Flowchart for Prompting Expressive Language (Appendix A, Form 9) for child with simple phrases.

Child's goal: Say the word 'ball' to request a ball

Activity: Ball play

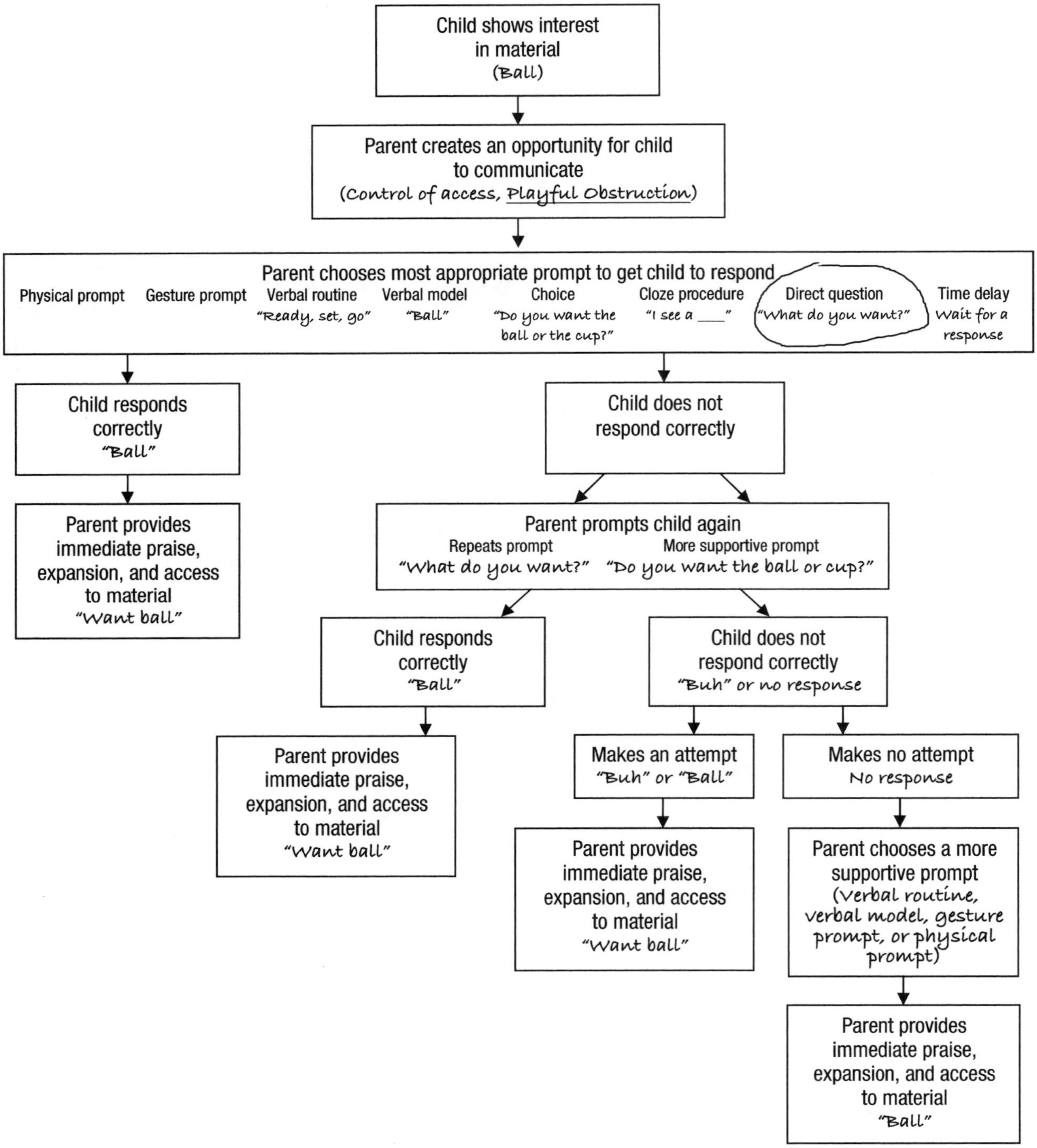

Figure S15–16.2. Example of completed Flowchart for Prompting Expressive Language (Appendix A, Form 9) for child with single words.

Child's name: *Point or use a single word to request an object*

Date: *Ball play*

Child shows interest
in material
(Ball)

Parent creates an opportunity for child
to communicate
(Control of access, Playful Obstruction)

Parent chooses most appropriate prompt to get child to respond

Physical prompt	Gesture prompt	Verbal routine	Verbal model	Choice	Cloze procedure	Direct question	Time delay
Help the child point	*Model a point*		*"Ball"*			*"What do you want?"*	*Wait for an initiation*

Child responds correctly
*Points to ball
or says, "Buh"*

Child does not
respond correctly

Parent provides
immediate praise,
expansion, and access
to material
"Ball"

Parent prompts child again

Repeats prompt
"Ball"

More supportive prompt
(Gesture prompt with verbal model)

Child responds
correctly
Points or "Buh"

Child does not
respond correctly
Partial point or no response

Parent provides
immediate praise,
expansion, and access
to material
"Ball"

Makes an attempt
Partial point

Makes no attempt
No response

Parent provides immediate
praise, expansion, and
access to material
*Points to the ball and
says, "Ball"*

Parent chooses a more
supportive prompt
(Physical prompt)

Parent provides immediate
praise, expansion, and
access to material
*Points to the ball and
says, "Ball"*

Figure S15–16.3. Sample Flowchart for Prompting Language for Preverbal Child.

157

use expressive language prompts. If she has trouble identifying three activities, you may wish to refer back to the Daily Activity Schedule and review ways to practice this during daily activities. Choose at least one play activity and one daily activity in which the parent can practice, and write this information on the homework sheet in the parent manual.

Next, help the parent identify the techniques she will use to create an opportunity for the child to communicate, the specific language skill she will model, and the type of prompt she will use. Write this information on the homework sheet.

Now read through the questions on the homework sheet and have the parent respond to the questions, based on her interaction with her child during this session. Some of the questions may not be applicable, because some types of prompts may not be beneficial for the child. For example, some children may not require a physical prompt, while other children may not yet be at the point of responding to questions. When this occurs, explain to the parent that the question is not applicable, and cross off the question. If the parent is unable to respond to the questions, ask probing questions or demonstrate the technique and have the parent identify the child's response. Instruct the parent to practice using the technique at home before the next session and to write down how her child responds to the technique. Explain that the homework will be reviewed at the beginning of the next session.

2. Have the parent read *Teaching Your Child Receptive Language* (Chapter 13 of the parent manual). Once the parent is effectively prompting expressive language, have her read *Teaching Your Child Receptive Language*. Explain to the parent that the receptive language prompts are used to improve the child's ability to understand language and follow directions. The parent should come to the session with any questions she may have about the technique. The parent does not complete the homework for the technique until it has been reviewed and practiced during the next session.

Troubleshooting Tips

Parents face several common challenges when they are beginning to use the direct teaching techniques. First, a parent can forget to use the interactive teaching techniques to gain her child's attention prior to prompting. When this occurs, the child is much less likely to respond appropriately. Thus it may be necessary to coach the parent on gaining the child's attention. To do this, give the parent a specific technique to use to create an opportunity to communicate, and one prompt to use that you are sure will elicit a response from the child. This type of practice allows the parent to become comfortable with the steps involved in prompting before she begins to focus on moving between prompts.

A second challenge is that the parent may observe an increase in her child's frustration when she begins to prompt language. This occurs when the child does not understand the expectations, has difficulty waiting, or the parent is prompting too much. If the child does not understand the expectations, review the necessity for clear and appropriate prompts, and provide the parent with a specific prompt to use (e.g., model the word and point to the object). When the child appears frustrated because of the amount of time he has to wait before receiving the item, cue the parent to begin with a prompt to which she knows the child will be able to respond successfully. For example, if the goal is for the child to point, have the parent use a physical prompt. If the goal is for the child to use a word, have the parent provide a verbal model. Once the routine is set, have the parent decrease support every third time. This strategy often decreases the amount of frustration. If the parent is prompting too much, remind the parent to return to using the interactive teaching techniques. Suggest that she prompt her child for a more complex response after only every third initiation.

A third challenge occurs when the parent has difficulty identifying when to provide reinforcement. Sometimes the parent reinforces the child for any behavior (as in the interactive teaching techniques), rather than requiring a more complex response. At other times, the parent has difficulty controlling access to the item and allows her child to grab it away before the child produced a more complex response. Finally, the parent may wait too long before providing reinforcement. If the parent has difficulty identifying an appropriate response for her child, remind her of what she is looking for before she prompts and cue her when the child has given that response. If the parent has difficulty controlling access to the item, recommend that she stand up or place the item in a place that the child cannot access when she is prompting.

Session 17

Teaching Your Child Receptive Language

Session Goal

1. Teach the parent strategies to improve her child's ability to understand language and follow directions.

Materials

1. Parent manual
2. Completed Goal Development Form (Appendix A, Form 4)
3. Number of highly preferred toys

Outline of Session

- Review homework from *Teaching Your Child Expressive Language* (10–15 minutes)
- Introduce the rationale for *Teaching Your Child Receptive Language* (5 minutes):

    It increases the child's ability to follow directions and understand language.

- Explain how this technique is used with previously taught techniques and how it differs from previously taught techniques (5 minutes).
- Discuss the key points of *Teaching Your Child Receptive Language* (5–10 minutes):

    Give clear directions:
        Gain the child's attention.
        Give direct commands.

Help the child respond:
    Physical prompt
    Visual prompt
    Verbal instruction
Provide reinforcement.

- Identify receptive language skills to prompt (5–10 minutes).
- Demonstrate use of *Teaching Your Child Receptive Language* (10–15 minutes).
- Have the parent practice *Teaching Your Child Receptive Language* while you provide feedback (30–40 minutes).
- Discuss and assign homework (10–15 minutes).
    1. Have the parent complete homework for *Teaching Your Child Receptive Language.*
    2. Have the parent read *Teaching Your Child Social Imitation* (Chapter 14 of the parent manual).

Review Homework
from *Teaching Your Child Expressive Language*

Begin the session by reviewing the homework from the previous session. Ask the parent whether she had difficulty using the prompts described in *Teaching Your Child Expressive Language*. Challenges at home are typically similar to the challenges discussed in the "Troubleshooting Tips" for Sessions 15–16, and are usually related to either parent frustration (because the child is not responding) or child frustration (because the parent is prompting too much or is not providing enough support). In both instances, it would be beneficial to review from Chapter 11 in the parent manual. This chapter explains the importance of monitoring the child's motivation and providing clear and appropriate prompts. Take time to describe the type of prompt the parent should use, to demonstrate its use, and to provide feedback before introducing *Teaching Your Child Receptive Language*.

Introduce the Rationale
for *Teaching Your Child Receptive Language*

This session is spent reviewing the different types of prompts the parent can use to improve her child's receptive language abilities. It is particularly important that the child is able to follow directions within daily routines.

It Increases the Child's Ability to Follow Directions and Understand Language

Children with ASD often have difficulty following directions because they are unable to understand the language used. This difficulty can make such a child appear noncompliant. One way to increase compliance with directions is to increase the child's comprehension of directions. This can be done through use of specific prompts.

Explain How This Technique Is Used
with Previously Taught Techniques and How It Differs
from Previously Taught Techniques

This technique differs from the other techniques presented in this program, because the parent is leading the interaction rather than the child. Explain to the parent that she will use this technique when the child is required to complete such activities such as putting his toys away or getting his shoes. The parent should continue to use techniques and strategies that are effective in gaining her child's attention (e.g., *Playful Obstruction*, control of access from *Communicative Temptations*) before giving the verbal instruction.

Discuss the Key Points of *Teaching Your Child
Receptive Language*

There are three steps involved in *Teaching Your Child Receptive Language*. The first step is to give clear directions; the second step is to help the child respond; and the third step is to provide verbal praise (reinforcement) after he responds. These steps are described in the parent manual and should be reviewed with the parent.

Give Clear Directions

Directions presented to the child should be clear. This is accomplished by first gaining the child's attention and then giving direct commands.

Gain the Child's Attention

As in giving expressive language prompts, it is important to gain the child's attention prior to presenting a verbal direction. If necessary, review the techniques that are effective in gaining the child's attention.

Give Direct Commands

Instruct the parent to use direct commands (e.g., "Come here") rather than indirect commands (e.g., "Would you come here?"), to improve her child's ability to follow directions. This strategy makes the expectations clear for the child and eliminates the possibility of an appropriate response (e.g., "No") that does not result in the child's following the direction.

Help the Child Respond

After the command is given, instruct the parent to use the least supportive prompt necessary to help the child respond correctly.

Physical Prompt

A physical prompt is the most supportive type of prompt and is essentially the same as the physical prompt used in prompting expressive language. To use this prompt, the parent physically assists the child to ensure that he follows the command or instruction. This type of prompt is used when the child does not follow a verbal direction paired with a visual prompt. Provide the parent with concrete examples of how and when she would use a physical prompt with her child. For example, after the command "Get your shoes," the parent can take the child's hand, bring him to his shoes, and help him pick them up.

Visual Prompt

Visual prompts are paired with a spoken command to help the child interpret the verbal message. A visual prompt can include pointing to the item, using a picture, or showing the child what is expected of him and having him imitate the action. Visual prompts help children who have difficulty understanding or attending to the verbal message. This type of prompt is used when the child does not follow the verbal instruction and before use of a physical prompt.

Verbal Instruction

Once the child is able to follow a direction when it is paired with a visual prompt, the parent should use the verbal instruction in isolation. If the child does not respond, the parent should add support by pairing the visual prompt with the verbal instruction. As the parent learns to implement these prompts, she will learn to move from one prompt level to another, to improve her child's ability to follow directions.

Provide Reinforcement

After the child follows the direction, either on his own or with help, the parent should provide verbal praise by telling him what it was that he did right (e.g., "Good job getting your shoes"). To provide natural reinforcement, the parent should use the receptive language prompts immediately before an enjoyable activity, such as going outside or having a snack. See this session's "Troubleshooting Tips" if the child has difficulty following directions or if you feel a tangible reinforcer may be required.

Identify Receptive Language Skills to Prompt

In many cases, goals have not been developed in this area, because this is the only technique that is used to address receptive language. If you do not have a language goal for improving the child's receptive language, work with the parent to identify goals that she would like to address. Take time to ask the parent whether there are specific directions that she would like her child to follow at home. Explain to the parent that, as with other skills taught in this program, she should prompt receptive language skills that are slightly above the level of the skills the child now uses on his own. For example, if the child is able to follow one-step directions, she might prompt two-step directions. Take time to help the parent identify skills she would like to target. Goals could include following one-step directions (e.g., "Get your shoes"), two-step directions (e.g., "Get your shoes and your jacket"), directions containing spatial concepts (e.g., "Put your plate on the table"), directions containing temporal concepts (e.g., "Get your shoes after you get your coat"), or directions containing two or more units of information (e.g., "Bring me the big red cup").

Demonstrate Use of *Teaching Your Child Receptive Language*

If possible, use the parent's goals for following directions to illustrate the techniques. If you are coaching in the home, take time to demonstrate *Teaching Your Child Receptive Language* during activities that take place within the home. Explain to the parent that she should balance the use of this technique with other techniques. Prompting the child to follow directions too often is likely to frustrate the child.

Next, demonstrate how to use the different strategies describe above to improve the child's ability to follow directions. For example, the trainer might say to Brian's mother:

"Brian was playing with the ball. I moved into his line of sight and stopped the movement of the ball to gain his attention. He looked at me. I gave him a verbal instruction: 'Throw the ball.' When he did not respond, I showed him how to throw the ball (a verbal prompt paired with a visual prompt). He continued to hold the ball, so I added more support by using the physical prompt and helping him throw the ball. I then reinforced him by providing verbal praise."

Explain how to add more support until the child is able to follow the direction. As with expressive language prompts, once the parent gives the verbal instruction, she should always add support until the child complies. Remind the parent that if she does not have time or does not want to follow through, she should use interactive teaching techniques (e.g., "I am throwing the ball"), which do not require a response from the child.

Have Parent Practice *Teaching Your Child Receptive Language* While You Provide Feedback

Have the parent practice for at least 30 minutes. Remind the parent to balance the use of *Teaching Your Child Receptive Language* with previous techniques. Provide the parent with specific techniques to use before she begins the interaction with her child—for example, "Remember to use direct commands that have one step. These could include 'Push the car,' 'Give me the car,' or 'Open the garage.' Remember to provide additional support until he follows the direction."

Provide the parent with positive and corrective feedback to help her use the appropriate prompt and to help her follow through once she has given the direction. It can also be helpful to give her a specific direction to use (e.g., "Push the red car"). In order for the parent to be successful, it may be necessary to provide coaching on gaining her child's attention prior to using a prompt. If the parent would like the child to get his coat, make sure to target this skill at the end of the session, when he would need to get these items. This technique can also be used to help the child clean up toys. If it is not possible to practice during daily activities, the parent should practice *Teaching Your Child Receptive Language* during play.

Discuss and Assign Homework

1. Have the parent complete homework for *Teaching Your Child Receptive Language*. Begin with a review of the rationale and the key points encompassed in *Teaching Your Child Receptive Language*. While reviewing the key points, remind the parent of any prompt rules she should use, and write the rules on the homework sheet. It is particularly important for the parent to gain her child's attention prior to giving a direction. As you complete the review, emphasize the types of prompts the parent should use by writing the number 1, 2, or 3 next to each prompt. Many children benefit from having a visual prompt paired with a verbal instruction.

Next, have the parent identify directions she would like the child to follow in the home. Examples could include getting his coat and shoes when it is time to go, cleaning up his toys, getting his clothes in the morning before getting dressed, or getting his cup when he is thirsty. Help the parent make the command direct and appropriate to the child's language level. For example, if the child is having difficulty following two-step directions, explain to the parent that she should provide a clear one-step direction (e.g., "Get your shoes").

Once you have identified the direction, have the parent respond orally to the questions on the homework sheet, based on her interaction with her child during this session. If the parent is unable to respond to the questions, ask probing questions or demonstrate the technique, and have the parent identify the level of prompting used to help the child follow the direction. Instruct the parent to practice at home and write down how her child responds to the technique. Remind the parent that she should balance use of this technique with previous techniques. Explain that the homework will be reviewed at the beginning of the next session.

2. Have the parent read *Teaching Your Child Social Imitation* (Chapter 14 of the parent manual). Have the parent read *Teaching Your Child Social Imitation* prior to the next session. Explain to the parent that this technique is used to teach her child to imitate others' behavior during play. Social imitation is an important skill in early development, because it gives the child a means to acquire new information (often referred to as *observational learning*) and a way to communicate interest in others (often referred to as *reciprocal imitation*). The parent should come to the session with any questions she may have about the technique. The parent does not complete the homework for the technique until it has been reviewed and practiced during the next session.

Troubleshooting Tips

The child may become frustrated when given a direct command, either because he does not understand the direction or because he does not want to comply with the direction. Regardless of the reason, once the parent presents a direct command, she should help her child follow the direction. One solution is to cue the parent to start with the prompt level at which she knows her child will have success. For example, if the goal is for the child to get an object, have the parent begin with a physical prompt and immediately provide reinforcement.

It may also be helpful to teach the parent to use artificial reinforcement after the child follows the direction. Explain to the parent that *artificial reinforcement* refers to use of a reward the child likes that is not related to the task (e.g., a food, toy, or sticker). This type of reinforcement is not used or recommended with other techniques in this program. Other direct teaching techniques begin with *Follow Your Child's Lead*, which allows the reinforcement to be directly related to the child's response (i.e., *natural reinforcement*). Natural reinforcement is preferred because it leads to better generalization and maintenance of skills. Unfortunately, natural reinforcement is not always possible with giving directions, because the parent is choosing what the child should do.

If the parent is prompting too much or the child becomes too frustrated, coach the parent to return to using the interactive teaching techniques in isolation until the child is engaged.

Session 18

Teaching Your Child Social Imitation

Session Goals

1. Teach the parent strategies to improve her child's spontaneous imitation skills.
2. Teach the parent strategies to improve her child's gesture use.
3. Teach the parent strategies to improve her child's reciprocity.

Materials

1. Parent manual
2. Completed Goal Development Form (Appendix A, Form 4)
3. Pairs of highly preferred toys

Outline of Session

- Review the homework from *Teaching Your Child Receptive Language* (10–15 minutes).
- Introduce the rationale for *Teaching Your Child Social Imitation* (5 minutes):

    It improves the child's spontaneous imitation skills.
    It increases the child's gesture use.
    It increases the child's social reciprocity.

- Explain how *Teaching Your Child Social Imitation* is used with previously taught techniques and how it differs from previously taught techniques (5 minutes).
- Discuss the key points of *Teaching Social Imitation* (5–10 minutes):

    Use *Imitate Your Child*.
    Describe your imitation.

> Model a skill you would like your child to imitate:
>> Model play actions with objects.
>> Model gestures.
>
> Describe the action.
> Use wait time.
> Prompt imitation.
> Give reinforcement.

- Demonstrate use of *Teaching Your Child Social Imitation* (5–10 minutes).
- Have the parent practice *Teaching Your Child Social Imitation* while you provide feedback (30–40 minutes).
- Discuss and assign homework (10–15 minutes):
    1. Have the parent complete homework for *Teaching Your Child Social Imitation*.
    2. Have the parent read *Teaching Your Child Play* (Chapter 15 of the parent manual).

Review Homework from *Teaching Your Child Receptive Language*

Begin the session by reviewing the homework from the previous session, and discuss whether the parent had any difficulty using the prompts described in *Teaching Your Child Receptive Language*. Frequent challenges at home are similar to the challenges discussed in "Troubleshooting Tips" for Session 17. These challenges are often intensified at home because of time constraints and previous patterns of interaction. Take time to talk through challenges and identify solutions. As discussed in Session 17, it may be beneficial in some cases to help the parent identify a reinforcer she can use after the child follows the instruction. Explain to the parent that she should show the child the reinforcer and provide a verbal instruction paired with the prompt that will enable the child to be successful. As soon as the child complies, even if it is with use of a physical prompt, the parent should provide the child with reinforcement. If necessary, take time during this session to demonstrate this sequence and to have the parent practice this sequence before introducing *Teaching Your Child Social Imitation*.

Introduce the Rationale for *Teaching Your Child Social Imitation*

This session is spent reviewing the different prompting and reinforcement strategies the parent can use to enhance her child's social imitation skills. As you explain the rationale, relate the technique's purpose to the parent's goals for her child.

It Improves the Child's Spontaneous Imitation Skills

Children with ASD often have difficulty watching others and imitating their behavior. The ability to observe and imitate others' behavior is very important for learning new skills. In fact, all of the modeling strategies in this program rely on the child's ability to imitate the parent's behavior. *Teaching Your Child Social Imitation* can improve the child's ability to imitate spontaneously (without a direct command to imitate), which will improve his ability to learn from his environment.

It Increases the Child's Gesture Use

Children with ASD have difficulty using gestures to enhance their communication. Teaching such a child to imitate a variety of descriptive gestures (gestures that describe actions, objects, or attributes) can improve this nonverbal aspect of language.

It Increases the Child's Social Reciprocity

Children also use imitation as means for interacting with others socially. Children with ASD have particular difficulty using imitation for this purpose. Teaching imitation as a back-and-forth interaction (i.e., the parent and child take turns imitating each other) can improve the child's social reciprocity.

Explain to the parent how this technique will address her child's individual goals. For example, when explaining the rationale to Brian's mother, the trainer might say: "We will use this technique to help Brian imitate gestures. We will focus on waving, pointing, and clapping, since those were the gestures we identified at the beginning of the program as imitation goals."

The trainer might say to Sam's mother: "We will use this technique to help Sam imitate play. We will focus on imitating pretend and symbolic actions with toys."

Explain How *Teaching Your Child Social Imitation* Is Used with Previously Taught Techniques and How It Differs from Previously Taught Techniques

Many of the strategies discussed in this session are similar to ones that have already been taught; however, the focus is slightly different. In this technique, the parent explicitly targets imitation as a skill in and of itself. In other words, the parent is trying to increase her child's ability to match her behavior, rather than use a specific language, gesture, or play behavior. Furthermore, the parent teaches imitation as a social behavior; thus she alternates between imitating her child and asking her child to imitate her.

To implement this technique effectively, the parent should continue to use *Follow Your Child's Lead* and to use a technique to gain the child's attention before she presents a behavior for the child to imitate. *Teaching Your Child Social Imitation* differs from other techniques involving the use of prompts, because the parent demonstrates the behavior she would like the child to imitate before prompting the skill.

Discuss the Key Points of *Teaching Your Child Social Imitation*

There are seven steps to *Teaching Your Child Social Imitation*. These steps are described in the parent manual and should be reviewed with the parent.

Use *Imitate Your Child*

The first step encompasses all of the elements that have been described for *Imitate Your Child*. The child chooses the activity, and the parent is face to face with the child. Imitation can include play with toys, gestures, body movements, or vocalizations. The interactive technique of *Imitate Your Child* is used to lay the groundwork for reciprocal imitation, in which the child learns that imitation is a back-and-forth interaction. The parent should be encouraged to use two of the same or similar toys, to enhance her ability to imitate her child's play with objects.

Describe Your Imitation

While the parent is imitating her child, she should describe what she and her child are doing, to highlight that they are doing the same thing. This strategy is the same as that discussed in *Modeling and Expanding Language*. Remind the parent to keep her language simple and repetitive. The goal of describing the behavior she is imitating is to increase the correspondence between the parent's and child's play, rather than to have the child imitate the parent's language.

Model a Skill You Would Like Your Child to Imitate

Explain to the parent that once she has imitated her child, she will model a new skill that she would like her child to use. Depending on the child's goals, she may choose to model play actions with objects or to model gestures. Many children will have goals in both areas; in this case, the parent can alternate between the skills she models and prompts.

Model Play Actions with Objects

This strategy is similar to the strategy of modeling play as described in *Balanced Turns*. However, in *Teaching Your Child Social Imitation*, the child is required to imitate the parent's model. The parent should have the same kind of toy that the child is playing with. To enhance the likelihood that the child will imitate, the parent should exaggerate her actions (*Animation*) and use a verbal label to describe her actions (see below). Instruct the parent to model the play action up to three times.

Model Gestures

The next strategy is similar to the strategy of using gestural cues as described in *Modeling and Expanding Language*. However, rather than targeting gestures to request (e.g., a point or sign for "more"), the parent is targeting gestures that convey conventional (e.g., "Where is it?" with palms upturned) and affective (e.g., "Oh, no" with hands on face) themes, as well as gestures that describe objects (e.g., "Airplane" with arms out), attributes (e.g., "Big" with raised arms), and actions (e.g., "Spin" with finger moving in a circle).

The parent should model gestures that are directly related to her child's play, paired with a verbal label. For example, if the child is playing with a baby doll, the parent might model a quiet gesture ("Shhh, baby's sleeping" with a finger over lips) or tired gesture ("Baby's tired" with a hand covering a yawn). Again, instruct the parent to model the gesture she would like her child to use up to three times. If the child does not imitate the gesture after the third model, the parent should prompt imitation (see below).

Descriptive gestures can be abstract and thus harder to imitate. Thus the parent should target gesture imitation only if the child already has some object imitation ability. Help the parent think of a number of descriptive gestures that she could use to describe her child's play.

Describe the Action

The parent should use a verbal label while she is modeling the play action or gesture, to cue the child to imitate her behavior without explicitly providing a command such as "Do this." This way the child will learn to imitate when the parent models an action and talks about it, rather than only when she tells him to do so. Verbal labels should be presented by using the same strategies emphasized in *Modeling and Expanding Language*: They should be short, be at or slightly above the child's language level, be said clearly and stressed, and describe the action without giving a command. If the parent models the play act or gesture more than once (providing three models and then prompting), the parent should be sure to keep the verbal label the same each time across those trials. However, to help the child imitate in many contexts, the parent should vary what she says if she models the same action at different times (e.g., she might say "Bounce" one time and "Boing" another time).

Use Wait Time

The purpose of *Teaching Your Child Social Imitation* is to have the child imitate the play or gesture without a direct prompt. Therefore, the parent should wait after each model to see whether her child will imitate the skill before she prompts imitation. As discussed for previous techniques, the amount of wait time will vary, depending on the child. Provide the parent with a concrete amount of time to wait (e.g., 3 seconds) before modeling the behavior again.

Prompt Imitation

If the child does not imitate the behavior after it is modeled three times, the parent should provide a prompt to help him imitate the action. Depending on the child's ability to respond, the first prompt might be a verbal instruction (e.g., "You do it") or a physical prompt (e.g., a movement to help the child push the car). For a child who has a lot of difficulty imitating during play, the parent should be encouraged to model actions that the child is highly motivated to imitate, such as actions that he already does with the toys. If the child has a very difficult time paying attention to what the parent is doing, she can say his name to get his attention first; however, she should avoid doing this every time, or the child will learn to imitate only when the parent says his name.

Give Reinforcement

Once the child imitates the behavior, either on his own or with the use of the prompt, the parent should immediately reinforce him by providing praise and allowing him to play with toys in the way he chooses.

Demonstrate Use of *Teaching Your Child Social Imitation*

Ask the parent whether there are specific behaviors she would like her child to imitate. The parent may choose either a play skill or a gesture. Once the parent has identified a skill to target, demonstrate how to use the different strategies, identifying each strategy, and the child's response. For example, the trainer might say to Brian's mother:

> "Brian was spinning the wheels on the car. I moved into his line of sight and began spinning the wheels on another car while I described our play. He looked at me. I then modeled a new way to play with the car by pushing it and saying, 'Drive car.' When he did not respond, I repeated the model two times. He continued to spin the wheels on the car, so I added more support by using the physical prompt to help him push the car. Once he used the new skill, I provided reinforcement by giving him praise and letting him choose how to play with the car. I then returned to imitating his play."

If appropriate, demonstrate use of the technique to prompt imitation of play and imitation of gestures.

Have the Parent Practice *Teaching Your Child Social Imitation* While You Provide Feedback

Have the parent practice use of the technique for at least 30 minutes. Prior to having the parent practice, ask her if she has any questions, and provide her with specific strategies to use—for example, "Remember to show him the skill three times. If he does not imitate the behavior, add support by giving him a physical prompt."

Provide feedback to help the parent alternate between imitating her child and asking her child to imitate her. You should also help the parent identify behaviors for the child to imitate. In order for the parent to be successful, it may be necessary to provide coaching on gaining attention prior to using a prompt.

Discuss and Assign Homework

1. Have the parent complete homework for *Teaching Your Child Social Imitation*. During this review, emphasize the rationale and the key points of *Teaching Your Child Social Imitation*. While reviewing the key points, write down on the homework sheet in the parent manual the type of prompt (verbal instruction or physical prompt) the parent should use if her child does not imitate her behavior.

Next, have the parent identify at least one goal she would like to address at home. This goal should be the imitation goal that was developed during the first sessions. Write the child's goal on the homework sheet. Once you have identified a goal or goals, have the parent choose at least two activities in which to teach imitation. If she has trouble identifying two activities, you may wish to refer back to the Daily Activity Schedule and review ways to practice this technique during daily activities.

Next, have the parent identify the types of skills she would like her child to imitate at home. Examples could include functional or pretend actions with a toy, greeting/parting gestures (e.g., waving, blowing kisses), gestures to display emotions (e.g., clapping, high fives), or gestures that describe actions (e.g., "Spin" with finger moving in a circle, "Stop" with palm out). Write the imitation skills (e.g., pretend play, emotion gestures, etc.) the parent would like to teach her child on the homework sheet.

Once you have identified the goal(s) and activities, have the parent respond orally to the questions on the homework sheet, based on her interaction with her child during this session. If the parent is unable to respond to the questions, ask probing questions or demonstrate the technique, and have the parent identify the level of prompting used to help her child imitate. Have the parent practice at home and write down how her child responds. Remind her that you will review her homework at the beginning of the next session.

2. Have the parent read *Teaching Your Child Play* (Chapter 15 of the parent manual). Have the parent read *Teaching Your Child Play* prior to the next session. Explain to the parent that this technique is used to increase the variety and complexity of her child's play. The parent should come to the session with any questions she may have about the technique. The parent will not complete the homework for the technique until it has been reviewed and practiced during the next session.

Troubleshooting Tips

Several common challenges can occur when parents are learning to use this technique. First, a parent may focus too heavily on having her child imitate. The goal is for imitation to be reciprocal; the parent and child should take turns imitating each other. If the parent requests imitation from her child too often, the child is likely to get frustrated and may be less likely to engage with the parent. If this occurs, remind the parent that she should only model a new behavior every 1–2 minutes, and the rest of the time she should be imitating her child. Second, the parent may have difficulty identifying behaviors to model that the child is likely to imitate. This may be the case with a child who has very limited imitation skills. If this occurs, have the parent stop and observe her child to see how he plays with toys. She can then model an action that she has already seen him use. This will increase the likelihood that he will imitate her behavior spontaneously (without a verbal or physical prompt), which she can then reinforce. Finally, the parent may have difficulty gaining the child's attention before modeling a new action, in which case he will not observe it or imitate it. If this occurs, encourage the parent to use *Playful Obstruction* to stop the child's play before she presents a model.

Teaching Your Child Play

Session Goals

1. Teach the parent strategies to increase the variety and complexity of her child's play.
2. Teach the parent strategies to increase her child's independent play skills.

Materials

1. Parent manual
2. Completed Goal Development Form (Appendix A, Form 4)
3. Number of highly preferred toys that can be used creatively
4. Blank Flowchart for Prompting Play (Appendix A, Form 10)

Outline of Session

- Review the homework from *Teaching Your Child Social Imitation* (10–15 minutes).
- Introduce the rationale for *Teaching Your Child Play* (5 minutes):

    It improves the variety and complexity of the child's play.
    It improves the child's independent play skills.

- Explain how *Teaching Your Child Play* is used with previously taught techniques (5 minutes).
- Discuss the key points of *Teaching Your Child Play* (5–10 minutes):

    Physical prompt
    Play model
    Verbal instruction
    Leading question
    Leading comment
    Wait time

- Identify play skills to prompt (5–10 minutes).
- Demonstrate use of *Teaching Your Child Play* (10–15 minutes).
- Have the parent practice *Teaching Your Child Play* while you provide feedback (30–40 minutes).
- Have the parent complete the Flowchart for Prompting Play (Appendix A, Form 10) (5–10 minutes).
- Discuss and assign homework (10–15 minutes):

    1. Have the parent complete the homework for *Teaching Your Child Play*.
    2. Have the parent read *Review of the Direct Teaching Techniques* (Chapter 16 of the parent manual).

Review Homework from *Teaching Your Child Social Imitation*

Read over the homework sheet in the parent manual; ask the parent to answer the questions even if she did not fill out the homework sheet. If the parent identifies challenges during the review of the homework, take time to provide solutions. One challenge can occur when the child does not engage well with toys; the parent may report difficulty knowing what to imitate or model. In this case, have the parent imitate her child's body movements and model gross motor movements, such as running across the room or spinning in a circle. Another challenge may be that the child remains engaged as long as the parent imitates his behavior; however, he leaves the interaction as soon as she models a different behavior. In this case, encourage the parent to follow through with the imitation by following her child to the new location, bringing the toy with her.

Introduce the Rationale for *Teaching Your Child Play*

This session is spent reviewing the different types of prompts the parent can use to enhance her child's play skills. In this technique, the parent is targeting the use of specific play skills, rather than increasing her child's ability to imitate her behavior (as in *Teaching Your Child Social Imitation*). However, the parent will still use imitation and physical prompting on occasion to help her child use new play forms. As you explain the rationale, relate the technique's purpose to the parent's goals for her child.

It Improves the Variety and Complexity of the Child's Play

Children with ASD often have delayed play skills. They may play with toys nonfunctionally (e.g., spinning the wheels on a toy car rather than pretending to drive it) or repetitively (e.g., setting up a tea party the same way over and over). Development of play skills is important for a variety of reasons. First, it can improve joint attention skills, because the child has to shift his attention between the toy and the person. Play is also an activity that children engage in with each other; by enhancing the child's play skills, the parent can increase his ability to interact with peers during play. Finally, play can be an excellent way to target problem solving and reasoning skills. The strategies encompassed within *Teaching Your Child Play* provide the child with specific cues to improve his play skills.

It Improves the Child's Independent Play Skills

Some children with ASD learn to play with their parents, but continue to have difficulty playing with peers. One reason is that a child becomes dependent on the parent's verbal and visual instructions telling him how to play; when this support is not available, the child may return to his atypical pattern of play or leave the activity. Like the expressive language prompts, the play prompts vary in the degree of support they provide, to help the child move toward developing independent play skills.

Explain to the parent how the prompts covered in *Teaching Your Child Play* are used to address her child's specific play goals. For example, when explaining the rationale to Brian's mother, the trainer might say: "Brian's play goal is to improve his ability to use toys for their intended purpose—that is, to improve his functional play skills. Today you will learn types of prompts to help him improve his functional play."

The trainer might say to Sam's mother: "Sam's play goal is to improve his ability to play with toys in a pretend manner. Today you will learn types of prompts to help him improve his pretend play."

Explain How *Teaching Your Child Play* Is Used with Previously Taught Techniques

The parent continues to use *Follow Your Child's Lead* to create interest and motivation, and to use other interactive teaching techniques to gain her child's attention. Once the child engages or communicates, the parent uses *Teaching Your Child Play* prompts to increase the complexity of her child's play skills. This procedure corresponds with the fourth and fifth steps of the procedure for the direct teaching techniques (i.e., prompt your child to use more complex language, imitation, or play, and provide a more supportive prompt as necessary). After the child uses the new play, the parent provides reinforcement by letting the child choose how to play next. The parent should prompt only one type of skill at a time; therefore, it is important to prompt a play or language skill, but not both skills at the same time.

Discuss the Key Points of *Teaching Your Child Play*

There are six types of prompts the parent can use to increase the complexity of her child's play. Each prompt is described in the parent manual, in order from the most supportive to the least supportive, and should be reviewed with the parent. Remind the parent to continue to use the interactive teaching techniques (i.e., to *Follow Your Child's Lead* and to create an opportunity for him to engage or communicate) before she prompts play.

Physical Prompt

The physical prompt is essentially the same for all direct teaching techniques: The parent provides physical assistance to help her child use a new skill. When prompting play, the parent physically helps the child play with a toy in a new way. This type of prompt is used when the child does not respond to the verbal instruction or model of play.

Play Model

Providing a model of play is essentially the same procedure described for increasing object imitation skills in *Teaching Your Child Social Imitation*. It is also similar to the modeling strategy described in *Balanced Turns: Modeling and Expanding Play*. The parent should model play with a toy in which the child is interested. However, unlike in that strategy, the parent adds more support by physically assisting her child if he does not imitate her play on his own. Depending on the child, the parent may add a verbal instruction (e.g., "Wash the car") or a physical prompt to help her child imitate the model. Take time to help the parent identify different ways she could play with toys that interest her child. Depending on the child's skill level, you might identify combinatorial play (e.g., nesting cups, stacking rings), functional play (e.g., throwing, kicking, or rolling a ball), pretend play (e.g., feeding a puppet or putting it to bed), or symbolic play (e.g., substituting one object for another or projecting emotions onto an object).

Verbal Instruction

Children who have difficulty generating ideas during play often benefit from a verbal instruction, because it gives them an idea of how to play with the toy. Like similar strategies in other techniques, this strategy is most effective if the parent provides instructions related to the child's activity of choice. In this technique, the strategy is used to help the child add another sequence to his play scheme or to bring new toys into his play. As with the verbal instruction used in *Teaching Your Child Receptive Language*, if the child does not respond to the instruction, the parent should add more support by modeling a play action or physically prompting the child.

Leading Question

The fourth type of prompt consists of asking the child an open-ended question (e.g., "What should Elmo do now?") and waiting to see whether he expands on his play. The child's response to the leading question may be nonverbal, because the goal in this case is to expand the child's play, not his expressive language. If the child has difficulty responding to the open-ended question, the parent should then provide her child with a choice (e.g., "Should Elmo eat or go to sleep?"). This strategy provides the child with ideas of play, but allows him to have the final decision on the play sequence or type of play that will be added. Leading questions are appropriate for children who have good receptive language skills but have difficulty expanding their play themes. This strategy is effective in increasing the complexity of the child's play and adding sequences to the child's play.

Leading Comment

Children with ASD often have difficulty responding to a comment, as this requires them to infer meaning from the verbal message. Because this skill can be difficult, the parent may pair a visual cue with *Animation* to improve the child's ability to respond to the leading comment. For example, the parent might say, "Baby looks hungry," and hold up a bottle to encourage her child to feed the baby. This technique is effective in improving the child's ideation with play, the child's play theme, and the child's ability to make inferences. This strategy is appropriate for children with good receptive language skills.

Wait Time

As in earlier techniques, wait time provides the child with an opportunity to initiate new play without a direct prompt. The parent should use this strategy once the child is able to use a new play skill with one of the strategies listed above. It is particularly important to use wait time with children who respond to leading comments. As discussed in the rationale, independent play skills are important to increase opportunities for peer interaction. Similar to the time delay strategy discussed in *Teaching Your Child Expressive Language,* the amount of wait time varies, depending on the child.

In today's session, the parent should learn to vary the types of play prompts she uses, to increase the complexity of her child's play and to encourage independent play skills (i.e., the ability to play without prompts).

Identify Play Skills to Prompt

As in prompting language and imitation skills, the parent should prompt play skills that are slightly above the level of the skills the child uses on his own. For example, if the child plays with toys in a functional manner, the parent will want to prompt pretend play. Review the ways that the parent can increase the variety and complexity of her child's play. These are outlined in the parent manual and include increasing the number of actions he does with a favorite toy, teaching him to play with new toys, increasing the developmental level of his play actions, and expanding the number of sequences he uses in his play. To help the parent identify appropriate skills to target, you may refer her to the chart of play development stages and the chart of play skills to model or prompt in the parent manual (Figures 1.3 and 8.2 there).

Demonstrate Use of *Teaching Your Child Play*

Take time to identify the play skill you will target and the type of prompt you will use to elicit the new play. Acknowledge that the parent may find play difficult, and take time to brainstorm play ideas prior to engaging in play with the child.

During the demonstration, identify the techniques you use and the child's response. For example, the trainer might say to Sam's mother:

> "Sam was playing with the cars. I moved into his line of sight and stopped movement of his car to gain his attention. He looked at me. I asked a question, 'Where should the car go?', and let go of the car. Sam did not respond. So I stopped the car again to gain his attention and presented him with a choice: 'Should the car go to the gas station or the car wash?' Sam responded by washing the car. I reinforced him by providing praise ('Yay, you washed your car!') and letting him play with the toy for a little while before providing another prompt."

Explain to the parent how to add more support until the child is able to increase the complexity of his play. As in using expressive language prompts, it is important that the parent elicit a response from the child once she has given a play prompt. Remind the parent that if she does not have time or does not want to follow through, she should use interactive teaching techniques (e.g., demonstrate washing the car and model language by saying, "I am washing my car"), which do not require a response from the child.

Have the Parent Practice *Teaching Your Child Play* While You Provide Feedback

Have the parent practice use of this technique for at least 30 minutes. Before the parent begins to practice, brainstorm with her the types of play skills that she may prompt. It can be difficult for the parent to think of how to play with a toy when she is involved in the interaction. Once you have identified a few play skills the parent can prompt, provide the parent with specific techniques to use—for example, "After you follow his lead to his play with cars, ask him, 'Where will the car go next?' (a leading question) to help him change his play."

Provide positive and corrective feedback to help the parent change the type of prompts she uses. It is also helpful to provide the parent with additional types of play to prompt. There may also be times when it is necessary to provide coaching on gaining the child's attention before using a prompt.

Have the Parent Complete the Flowchart for Prompting Play (Form 10)

Review Appendix A, Form 10, with the parent, using real examples from the session. This will help the parent visualize how the strategies are used together for her child. However, if the parent did not find this to be helpful with *Teaching Your Child Expressive Language,* this step should be omitted. If you choose to complete this flowchart, the first step is to have the parent identify the goal she would like to address, the play activity, and the strategy she will use to gain her child's attention. Write this information down on the flowchart. Next, have the parent identify the prompts she will use to address the goal. If the parent is unable to respond to the open-ended questions, ask probing questions to help her complete the flowchart, as in this example:

PARENT TRAINER: What play goal would you like to address with your child?

PARENT: I would like him to do more with the squishy balls he likes to hold. Right now he holds them and walks around.

PARENT TRAINER: What do you think about trying to get him to add an action to his play with balls?

PARENT: That sounds good.

PARENT TRAINER: What interactive teaching technique will you use to gain his attention?

PARENT: I think *Playful Obstruction,* because he often looks at me when I do that.

PARENT TRAINER: Great idea. Once you have his attention, what type of prompt will you use first?

PARENT: Maybe I should start with a leading question.

PARENT TRAINER: Great idea. Let's say that you will start with a leading question. Perhaps we could work on getting him to throw the ball in a basket. Your leading question could be "Where does the ball go?" If he responds, you want to reinforce that by providing praise and letting him play with the toy however he wishes. If he does not respond, what type of prompt will you use?

PARENT: Looking at the chart, maybe I could use a verbal instruction. I might say, "Make a basket."

PARENT TRAINER: That is a great idea. If he responds by throwing the ball in or toward the basket, you will immediately reinforce him and then let him play with the toy however he wishes. If he does not respond, what type of prompt will you use?

PARENT: It looks like I could model the play.

PARENT TRAINER: Excellent. Again, if he responds by throwing the ball, you will want to reinforce him. If he does not, what type of prompt will you use?

PARENT: A physical prompt to help him make the basket.

PARENT TRAINER: That sounds great, since you know that will enable him to expand his play.

Write down the examples on the flowchart, and have the parent practice this at home. Figure S19.1 illustrates how this information is written on the flowchart. Notice that the leading question is circled under "Parent chooses most appropriate prompt to get child to respond," to help the parent remember where to start. However, the less supportive prompt of a leading comment is also filled in. It is important to provide suggestions for all types of prompts, because the parent may be able to decrease the amount of support she gives as she practices at home.

Discuss and Assign Homework

1. Have the parent complete homework for *Teaching Your Child Play*. Review the rationale and the key points of *Teaching Your Child Play*. While reviewing the key points, remind the parent of any prompt rules she should use, and write the rules on the homework sheet in the parent manual. Help the parent identify the types of play prompts she will use, and highlight the prompts on the homework sheet.

Next, review the child's play goals and have the parent identify one to two goals she will practice at home. Play goals could include increasing the complexity of the child's play (e.g., use of pretend play), increasing the number of sequences used in play, or increasing the number of toys with which the child plays. Choose from the play goals that were developed during the first session.

Next, help the parent identify at least one play activity in which she will practice these goals. This should be an activity that the child enjoys at home. Once you have identified the activity, help the parent identify the type of play she will teach. For example, if the parent chooses to teach her child pretend play during play with cars, help her identify specific play with cars. This could include pushing the car to the gas station, washing the car, fixing a part of the car, and so

Child's goal: New action with a ball (make a basket)

Activity: Ball play

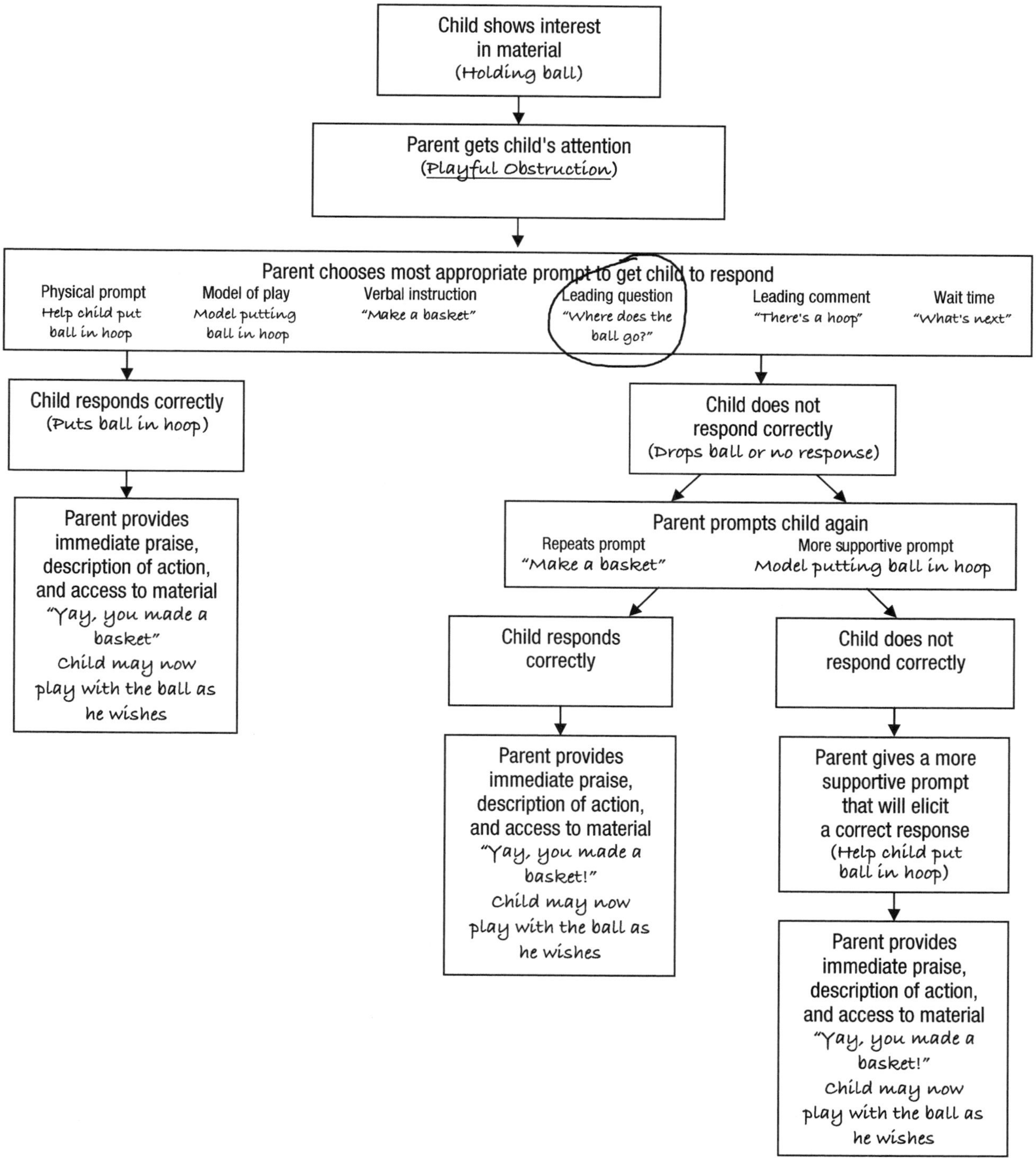

Figure S19.1. Example of completed Flowchart for Prompting Play (Appendix A, Form 10).

on. Write these ideas on the homework sheet. You will also want to help the parent identify the type of prompt with which she will start.

Once you and the parent have determined the goals, activities, and types of prompts, review the questions outlined on the homework sheet for *Teaching Your Child Play* and have the parent respond orally to the questions, based on her interaction with her child during this session. Some of the questions may not be applicable, because some specific prompting strategies may not be beneficial for the child. For example, some children may not require a physical prompt, while others may not yet be able to respond to leading questions. When this occurs, explain to the parent that she should not use that type of prompt, and cross off the question. If the parent is unable to respond to the questions, ask probing questions or demonstrate the strategies and have the parent identify the child's response. Instruct the parent to practice at home before the next session and to write down how her child responds. Explain that you will review the homework at the beginning of the next session.

2. Have the parent read *Review of the Direct Teaching Techniques* (Chapter 16 of the parent manual). Explain to the parent that the next session will be spent reviewing the direct teaching techniques. The format for this session is the same as that for the *Review of the Interactive Teaching Techniques*. The parent should come to the session with questions about the direct teaching techniques. The parent does not complete the homework for these techniques until the techniques have been reviewed and practiced during the session.

Troubleshooting Tips

Some children with ASD may become frustrated when their parents attempt to change their play. This is particularly true for children who have specific actions or patterns they like to complete with a toy (i.e., repetitive play). There are two possible solutions to this problem. The first is to remove toys that cause frustration from the environment. The second is to have the parent provide a quick prompt to the child at a level that she knows he can respond to, and then to allow the child to play with the toy his way. For example, if the goal is for the child to use a new play action, have the parent begin with a physical prompt. Once the routine is set, have the parent decrease support every third time. This strategy often decreases the amount of frustration for the child.

Another challenge is that it can be difficult to think of new ways to play with toys. When this occurs, take time to help the parent identify actions she can complete with the toys, new toys that could be added to expand the play theme, or emotions that could be brought into play. If the child has a sibling, or the parent has the occasion to be with other children, instruct her to observe how other children play with the toys. This often leads to additional ideas on how to play with toys. If you are providing training in a clinic or school setting, and you anticipate that the parent will have difficulty with thinking of play ideas at home, suggest that she bring some of her child's favorite toys with her to the next coaching session.

Review of the Direct Teaching Techniques

Session Goals

1. Improve the parent's ability to use the direct teaching techniques to enhance her child's social-communication skills.
2. Determine whether an additional session should be spent on the direct teaching techniques.

Materials

1. Parent manual
2. Completed Goal Development Form (Appendix A, Form 4)
3. Number of highly preferred toys
4. Variety of clear storage containers (e.g., jars with screw lids, Ziploc bags, large bins, shelving) in which to place desired items
5. Direct Teaching Techniques Review Sheet (Appendix A, Form 11)
6. Video-recording equipment
7. Direct Teaching Techniques Video Review Form (Appendix A, Form 12)
8. Individual Format Coaching Form (Appendix A, Form 8)

Outline of Session

- Explain the format of the session (3 minutes).
- Review the homework from *Teaching Your Child Play* (10–15 minutes).
- Discuss the direct teaching techniques, using Appendix A, Form 11 (10–15 minutes):
  1. Use *Follow Your Child's Lead*.
  2. Create an opportunity for your child to communicate.
  3. Wait for your child to communicate.
  4. Prompt your child to use more complex language, imitation, or play.
  5. Provide a more supportive (helpful) prompt as necessary.
  6. Reinforce and expand on your child's response.
- Demonstrate the direct teaching techniques (5–10 minutes).
- Have the parent practice the direct teaching techniques while you provide feedback (5–15 minutes).
- Record the parent–child interaction on video (5 minutes).
- Review the video with the parent (15 minutes).
- Discuss and assign homework:
  1. Have the parent complete homework for *Review of the Direct Teaching Techniques*.
  2. Have the parent read *Putting It All Together* (Chapter 17 of the parent manual).

About This Session

The purposes of this session are to improve the parent's ability to use the direct teaching techniques together, and to determine whether additional time should be spent on them. Before she begins *Putting It All Together*, the parent should be using *Follow Your Child's Lead*; using techniques to create an opportunity for her to communicate (*Playful Obstruction, Balanced Turns,* and *Communicative Temptations*); waiting for her child to communicate; prompting a more complex language, imitation, or play skill; adding more support as necessary to help the child respond; and reinforcing and expanding on her child's response. These steps are outlined in the parent manual and are reviewed in this session with the parent.

Explain the Format of the Session

Explain to the parent that this session will be spent practicing the use of the direct teaching techniques to increase the complexity of the child's skills and to decrease the child's reliance on prompts. The format of this session is essentially the same as the format that was used for the *Review of the Interactive Teaching Techniques.* Explain that you will provide a brief overview and demonstration of the techniques, and then the parent will practice the techniques while you record the parent–child interaction on video. Then you and the parent will review the video. The purpose of the video review is to help the parent begin to identify the techniques she uses and the effects they have on her child's behavior. Inform the parent that it may take two sessions to complete the steps of the review, particularly if two parents attend or if the parent is having difficulty with one or more aspects of the direct teaching techniques.

Review Homework from *Teaching Your Child Play*

Read over the homework with the parent. If the parent identifies challenges during the review, take time to provide solutions. One common challenge is thinking of new ways to play with toys. To help, ask the parent to describe the child's typical play and provide her with ways to expand it. Ask questions to help her identify actions, sequences, or emotions that could be brought into the play. If she has brought in some of her child's favorite toys, take time to help her identify actions for them. Another challenge occurs when the child has a specific way in which he prefers to play (e.g., repetitive play). As discussed in "Troubleshooting Tips" for Session 19, the parent could either remove the toys or provide a quick prompt to her child at a level that she knows he can successfully respond to, and then allow her child to play with the toy his way. If necessary, take time to review play prompts and to provide feedback.

Discuss the Direct Teaching Techniques, Using Form 11

Go through the Direct Teaching Techniques Review Sheet (Form 11) with the parent. This form can be found in Appendix A of this manual, as well as in the parent manual (Form 16.1 there).

Use this form to provide a brief review of the techniques. Allow the parent ample time to ask questions about the techniques before your demonstration. If the parent has questions about a specific technique or strategy, take this time to review it, demonstrate its use, and have the parent practice its use in isolation. It is important that the parent understands how to use all of the techniques before she attempts to use them together.

Review the six-step procedure the parent follows when using the direct teaching techniques:

1. Use *Follow Your Child's Lead*.
2. Create an opportunity for your child to communicate.
3. Wait for your child to communicate.
4. Prompt your child to use more complex language, imitation, or play.
5. Provide a more supportive prompt as necessary.
6. Reinforce and expand on the child's response.

Ask the parent to identify the techniques she will use for each step. When discussing Step 4, remind her to prompt only one type of skill at a time. Ask her to identify the prompts she will use when teaching each type of skill (language, imitation, and play).

Demonstrate the Direct Teaching Techniques

Ask the parent which specific goal she would like you to target in your demonstration of the techniques. Then explain the type of prompt you will use to target the goal. During the demonstration, identify each technique or strategy you use and the child's response. For example, the trainer might say to Sam's mother:

> "Sam was playing with the cars. I moved into his line of sight and held up more cars to gain his attention. He looked at me. I prompted language by asking a question: 'What do you want?' He said, 'Car.' I reinforced and expanded his response by giving him the red car and saying, 'Red car.'"

Take time to demonstrate any technique or strategy that has been difficult for the parent to implement. Once you have provided two to three demonstrations, have the parent identify the techniques or strategies you used for each step. Because the interaction moves quickly, have the parent focus on one step at a time—for example,

> "Watch to see which strategy I use to prompt language."
> "What technique did I use?"
> "How did he respond?"

This approach helps the parent begin to observe how specific techniques and strategies affect her child's social-communication skills.

Have the Parent Practice the Direct Teaching Techniques While You Provide Feedback

Suggest specific techniques and strategies for the parent to use for the practice—for example,

> "After you follow Sam's lead to an activity and gain his attention, use a question to increase his use of verbs. For example, if he is playing with the cars, you could stop the car and say, 'What do you want the car to do?' His response might be 'Drive,' 'Push,' or 'Crash.'"

Plan what additional support to use if the child does not respond, and remind the parent to reinforce the child. Have the parent practice for at least 5 minutes and until she is successful.

Record the Parent–Child Interaction on Video

Record the parent–child interaction on video for 5 minutes. Again, if two parents are present, separate them to allow for individual practice. Provide a clear transition statement to the parent before you begin the recording, and instruct the parent to use the direct teaching techniques to increase her child's language, imitation, or play skills. Remind her to prompt only one type of skill at a time. Complete the Individual Format Coaching Form (Form 8 in Appendix A), while you observe and record the interaction in lieu of providing live feedback. This form helps you identify any direct teaching techniques that may require additional coaching. This form is for your reference and is not shared with the parent.

Review the Video with the Parent

The purpose of reviewing the video with the parent is to help her identify which techniques and strategies she is using and how they affect her child's behavior. This is accomplished by watching the video together, having the parent complete the Direct Teaching Techniques Video Review Form (Appendix A, Form 12), and asking open-ended and probing questions.

Begin by giving the parent Form 12 in Appendix A. Explain to the parent that you will watch the video together, and instruct her to look for examples of when she used particular techniques or strategies to prompt a skill and the child's response. Because the interactions happen so fast, you should pause the video and watch the clips a number of times. Have the parent tell you if she would like you to stop the video to review any aspect of the interaction. If the parent does not have you stop the tape after 2 minutes, stop it and ask the parent an open-ended question (e.g., "What did you observe?"). If she is unable to respond, provide her with a specific behavior to look for while she watches the tape—for example, "Let's watch the tape and pause it when you use a strategy to prompt language."

It is also helpful to have the parent watch a clip of when she used all of the steps encompassed in the direct teaching procedure. When doing this, ask the parent the following questions, and watch the same clip a number of times to provide her with the opportunity to observe each step.

1. "What techniques did you use to create an opportunity for your child to communicate?"
2. "How did your child communicate with you?"
3. "What type of language/imitation/play did you prompt?"
4. "How did your child respond?"

Continue to watch the remainder of the video. Provide the parent with specific behaviors to look for as she watches the video, and pause it when these behaviors are noticed. The feedback during the review of the video should be primarily positive. However, if the parent has difficulty with a specific technique or strategy and you do not think she is aware of it, the video can be used to provide feedback. For example, if the parent provides a prompt before she has her child's attention, pause the video when you observe this, and ask the parent why she thinks her child does not respond. Have the parent compare her child's response to the response at a time when she gains the child's attention before she prompts.

Discuss and Assign Homework

1. Have the parent complete the homework for *Review of the Direct Teaching Techniques*. Begin by reviewing the rationale and steps involved in the direct teaching techniques. Ask the parent to identify the techniques and strategies she feels may be most effective for each of the steps included in the direct teaching techniques, and write these on the homework sheet in the parent manual. For example, ask the parent to identify the techniques she feels may be most effective in creating an opportunity for her child to communicate. These could include *Playful Obstruction, Balanced Turns,* and/or any of the *Communicative Temptations.* Write these down next to "Create an opportunity for your child to communicate." Continue this process and write down next to each step any technique or strategy on which the parent should focus. For example, if the child responds well to the *cloze procedure*, write this strategy next to "Give a least supportive prompt."

Review the child's individualized goals and identify at least one language, imitation, and play goal the parent would like to address at home. Write the goals on the homework sheet next to "Child's goals." Next, help the parent identify activities and daily routines in which she can target the goal. Try to identify at least one activity and one daily routine for each goal, to help the parent use techniques across settings. If necessary, refer to the Daily Activity Schedule to identify activities the child enjoys.

The next step is to determine the type of prompt the parent will use to teach each identified child goal. Assist the parent by making sure the prompt is appropriate to the child's skill level. Instruct the parent to practice these techniques at home and to write down how her child responds. Explain that homework will be reviewed at the beginning of the next session.

2. Have the parent read *Putting It All Together* (Chapter 17 of the parent manual). Explain to the parent that the next session will be spent learning to use the interactive and direct teaching techniques together, and determining the best time to use the different types of techniques. The parent should come to the session with any questions she may have. The parent should not complete the homework for *Putting It All Together* until it has been reviewed and practiced during the session.

Troubleshooting Tips

When a parent does not want to be recorded on video, observe her interacting with her child, and complete Appendix A, Form 12, on that basis. Model a variety of examples to help the parent identify how the techniques affect her child's communication. During parent practice, you should continue to provide feedback in the same manner as during previous sessions.

Another challenge is that some parents change their interaction style while being recorded. In this case, pause the camera, provide feedback, and then resume recording. It is important to have positive examples for the parent to view on video. One of the most frequent changes in parent behavior is an increase in the use of prompts and a decrease in the use of interactive teaching techniques. This causes problems for two reasons: (1) The parent does not have the child's attention before she prompts, and (2) use of the direct teaching techniques more than one-third of the time can cause child frustration and increase the child's reliance on prompts. To address the first challenge, remind the parent to use *Follow Your Child's Lead* to determine what the child is interested in before creating an opportunity for the child to communicate. This step increases the effectiveness of the direct teaching techniques. To address the second challenge, remind the parent to use the direct teaching techniques only about a third of the time. This aspect is important to decrease frustration and to increase the child's ability to communicate without support.

Sessions 21–22

Putting It All Together

Session Goal

1. Teach the parent to use the interactive teaching techniques and direct teaching techniques together to enhance her child's social-communication skills.

Materials

1. Parent manual
2. Completed Goal Development Form (Appendix A, Form 4)
3. Number of highly preferred toys
4. Variety of storage containers (e.g., clear containers with screw lids, Ziploc bags, large bins, shelving) in which to place desired items
5. *Putting It All Together* Review Sheet (Appendix A, Form 13)

Outline of Session

- Explain the format of these sessions (5–10 minutes).
- Review homework (10–15 minutes each session):

> *Review of the Direct Teaching Techniques* (Session 21)
> *Putting It All Together* (Session 22)

- Introduce the rationale for *Putting It All Together* (5 minutes, Session 21):

  It improves the child's social engagement.
  It improves the complexity of the child's social-communication skills.
  It decreases the child's frustration and reliance on prompts.

- Discuss the key points of *Putting It All Together* (5–10 minutes):

  Use *Follow Your Child's Lead.*
  Create an opportunity for your child to engage or communicate.
  Wait for your child to engage or communicate.
  Choice point: Model *or* prompt a more complex response.
  Reinforce and expand on your child's response.
  Pace the interaction to keep your child engaged and learning.

- Discuss when to use interactive techniques and when to use direct techniques:

  Emphasize the role of the environment.

- Demonstrate use of *Putting It All Together* (5–10 minutes):

- Have the parent practice *Putting It All Together* while you provide feedback (30–45 minutes each session).

- Discuss and assign homework (10–15 minutes):

  1. Have the parent complete homework for *Putting It All Together.*

- Discuss the format of the remaining sessions (2 minutes).

Explain the Format of These Sessions

Now that the parent has learned to use all of the techniques encompassed in this program, the remaining sessions are spent in improving the parent's ability to use the techniques together, updating the child's goals, and developing new goals. The parent should be able to use the techniques together before the goals are updated. The amount of time spent helping the parent use the techniques together may vary from one to two sessions, depending on the parent's skills.

Review Homework from *Review of the Direct Teaching Techniques* (Session 21)

Begin the session by reviewing the homework from *Review of the Direct Teaching Techniques.* Any challenges usually occur because the parent is unable to elicit a specific skill or the child becomes frustrated. Take time to help the parent identify solutions. Reasons why the child does not respond or gets frustrated are often similar and can be related to the child's lack of motivation or inability to respond (e.g., because he is not given enough support). If the child is not motivated, it may be because he is not interested in the object or because he already has access to the object he wants. In this case, remind the parent to follow the child's lead and use a technique like *Communicative Temptations* to ensure that the child is motivated before she prompts. If the child needs more support to respond, tell the parent the type of prompt she should use (e.g., a physical prompt).

Review Homework from *Putting It All Together* (Session 22)

Review the homework from *Putting It All Together*. Challenges are usually related to the parent's having difficulty knowing when to use the interactive versus direct teaching techniques. Take time to help the parent identify solutions by providing concrete suggestions for which techniques are best suited to specific daily activities.

Introduce the Rationale for *Putting It All Together*

Use the pyramid diagram in the parent manual (Figure 1.1 there; Figure S1.3 in Session 1, this manual) to help the parent visualize how the techniques are used together. Now that the parent is familiar with all of the techniques, she should move up and down the three levels of the pyramid during interactions with her child. Explain to the parent that if she spends too much time at the top level of the pyramid, her child will become frustrated; however, if she spends too much time using only the techniques at the lower level, her child may not be challenged enough. The goal of this session is to learn to balance the use of the techniques in order to keep the child optimally engaged in the interaction, while teaching him new skills.

It Improves the Child's Social Engagement

The interactive teaching techniques are used to increase the child's social engagement and initiation skills. They also lay the groundwork for the direct teaching techniques. If the child is not engaged or communicating, the direct teaching techniques will not be as effective.

It Improves the Complexity of the Child's Social-Communication Skills

The direct teaching techniques are used to elicit specific language, imitation, or play skills. Providing a balance between the interactive and the direct teaching techniques increases the child's engagement and spontaneity.

It Decreases the Child's Frustration and Reliance on Prompts

Children learn and maintain skills best when they are motivated and engaged in an activity. Learning when to respond to a child's initiations and model a more complex response, and when to prompt, helps to increase the child's motivation, decrease reliance on prompts, and decrease frustration.

Discuss the Key Points of *Putting It All Together*

Refer to the *Putting It All Together* Review Sheet (Form 13) in Appendix A of this manual; see also Form 17.1 of the parent manual) to help the parent identify techniques to use for each of the steps listed below. Emphasize that the first three steps are the same, regardless of the type of teaching technique chosen (interactive or direct). These three steps lay the foundation for the program and focus on increasing engagement, motivation, and spontaneous skills. Once the child is engaged, the parent can choose to continue with an interactive technique (modeling a language or play skill without requiring a specific response) or a direct teaching technique (prompting a more complex language, imitation, or play response).

Use *Follow Your Child's Lead*

The *Follow Your Child's Lead* technique is used with both interactive and direct teaching techniques (except for *Teaching Your Child Receptive Language*) to increase engagement and motivation. It is also effective in increasing the length of the interaction.

Create an Opportunity for Your Child to Engage or Communicate

Discuss the interactive teaching techniques that are most effective in increasing engagement (*Imitate Your Child, Animation*) and obtaining communication from the child (*Playful Obstruction, Balanced Turns, Communicative Temptations*), and circle these techniques on the review sheet.

Wait for Your Child to Engage or Communicate

The parent should wait for her child to engage or communicate before she chooses to model or prompt. Whether the child responds and if so, how, informs the choice of what to model or prompt. It also ensures the child is motivated.

Choice Point: Model *or* Prompt a More Complex Response

Once the parent determines what the child is interested in, she will choose either an interactive or a direct teaching technique. When using an interactive technique, the parent models a new skill at the same time she reinforces the child for initiating. When using a direct technique, the parent prompts a new skill and only provides reinforcement after the child uses the new skill. Remind the parent that if she starts with a direct teaching technique (e.g., asking a direct question as part of *Teaching Your Child Expressive Language*), she must follow through, making sure the child succeeds before providing the reinforcement.

Reinforce and Expand on Your Child's Response

When using either set of techniques, the parent should provide her child with the desired object and expand on his response.

Pace the Interaction to Keep Your Child Engaged and Learning

The overall goal is to balance the use of the techniques. The interactive techniques keep the child optimally aroused and in the interaction; they do not push too hard. The direct techniques increase the complexity of the child's skills; they make sure to push him to the next level.

Discuss When to Use Interactive Techniques and When to Use Direct Techniques

Review with the parent when to use interactive versus direct teaching techniques. Interactive teaching techniques are used to elicit engagement, to increase motivation, and to create spontaneity. Since the child is not required to produce a specific response, these techniques are easier for the child. Therefore, if the child is highly frustrated, the parent would want to use the interactive teaching techniques to elicit engagement. In addition, since the interactive techniques do not use prompting to elicit a specific behavior, they are helpful for building spontaneous skills and should be used once a child has begun using a new skill with least supportive prompts.

Direct teaching techniques are most effective when the child is motivated, the parent has time to follow through, and the parent can control access to the object or activity that the child wants. The one exception to this rule is that the parent should use direct teaching techniques if the child is using an inappropriate behavior that needs to be changed. For example, if the child is hitting the parent to gain the parent's attention, the parent should use a verbal or physical prompt to get her child to use an appropriate behavior (e.g., a word or tap on the arm), and only then give the child her attention.

Emphasize the Role of the Environment

Discuss with the parent the role the environment plays in the choice of techniques. It is often difficult to prompt a child in uncontrolled and public environments. These environments are challenging not only because of the number and degree of stimuli they involve, but because the parent may have difficulty controlling access to reinforcers. Such access is critical to success of the direct teaching techniques. The parent should choose to use the interactive teaching techniques when there are time constraints (i.e., they are waiting in line, the store is closing), when she is in an uncontrolled environment, when she is unable to gain the child's attention, and/or when the child is highly frustrated.

Remind the parent that she should use direct teaching techniques only about one-third of the time. If these techniques are used more often, it may cause the child to become dependent on prompts or highly frustrated.

Demonstrate Use of *Putting It All Together*

Ask the parent whether there is a specific goal she would like you to target, and explain how you could use both the interactive and the direct teaching techniques to target the goal. For example, if the goal is to increase the child's use of single words, explain that after using *Follow Your Child's Lead* and creating an opportunity for the child to engage or communicate, you could respond to the child's communication by modeling the new word (an interactive teaching technique), or you could prompt with choices and a verbal model (a direct teaching technique) to elicit the new word. Reiterate to the parent that you would use interactive techniques approximately two-thirds of the time, and direct techniques approximately one-third of the time. This balance increases the child's use of new skills and decreases his reliance on prompts.

After discussing these issues with the parent, demonstrate the use of the techniques together. Identify the techniques as you use them and the child's response. For example, the trainer might say to Sam's mother:

> "Sam was playing with the cars. I moved into his line of sight and held up more cars to gain his attention. He said, 'Can I have the car?' I used the direct technique of *Teaching Your Child Expressive Language* to expand his language. I began by asking a direct question: 'Why? He said, 'Can I have the car?' I added more support by using the cloze procedure: "Because … ?" Again he said, 'Can I have the car?' I used a choice to add more support to help him respond: 'Because you want to play or sleep?' He said 'To play.' I gave him the red car and expanded on his response: 'Why do you want the car? Because you want to play.'"

The trainer would then explain why she chose to use the direct teaching technique. Alternatively, she could discuss how an interactive teaching technique could be used to address this goal:

> "Sam was playing with the cars. I moved into his line of sight and held up more cars to gain his attention. He said, 'Can I have the car?' I used *Modeling and Expanding Language*. That is, I responded to his communication by giving him the car, and expanded by saying, '*Why* do you want the car? Because *you* want to *play* with the car.'"

Have the Parent Practice *Putting It All Together* While You Provide Feedback

Announce to the parent that she should now practice the techniques to address her child's goals. Ideally, the parent will be able to use the direct and interactive teaching techniques together. However, if the parent is having difficulty balancing the use of the techniques, it may be helpful to give her a concrete rule to follow—for example, "Demonstrate a new skill three times and then prompt it. This balance will increase his engagement and decrease his frustration."

At this point in the program, you should be primarily giving positive feedback. When you give corrective feedback, it should describe the situation but should not tell her a specific technique or strategy to use. Less directive corrective feedback can be given in the form of a question (e.g., "Why do you think Sam is having difficulty responding to you?") or a comment (e.g., "Sam is playing with the car"). This type of feedback helps the parent move toward independence.

Discuss and Assign Homework

1. Have the parent complete homework for *Putting It All Together*. The homework sheet remains the same for both sessions of *Putting It All Together*. Make a photocopy of the homework sheet in the parent manual, so the parent has a clean copy to complete after the second session.

Review the key points of *Putting It All Together* with the parent, and write down on the homework sheet any techniques on which the parent should focus. Because you typically spend two sessions on *Putting It All Together*, it can be effective to choose one or two steps for the parent to practice after each session. Circle the steps the parent should focus on after each session. For example, if the parent does not always gain her child's attention, circle "Create an opportunity for your child to engage or communicate," and write down techniques she should use next to this step. At this point, the parent should take the leading role in identifying the techniques and strategies she will use for each step.

Next, help the parent identify the goals she would like to address at home, and to select at least three activities in which she will practice the techniques across settings. If necessary, refer to the Daily Activity Schedule and help the parent identify activities her child enjoys. Once the parent has identified each goal and activity, have her identify the techniques she will use to achieve the goal. This information should also be written on the homework sheet.

Review the questions on the homework sheet and have the parent respond orally to the questions, based on her interaction with her child during this session. Instruct the parent to practice the techniques at home and to write down her response to the questions, based on her interactions with her child during a variety of activities.

Discuss the Format of the Remaining Sessions

Depending on the parent's ability to implement the techniques, the next session may be spent completing one of the following activities:

1. Have the parent continue to practice techniques; this may include a home visit or a video review of the parent using the techniques at home.
2. Update the child's goals.
3. Devise new goals.

Strategies to implement the second and third activities are outlined in Session 23. If you feel the parent should have additional time to practice the techniques (the first activity), follow the format for Sessions 21–22.

Troubleshooting Tips

The most common challenge that occurs in *Putting It All Together* is that the parent uses one type of technique more than another. When this occurs, prompt the parent to move between the two types of techniques. It may also be helpful to record the parent–child interaction on video and then to review the video. During this review, have the parent identify when she uses the interactive techniques and when she uses the direct techniques.

If the parent reports difficulty with use of the techniques at home, it may be beneficial to set up a home visit. If possible, schedule the home visit during a daily activity that is particularly challenging for the parent, to help her use the techniques. During the home visit, follow the usual practice of first explaining the techniques you will use, then demonstrating them, and then having the parent practice while you give feedback. If you are unable to make a home visit and the parent has access to a video camera, have her record the interaction, and review the video with her during the next session.

Update Goals

Session Goals

1. Help the parent update her child's goals.
2. Help the parent develop goals to target at home after the program is complete.

Materials

1. Parent manual
2. Completed Goal Development Form (Appendix A, Form 4)
3. Two copies of Session Data Sheet (Appendix A, Form 14)
4. Number of highly preferred toys
5. Variety of clear storage containers (e.g., jars with screw lids, Ziploc bags, large bins, shelving) in which to place desired items
6. Video-recording equipment
7. Blank Goal Development Form (Appendix A, Form 4)

Outline of Session

- Explain the format of the session (5 minutes).
- Review the homework from *Putting It All Together* (10–15 minutes).
- Review and update goals (30–40 minutes):

    Choose a goal to update.
    Assess the child's progress toward achieving the goal.
    Update the goal when appropriate.
    Have the parent practice the techniques to target the updated goal while you provide feedback.
    Repeat this process to update all goals.

- Record the parent–child interaction on video (5 minutes).
- Develop goals to target at home (5 minutes)
- Discuss and assign homework (10–15 minutes):

    1. Have the parent complete homework for *Moving Forward*.

- Explain the format of the final session.

Explain the Format of the Session

The purposes of this session are for the parent to update one or more of her child's goals, and to determine how to target those goals for practice between this session and the follow-up session. You will do the following:

1. Help the parent select a goal to assess and update.
2. Assess the child's progress toward achieving the goal while the parent records data on the child's performance.
3. Update the goal when appropriate.
4. Have the parent practice the techniques to target the updated goal while you provide feedback.

During this session, you can also record the parent–child interaction on video. The video is used to improve the parent's use of the techniques and her ability to provide feedback to herself.

Review the Homework from *Putting It All Together*

Review the homework for *Putting It All Together*. If the parent has recorded an interaction at home, take time to review the video and provide feedback to the parent. The format of the video review should be similar to the format used in the *Review of the Interactive Teaching Techniques* and *Review of the Direct Teaching Techniques* sessions. Ask the parent to identify techniques that worked well and to provide possible solutions when the techniques were not effective.

Review and Update Goals

Most of this session is spent reviewing and updating goals. Select one goal at a time to update; demonstrate how to use the techniques to address the goal; and then have the parent practice using the techniques to address the selected goal while you provide feedback. Target each goal individually to help the parent adapt her use of the techniques. This helps the parent become more comfortable with the techniques and increases the parent's ability to generalize use of the techniques for a wide range of goals.

Choose a Goal to Update

Have the parent review her child's original goals, and then help her identify a measurable goal to update. Begin with the goal that the child has made the most progress toward achieving throughout the program. For example, in the case of Brian, the following measurable goals were developed in Session 1:

1. Brian will increase the amount of time he is engaged with a play partner to at least 5 minutes.
2. Brian will use a point, vocalizations, or single word to initiate requests for actions or objects at 5 out of 10 opportunities.
3. Brian will imitate conventional gestures (e.g., wave, point, clap) at 3 out of 6 opportunities.
4. Brian will use toys for their intended purpose at least 50% of the time when provided with a model.

Brian has made the most progress toward achieving the second goal, his expressive language goal. Therefore, the trainer would suggest updating this goal, while also asking the parent whether she would prefer to begin updating one of the other goals.

Assess the Child's Progress toward Achieving the Goal

Explain to the parent that you will use the various types of prompts to target the child's progress toward meeting the selected goal. She is to observe and mark the child's response to the prompts on a copy of the Session Data Sheet (Appendix A, Form 14). First, have the parent write the goal selected for updating on the form under the "Goal" heading. Then instruct the parent to make a "+" in the appropriate column for those prompts that are effective with the child. If you use an interactive teaching technique (no prompts) and the child is able to use the skill, the parent should mark a "+" under the "Spontaneous" heading. As you interact with the child, explain the techniques you are using and the child's responses.

The completed Session Data Sheet lets you and the parent know what prompt level the child requires to meet the goal. If the child is able to use the skill spontaneously the majority of the time, then the goal has been met, and new goals should be developed. Explain to the parent that if time permits, all of her child's measurable goals will be updated. Your demonstration for each goal should last no more than 5 minutes.

Update the Goal When Appropriate

Depending on the child's progress, some of the goals may remain the same. The number of goals developed varies, depending on the family, and may range from one to four. Goals should be directly related to the child's skills at home. Write the new goals down on the homework sheet for *Moving Forward* (see "Discuss and Assign Homework," below) and on a blank copy of the Goal Development Form (Appendix A, Form 4). This new Goal Development form will be referred to during the final and follow-up sessions to help track progress.

Have the Parent Practice the Techniques to Target the Updated Goal While You Provide Feedback

The majority of the session should be spent on having the parent interact with her child and receive feedback. Feedback should be directly related to her use of the techniques and her child's response. While the parent has learned to use all of the techniques together, it continues to be important to coach on only one to two techniques at a time. Select the technique that will lead to the most success for the parent and the child, emphasize that technique, and provide coaching on that technique. As the parent practices and you provide feedback, collect data with the Session Data Sheet (Appendix A, Form 14).

Repeat This Process to Update All Goals

If time permits, repeat the process described above until all goals have been updated. Having the parent become part of the process improves her ability to track her child's progress in this program and in other programs. This element is important, because it empowers the parent to take the lead in programming decisions for her child.

Record the Parent–Child Interaction on Video

Once the parent is successfully using the interactive and direct teaching techniques together, record a 5-minute parent–child interaction on video. The purpose of this video is to emphasize the techniques that work well with the child, improve the parent's ability to evaluate her use of techniques, and demonstrate to the parent the change in her child's skills as a result of her work. If applicable, inform the parent that this video will be reviewed during the last treatment session.

Discuss and Assign Homework

1. Have the parent complete homework for *Moving Forward*. The homework sheet is the same for this sessions as for the final session (*Moving Forward*), because the parent is practicing use of the techniques together. Make a photocopy of the *Moving Forward* homework sheet in the parent in manual, so the parent has a clean copy to complete after the final session.

Begin by reviewing the intervention procedure. Ask the parent to identify the techniques she feels may be most effective for each of the steps of this intervention, and write these down on the homework sheet. For example, ask the parent to identify the techniques she feels may be most effective in creating an opportunity for her child to engage (*Imitate Your Child, Animation*) or communicate (*Playful Obstruction, Balanced Turns*, and/or any of the *Communicative Temptations*). Write these down next to "Create an opportunity for your child to engage or communicate." Continue this process, and write down next to each step any technique or strategy on which the parent should focus. For example, if the child responds well to the *Teaching Your Child Expressive Language* prompt of choices, write this down next to "Model *or* prompt a more complex response." If you feel the parent requires more practice with either the interactive or direct techniques, circle the corresponding word (i.e., "model" or "prompt") and identify the techniques she should use.

If applicable, review the child's new individualized goals that were developed during the session and written on the homework sheet. Have the parent identify activities in which she can target the goals at home. Try to identify at least three activities for each goal, to help the parent use techniques across settings. If necessary, refer to the Daily Activity Schedule to identify activities the child enjoys.

Next, have the parent identify the techniques she feels may be most effective to address each goal. Write these down next to "Intervention techniques to achieve goal."

Instruct the parent to practice these techniques at home and to write down how her child responds. Inform the parent that if she is having difficulty implementing any of the techniques at home, she can record the interaction on video and bring the video to the next session for feedback. As discussed in *Putting It All Together*, you may also schedule a home visit to help the parent use the techniques at home.

Explain the Format of the Final Session

The format of the final session may vary, depending on the parent's needs. Typically, this session is spent practicing the techniques the parent can use over the next month. In some cases, you may choose to watch the videos of the initial and final parent–child interactions, to show the parent the progress her child has made over the course of the program. Take time to let the parent know what to expect during her final session.

Session 24

Moving Forward (Final Session)

Session Goals

1. Improve the parent's independent use of the interactive and direct teaching techniques, to enhance her child's social-communication skills.
2. Help the parent observe her child's progress.

Materials

1. Parent manual
2. Completed Goal Development Form (Appendix A, Form 4) from Session 23
3. Number of highly preferred toys
4. Variety of clear storage containers (e.g., jars with screw lids, Ziploc bags, large bins, shelving) in which to place desired items
5. Video recordings from Sessions 1 and 23, and player (optional)
6. Parent Satisfaction Survey (Appendix A, Form 15)

Outline of Session

- Review the *Moving Forward* homework sheet from *Update Goals* (10–15 minutes).
- Have the parent practice using the intervention while you provide feedback (30–45 minutes).
- Review video clips (10–15 minutes).
- Have the parent complete the Parent Satisfaction Survey (5–10 minutes).
- Schedule follow-up sessions.
- Discuss and assign homework (10–15 minutes):
    1. Have the parent complete another homework sheet for *Moving Forward*.

Review the *Moving Forward* Homework Sheet from *Update Goals*

Begin the session by reviewing the homework from the previous session and discussing whether the parent had any difficulty using the techniques at home. At this point in the program, challenges typically involve use of a technique at home or during a particular activity. Ideally, you can set up a home visit or review a video of the interaction with the parent. When these options are not possible, use this session to discuss solutions, provide a demonstration of techniques that are difficult to implement, and provide feedback to the parent as she uses the techniques.

Have the Parent Practice Using the Intervention While You Provide Feedback

At this point, demonstration of techniques is no longer required. However, if the parent is having difficulty implementing a particular technique or has questions, it may be beneficial to demonstrate the skill quickly and then have the parent practice. The type of feedback should be primarily positive, to emphasize the techniques that work well with the child. Emphasizing what works well improves the likelihood that the parent will use these strategies at home.

Review Video Clips

Review the video from Session 23 with the parent. Help the parent identify techniques that are effective with her child, techniques that are not effective, reasons why the latter techniques may not be effective, and additional ways she could enhance the effectiveness of the techniques. This is accomplished by asking open-ended questions (e.g., "What did you notice in that interaction?") and probing questions (e.g., "What technique could you use to gain his attention?").

In many cases, it can be valuable to show the parent the video from Session 1 and compare that to the video from Session 23. This comparison will allow the parent to observe the changes in her child's skill level. If you choose this option, it is recommended that you preview both videos before the session, to ensure that the parent will observe positive changes. Allow the parent to watch 2–3 minutes of each clip, and ask her what she notices about her own and her child's behavior. It is important that the parent end the program feeling successful about her ability to affect her child's development, or she is unlikely to continue using the intervention techniques.

Have the Parent Complete the Parent Satisfaction Survey

Take time at the end of the session to have the parent complete the Parent Satisfaction Survey (Form 15 in Appendix A). This will give you important information on ways to improve your parent training skills.

Schedule Follow-Up Sessions

Follow-up sessions are scheduled once a month as needed, to help the parent continue to use techniques to address her child's goals. Clinical experience reveals that if a parent does not return for follow-up sessions, her use of the techniques declines significantly. However, with attendance at follow-up sessions, parents are able to maintain use of the techniques and thus to continue increasing their children's social-communication skills. Ideally, follow-up sessions are conducted in the home; however, the clinic setting is effective if this is not possible.

Discuss and Assign Homework

1. Have the parent complete another homework sheet for *Moving Forward*. Have the parent identify at least two goals that she will target over the next month. Write down the activities and the techniques she will use to address the goals. Instruct the parent to write down at home how her child responds. This homework is reviewed during the first follow-up coaching session, if applicable. The parent may choose to video-record an interaction over the next month and receive feedback on the interaction during the follow-up session.

Follow-Up Session

Session Goals

1. Maintain the parent's ability to implement the intervention.
2. Review and update goals.
3. Teach the parent to use the techniques to address new goals.

Materials

1. Parent manual
2. Completed Goal Development Form (Appendix A, Form 4)
3. Social-Communication Checklist (Appendix A, Form 3)
4. Blank Goal Development Form (Appendix A, Form 4)
5. *Putting It All Together* Review Sheet (Appendix A, Form 13)
6. Five to six highly motivating toys and activities, including two sets of some toys, and some toys the child needs help to use
7. Variety of storage containers for holding desired items (e.g., clear plastic containers with screw lids, Ziploc bags, large bins, shelving)
8. Homework: *Follow-Up Session* (Appendix A, Form 16)

Outline of Session

- Review homework from the last treatment session (10–15 minutes).
- Review and update the child's goals (10–15 minutes):

    Have the parent report on the child's current skills.
    Observe a brief parent–child interaction and complete the Social-
       Communication Checklist.
    Update goals for the child with the parent.

- Provide a brief review of *Putting It All Together* (5 minutes).
- Demonstrate use of techniques to target updated goals (10–15 minutes).
- Have the parent practice the techniques while you provide feedback (30–40
  minutes).
- Discuss and assign homework (10–15 minutes):

    1. Have parent complete Homework: *Follow-Up Session* (Appendix A,
       Form 16).

Review Homework from the Last Treatment Session

Begin the session by asking the parent an open-ended question about how things have gone at home since the last coaching session. Next, review the homework sheet completed after the *Moving Forward* session. Review of this homework allows you to assess the parent's needs and informs the session. This review may take longer than previous sessions, given the amount of time between sessions. If the parent did not complete the homework, read over the questions and have the parent respond orally. If the parent reports significant challenges with a technique or goal, take time to discuss the goal or technique, demonstrate use of the techniques to address the goal, and have the parent practice. If the parent has brought a video to review, take time to review the video, answer any questions, and provide feedback before you update the child's goals.

Review and Update the Child's Goals

Have the Parent Report on the Child's Current Skills

Review the child's current goals, as recorded on the homework sheet for *Moving Forward* and on the Goal Development Form from Session 23. Ask the parent to report how the child has progressed on these goals since the last coaching session. For example, you might ask:

- "You were working on increasing your child's single words. How is he communicating now?"
- "You were working on increasing your child's functional play. How is he playing now?"

Observe a Brief Parent–Child Interaction and Complete the Social-Communication Checklist

Have the parent use the intervention techniques with her child while you observe. This observation will help you determine the child's current skill level, as well as the parent's continued ability to use the intervention techniques. While she interacts with her child, use the Social-Communication Checklist (Appendix A, Form 3) to record information on the child's use of skills in each of the four core areas.

Update Goals for the Child with the Parent

Based on the parent's report and your observation of the parent–child interaction, you may choose to develop new goals for the child. In this event, write the updated goals on a new copy of the Goal Development sheet (Appendix A, Form 4) and on the homework sheet that you will be sending home with the parent at the end of the session. If you feel that the current goals are appropriate and the parent would like to continue targeting these goals at home, keep the same Goal Development Form and write the goals on the homework sheet that you will send home with the parent.

Provide a Brief Review of *Putting It All Together*

Briefly review the key points of techniques, using the *Putting It All Together* Review Sheet (Appendix A, Form 13). Give the parent an opportunity to ask any questions she might have about any of the techniques or how to use them at home to address her child's goals.

Demonstrate Use of Techniques to Target Updated Goals

Demonstrate use of the intervention techniques to target any new goals the parent has identified or goals that have presented a challenge at home. During the demonstration, identify the techniques you use and the child's response. It is also important to identify how both the interactive and direct teaching techniques can be used to address the child's updated goals. This explanation helps the parent to continue balancing the use of the techniques. If the parent has reported difficulty with any specific intervention techniques or strategies, be sure to demonstrate them with the child.

Have the Parent Practice the Techniques While You Provide Feedback

Parent practice should make up the majority of the session. Have the parent practice using either techniques that have been challenging at home or ones that are needed to address new goals. Remember that feedback should not be provided on too many techniques at once. If you notice that the parent is having difficulty with a particular technique, focus on that technique.

Discuss and Assign Homework

1. **Have the parent complete Homework:** *Follow-Up Session* (Appendix A, Form 16). Review the goals that the parent has identified during the session, and ask the parent whether

there are additional goals she would like to address. Write any additional goals on the homework sheet and on the child's current Goal Development Form. Next, have the parent identify the activities in which she will use the techniques, and the techniques she will use to address the goals. The number of goals identified should be individualized for the family and should range from one to four. If the parent is struggling with a specific technique or behavior during certain activities, have the parent record an interaction on video and bring the video to you to review during an additional follow-up session.

PART III

Group Parent Training Program Session Guidelines

Parents who receive training in the group format should attend a total of 12 sessions. Six of these are 2-hour group sessions (for parents without children), and six are 45-minute individual coaching sessions (for each parent and child). Research suggests that individual practice with feedback is essential for helping parents learn to use intervention strategies, and thus we do not recommend the group format without individual coaching. Ideally, the program is conducted over the course of 12 weeks, with a session (group or individual) scheduled each week (see Table III). However, we recognize that each practitioner's constraints are different, and thus that the program may need to be presented in a shorter or longer period of time. If the length of time needs to be condensed, we recommend running the program over the course of 6 weeks, with each group presentation preceding the coaching session on the same topic by several days, to give parents the opportunity to practice at home before receiving feedback.

We recommend that you hold the group sessions in the evening. If possible, plan to provide child care. We recommend that the individual coaching sessions be held during the daytime—possibly all on the same day—for 45 minutes each, with 15-minute breaks between families. Upon completion of this parent training program, we recommend that you provide follow-up sessions to each family once every 1–3 months for up to a year, to encourage each parent to maintain her use of the intervention, address any new concerns, and help her understand how the techniques can address new goals. This is particularly helpful for families receiving the group training format, as they will have had fewer opportunities to practice and receive feedback than families who receive individual training.

We have found that the ideal group size is about 6–8 parents. We recommend keeping the group size no larger than 12 participants, in order to have time for all parents to participate.

Because the techniques build upon each other, it is important for the same parent from each family to be present for all sessions. This requirement does not preclude additional family members from attending sessions with each primary parent as their schedules permit. However, attendance without the primary parent is not recommended, because the other family members will not have received the background on previously taught techniques.

About the Group Sessions

The group sessions are conducted to teach parents the intervention techniques, allow parents to share their experiences with other parents, and provide opportunities to answer parents' questions. Each of the six group sessions is designed to be taught using the PowerPoint slide presentations and video

Table III.1. Sequence of Sessions for Group Training Format

Session	Format	Topic
1	Group	*Overview of the Program* and *Set Up Your Home for Success*
2	Coaching	Review of *Set Up Your Home for Success* and *Goal Development*
3	Group	*Make Play Interactive* and *Modeling and Expanding Language*
4	Coaching	Review of *Make Play Interactive* and *Modeling and Expanding Language*
5	Group	*Create Opportunities for Your Child to Engage or Communicate* and *Overview of the Direct Teaching Techniques*
6	Coaching	Review of *Create Opportunities for Your Child to Engage or Communicate*
7	Group	*Teaching Your Child Expressive and Receptive Language*
8	Coaching	Review of *Teaching Your Child Expressive and Receptive Language*
9	Group	*Teaching Your Child Social Imitation and Play*
10	Coaching	Review of *Teaching Your Child Social Imitation and Play*
11	Group	*Putting It All Together*
12	Coaching	Review of *Putting It All Together*

clips included on the DVD that accompanies this manual. Because parents attend the group sessions without their children, the video clips allow you to introduce each technique and show a video demonstration of it. Each session's PowerPoint slide presentation is reproduced on the following pages, along with a suggested script and notes for points to make for each slide.* Review the session slide presentations and the script and notes before you present the information to families, to familiarize yourself with the content. Although the script contains all of the necessary information for the presentation, you are encouraged to present the information in your own words and generate your own examples. This approach will enrich the presentation and make it more personal.

When presenting the information, make sure to speak loudly and slowly. You should also visually "check in" with the audience to ensure that each parent is following along. People making a presentation have a tendency to deliver the presentation to members of the audience who are most responsive and participative. By visually checking in with all audience members, you can encourage shyer members to participate.

You should be comfortable with facilitating group discussion. The script and notes for each session include a number of probe questions that you can ask parents during the presentation, to help them apply the material to their own situations and facilitate discussion. Again, these questions are only suggestions, and you are encouraged to add information to make the presentation your own. Parents may be uncomfortable speaking in group sessions and may take a little while to respond to your questions, especially in the beginning. Therefore, after you present a question, allow adequate time for parents to respond.

Many parents are hesitant to ask questions in a group setting. Thus it is important to check periodically for understanding. By taking a brief break and asking parents whether they have any questions, you can encourage the parents to ask for clarification on points they are unsure about. When a parent does ask a question, repeat the question before answering it, to make sure all parents have heard and understood it. If a question is slightly off topic, try to relate it to the current material. If the question is substantially off topic, offer to discuss the issue with the parent during the break or after the session.

You should encourage parents to give feedback to each other during the homework review. However, make sure that this feedback stays positive,

---

*A note on pronouns in the suggested script is in order: Unlike our usage in other Project ImPACT materials, we use "he or she" for a child with ASD in this material, which is intended to be *spoken to* parents.

remains on topic, and is consistent with the correct implementation of intervention techniques. If a parent becomes overly negative, goes off topic, or makes repeated suggestions that involve incorrect use of the strategies, you should add more structure to the feedback portion of the session. For example, you might mention that although there have been a number of good suggestions, only you will provide feedback to families, for the sake of saving time.

Many families want to know how this intervention relates to other therapies that they have heard of or used with their children. Thus it is important to have an understanding of the theoretical basis of Project ImPACT, and to be able to explain how this approach relates to and may complement other interventions for children with ASD. A discussion of the theoretical foundation of Project ImPACT and how it relates to other developmental and behavioral interventions can be found in Part I, Chapter 1.

Group Session Format

Except for the initial session, each group session should begin with parents' asking questions and sharing their experiences of using the techniques at home. During this discussion, you should help parents see common themes in their experiences and relate them back to the techniques being covered. Halfway through each session, take a short break to allow parents to absorb the information, meet other parents, and ask specific questions. The trainer notes suggest a stopping point for the break; however, you may find it better to break at a different point in the presentation. At the end of each session, give parents time to write down homework goals and ask any additional questions they have.

Homework sheets for the group training format can be found in Appendix A of this manual. They should be copied and distributed to parents at each session. Each of these homework sheets cover multiples techniques. However, you may choose to have parents complete the individual homework sheets in the parent manual instead.

Although flexibility is necessary, you should try to maintain the following format:

1. Review homework from the previous coaching session (15–20 minutes).
2. Conduct first half of presentation (30–45 minutes).
3. Take break (10 minutes).
4. Conduct rest of presentation (30–45 minutes).
5. Discuss and assign homework (10 minutes).

The Fidelity of Implementation for Group Sessions Form (Form 29) is a checklist of critical steps that need to be implemented when you are conducting the group sessions. The form can be found in Appendix A of this manual. This checklist can be used by you or your supervisor to ensure that you are implementing the group sessions with fidelity.

About Individual Coaching Sessions

Each parent attends the individual coaching sessions with her child. These sessions are conducted to give parents an opportunity to practice the techniques they are learning in the group sessions. The outlines for these sessions include what to model and provide feedback on. The PowerPoint slides are not used, and the video clips are generally not needed, for these coaching sessions.

Coaching Session Format

The sessions should focus on teaching the parent the intervention techniques, using discussion, demonstration, parent practice, and feedback. Homework should be given at the end of each coaching session to ensure that the parent practices at home. The parent should be given a copy of the homework sheet for the techniques to be practiced. Although flexibility is necessary, you should try to maintain the following format:

1. Review homework from previous session (5 minutes).
2. Provide a brief review of techniques (5 minutes).
3. Demonstrate techniques with child (5 minutes).
4. Have parent practice techniques while you give feedback (20 minutes).
5. Discuss and assign homework (10 minutes).

The coaching environment should be structured to facilitate parent–child interactions: It should have a defined physical space, limited distractions, and highly motivating toys.

The Fidelity of Implementation for Coaching Sessions Form (Form 30) is a checklist of critical steps that need to be implemented when conducting the individual coaching sessions. Like the other forms, it can be found in Appendix A of this manual. This checklist can be used by you or your supervisor to ensure that you are implementing the coaching sessions with fidelity.

Steps to Complete Prior to the First Session

Select the dates and times for the group program. Three to four weeks prior to the start date, send parents the introduction letter (Appendix A, Form 17) that describes the program and includes registration information. Then send parents the Daily Activity Schedule (Appendix A, Form 5) to arrive 2–3 days before the first group session. Request that parents complete it and bring it to the first session. It is also possible to have the parents complete the Daily Activity Schedule during the first group session; however, having parents complete the form before this session allows more time for discussion during the session.

Overview of the Program
and *Set Up Your Home for Success*

Session Goals

1. Help parents understand the rationale for parent training.
2. Provide an overview of the program's goals and training format.
3. Give an overview of the intervention strategies.
4. Teach parents to set up their home environment for successful interactions.
5. Help parents identify routines in which to teach their children.

Materials

1. DVD
2. Parent manuals
3. Copies of homework for Group Format: *Set Up Your Home for Success* (Appendix A, Form 22)

Outline of Session

- Introduce session agenda and conduct trainer and parent introductions (Slide 1).
- Explain goals and benefits of parent training (Slides 2–5).
- Provide overview of program (Slides 6–8).
- Introduce intervention techniques (Slides 9–20):

     Provide overview of interactive teaching techniques (Slides 11–14).
     Show video clips of interactive teaching techniques (at Slide 15).
     Provide overview of direct teaching techniques (Slides 16–18).
     Show video clips of direct teaching techniques (at Slide 19).

- Take Break.
- Present *Set Up Your Home for Success* (Slides 21–25).
- Pass out parent manuals.
- Discuss Daily Activity Schedule (Slide 26).

     Have parents complete the Daily Activity Schedule in the parent manual.

- Discuss and assign homework (Slide 27):

     1. Pass out Homework for Group Format: *Set Up Your Home for Success* (Appendix A, Form 22) and have parents fill out "Goals of the Week."
     2. Instruct parents to practice this homework over the next week and answer the questions.
     3. Have parents read *Overview of the Program* and *Set Up Your Home for Success* (Chapters 1 and 2 of the parent manual).

- Review format of the individual coaching sessions.
- Have parents sign up for an individual coaching session.

Introduce Session Agenda and Conduct Trainer and Parent Introductions

Slide 1

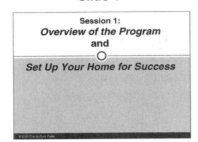

Welcome. Thank you for coming. You are all here because you have a child with an autism spectrum disorder or ASD, or a child who has other difficulties with social-communication skills. Today's session will be 2 hours long. It will provide an overview of this intervention program, Project ImPACT, and will discuss ways to set up your home to increase positive social interactions with your child.

I'd like to start by introducing myself.

> **Note to Trainers:** Parent trainers should introduce themselves and briefly describe their experience with parent training.

To help us get to know each other, I would like to have each of you introduce yourself. Please tell everyone your name and your child's name. I would also like you to describe one of your child's strengths, as well as an area in which he or she struggles. Finally, I would like you to describe what you hope to gain from this program.

> **Note to Trainers:** Another strategy for encouraging parents to develop rapport with each other is "pair and share." Have each parent pair up with someone she doesn't know. Each partner should then introduce herself and answer the questions above. Then each parent should take a turn introducing her partner to the group. This strategy is often successful for parents who may be uncomfortable addressing the group initially.
>
> As parents bring up goals related to improving their children's social-communication skills, let them know that this program will address these goals. If they bring up goals that involve decreasing problem behaviors, such as tantrums, mention that although this program does not directly address behavior management, improving social-communication skills can often decrease problem behavior. If they mention more specific behavior management goals or self-help goals, such as toilet training, let them know that this program will not address these issues, but that you can identify resources to help them with these concerns.
>
> Introductions should take approximately 10–15 minutes.

Explain Goals and Benefits of Parent Training

Slide 2

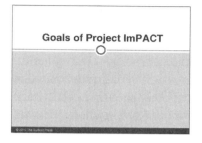

Project ImPACT is an evidence-based parent training intervention for families of young children with autism spectrum disorders (ASD). The ImPACT in Project ImPACT stands for Improving Parents As Communication Teachers.

This program is based on the philosophy that parents are their children's best teachers. Parents know their children the best.

Children with ASD have difficulty learning in the same way as typically developing children. For this reason, parents often need to use different ways of interacting with their children with ASD in order to help the children reach their potential.

This program teaches you strategies for teaching your child social-communication skills, such as how better to engage and communicate with you. These are many of the same proven techniques used by specialists who work with children with ASD.

Once you are trained, you can provide important therapy to your child. This "parent-implemented" therapy will complement what your child learns at school and in other interventions. By working together with your child's other therapists, you can ensure that your child gets the 25 hours per week of intervention recommended for children with ASD.

Slide 3

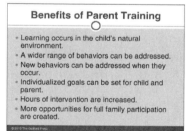

There are many good reasons for learning to teach your child with ASD.

What children learn in their families is often more important than what they learn in school. That's because the goal is for them to be able to interact and communicate with the people most important to them. When you learn the techniques in this program, you can increase the effectiveness of your child's interactions.

At home, many "teachable moments" occur that do not occur at school, such as at bathtime and bedtime. Parent training allows you to make the most of these moments.

If you have training, you can also work with your child when new behaviors occur. For example, if your preverbal child begins to use single words over summer break, you will know how to promote more advanced language rather than waiting for school to start again.

With parent training, you can select the strategies that work best for both your child and you. For example, some parents prefer to use pictures, while others prefer to use signs with their preverbal children.

Once you have learned to use effective intervention strategies, you can increase the number of hours of intervention your child receives by providing intervention throughout your child's day.

Once you have been trained, you can teach other family members (partners, grandparents, and siblings) to use these techniques with your child, expanding the number of "therapists" your child has.

Slide 4

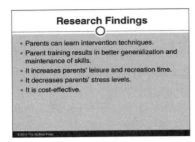

Research shows that parent training is a very effective intervention approach, both for children with ASD and for their families.

Studies have shown that, with training, parents can learn to use the same intervention techniques as specialists, and can be just as effective (if not more so!).

Children with ASD have particular difficulty with generalization. This means that skills they learn in one situation, such as the classroom, don't get used in other situations, such as at home. They also have difficulty maintaining these skills when intervention stops, such as during winter or summer breaks. Research shows that when parents—and not just specialists—use these techniques, their children are more likely to apply their learning to new situations and to remember and use what they learn over time.

Parent training takes time, and it may seem to add stress to parents' already hectic lives. But research has found that parents who learn and use these techniques have more time for recreation and lower stress levels than parents who have not been trained.

Finally, research has shown that children who received 1 hour of parent training per week made similar gains as children who received 5 hours per week from a specialist, making parent training more cost-effective.

Slide 5

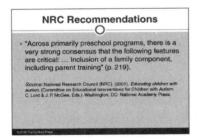

The National Research Council or NRC examined the research on several state-of-the-art intervention programs for children with ASD. Based on its review, the NRC concluded that parent training was a critical part of high-quality intervention programs for children with ASD.

> **Note to Trainers:** If parents are interested, the NRC report can be purchased at Amazon.com or on the National Academies Press website (*www.nap.edu*). Parents can find full publication information in the "Further Reading" section of the parent manual.

Provide Overview of Program

Slide 6

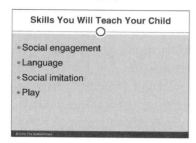

Children with ASD have particular difficulty with social communication. This includes trouble using language, eye contact, and gestures as ways to engage socially with others.

The goal of this program is to teach you strategies to improve your child's social-communication skills. It targets four core social-communication skills.

• *Social engagement.* The first core skill is social engagement. Children with ASD have much difficulty with this. It includes trouble taking turns, using language spontaneously, or playing with others. It also includes trouble responding to others, seeking and getting another's attention, and then staying engaged for any length of time.

The starting point of this program is to teach you to increase your child's social engagement. It is the foundation of all other social-communication skills. All children are more likely to learn when they are actively engaged.

• *Language.* The second core skill is language: Children with ASD have difficulty learning to speak and understanding others' speech. They may struggle to use words or to combine them into sentences.

They also have difficulty understanding why people communicate and using language for these different functions—for example, to protest, request, gain attention, maintain attention, label, describe, respond to a question, greet, give a direction, solve a problem, share experiences, and express feelings and interests. Their language often involves unusual features, such as *echolalia* (the nonfunctional repetition of previously heard speech). They also have difficulty using nonverbal language, such as eye contact and gestures. This means that children who have good spoken language skills still struggle to use language in a social way.

This program places a strong emphasis on teaching expressive or spoken language skills, including nonverbal language (gestures)—and, to a lesser extent, receptive language or understanding and following directions.

• *Social imitation:* The third core area is social imitation. Imitation is a very important, since children learn new skills by watching and imitating others. Children with ASD have difficulty imitating others, including imitating others' object use, gestures, language, and facial expressions. This program teaches social imitation—that is, imitation during play.

• *Play.* The last core area is play. Play is important for developing social and language skills, imaginative abilities, problem solving, perspective taking, and fine and gross motor skills. Children with ASD have trouble playing appropriately with toys. Some show no interest in toys, while others prefer to engage in nonfunctional play (such as lining up toys or spinning the wheels of a car) or repetitive play. Other children have difficulty playing with toys in a pretend or symbolic manner, such as pretending that a block is an apple.

This program focuses on improving the variety and complexity of your child's play skills.

Slide 7

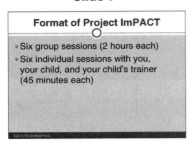

This program consists of six group sessions and six individual sessions.

In the six group sessions, you will learn to set goals for your child and learn the teaching techniques for reaching those goals. Group sessions will be a combination of lecture, video examples, and discussion.

In the six individual sessions you will practice the techniques learned during the group sessions and receive coaching and feedback from me [the parent trainer].

You are strongly encouraged to attend both group and individual sessions. Both are important for learning the techniques. It is also important that at least one parent or caregiver from each family commit to attending all of the training sessions, because the sessions—and the techniques—build on each other.

Slide 8

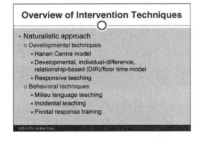

- *Parent's role:* Your interactions with your child are more important than my [the parent trainer's] interactions with your child. The best way for you to learn new skills is to practice and receive feedback.

Therefore, in this program, you will take the primary role of working with your child. You will be the primary intervention provider and should use the techniques at home and in your community.

- *Trainer's role.* I [the trainer] take a coaching role. When I meet individually with you and your child, I will briefly demonstrate techniques with your child, but then you will practice the techniques with your son or daughter while I provide you with feedback.

Introduce Intervention Techniques

Slide 9

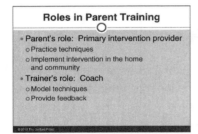

- *Naturalistic approach.* This program uses a *naturalistic* approach. This means that the techniques are used during your daily routines and natural interactions with your child, rather than during structured teaching sessions. You may need to set aside time to practice while you are learning, but the techniques are meant to be woven into your everyday life.

- *Developmental and behavioral techniques.* The specific techniques in this program were drawn from other naturalistic intervention programs designed for children with ASD as listed on the slide. Some of these programs consider themselves to be *developmental*, while others consider themselves to be *behavioral.* The specific techniques in this program have all been shown to be effective with children with ASD and are used together to teach social-communication skills.

[Ask parents:] Have you heard of or used any of these approaches? [If so, ask:] Which ones?

> *Note to Trainers:* If parents have received previous training in one of more of these programs, mention that although some of the techniques may be similar, they are also likely to seem a little different. That is because this program combines developmental and behavioral techniques. Parents should still be able to benefit from this program.

Slide 10

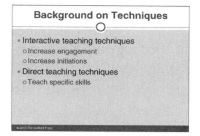

This program will train you in two sets of naturalistic teaching techniques. The first set—the *interactive teaching techniques*—have been drawn from developmental research. The second set—*the direct teaching techniques*—are drawn from behavioral research.

The interactive teaching techniques are used during child-directed activities to enhance your responsiveness to your child's behavior. They have been shown in research to increase children's engagement with others and increase their spontaneous communication.

The direct teaching techniques are used to teach language, imitation, and play skills by using prompting and reinforcement.

Provide Overview of Interactive Teaching Techniques

Slide 11

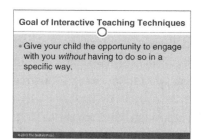

Children with ASD have difficulty interacting with other people. In particular, they can have trouble responding when others want to engage them. They tend not to initiate social engagement on their own, or stay engaged with others for very long. These are basic social engagement skills, and without them, it's hard to learn from other people.

Interactive teaching techniques are used to increase your child's engagement with you, to increase his or her initiation of social interactions, turn taking, language, and imitation skills.

When you use the interactive teaching techniques, your goal is to respond to all of your child's behaviors—even those that are unusual or not yet intentional. You provide opportunities for your child to interact with you, and you respond to all of your child's behaviors in a meaningful way.

By doing this, you increase your child's motivation to engage with you, and you teach your child that his or her behaviors carry meaning.

Slide 12

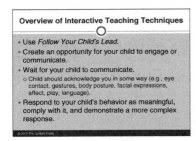

We will be learning a variety of interactive teaching techniques in this program. You will learn each one step by step. The goal is for you then to use them together in the following sequence.

You begin by using a technique called *Follow Your Child's Lead,* which means that you let your child choose the activity and you join him or her in it. When you do this, you can be sure that your child is interested in the activity. All the other techniques build on *Follow Your Child's Lead.*

Once you have joined your child in his or her choice of activities, you create an opportunity for your child to communicate with you. You then should wait to see if he or she does. The goal here is to get your child to acknowledge your involvement in the activity—even if it's just a brief flicker. Your child can acknowledge your involvement in many ways, including eye contact, gestures, body postures, facial expressions, change in affect or play, or language.

When your child seems to acknowledge you, you then treat the behavior as meaningful and respond to it appropriately. This helps your child understand that his or her behavior carries meaning and can have an effect on you. Many children with ASD don't realize this automatically. When you respond to your child's behavior as meaningful, you also want to model a more complex way for your child to acknowledge you in the future. *More complex* means a more developed response.

Slide 13

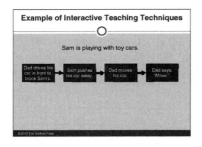

Let's look at an example of how the interactive teaching techniques are used together.

Sam is a 4-year-old boy with some single words. He is playing by himself with cars, by rolling one back and forth in front of his eyes.

His dad follows his lead by taking another car and joining Sam in his play. Dad rolls his car back and forth just as Sam is doing.

When Sam does not engage with his dad, his dad provides another opportunity for Sam to respond to him by blocking Sam's car with his car.

Sam responds by pushing his dad's car away. This may not be the way his dad would prefer Sam to respond. For example, Dad might prefer Sam to ask him politely to move his car. But Sam's response is communication with his dad, and this is what we want to increase. Thus his dad responds to Sam's push as meaningful and moves his car.

As his dad moves his car, he also models a more complex response for Sam by saying, "Move." This is closer to how he would like Sam to respond. However, at no point in the interactive teaching techniques does Dad require Sam to say, "Move."

Slide 14

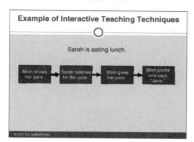

Let's look at another example of how the interactive teaching techniques are used together. Sarah is a 2-year-old girl who is preverbal. She is eating lunch at the table. Sarah's mother provides an opportunity for Sarah to communicate with her by showing her the juice but holding it out of Sarah's reach.

Sarah responds by reaching for the juice. Again, this might not be the ideal response that her mother wants. Mom might have preferred a more specific gesture, such as a point); however, it is a response. Thus her mother responds to Sarah's behavior as meaningful and gives her the juice.

At the same time, her mom also models a more complex response by pointing to the juice and saying, "Juice." Pointing is a more complex—that is, more developed—communication than reaching. Single words are more complex than gestures. The interactive teaching techniques can be adapted for children at many different language levels—or for the same child as he or she learns more.

I'll next show some video clips of these techniques being used with children at different language levels.

Show Video Clips of Interactive Teaching Techniques

Slide 15

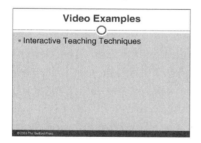

Note to Trainers: Prepare to show video clips (Session 1, interactive teaching techniques, 3 clips).

Before showing each clip, tell the parents to look for these things:

> How the parent follows the child's lead and creates opportunities for the child to respond.
> How the child responds to the parent.

After each clip, ask parents:

> "How did the parent follow the child's lead?"
> "How did the parent provide opportunities for the child to respond?"
> "How did the child respond?"
> "How did the parent respond to the child's response?"

The important techniques to highlight and the children's responses are outlined below.

• *Preverbal.* The parent uses several interactive teaching techniques to encourage her son to interact with her. She uses *Follow Your Child's Lead,* staying face to face with him. She uses simple and repetitive language to talk about his focus of interest. She also responds to his behavior as meaningful. For example, at one point when her son vocalizes ("Ga ga"), she responds by saying, "Ga ga, glasses." Her son responds with increased attention, eye contact, and positive affect. He also vocalizes again ("Ga ga").

• *Single words to complex phrases.* The father uses *Follows Your Child's Lead*, sitting face to face. He also uses a *Communicative Temptation* (controlling access) to encourage his son to communicate with him. Throughout the interaction, the father models simplified and repetitive language around his son's attentional focus. He also treats his son's actions as purposeful. For example, when the child says, "Peas," his father responds by repeating the child's language and handing him the peas. The child remains in the interaction, and responds with eye contact and by imitating words.

• *Complex phrase speech.* The mother uses *Follow Your Child's Lead* by playing with the umbrella. She provides language models ("It's raining, I need an umbrella, I'm getting all wet") around her son's play. In addition, she responds to all of his communicative attempts. She also uses a *Communicative Temptation* (pretending she doesn't have an umbrella) to encourage her son to initiate, which he does by telling her to get her umbrella. He also uses eye contact, gestures, and language throughout the interaction.

Provide Overview of Direct Teaching Techniques

Slide 16

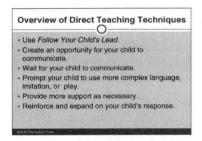

The direct teaching techniques are the second set of techniques you will learn in this program. They build on the interactive teaching techniques.

Children are likely to learn more when they are actively engaged. The interactive teaching techniques work to increase your child's social engagement. The direct teaching techniques use that engagement to teach your child new behaviors directly. The new elements in the direct teaching techniques are *prompts* and *reinforcement*.

Prompts are cues that help your child succeed in giving you a more complex—or more developed—response.

Reinforcement is how you reward your child for giving you that more complex response. We saw some examples of reinforcement in the video clips on the interactive techniques; we just didn't use the word. Getting what you ask for—like Sarah reaching for juice—is reinforcing.

As in the interactive teaching techniques, you will continue to use *Follow Your Child's Lead* to provide your child with an opportunity to communicate with you, and then to wait for a response. However, unlike in the interactive techniques, you will next use prompts to increase the complexity of your child's response before reinforcing your child's behavior.

You will adjust the amount of support—or help—that you give your child to use the more complex response.

After your child produces the more complex response, you will provide reinforcement and expand on your child's response by modeling an even more complex response.

Slide 17

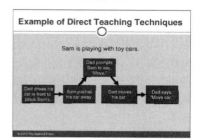

Let's look at an example of how the direct teaching techniques are used together. Again, Sam is playing with the cars. His dad follows his lead by taking another car and joining Sam in rolling the car back and forth.

When Sam does not respond, his dad provides another opportunity for Sam to respond by blocking Sam's car with his car.

Sam communicates by pushing his dad's car away.

This time, his dad doesn't move his car right away. Instead, Dad prompts Sam to say, "Move." The word is a more complex response than the pushing gesture

After Sam says, "Move," his father reinforces Sam's response by moving his car.

As his dad moves his car, he also models an even more complex response for Sam by saying two words: "Move car."

The key differences between the interactive and direct teaching techniques are the prompts and reinforcement. The direct teaching techniques use prompts to get a specific response from the child, and the child is reinforced only after he or she has succeeded in giving the appropriate response.

Slide 18

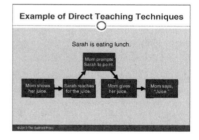

Let's look at another example of direct teaching techniques used together. Again, Sarah is eating lunch at the table. Sarah's mother provides an opportunity for Sarah to respond by showing her the juice and holding it out of her reach.

Sarah responds by reaching for the juice. This time her mom prompts Sarah to point to the juice. Pointing is a more complex ways of requesting.

Once Sarah points, her mom gives her the juice, thus reinforcing Sarah's pointing. At the same time, her mom also models an even more complex response by saying the word "Juice."

Next, we will look at video clips of the direct teaching techniques being used with children at different language levels.

Show Video Clips of Direct Teaching Techniques

Slide 19

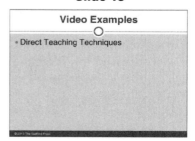

Note to Trainers: Prepare to show video clips (Session 1, direct teaching techniques, three clips).

Before showing each clip, tell parents to look for these things:

How the adult continues to use interactive teaching techniques by following the child's lead and creating opportunities for the child to engage with the parent.

How the child initially responds.

How the parent then prompts or cues the child to use a more complex response.

After each clip, ask parents:

"How did the parent follow the child's lead?"

"How did the parent provide opportunities for the child to respond?"

"How did the child respond?"

"How did the parent prompt a more complex response?"

"How did the child respond?"

"How did the parent respond to the child's more complex response?"

The important techniques to highlight and the children's responses are outlined below.

- *Preverbal.* The mother continues to use interactive teaching techniques to engage with her son and encourage initiations. These include *Follow Your Child's Lead,* assistance (a *Communicative Temptation*), and *Modeling and Expanding Language.* She also uses some direct teaching techniques to teach her son to increase the complexity of his request, by prompting him to use his sign for "More" before blowing the bubbles. Her son responds by signing "More."

- *Single words to complex phrases.* The father continues to use interactive teaching techniques to engage with his son, particularly using toys that he needs assistance with (balloon) and remaining face to face. The father also uses several direct teaching techniques to help him increase the complexity of his language skills. He uses a variety of language prompts, including direct questions, verbal model, and verbal routine, to increase the complexity of his response and decrease reliance on prompts. The child responds to the father's prompt by using a longer sentence ("I want blow balloon").

- *Complex phrase speech.* The mother uses a variety of interactive teaching techniques to engage with her son and to encourage initiations, including being face to face, using silly situations (pretending she will eat the fruit leather), and providing assistance (waiting for him to initiate before opening the fruit leather). Once he initiates, she uses direct teaching techniques to get a more complex response. For example, the child says, "Open," and Mom uses a time delay and direct question to get him to say "Mommy, open the fruit leather." The child responds by expanding the length of his utterance.

Slide 20

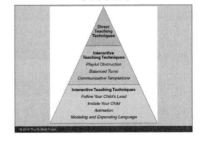

As you go through the program, the techniques you learn will build on each other. At the end of the program, you will understand how to use each technique, when to use each technique, and how they are used together. As shown in this diagram, the interactive teaching techniques lay the groundwork for all types of teaching. Therefore, the first part of the program will focus on implementing these techniques.

The bottom section of the pyramid includes the interactive

teaching techniques that are almost always used, such as *Follow Your Child's Lead, Imitate Your Child, Animation,* and *Modeling and Expanding Language. Imitate Your Child* and *Animation* are ways to create an opportunity for your child to engage with you. All four of these techniques increase your responsiveness to your child. You should use these techniques throughout the interaction with your child.

The middle section includes additional interactive teaching techniques: *Playful Obstruction, Balanced Turns,* and *Communicative Temptations.* You will use these techniques if the ones in the bottom section are unsuccessful at getting your child to engage with you or communicate. These techniques are more insistent at gaining your child's attention and getting a response. The two sections of interactive teaching techniques should be used during about two-thirds of the interactions with your child.

The top section of the pyramid represents the direct teaching techniques, all of which include the use of prompting and reinforcement. These techniques are used to help your child increase the complexity of his or her response. You should use the direct teaching techniques during about one-third of the interactions with your child.

By the end of the program, you will learn how to move up and down the pyramid's three sections during the interaction. If you spend too much time at the top, your child will get frustrated. If you spend too much time at the bottom, you won't challenge your child enough.

Take Break

Present *Set Up Your Home for Success*

Slide 21

A first step in teaching your child is to set up your home to increase the opportunities for successful interactions. Many children with ASD have difficulty engaging with other people when there are a lot of distractions. The following strategies will help you structure your home in a way that helps your child to engage with you.

Slide 22

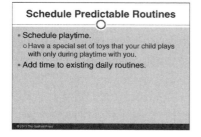

Many of the intervention techniques in this program are focused on promoting social interaction during play. Therefore, it is very important to set aside time to play with your child each day. Practice using the techniques with your child for 15–20 minutes each day during a play period. This can be done during a single session, or it can be spread out over several different sessions.

Make playtimes predictable, such as always before or after mealtime, right before bedtime, or in the morning after breakfast. This way, it will be easier for you to find time to play, and it can help your child stay in the interaction with you during these play periods.

If your child has difficulty playing with you, have a set of special toys that your child only gets to play with during playtime with you. The toys will then be more exciting, and your child may become more engaged. In addition, your child may begin to associate you with the favorite toys and may become more excited to play with you since, he or she will also get to play with those toys. However, if your child is so interested in his or her special toys that it makes playing with you difficult—for example, your child has a tantrum when you try to take a turn—you may not want to use those toys.

In addition to playtime, you should use the teaching techniques during daily caregiving routines, such as dressing, bathing, and meals. Since your child is already familiar with his or her daily routines, these activities are likely to be personally meaningful and offer the best opportunities for learning. If you can add just 5–10 minutes to a routine that you have to do anyway, you are more likely to use the techniques with your child throughout the day. This approach is much easier than trying to fit longer "work periods" into your already hectic lives.

Slide 23

The closer in proximity you are to your child, the more likely he or she is to engage with you. However, some children have difficulty staying in proximity to others, and will leave the space as soon as their parents attempt to join them. This may be particularly true in homes and other settings in which there is a lot of open space. You may then find yourself having to constantly move after your child to stay near him or her.

[Ask parents:] Do any of your children do this?

When you set up a defined space with visual and physical boundaries, your child is more likely to stay in proximity to you, and thus to engage with you. The space should be limited by physical boundaries, and ideally, the child should not be able to see outside the space. Many parents choose to use a small room or the child's bedroom. Some parents who don't have a separate room available have used a walk-in closet, or set up a tent, or worked under the dining room table. These were all confined spaces that the children enjoyed. Other parents have rearranged furniture in a larger room to create a smaller space and to eliminate "runways."

[Ask parents:] How could you set up a defined space in your home?

Slide 24

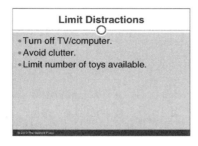

It is also important to limit distractions when you are trying to interact with your child. Children with ASD often get easily distracted by "competitors" for their attention. This is especially true when the "competitors" are very reinforcing for the child, such as TV or the computer.

[Ask parents:] What are the major distractions in your home?

It is also a good idea to limit the number of toys that are available to your child at any one time. Many parents buy their children a large number of toys in an attempt to keep them engaged. However, when all the toys are available, a child may flit from toy to toy without engaging for any length of time. This behavior may increase as the parent attempts to join the child in his or her play.

[Ask parents:] Do any of your children do this?

For this reason, it is highly recommended that you limit the number of toys available. We recommend that you have no more than about six preferred toys available at any time. For some children, even fewer toys may be best. The rest of the toys should be boxed up and placed out of your child's reach.

When you are playing with your child, you can place the toys you want to use in a big plastic bin or box, so that you take out only one or two at a time. This will help your child engage with you rather than moving from toy to toy.

[Ask parents:] How might you limit distractions in your home?

Slide 25

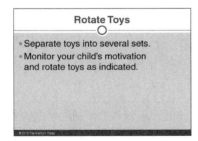

Children often get bored with toys that they see frequently. We recommend you separate your child's toys into several sets. Have only one set available at a time. Rotate toy sets whenever your child seems to be losing interest. A good length of time for each set is 2–3 weeks. This keeps old toys "fresh" and exciting, and may greatly improve your child's engagement with toys.

Children with ASD who have limited play skills may be even less inclined to stay engaged with toys once they are no longer novel. By rotating toys, you can increase the novelty of your child's toys without having to continually buy new ones.

This technique also helps limit distractions by having a limited number of toys present at a time (that is, it limits visual stimuli).

[Ask parents:] Have any of you tried this? [If so, ask:] How does your child respond?

Pass Out Parent Manuals

Discuss Daily Activity Schedule

Slide 26

Each family should have received a copy of the Daily Activity Schedule. If you do not yet have a copy, one can be found in the parent manual.

Note to Trainers: Provide time for parents to fill out the Daily Activity Schedule (Appendix A, Form 5) if they haven't already.

If you haven't already completed this form, write down the daily routines that you use with your child. Include when they typically occur and how long they typically last. Then write a brief description of what each routine looks like. For example, "Wake-up time," you might write: "I go into Jason's room and turn on the lights. I get in bed with my child and rub his back until he wakes up. Then I get him up and bring him to the living room." Finally, indicate whether your child enjoys, tolerates, or resists the routine.

This information will help you identify the best caregiving routines to teach within. You should start with activities that your child enjoys or at least tolerates, and to which you have the ability to add 5–10 minutes.

You will notice just how much time you already devote to interacting with your child during the day. Our goal is to teach you intervention techniques and strategies that you can use during these times to help your child engage and communicate better.

Discuss and Assign Homework

Slide 27

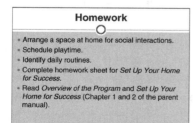

Homework

- Arrange a space at home for social interactions.
- Schedule playtime.
- Identify daily routines.
- Complete homework sheet for *Set Up Your Home for Success.*
- Read *Overview of the Program* and *Set Up Your Home for Success* (Chapter 1 and 2 of the parent manual).

Note to Trainers: Pass out copies of Homework for Group Format: *Set Up Your Home for Success* (Appendix A, Form 22).

Think about your home. How will you will arrange your home to set up a defined space and limit distractions during play? Look at your Daily Activity Schedule. I would like each of you to identify times when you can schedule a daily playtime (15–20 minutes). I would also like you to identify daily routines that you can add time to for using the techniques.

Note to Trainers: If time permits, have each parent report. Give feedback as necessary.

I would like you to implement these changes over the next week and to respond to the questions on your homework sheet.

We will discuss your homework during your first individual session next week, as well as at the beginning of the next group session.

Please read Chapters 1 and 2 (*Introduction* and *Set Up Your Home for Success*) of the parent manual for next week.

The next individual session will be spent reviewing your homework and developing individual goals for your child. You should come to the session with questions you have about the intervention or social-communication skills taught in this program, as well as setting up your home for success.

> **Note to Trainers:** Have parents sign up for the individual session if they haven't already been scheduled.

Session 2 (Coaching)

Review of *Set Up Your Home for Success* and *Goal Development*

Session Goals

1. Help the parent to set up the home environment for successful interactions.
2. Develop goals for the child.

Materials

1. Parent manual
2. Goal Development Form (Appendix A, Form 4)
3. Two copies of Social-Communication Checklist (Appendix A, Form 3)
4. Toys to keep child occupied

Outline of Session

- Prior to session, arrange the coaching space to facilitate parent–child interactions.
- Review homework from preceding group session (5 minutes).
- Set goals for the child:

    Have parent complete Social-Communication Checklist while you interact with child (10 minutes).

    Complete Social-Communication Checklist based on your interaction and observation of parent–child interaction (10 minutes).

    Write goals for the child with the parent (20 minutes).

- Discuss and assign homework (2 minutes):
    1. Have the parent read *Follow Your Child's Lead, Imitate Your Child, Animation,* and *Modeling and Expanding Language* (Chapters 3–6 of the parent manual).

Prior to Session, Arrange the Coaching Space to Facilitate Parent–Child Interactions

Create a defined physical space, limit distractions, and select highly preferred toys.

Review Homework from Preceding Group Session

Review the questions from the homework sheet for *Set Up Your Home for Success* (Appendix A, Form 22). If the parent had difficulty creating a space at home, take time to help her identify possible solutions. If there is still a problem, it may be necessary to make a home visit to assist in creation of an appropriate environment in the home setting. Let the parent know that you will review the homework for *Set Up Your Home for Success* at the next group session as well.

Set Goals for the Child

The goals for the child are developed on the basis of the parent report, your own interaction with the child, and your observation of a parent–child interaction. These goals will be used throughout the program.

Have Parent Complete Social-Communication Checklist While You Interact with Child

Explain to the parent that the Social-Communication Checklist (Appendix A, Form 3) is used to determine her understanding of her child's social engagement, language, social imitation, and play skills at home, and thus to help in the development of goals. Be available to the parent while she completes the checklist, to respond to any questions that may arise and to obtain clarification of any responses that may be vague or difficult to interpret. When two parents attend the training, ask them whether they want to complete a checklist together or independently. Acknowledge that sometimes children interact differently with different adults and in different situations.

While the parent completes the Social-Communication Checklist, interact with the child to gain a brief understanding of his social engagement, language, social imitation, and play skills. Take this time to determine which techniques are most effective with the child. This knowledge is helpful when you demonstrate use of the techniques at the end of this session.

Complete Social-Communication Checklist Based on Your Observation of Parent–Child Interaction

Instruct the parent to play with her child as she would at home. Explain to the parent that this interaction will be used to collect baseline data. While she interacts with her child, use the Social-Communication Checklist to record information on the child's use of skills with you and with the parent in each of the four core areas. It is also beneficial to note any techniques the parent is using and their effect on the child's behavior. This information will be useful when you are describing the treatment techniques in subsequent sessions.

When two parents are present, allow each to interact individually with the child for 5 minutes. Clearly announce transitions between your interaction with the child and each parent's interaction. For example, with two parents present, you might say: "Molly, you can begin the interaction with your son. Jim, you can come stand with me and observe the interaction. ... Thank you, Molly. Jim, now it is your turn to play with your son as you would at home. Molly come stand with me to watch them play." A clear transition statement sets the precedent for separating parents throughout the program while they practice and receive feedback. This ensures that each parent has time to practice and receive feedback.

Write Goals for the Child with the Parent

Goals are developed with the Goal Development Form (Appendix A, Form 4). The first step is to determine one to two global goals the parent would like to address in each of the four core areas. To determine the parent's goals, ask the parent about her goals for her child. If the parent does not have a goal for each of the four areas, ask probing questions, suggest a goal, and then ask the parent whether she agrees. Here are some sample questions:

1. "I notice that Brian often leaves the interaction when you join in his play. Is this something you would like to address? How would you feel about a goal to increase the length of time he plays with others?"
2. "As we discussed earlier, Sam does not use phrase speech on his own; rather, he reaches toward an object and waits for you to say the phrase and repeats what you said. How would you feel about adding a goal to increase his spontaneous use of two- to three-word phrases?"
3. "Sam appears to have difficulty playing with toys in a pretend manner. Do you find this to be true at home? How would you feel about adding a goal to increase his pretend play?"

Write these goals on the Goal Development Form under "Global Goals."

The next step is to help the parent understand her child's current level of functioning each area. The current level of functioning is determined by comparing the parent's and your completed Social-Communication Checklists and by reviewing previous evaluations or IFSP/IEP goals. Many times you will find consistency across the two checklists and previous evaluations or goals, which will make identifying the child's skill level relatively easy. However, sometimes there are differences that need to be reconciled before goals can be developed. Differences in reports and observations usually occur when (1) the child has difficulty engaging and communicating in a new environment, and therefore does not display his typical skills; (2) the parent has a different interaction style when being watched; and/or (3) the parent is unaware of the child's level of functioning and the amount of support she provides. If the information on the parent's checklist is significantly different from your observation, this difference can be explored by asking open-ended and probing questions. Questions can help clarify the parent's responses and inform you whether the observation is typical of the child's performance. Here are some sample questions:

1. "Did this seem to be typical of play at home with your child? If no, how was it different?"

2. "I notice you reported that your child uses two to three words to communicate at home. He seemed to be fairly quiet today. Can you give me some examples of his language at home?"

3. "Today your child appeared to repeat language he heard. I did not hear him say anything without you saying it first. Do you find this to be true?"

4. "Your child seems to ask questions even when he knows the answer. Do you find this to be true?"

Once you and the parent agree on the child's current level of functioning, it should be written on the Goal Development Form under "Current Skills."

The last step is to translate the targeted behaviors into specific goals that are measurable and appropriate for the child's skill level. You should write these specific goals to be consistent with your current method of data collection, so that you can document the child's progress. The specific goals should be written under "Measurable Goals" on the Goal Development Form. Be sure to check in with the parent to confirm that she is in agreement with these goals. Once you have measurable goals, you can write them on Form 1.1, Child Goals (in the parent manual), for the parent to keep with her. Be sure to keep your copy of this form for future sessions, in case the parent forgets to bring her manual

See Part II, Session 1, for case examples of goal setting. Part I, Chapter, 2 contains additional information regarding goal setting, as well as sample goals for the four core areas targeted in this program.

Discuss and Assign Homework

1. **Have the parent read** *Follow Your Child's Lead*, *Imitate Your Child*, *Animation*, **and** *Modeling and Expanding Language* (Chapters 3–6 of the parent manual). Explain to the parent that the first set of interactive teaching techniques will be introduced during the next group session. These techniques focus on increasing child engagement and motivation. The parent should read the techniques, but should not complete the homework until after the next group session.

Troubleshooting Tips

A parent may report having difficulty interacting with her child while a sibling is present. To address this concern, ask the parent to describe the sibling interaction and see whether the sibling could be involved in play. If this is not feasible for either or both children, review the parent's schedule to see whether she can identify a 10-minute period in which to play with each child separately.

Parents also frequently have trouble fitting playtime into an already demanding schedule. To address this concern, review the Daily Activity Schedule to determine whether play can fit within already existing daily activities. Help the parent identify activities with which her child may be able to help. Examples could include cooking, washing the dishes, or separating the laundry. When you are helping the parent identify an activity, it is important to take into consideration the individual needs and skills of her child. If the child's involvement in daily chores would not work because the parent needs to accomplish the task quickly, then identify an activity the child likes (e.g., balloons, bubbles, etc.) and ask whether the parent can play one of these activities with the child for 5 minutes after mealtime before she cleans up.

Session 3 (Group)

Make Play Interactive and *Modeling and Expanding Language*

Session Goals

1. Help parents understand why they may need to use different techniques to interact successfully with their children.
2. Teach parents techniques that can improve their interactions with their children.
3. Teach parents to change the way they speak, to improve their children's understanding and use of language.

Materials

1. DVD
2. Copes of homework for Group Format: *Make Play Interactive* and *Modeling and Expanding Language* (Appendix A, Form 23)
3. Whiteboard or large sheets of paper to review and introduce homework

Outline of Session

- Introduce session agenda (Slide 1).
- Review homework from Session 1 (Slide 2).
- Introduce rationale for *Follow Your Child's Lead, Imitate Your Child,* and *Animation* (Slides 3–6).

- Present *Follow Your Child's Lead, Imitate Your Child,* and *Animation* (Slides 5–15).
- Show video clips of *Follow Your Child's Lead, Imitate Your Child,* and *Animation* (at Slide 16).
- Take break.
- Introduce rationale for *Modeling and Expanding Language* (Slides 17–18).
- Present *Modeling and Expanding Language* (Slides 19–25).
- Show video clips of *Modeling and Expanding Language* (at Slide 26).
- Discuss and assign homework (Slide 27):
  1. Pass out Homework for Group Format: *Make Play Interactive* and *Modeling and Expanding Language* (Appendix A, Form 23) and have parents fill out "Goals of the Week."
  2. Instruct parents to practice this homework over the next week and answer the questions.
- Have parents sign up for an individual coaching session.

Introduce Session Agenda

Slide 1

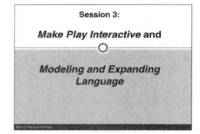

We will begin with the homework from the last session and then cover the most basic interactive teaching techniques. These techniques are the basis for all of the other intervention techniques that will be covered.

Review Homework from Session 1

Slide 2

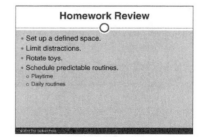

Note to Trainers: Read through the homework given in the first group session (Appendix A, Form 22) and ask parents to respond.

Use a whiteboard to record parents' responses. Make three columns: "Successes," "Challenges," and "Suggestions." If a parent reports successful use of a technique, write it on the whiteboard under "Successes" (e.g., "Putting away most of child's toys increased length of play with parent"). Ask if any other parents had a similar success, in order to encourage group discussion.

If a parent reports difficulty using a technique, write it under "Challenges." Lead a discussion of what could be done to overcome the challenge. Based on the other parents' responses (or your own), write the best suggestions under the "Suggestions" column next to the specific challenge. (See Part II, Session 2, "Troubleshooting Tips" for some common challenges and solutions.)

Point out any main themes parents report.

Introduce Rationale for *Follow You Child's Lead, Imitate Your Child,* and *Animation*

Slide 3

Why is playing often so difficult?
• Child's difficulty with social engagement
• Child's difficulty with play skills
• Child's difficulty with initiating
• Our own difficulty remembering how to play
• Emotions we experience when our child prefers not to play with us

[Ask parents:] Is it difficult to play with your child with ASD?

Play is supposed to be fun. However, playing or engaging with a child with ASD is often difficult, and this may lead to feelings of guilt or frustration. However, the difficulty is not due to poor parenting; it is due to the child's limitations.

What are these limitations? Children with ASD have difficulty with social engagement. They may not respond to your play suggestions or may prefer to play alone. Some children even get upset when someone else tries to play with them, making it difficult to have fun.

In addition, children with ASD often don't know how to play. They may not think to combine toys, like putting blocks in a jar or putting toy people into cars or even making a toy car go somewhere. Instead, their play may be odd or repetitive, such as lining toys up, or spinning the wheels of a car rather than pushing it. Some children don't play with toys, preferring to run back and forth, jump on the furniture, or turn the lights on and off. When your child has difficulty playing in appropriate ways, it can be difficult to play with him or her.

Children with ASD also have trouble initiating interactions or communication with other people. They might respond when you solicit their attention or ask a question, but they may have difficulty starting an interaction or sharing their interests or needs without being asked. Therefore, play with your child may feel very "one-sided," with you doing all of the work.

Most parents take their lead in play from the child they are playing with. If you don't remember how to play, it may be difficult to know how to join a child who plays in unusual ways.

For all these reasons, it is often difficult just to sit and play with a child with ASD in the same way you might with a typically developing child. Often this difficulty can lead parents to feel frustrated and rejected. They may stop trying to play with their child, particularly if he or she prefers to play alone.

This session teaches you to make small changes in the way you interact with your child. These changes help make play more interactive and more enjoyable for you and your child.

Slide 4

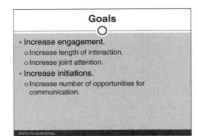

The techniques discussed in the first half of today's session can be used to increase your child's engagement with other people. This often means increasing the length of time your child is engaged with others, as well as his or her ability to use joint attention. *Joint attention* involves paying attention to a toy and a person at the same time. Children with ASD have particular difficulty with joint attention. But it's important for developing other social-communication skills.

These strategies are also effective for increasing the number of times your child initiates an interaction. This is another important goal. The more often your child initiates communication, the more opportunities you have to teach more advanced communication skills.

Slide 5

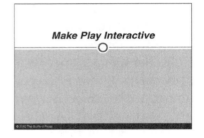

The first techniques we will discuss are called *Follow Your Child's Lead, Imitate Your Child,* and *Animation*. They are used to increase your child's motivation and to encourage him or her to interact with you.

Slide 6

The interactive teaching techniques we will discuss today are at the base of the pyramid.

As we discussed last session, the techniques in the bottom section lay the groundwork for the entire intervention and should be used throughout the interaction with your child.

Present *Follow Your Child's Lead, Imitate Your Child, and Animation*

Slide 7

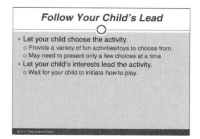

What does *Follow Your Child's Lead* mean? It means that you allow your child to choose the toy or activity, and you follow and join your child in play.

Why?

Children must be motivated and engaged to learn. Children with ASD are often not motivated in the same ways as typically developing children. When you use *Follow Your Child's Lead,* you are joining the child in what he or she is interested in doing. This is likely to increase your child's engagement, attention, and motivation. When your child is motivated and engaged, you can take advantage of these opportunities to teach new skills.

Typically developing children are often interested in whatever we are interested in. But children with ASD are often not interested in what we want to show them, and they may be interested in some unusual activities. Rather than trying to get your child to play with what you think would be fun, observe how the child plays and join him or her in whatever is going on, even if it seems unusual.

[Ask parents:]

What activities does your child like to do?
How can you join in these activities?
Have any of you tried this? [If so, ask:] How does your child respond?
How could you use this technique with your child?

Slide 8

When?

You can use *Follow Your Child's Lead* during any activity in which it is OK for your child to direct the interaction, such as play, trips to the park, walks in the neighborhood, and even bathtime if your child enjoys the tub.

Plan at least 15–20 minutes each day to use *Follow Your Child's Lead* during his or her choice of activities. During this time, you should avoid interruptions and avoid activities that are usually solitary, such as TV, videos, and computer games.

It is important that these experiences remain positive. Thus, if 20 minutes is too long at first, start with several shorter interactions throughout the day and gradually increase the length of each. Although it is important to use *Follow Your Child's Lead,* you will also have times when your child needs to follow your lead. Thus this technique is not appropriate when you need your child to complete an undesired activity or when you are on a schedule. At these times, you should not allow your child to "run the show."

Slide 9

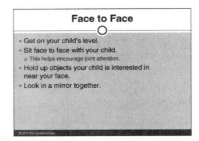

How?

Let's look now at how to use *Follow Your Child's Lead*. First, get face to face with your child. Get on your child's level so that your face is in his or her line of sight. Why? Because eye contact is a very important behavior that indicates social engagement. Children with ASD often have difficulty engaging in face-to-face gaze. By being in your child's line of sight, you make it easier for your child to make eye contact with you and use joint attention. If your child prefers to sit on your lap, or consistently faces away from you, be persistent. Move so that you can stay face to face.

You can also hold up objects that your child is interested in near your face, so that when the child looks at the object, he or she can make eye contact with you more easily.

For some children with ASD, it can be too intense to sit face to face with another person. If this is the case, try looking into a mirror together. This way your child can also watch him or herself in the mirror, which many young children enjoy, while also making eye contact with you without needing to shift his gaze very far.

[Ask parents:] Have any of you tried this? [If so, ask:] How does your child respond?

Slide 10

Join in your child's play by becoming a necessary part of it. For example, if your child is building a tower, hand him or her the pieces one at a time. You can also add to your child's play by expanding it slightly. For example, if your child is pushing a car, you can put a driver in the car.

Some children who are very hard to engage respond very well to physical or sensory play. For example, if your child likes to climb, engage in rough-and-tumble play; if your child likes to spin, spin him or her in a chair; if your child likes to touch textures, give him or her a lotion rub; if your child likes to stare at lights, play with flashlights together. By providing a positive sensory experience to your child, you are working to make yourself part of the experience.

[Ask parents:]

Have any of you tried this? [If so, ask:] How does your child respond?
Let's go back to some of the activities you reported were favorites of your child's. How could you use this technique with your child?

Slide 11

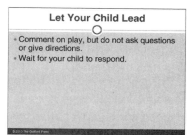

A purpose of this technique is to increase the times your child engages and initiates communication with you. So do not ask your child questions or give directions. This can sometimes be difficult if you are used to helping structure your child's play or asking your child to communicate. However, asking lots of questions and giving directions takes the lead away from your child. Instead, simply comment on your child's play, to indicate your interest in his or her choice of activities.

Responding to questions and demands is also an important aspect of language development. However, it will be covered in the direct teaching portion of this program.

Next, wait and see how your child responds to your joining his interests. Does your child make eye contact? Use gestures? Change his or her body posture, facial expression, play, or language? Remember, all of these behaviors indicate that your child is engaged with you in some way.

[Ask parents:] Have any of you tried this? [If so, ask:] Is it hard to avoid questions and directions? And how does your child respond?

Slide 12

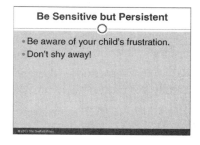

Because many children with ASD would rather play alone, your child may actively avoid you when you try to engage. This may make you feel discouraged and cause you to "back off."

While it is important to monitor your child's frustration so that you don't push him or her to the point of a "meltdown," you should also be persistent when your child avoids the interaction and should work through minor protests. It is OK for you to pursue play with your child even if your child would rather play alone.

Slide 13

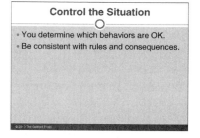

Follow Your Child's Lead does *not* mean that anything your child wants to do is OK. If your child is behaving inappropriately (being dangerous, destructive, unpleasant, etc.), do not allow this to continue. It is important to be consistent about what is and is not OK for your child to do.

For example, if you decide that it is not OK to throw toys, and throwing toys means that your child needs to put the offending toy away, you should be consistent about this rule. If your child throws a toy, he or she needs to put it away.

Your child may be able to share some activities with you for a period of time, but the activities may stop being interactive if they continue for too long, are too repetitive, or are too absorbing. It is OK to be "all done" with these activities when they interfere with your child's being able to interact with you.

Slide 14

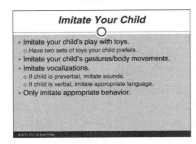

Another technique that you can use to engage with your child is to *Imitate Your Child*.

Why?

Children learn through imitation. But children with ASD often have difficulty imitating others. *Imitate Your Child* is one way to enhance your child's imitation skills, by making him or her more likely to imitate you.

It also improves joint attention, social responsiveness, play, spontaneous language, and verbalizations. *Imitate Your Child* is also a great way to follow his or her lead. If you are doing the same thing as your child, you will be joining him or her in his choice of activity.

How?

You can start by imitating your child's play with toys. This is much easier if you have two sets of the same toy. This works great for some cheaper items, such as Slinkies, balls, and pull tubes. However, you don't need to go out and buy two of everything. Instead, try having toys available with multiple pieces, such as blocks and stacking cups.

You can also imitate your child's gestures and body movements. This can be particularly effective when your child is not engaged with toys or is wandering aimlessly. When doing this, try overexaggerating your imitations of gestures, to help your child notice that you are copying him or her.

You can also imitate the sounds or words your child makes. If your child is not yet speaking, imitating your child's vocalizations can increase his or her vocalizations. If your child is using some words or phrase speech, imitating your child's language can show your interest in his or her play and can help promote language growth. Be sure to imitate only language that is appropriate to the play.

Imitate Your Child often increases the behaviors you are imitating. This is why it can be a great way to increase play and language skills. To avoid increasing inappropriate behaviors, do not imitate any inappropriate behaviors or any other behaviors you are trying to decrease. If your child uses behaviors that you don't want to see increase, you can imitate the emotion while shaping it into something more appropriate. For example, if your child is flapping his or her hands to show excitement, you could clap your hands instead.

[Ask parents:]

Have any of you tried imitating your child? [If so, ask:] How does your child respond?
Let's go back to some of your child's favorite activities. How could you use this technique with your child?

Slide 15

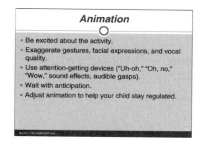

Another technique is to use heightened *Animation*.

Why?

Children with ASD often have difficulty understanding and using nonverbal language. Exaggerating the nonverbal aspects of language is one way to increase your child's skills in these areas. It also makes the interaction more fun and so helps keep your child motivated to stay in the interaction.

How?

Be excited about the activity, even if you are not really enjoying it. Let your child know that you enjoy being with him or her by being excited. Being excited makes your child more interested in sharing his or her enjoyment with you.

Make the nonverbal aspects of your communication "bigger" and easier to interpret by exaggerating your gestures, facial expressions, and vocal quality (rate, tone, volume).

Use attention-getting words and devices, such as "Wow," "Uh-oh," sound effects, or gasping audibly. This can increase your child's attention to your face.

Wait with anticipation. After doing an activity your child enjoys several times, such as tickles, chase, or throwing a ball, pause with an expectant look to see if your child indicates a wish to continue.

Adjust your animation to help your child stay regulated. Children learn best when they are regulated or in a balanced state of arousal—neither too up nor too down. Some children may become too revved-up when their parents are highly animated. If this happens, you would want to decrease gestures, vocal volume, and facial expressions to help your child calm down.

On the other hand, if your child is quiet, withdrawn, or sleepy, you can increase your child's arousal by exaggerating your gestures and facial expressions while increasing your vocal volume.

[Ask parents:]

Have any of you tried this? [If so, ask:] How does your child respond?

Let's go back to some of the activities you reported were favorites of your child's. How could you use this technique with your child?

> **Note to Trainers:** Discuss with parents their children's regulatory patterns. Identify how parents should implement this technique, depending on their children's tendencies.

Show Video Clips of *Follow Your Child's Lead,* *Imitate Your Child,* and *Animation*

Slide 16

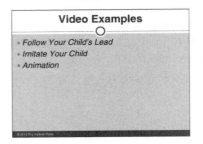

Note to Trainers: Prepare to show video clips for Session 3: *Follow Your Child's Lead, Imitate Your Child,* and *Animation.* There is not a specific clip for *Follow Your Child's Lead,* since this technique is demonstrated in the other techniques.

Before each clip, tell parents to notice these things:

How the parent uses *Follow Your Child's Lead.*
How the parent uses the other two techniques to make it interactive.

After each clip, ask parents:

"How did the parent use each technique?"
"How did the child respond?"

The important techniques to highlight and the children's responses are outlined below.

Imitate Your Child

• *Preverbal.* The father sits face to face with his son and alternates between modeling new play and imitating his son's play with blocks. The child is not very attentive when the father is modeling new play; however, he becomes more responsive once his father begins to imitate him. During this time, he watches his father's play, and his play becomes more purposeful. He also demonstrates positive affect during the imitation.

• *Emerging language.* The mother sits face to face with her daughter and imitates her daughter's play with the toy food. Her daughter responds to her mother's imitating her by using increased eye contact and positive affect.

• *Single words to simple phrases 1.* The child is playing with the beads by running them through her fingers. The mother imitates the child's play, expanding it ever so slightly. The child responds by using eye contact.

• *Single words to simple phrases 2.* The child is wandering aimlessly. The mother begins to imitate her body movements, gestures, and vocalizations. The child responds by engaging with her mother.

Animation

• *Preverbal.* The mother sits face to face, exaggerates her vocal quality, and pauses with an expectant look. Her child responds with increased attention and eye contact, as well as positive affect. He also initiates play during his mother's pauses, initially with gestures (reaching for her toy) and, after several turns, eventually with a vocalization.

   • *Complex phrase speech.* The mother sits face to face with her son and exaggerates her vocal quality, gestures, and facial expressions. Throughout the interaction, she uses heightened affect. Her son responds with increased eye contact, anticipation, and positive affect.

Take Break

Introduce Rationale for *Modeling and Expanding Language*

Slide 17

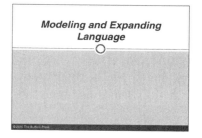

Once you are following your child's lead, you can begin to adjust your language to facilitate your child's language development. The technique of *Modeling and Expanding Language* will help you use language most effectively. The word *Modeling* is used here to mean showing or demonstrating.

Slide 18

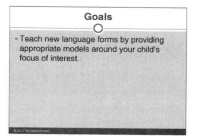

Why?

Children with ASD often have delayed language skills. You can improve your child's skills for understanding and expressing language by modeling—that is, showing—the use of a gesture, word, or phrase. These techniques build on the previous techniques: You use *Follow Your Child's Lead,* wait for your child to engage with you, and then model a more complex (developed) response.

Present *Modeling and Expanding Language*

Slide 19

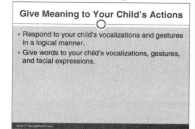

Why?

The behaviors of some children with ASD do not appear to be intentional. Treating your child's actions as purposeful is one way to increase your child's intentional use of language and play.

How?

To do this, respond to your child's vocalizations and gestures in a logical manner. For example, if your child puts your hand on the doorknob, respond to your child in a logical way by opening the door. This teaches your child that his or her behaviors carry meaning and elicit a specific response from you.

You can then teach your child a more appropriate way to communicate by putting gestures and words to your child's nonverbal behavior or vocalizations. For example, if your child puts your hand on the doorknob, tap on the door and say, "Open," before you open the door. This will show the child a more appropriate way to get you to open the door.

Slide 20

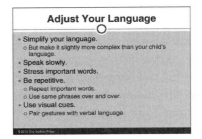

Why?

Children with ASD often have difficulty understanding the language they hear around them. This may be because it takes them more time to process what they hear. If you use big words, speak quickly, and let your words run together, your child may have much more difficulty understanding you. Adjusting how you speak to your child will help him or her understand language more clearly.

How?

Simplify your language so that is only slightly more complex than your child's language. If your child is preverbal, use single words. If your child uses single words, use two- to three-word phrases. Speak slowly to your child.

Stress important words, and segment your speech so that your words do not run together.

Repeat important words many times, and use the same phrases over and over. For example, if your child is playing with a car, you might say, "Car. Drive car. Car. Drive car."

Use gestures or other visual cues to help your child understand you. For example, when you say, "Baby," point to the baby.

Slide 21

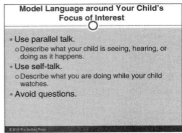

Why?

Your child is much more likely to learn language that relates to his or her personal experience. So speak about the things your child is paying attention to.

How?

Use *parallel talk*. That is, comment on or describe what your child is seeing, hearing, or doing. You might imagine yourself as a "sports announcer" describing everything that your child is experiencing.

Use *self-talk*. That is, describe what you are doing while your child watches. For example, in the video clips, we saw parents saying the word "Pop" as they popped bubbles, or saying the word "Stack" as they stacked blocks.

Don't ask questions; instead, make comments and provide labels. This provides your child with an opportunity to communicate and a model of the language he or she might use. When a child is not very responsive, parents can be tempted to fill up space with rhetorical questions—that is, questions that don't require an answer (e.g., "Is the boy going down the slide?", "Are you having fun?"). Instead rephrase rhetorical questions as comments (e.g., "The boy is going down the slide," "You are having fun").

You should also avoid asking "test" questions, or questions that only serve to demonstrate your child's knowledge (e.g., "What color is the ball?", "How many blocks do you have?"). Some children respond well to these types of questions if they know the answers. While there is a place for these questions, they do not promote reciprocal interactions. Imagine if every time you spoke to your partner, all he or she did was ask you test questions. The conversation would feel very one-sided. Thus it is important to avoid these types of questions, especially at the beginning. We will cover how to ask questions and get a response when we discuss the direct teaching techniques.

Slide 22

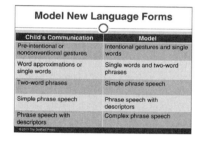

What to Model: Language Forms

How children communicate can take several different forms, such as eye contact, gestures, signs, words, and phrases.

This slide shows a broad overview of the development of language forms. The goal is to model behaviors that are slightly above the forms your child is currently using. For example, if your child is using a nonconventional gesture (such as leading you by the hand to what he or she wants), you should model a more conventional gesture (such as a tap or point). If your child is vocalizing, you should model single words.

[Ask parents:]

How does your child usually communicate?
What new language form could you model for your child?

Slide 23

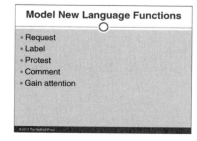

What to Model: Language Functions

You should be aware of how your child communicates and the form of language you will model. It is also important to determine why your child is communicating and to model language that increases the functions for which your child uses language.

There are many different reasons why children communicate. These include to request, label, comment, protest, and gain attention.

[Ask parents:]

Why does your child usually communicate?
What new language functions could you model?

Slide 24

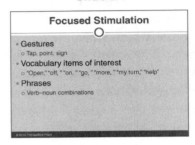

Focused stimulation means concentrated, repeated modeling of a small set of language forms or functions. Providing focused stimulation increases the likelihood that your child will learn these particular new forms of communication.

Pick several new gestures, words, or phrases that are related to your child's interests, and model them 15–20 times a day.

Remember the discussion of *how* your child is communicating and what you might model for him or her. For example, if your child is reaching, model a point and a single word.

[Ask parents:] What specific communication will you model over the next week?

Slide 25

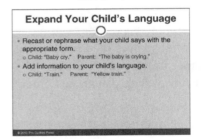

You can improve your child's appropriate language by recasting or rephrasing what he or she has said with appropriate grammar or syntax. For example, if your child says, "Baby cry," you could respond by saying, "The baby is crying." In this way, you revise and complete your child's speech without direct correction. It also indicates to your child that you have heard and understood him or her.

You can also add a word or two to what your child has said, to add new words and concepts to your child's language. For example, if your child says, "Train," you could respond by saying, "Yellow train."

These techniques are particularly useful for children who are beginning to use phrase speech.

Show Video Clips of *Modeling and Expanding Language*

Slide 26

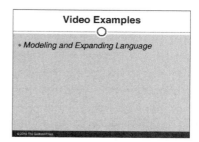

Note to Trainers: Prepare to show video clips for Session 3: *Modeling and Expanding Language.*

Before each clip, tell parents to notice:

How the parent adjusts his or her language when talking about what the child is attending to.
How the parent expands on the child's language.

After each clip, ask parents:

"How did the parent adjust his or her language?"
"What did the parent model for the child?"
"How did the child respond?"

The important techniques to highlight and the children's responses are outlined below.

• *Preverbal.* The mother uses *Follow Your Child's Lead,* staying face to face with him. She uses simple and repetitive language to talk about his focus of interest. She also responds to his behavior as meaningful. For example, at one point when her son vocalizes ("Ga Ga"), she responds by saying, "Ga ga, glasses." Her son responds with increased attention, eye contact, and positive affect. He also vocalizes again ("Ga ga").

• *Emerging language.* The mother talks about her daughter's focus of interest, using simple and repetitive language. She also overlays language on her daughter's point for the bubbles and gesture for "All done." She uses expansion to correct her daughter's verbalization ("Baby" instead of "Mama"). Her daughter responds by imitating her mother's language and adding a gesture.

• *Single words to simple phrases 1.* The father sits face to face with his son and models simple and repetitive language around his son's focus of attention, using exaggerated vocal quality. His son responds by imitating his father's language and using some words spontaneously.

• *Single words to simple phrases 2.* The mother imitates the child's language ("Open") as she responds to her request. She then uses simplified language around her child's focus of attention. The child responds by imitating the mother's language ("Turn").

• *Complex phrase speech.* The mother sits face to face with her son and uses self-talk and parallel talk to describe her own and her son's actions, along with an exaggerated vocal quality. She emphasizes descriptive words ("big" and "bigger") and expands on her son's language to add more parts of speech ("We all done balloon" becomes "You're all done *with the* balloon"). Her son is attentive and uses language.

Discuss and Assign Homework

Slide 27

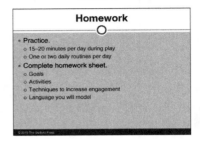

Note to Trainers: Pass out copies of Homework for Group Format: *Make Play Interactive* and *Modeling and Expanding Language* (Appendix A, Form 23).

I would like each of you to think of one to two goals that you will target this week. These goals should be related to increasing your child's social engagement (such as making eye contact during play or playing for an increased length of time) and language (such as using a gesture or words). Write your goals on your homework sheet. Also think of the type of language that you will model for your child during the week (focused stimulation), and write it on your homework sheet.

Next, think about the techniques that we talked about today for providing an opportunity for your child to engage. These include *Follow Your Child's Lead, Imitate Your Child,* and *Animation.* Choose one or more techniques that you will use to increase your child's engagement, and write these down on your homework sheet.

You should plan to practice these techniques for 15–20 minutes per day during play, as well as during one or two daily activities. So think about a play activity and one or two daily routines during which you can practice these techniques. Remember that you may need to add several minutes to your daily routines in order to have time to use the techniques. Once you decide on the activities, write them down on your homework sheet.

Note to Trainers: If time permits, have each parent report. Give feedback as necessary.

I would like you to practice these techniques over the next week and to respond to the questions on your homework sheet.

We will discuss your homework during your individual coaching session next week. You should come to the session with any questions you have about *Follow Your Child's Lead, Imitate Your Child, Animation,* and *Modeling and Expanding Language.*

Note to Trainers: Have parents sign up for the individual session if they haven't already been scheduled.

Review of *Make Play Interactive* and *Modeling and Expanding Language*

Session Goal

1. Improve the parent's ability to use interactive teaching techniques.

Materials

1. Parent manual
2. Completed Goal Development Form (Appendix A, Form 4)
3. Interactive Teaching Techniques Review Sheet I (Appendix A, Form 19)
4. Group Format Coaching Form (Appendix A, Form 18)
5. Five to six highly motivating toys and activities, including two sets of some toys
6. Homework for Group Format: *Make Play Interactive* and *Modeling and Expanding Language* (Appendix A, Form 23)

Outline of Session

- Prior to session, arrange the coaching space to facilitate parent–child interactions.
- Review homework from preceding group session (5 minutes).
- Provide a brief review of *Make Play Interactive* and *Modeling and Expanding Language* (5 minutes).
- Demonstrate use of *Make Play Interactive* and *Modeling and Expanding Language* with the child (5 minutes).
- Have the parent practice *Make Play Interactive* and *Modeling and Expanding Language* while you give feedback (20 minutes).
- Discuss and assign homework (10 minutes):
  1. Give out Homework for Group Format: *Make Play Interactive* and *Modeling and Expanding Language* (Appendix A, Form 23) and have to parent fill out "Goals of the Week."
  2. Instruct the parent to practice this homework over the next week and answer the questions.
  3. Have the parent read *Playful Obstruction, Balanced Turns, Communicative Temptations,* and *Overview of the Direct Teaching Techniques* (Chapters 7–9 and 11 of the parent manual).

Prior to Session, Arrange the Coaching Space to Facilitate Parent–Child Interactions

As described earlier, the coaching space should have physically defined boundaries. Again, too, limit distractions and select highly preferred toys.

Review Homework from Preceding Group Session

Begin the session by discussing the parent's answers to each of the homework questions from the copy of Appendix A, Form 23, that she received in the preceding group session (Session 3). If the parent did not write down her answers, review them orally with her now. If the parent had difficulties, brainstorm solutions. One challenge that frequently arises is that the parent is unable to interact with her child because he will not stay in one place. In such cases, brainstorm ways the parent can create a smaller and more intimate space at home.

Provide a Brief Review of *Make Play Interactive* and *Modeling and Expanding Language*

Briefly review the critical elements of techniques, using the Interactive Teaching Techniques Review Sheet I (Appendix A, Form 19). Explain that you will demonstrate these techniques and then have her practice while receiving feedback. These elements are also discussed in Chapters 3–6 of the parent manual (*Follow Your Child's Lead, Imitate Your Child, Animation,* and *Modeling and Expanding Language*). Give the parent an opportunity to ask questions before demonstrating use of the techniques.

Demonstrate Use of *Make Play Interactive* and *Modeling and Expanding Language* with the Child

Briefly model the techniques while explaining the targeted goals (e.g., making eye contact, maintaining the interaction), the techniques used (e.g., *Imitate Your Child, Animation*), the child's response (e.g., eye contact, gesture, words), and the type of communication form being modeled (e.g., point, single word). For example, the trainer might say to Brian's mother (see Part II, Session 1, Case Study 1): "Brian was rolling a car back and forth. I moved into his line of sight and began rolling another car while saying, 'Roll, roll.' He looked at me and said, 'Ro.'"

There are four interactive teaching techniques to demonstrate in this session. Given the fact that you have limited time to teach all techniques and that these particular techniques can be used together quite easily, it is recommended that you use them together. However, it might not be clear to the parent which ones you are modeling. Be sure to point out to the parent how you are combining techniques. For example, the trainer might say to Sam's mother (see Part II, Session 1, Case Study 2): "Sam was lining up his cars. I joined him by lining up cars with him.

Each time he or I added a car, I pointed to the car and said, 'More cars.' Notice that I used simple language and lots of animation."

If the parent is having difficulty recognizing the different techniques, you may choose to model each one separately for a few minutes.

Have the Parent Practice *Make Play Interactive* and *Modeling and Expanding Language* While You Give Feedback

Since the preceding group session has covered several different interactive techniques, you may need to guide the parent on what to practice. It is often good to start with *Imitate Your Child*, since this technique is often successful at developing the child's attention to the parent, and the child usually enjoys it. After the parent has had some success with this, you might suggest ways to use *Follow Your Child's Lead* or *Animation*. Once the parent is successful at using these techniques, you should have her focus on combining them with *Modeling and Expanding Language*. The parent should have at least 20 minutes to practice the intervention techniques.

If you are providing coaching in the home, you should have the parent practice using the techniques in the controlled environment that was chosen during Session 2. If you are coaching in a clinic or school, you should have the parent practice with a limited number of toys available. This will help to decrease the movement of the child between activities.

Use the Group Format Coaching Form (Appendix A, Form 18) to help you provide specific feedback on the techniques and to recognize the parent's strengths and weaknesses. Feedback should be specific, mostly positive, and related to technique use or to goals the parent could be targeting. The coaching form can be filled out during or immediately after the coaching session. Use the "Notes" portion of the form to record information for the next coaching session, including which techniques the parent is using well, which techniques should be targeted in the next session, and how the child is responding.

Discuss and Assign Homework

1. Give out Homework for Group Format: *Make Play Interactive* **and** *Modeling and Expanding Language* **and Have the Parent Fill Out "Goals of the Week."** Give the parent a fresh copy of Appendix A, Form 23, and help her fill out the "Goals of the Week" portion. First, help the parent identify one to two goals she will target this week and the specific language forms that she will model. Have the parent choose the techniques that were most effective at increasing engagement during the individual coaching session. Discuss ways in which the parent can use these techniques practiced during the individual coaching session during her daily routines with her child at home. To facilitate this discussion, you may wish to refer to the Daily Activity Schedule to identify specific routines. *Follow Your Child's Lead, Imitate Your Child,* and *Animation* are most likely to be effective during child-led activities such as fine or gross motor play, songs, and social games. *Modeling and Expanding Language* can be used during any activity. Ask the parent to identify one or more activities in which she will practice using this intervention. Activities should include a play activity as well as a daily routine.

2. Instruct the parent to practice this homework over the next week and answer the questions. Remind the parent that she should be practicing for 15–20 minutes a day during play, and also during her chosen daily routines. Mention that you will be discussing the homework at the beginning of the next group session.

3. Have the parent read *Playful Obstruction, Balanced Turns, Communicative Temptations,* **and** *Overview of the Direct Teaching Techniques* (Chapters 7–9, 11 of the parent manual). *Playful Obstruction, Balanced Turns,* and *Communicative Temptations* are all used to create opportunities for the child to engage or communicate, and are effective in gaining the child's attention and increasing the child's ability to initiate. The direct teaching techniques are used to teach the child specific language, imitation, and play behaviors. Explain to the parent that these topics will be discussed during the next group session. The parent should not complete the homework for these topics until they have been reviewed during the next session.

Troubleshooting Tips

One challenge in coaching a parent to use the first set of interactive teaching techniques is that they may elicit less interaction than the parent is used to receiving from her child. This is why the subsequent techniques focus on eliciting initiations. This may be frustrating for some parents, especially those who have difficulty letting their children lead the interaction. A parent who is used to structuring her child's play, asking a lot of questions, and giving directions may not understand why she should stop asking questions or giving directions, especially when the child has some language and can respond. If this occurs, explain that responding to questions and directions is only one kind of skill. The child also needs to learn other skills. These techniques ensure that the child is motivated; they improve the child's social engagement skills; and they increase the child's ability to initiate an interaction or to communicate spontaneously. Furthermore, these techniques make the direct teaching techniques more effective. Assure the parent that you will eventually get back to asking questions and giving directions when you cover the direct teaching techniques. For "Troubleshooting Tips" on individual techniques, refer to Sessions 3–7 in Part II.

Create Opportunities for Your Child to Engage or Communicate and Overview of the Direct Teaching Techniques

Session Goals

1. Teach parents to provide opportunities for their children to engage or communicate.
2. Provide parents with an overview of the direct teaching techniques, which will be taught during the next four sessions.
3. Teach parents how to prompt new skills effectively.
4. Teach parents how to provide reinforcement to increase the likelihood that their children will use a specific behavior.

Materials

1. DVD
2. Copies of Homework for Group Format: *Create Opportunities for Your Child to Engage or Communicate* (Appendix A, Form 24)
3. Whiteboard or large sheets of paper to review and introduce homework
4. Items children have trouble using alone (e.g., bubbles, tops, wind-up toys)
5. Variety of storage containers (e.g., clear plastic containers with screw lids, Ziploc bags, large bins, shelving) to illustrate techniques

Outline of Session

- Introduce session agenda (Slide 1).
- Review homework from preceding individual coaching session (Slide 2).
- Introduce rationale for *Playful Obstruction, Balanced Turns,* and *Communicative Temptations* (Slides 3–4).
- Discuss *Playful Obstruction, Balanced Turns,* and *Communicative Temptations* (Slides 5–14).
- Show video clips of *Playful Obstruction, Balanced Turns,* and *Communicative Temptations* (at Slide 15).
- Take break.
- Present *Overview of the Direct Teaching Techniques* (Slides 16–21).
- Show video clips of *Overview of the Direct Teaching Techniques* (at Slide 22).
- Explain how to make prompting and reinforcement effective (Slides 23–24).
- Discuss and assign homework (Slide 25):
  1. Pass out Homework for Group Format: *Create Opportunities for Your Child to Engage or Communicate* (Appendix A, Form 24) and have parents fill out "Goals of the Week."

249

2. Instruct parents to practice this homework over the next week and answer the questions.

- Have parents sign up for individual coaching session.

Introduce Session Agenda

Slide 1

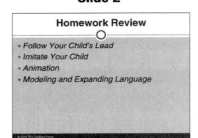

Today we will be discussing some additional interactive teaching techniques that can be used to encourage your child to engage with you and to initiate communication.

In the second half of the session, I will provide a brief overview of the direct teaching techniques, to acquaint you with the basics of prompting and reinforcement. At the next group session, we will provide more detail on the direct techniques and how to use these to teach specific social-communication skills.

Review Homework from Preceding Individual Coaching Session

Slide 2

Homework Review

- Follow Your Child's Lead
- Imitate Your Child
- Animation
- Modeling and Expanding Language

Note to Trainers: Review the homework given during the preceding individual session (Appendix A, Form 23). Read through the homework questions and ask parents to respond.

Use a whiteboard to record parents' responses. Make three columns: "Successes," "Challenges," and "Suggestions." If a parent reports successful use of a technique, write it on the whiteboard under "Successes." Ask whether any other parents had a similar success, in order to encourage group discussion.

If a parent reports difficulty using a technique, write it under "Challenges." Lead a discussion of what could be done to overcome the challenge. Based on the other parents' responses (or your own), write the best suggestions under the "Suggestions" next to the specific challenge.

Point out any main themes parents report.

Introduce Rationale for *Playful Obstruction, Balanced Turns,* and *Communicative Temptations*

Slide 3

We discussed the interactive teaching techniques at the base of the pyramid in the last two sessions. These techniques are designed to increase your child's social engagement and motivation. You allow your child to choose the activity and then join him or her in a highly engaging way. Use these techniques throughout your interactions with your child.

These techniques are likely to increase the amount of time that your child stays in an interaction with you. These techniques can lead some children with ASD to initiate social interactions and communication. However, for many children with ASD, they are not enough to encourage these initiations.

Thus, this week we will discuss the interactive teaching techniques in the middle of the pyramid. These techniques are used to provide your child specific opportunities to engage with you and to initiate communication, by interrupting your child's activity or controlling access to or "holding back" items that your child wants. They are used when the previous techniques are unsuccessful at getting your child to engage with you. They should be used in conjunction with the previous techniques, but not as often—more like two-thirds of the time.

Slide 4

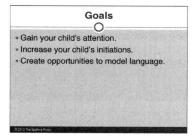

Why?

The following techniques are good at gaining your child's attention because, when you interrupt what your child is doing, he or she is more likely to pay attention to you.

Also, when you control access to or "hold back" the things that your child wants, your child will be more likely to initiate communication with you to obtain them.

Since these techniques increase your child's attention and initiations, they also provide opportunities for you to model a more complex response.

How?

As with all of these techniques, you use *Follow Your Child's Lead* to ensure that the items and activities are ones that your child chooses and is motivated by. If your child does not acknowledge your involvement on his or her own, you then use one of three techniques to provide a specific opportunity for him or her to engage with you.

Discuss *Playful Obstruction, Balanced Turns,* and *Communicative Temptations*

Slide 5

> **Playful Obstruction**
> ○
> * Prevent your child from doing what he or she wants by "playfully" blocking your child from completing a goal.
> * Use an anticipatory phrase.
> * Then present the playful obstruction.
>   ○ Block your child's play with your hand.
>   ○ Use a puppet or blanket to block your child's play.
>   ○ If your child is not engaged, block his or her path.
> * Wait for your child to communicate.
> * Respond to your child's communication.

The first technique is *Playful Obstruction.*

Why?

Many children with ASD have difficulty engaging with people when they are engaged in an activity. By playfully interrupting or obstructing what your child is doing, you can encourage your child to engage with you.

How?

Use an *anticipatory phrase,* such as "Here I come" or "I'm going to get the ball," before interrupting your child's play. This gives him or her a warning that something is about to change. Try to use the same phrase every time you use this technique. Be animated with your voice, face, and gestures when you use the anticipatory phrase.

Then *playfully obstruct* your child. You can do this in a variety of ways. The most simple is to block your child's play with your hand. For example, if your child is putting a ball in a ball chute, you could cover the hole in the ball chute with your hand so that your child can't put the ball down. Or, if your child is pushing a car, you could put your hand over the car so that your child can't move it.

Sometimes children get frustrated when someone else blocks their play. In this case, it can help to use a puppet, blanket, or some other object to block your child's play instead. Then he or she perceives the "culprit" to be an object rather than you.

Many children with ASD don't engage with toys, preferring to wander aimlessly or run back and forth. When this is the case, you can playfully obstruct your child by blocking your child's path, beating him or her to the intended spot, or simply stopping your child from moving with your hands. When doing this, be sure to keep it playful and try to turn it into a game. For example, if your child is running back and forth, you could briefly stop him or her from running and say, "Stop," wait for the child to engage, and then let him or her go while you say, "Go."

Next, *wait for your child to communicate.* Look for eye contact, shifts in body posture, gestures (points or hand leading), vocalizations, or words. These behaviors can indicate your child is aware that you are interacting with him or her.

Respond to your child's communication by giving him or her the desired item or stopping the interruption. If the child protests before you obstruct the play, then do not obstruct it.

[Ask parents:]

Have any of you tried this? [If so, ask:] How does your child respond?
Let's go back to some of the activities you reported were favorites of your child's. How could you use this technique with your child?

Slide 6

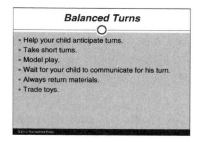

The second technique is *Balanced Turns.*

Why?

Children with ASD often have difficulty taking turns with others. By taking turns with your child, you can teach important early social skills. In addition, it provides an opportunity for you gain your child's attention, since you will have access to the toy that he or she wants.

How?

Help your child anticipate turns by first saying, "My turn." Then take the toy from the child, play with it briefly, and give it back, saying, "Your turn" or "John's turn."

When you start to take turns, make sure your turns are very short, to prevent your child from becoming too frustrated. When you can take a longer turn, take the opportunity to model a different way to play with the toy.

Wait for your child to initiate his or her turn.

Always return the item after your turn, even if your child does not initiate his or her turn or loses interest in the toy. This will teach your child that he or she will always get the toy back.

If your child becomes very frustrated when you take a turn, you can start by trading similar toys. Gradually increasing the amount of time that your child needs to wait before getting his or her toy back.

Slide 7

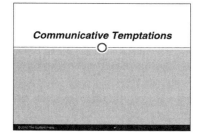

The third technique is *Communicative Temptations.* This is a set of strategies for controlling access to materials that your child wants. Most of these strategies involve setting up the environment ahead of time to encourage your child to initiate communication with you.

Slide 8

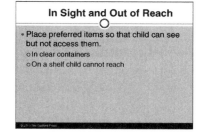

Increase your child's initiations by arranging preferred items so your child can see them but not get to them. In other words, they are *in sight*—but not accessible without your help.

Organize toys into clear containers that limit free access. Your child may also be more likely to play with this one toy for a longer period of time, increasing his or her engagement.

For a child who is not yet able to communicate intentionally, try placing desired toys in a tightly sealed container that the child has access to but cannot open. Sit facing your child.

Once your child realizes that he or she cannot open the container without your help, encourage the child to give you the container and open it for him or her. Over time, your child will learn that he or she can get a favorite toy by communicating with you (giving you the container).

> **Note to Trainers:** Show containers that can be used and discuss where they can be purchased.

For a child who is starting to gesture or use language intentionally, try storing some of your child's favorite toys on a special shelf that the child cannot reach. Your child then has the opportunity to initiate with you throughout the day whenever he or she wants the favorite toys. However, beware of climbing!

[Ask parents:]

Have any of you tried this? [If so, ask:] How does your child respond?
Let's go back to some of the activities you reported were favorites of your child's. How could you use this technique with your child?

Slide 9

Control Access
○
• Hold items your child wants so that he or she cannot access them.
• Only have one or two toys out at a time.

Control access means holding items that your child wants so that the child cannot reach them on his or her own. By holding the desired item near your eyes, you can encourage your child to look at you to indicate that he or she wants the item.

Be sure to only have one or two items available at a time, or your child is likely to switch to another toy as soon as you make him or her work for it.

It is OK to give your child the item when the child indicates he or she wants it by reaching. However, do not let your child grab the item out of your hands, or he or she will learn that this is an acceptable behavior. If your child attempts to grab the item away, you can stand up or hold the item out of arm's reach.

[Ask parents:]

Have any of you tried this? [If so, ask:] How does your child respond?
Let's go back to some of the activities you reported were favorites of your child's. How could you use this technique with your child?

Slide 10

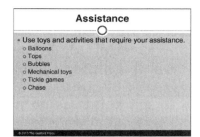

Choose highly motivating toys to play with that require your *assistance,* such as balloons, tops, bubbles, and mechanical toys. These items create natural opportunities for your child to initiate a request for your help. They are especially good to use with children who get very frustrated when you try to control their play. Also, while you are holding the item, your child is more likely to attend to you. We have already seen examples of this on the video clips of parents blowing bubbles and balloons. You can also use activities that require your participation, such as tickles or chase, and then wait for your child to communicate for more.

[Ask parents:]

Have any of you tried this? [If so, ask:] How does your child respond?
Let's go back to some of the activities you reported were favorites of your child's. How could you use this technique with your child?

Slide 11

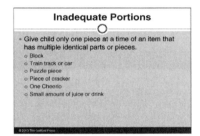

Use *inadequate portions* by providing your child only one piece at a time of an item that has multiple identical parts or pieces, such as blocks, trains, or puzzles. After giving a piece, wait for your child to initiate a request for more. This strategy is particularly effective with snacks or other food items when your child is motivated to eat. For example, rather than giving your child a whole bowl of fish crackers or Cheerios for a snack, give him or her only three pieces and hold the rest where your child can see them. You can also pour your child a small amount of juice rather than filling the cup. When using this strategy, be sure that you are present the entire time and have the item in sight and out of reach, so that your child realizes that he or she can get more.

[Ask parents:]

Have any of you tried this? [If so, ask:] How does your child respond?
Let's go back to some of the activities you reported were favorites of your child's. How could you use this technique with your child?

Slide 12

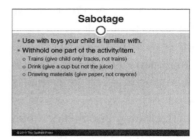

Use *sabotage* when your child knows the multiple parts of a familiar activity. Withhold a part of the activity to encourage your child to request the missing item. For example, give your child a train without the tracks. Give your child a cup, but not the juice. Give your child paper, but no crayons. This strategy is especially effective for teaching your child to ask questions (e.g., "Where is the _____?"). In order for sabotage to be effective, your child must know what particular item is missing.

For children who do not yet have a concept of all of the parts of an activity, inadequate portions is more effective. In this case, remain in your child's visual field with the missing items visible. Show the items to your child if he or she does not spontaneously initiate.

[Ask parents:]

Have any of you tried this? [If so, ask:] How does your child respond?

Let's go back to some of the activities you reported were favorites of your child's. How could you use this technique with your child?

Slide 13

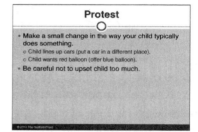

Use *protest* to teach your child how to say words such as "No" or "Stop" appropriately. Make a small change in the way your child typically likes to do something—a change that is likely to encourage a response. For example, if your child likes to line up cars, put a car in a different place. If your child wants a red balloon, offer a blue balloon.

This strategy is good to use with children who need to learn a more appropriate way to protest—for example, pushing a hand away instead of having a tantrum, or saying "No" instead of screaming.

When using this approach, make sure to model the appropriate language and or gesture immediately. For example if you move a favorite toy and your child gets upset, then as soon as your child begins to protest (fuss), model the correct target behavior ("Stop") and then put the toy back.

This strategy is often very effective at eliciting a response, but can also be frustrating to your child. So be sure not to use this strategy too often or to upset your child too much.

[Ask parents:]

Have any of you tried this? [If so, ask:] How does your child respond?

Let's go back to some of the activities you reported were favorites of your child's. How could you use this technique with your child?

Slide 14

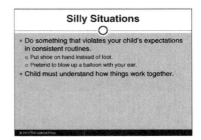

Silly situations involves completing a familiar activity or routine in a silly, obviously wrong way. This encourages your child to initiate for the right way. For example, put your child's shoe on his or her hand instead of his or her foot. Pretend to blow up a balloon with your ear.

This strategy requires that your child have a concept of the right and wrong ways to complete activities, and thus it may not be effective for younger or lower-functioning children.

When using this approach, you should use animation and emphasize that your behavior is "wrong." Many children find this strategy to be funny, and it can be used to develop shared positive feelings.

If your child does not respond, explain visually and verbally how the situation was "silly"—for example, "That's silly. Shoes go on our feet, not our hands!"

[Ask parents:]

Have any of you tried this? [If so, ask:] How does your child respond?
Let's go back to some of the activities you reported were favorites of your child's. How could you use this technique with your child?

Show Video Clips of *Playful Obstruction, Balanced Turns,* and *Communicative Temptations*

Slide 15

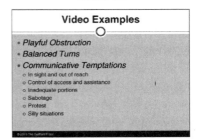

Note to Trainers: Prepare to show video clips for Session 5: *Playful Obstruction, Balanced Turns,* and *Communicative Temptations.*

Before each clip, ask parents to watch for these things:

How the parent uses the particular technique.
How the child responds.

After each clip, ask parents:

"Did you notice how the parent provided an opportunity for the child to communicate?"
"What behaviors did the child use to indicate what he or she wanted?"

The important techniques to highlight and the children's responses are outlined below.

Playful Obstruction

- *Single words to simple phrases 1.* The mother uses *Playful Obstruction* by interrupting her daughter's play with the beads to encourage engagement. She makes the obstruction "playful" by using a puppet. She also uses *Animation* and an anticipatory phrase ("Ready, set, stop") to help her daughter anticipate the disruption. The child responds by making eye contact and showing positive affect. After several times, the child anticipates the disruption and initiates by making eye contact and saying, "Ready."
- *Single words to simple phrases 2.* The mother uses *Playful Obstruction* again with a puppet to encourage her daughter to engage with her. She does not move her hand until her daughter responds to her in some way. The child responds with a change in affect (laughter) and sometimes eye contact.

Balanced Turns

- *Single words to simple phrases 1.* The mother joins her daughter's play with the beads. She takes a turn and models a new way to play with the beads. Her daughter responds by imitating her. Her mother then attempts to engage with her daughter by imitating her daughter's play with the beads. Her daughter does not respond by increasing engagement or initiating. Thus the mother takes another turn with the beads, so that the child loses access to the beads for a moment. The child responds by using language (imitates "My turn" and spontaneously says, "A pumpkin").
- *Single words to simple phrases 2.* The mother takes turns with her daughter with the bracelets. She uses a simple phrase ("My turn") to help her daughter anticipate the disruption. During the mother's turn, she models a new way to play with the bracelets, but keeps her turns short. Her daughter responds by using language (she says, "My heart," during the first turn and imitates "on" during the second turn). The mother also uses *Playful Obstruction* to help her daughter engage with her when her daughter is spinning, by physically stopping her in a playful way. Her daughter responds with positive affect (laughing).

Communicative Temptations

- *In sight and out of reach—Emerging language.* The mother uses in sight and out of reach by having the bubbles and stroller on shelves that are visible but out of reach. The mother waits for her daughter to direct her communication to her (social communication) before responding. The child responds by using words and gestures to request these toys. When her mother waits, she responds by directing her communication toward her mother (not just at the toy). She also imitates her mother's words.
- *Control of access and assistance—Complex phrase speech.* The mother uses several *Communicative Temptations* to engage with her son and to encourage initiations. She uses control of access by holding the fruit leather out of his reach and assistance by handing him a snack that he cannot open on his own. She also uses silly situations by pretending she will eat the fruit leather. The child responds by initiating more communication.
- *Inadequate portions—Preverbal.* The mother uses inadequate portions in order to

encourage her child to initiate by only providing her son with one block at a time. She eventually extends the interaction by using *Balanced Turns*. Her child responds by using a gesture (reach) to indicate that he wants more blocks. Eventually he is able to engage in turn taking with support.

- *Sabotage—Single words to simple phrases.* The mother uses sabotage to encourage her son to initiate by having some of the toys (the potty and the Dora character) missing when she gives him the set of toys. (This is a set of toys that he is familiar with, so he knows they are missing.) She also uses in sight and out of reach by having the toys on a shelf that he can see but cannot access on his own. He responds by using a gesture (point) and words (although they are unclear) to ask for the missing items.

- *Protest—Single words to simple phrases.* The mother uses protest by offering her son objects other than the one he requested (roller skates). When offering the wrong items, she is animated and models the correct response ("Is this the roller skate? No!") to avoid frustrating him. The child responds by initiating and eventually imitates the mother's language ("Is this the roller skate? Yes!").

- *Silly situations—Complex phrase speech 1.* The mother uses silly situations by pretending to blow up a balloon with her ear. To emphasize the "silliness," she uses *Animation*. Her son responds by using language to instruct his mother how to blow up the balloon properly. He is also very engaged and uses a lot of positive affect in response to his mother's silly situation.

- *Silly situations—Complex phrase speech 2.* The mother uses a silly situation by putting her son's shoes on his hands and then on her feet, instead of on his feet. Her son uses varied language and initiates multiple times to correct her. If his mother had just put his shoes on, it would have been the end of the interaction.

Take Break

Present *Overview of the Direct Teaching Techniques*

Slide 16

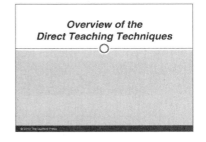

Up to this point, the main focus has been on increasing your responsiveness to your child's behavior and increasing the number of opportunities your child has to engage and initiate with you. Now we are going to focus on how to increase the complexity of your child's response after he or she has initiated.

We do this through the direct teaching techniques, which all involve the use of prompting and reinforcement. Today we will provide a brief overview of how to use the direct teaching techniques. You will not be expected to use these techniques until after the following group session, in which we will cover the specifics of how to prompt and reinforce more complex social-communication skills.

Slide 17

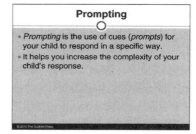

Why?

Direct teaching techniques teach new, specific language, imitation, and play skills. The techniques have been shown to be effective in promoting social-communication development. They increase various forms of expressive language, such as pointing, signs, words, and word combinations. The techniques also promote your child's understanding of language (receptive language), as well as social imitation and play skills, which are building blocks for further language development.

How?

Direct teaching techniques build on the techniques you have already been learning. You are going to continue to *Follow Your Child's Lead* and create opportunities for him or her to engage or communicate; however, you will then use prompting and reinforcement as sets of strategies to teach new social-communication skills.

Slide 18

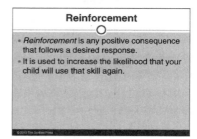

Prompting is the use of cues (*prompts*) to help your child produce a specific response. The specific response you prompt should be slightly more complex than what your child uses on his or her own. This helps your child increase the complexity of his or her language, imitation, and play behavior.

Prompts can differ in the level of help—or support—they give your child.

Slide 19

Reinforcement is a positive consequence that follows a behavior.

Once your child produces the response you have prompted, you will provide him or her with reinforcement.

Since your teaching will center around your child's interests, the positive consequence you provide as reinforcement will be related to the activity or item that your child wants. For example, if your child wants the bubbles and you prompt him or her to say, "Bubbles," the reinforcement would be the bubbles rather than an unrelated positive consequence, like candy.

By reinforcing your child's behavior, you increase the likelihood that your child will behave that way again.

Slide 20

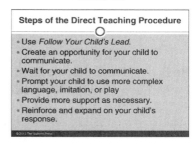

Let's now go over the six steps of the direct teaching procedure. Begin by using *Follow Your Child's Lead*. The more motivated and engaged your child is, the more likely he or she is to learn.

Next, create an opportunity for your child to communicate with you. This ensures that you have your child's attention before you provide the prompt. You will want to use *Playful Obstruction, Balanced Turns,* and *Communicative Temptations* to encourage your child to communicate with you if he or she hasn't done so spontaneously.

Once your child has initiated communication, you will then prompt your child to produce a more complex response. You begin with the *least supportive* prompt—that's the prompt that gives the least amount of help. This lets you see what your child can do on his or her own. You then add more support as necessary to help child respond appropriately.

After your child produces the desired response, you provide reinforcement. This means you will deliver the desired item or activity and praise your child. You will also expand on your child's response, as you have learned to do in *Modeling and Expanding Language*.

Slide 21

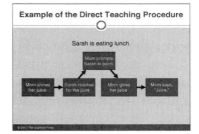

For example, Sarah routinely requests by reaching. Mom wants to teach her to point, a slightly more complex skill. Now Sarah is eating lunch at the table. Sarah's mother encourages her to initiate communication by showing her the juice but having it out of her reach. This is in sight and out of reach, a *Communicative Temptations* strategy.

Sarah initiates communication by reaching for the juice. Sarah's mom now uses a prompt to help Sarah point. Mom starts with a least supportive prompt and models a point. If Sarah imitates her mother's point (correct response), her mother will reinforce Sarah by giving her the juice and praising her. If Sarah does not imitate the point, Sarah's mother will increase her support and physically assist Sarah to point. This ensures that Sarah points, and her mother then provides reinforcement by giving her the juice and providing praise. Mom also expands on Sarah's response by saying, "Juice."

Show Video Clips of *Overview of the Direct Teaching Techniques*

Slide 22

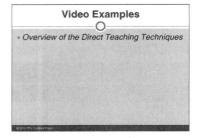

Note to Trainers: Prepare to show video clips for Session 5: *Overview of the Direct Teaching Techniques* (three clips).

Before each clip, tell parents to look for how the parent uses prompting and reinforcement.

After the clip, ask parents:

"How did the parent encourage an initiation?"
"After the child initiated, what did the parent do [the prompt]?"

"How did the child respond?"
"After the child responded with a more complex response, what did the parent do [the reinforcement]?

The important techniques and strategies to highlight and the children's responses are outlined below.

• *Preverbal.* The mother uses a *Communicative Temptation* (in sight and out of reach) to encourage her son to initiate by placing balls in a jar that her son cannot open on his own. Once he initiates, his mother prompts him to increase the complexity of his initiation. She prompts him to tap the jar by asking, "Do you want to open?", and patting the jar top. By modeling a gesture for her son to imitate (patting the jar), the mother prompts or cues her son to use a specific communication behavior (tapping). Once her son responds correctly by tapping the jar, the mother provides immediate reinforcement by opening the jar. The mother also uses *Balanced Turns* ("My turn") to encourage her son to initiate. She then prompts him to sign "My turn" by asking him, "Do you want your turn? What do we say?", and modeling the gesture for him to imitate (prompt). When he does not imitate on his own, she prompts him to use the sign by physically assisting him. She reinforces him by giving him the toy and praising him ("My turn. Good boy"). She also monitors his motivation and provides more support as necessary by moving to a physical prompt with "My turn," to ensure that her son knows how to get the ball back. Her son responds by using more complex communication (a tap for "Open" and a gesture for "My turn"). During the physical prompt, he also makes a verbal approximation of "My turn."

• *Single words to phrase speech.* The father uses a *Communicative Temptation* (assistance) to encourage his son to initiate by using a balloon that his son is unable to blow up on his own. Once his son initiates, the father prompts him to use more complex language by asking a question ("What do you want?"), waiting, and modeling language for him to imitate ("I ... want ... blow ... Balloon," and "One, two, three—"). As soon as his son responds correctly, the father reinforces him immediately by letting the balloon fly and saying, "Fly away." The child responds by using more complex language ("I want blow balloon," "Blow," and "Fly").

- *Complex phrase speech.* The mother encourages her son to initiate by using *Communicative Temptations*—having toys in a box with a lid (in sight and out of reach) and holding up the girl toy (control of access). After her son initiates, she prompts him to use more complex language by asking him a question ("What do you want, Isaac?"), helping him increase the specificity of his request ("More what?"), and giving him a choice ("Animals or girl?"). Once he responds correctly, she immediately reinforces him with access to the toy and praise ("Good asking"). The child responds by increasing his language complexity through using a label ("girl").

Explain How to Make Prompting and Reinforcement Effective

Slide 23

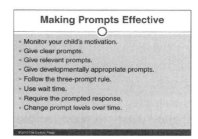

There are several "rules" to follow to make prompting most effective.

First, *monitor your child's motivation.* When children are very motivated for an activity, it is easy to push them to use a new skill. However, when they are not motivated or if the task becomes too hard, it is often difficult to get them to work harder. Motivation needs to be relatively high for the direct teaching techniques to be effective. Times when your child enjoys an activity are good times to prompt, because you can be sure your child is interested in and motivated by the activity; therefore, learning is more likely to take place. By *Follow Your Child's Lead,* you can be sure that your child is interested in the activity. However, even when you use *Follow Your Child's Lead,* there are times when he or she may not be motivated to play, interact, or communicate. If your child is not interested in the available materials; does not enjoy the task; or is feeling unhappy, frustrated, tired, or sick, then alter the interaction to increase motivation prior to using a prompt.

You should also *make sure that your prompts are clear,* so that your child understands what you are asking him or her to do. One common mistake is to ask rhetorical questions without intending that your child respond, such as "Are you driving your car?" Another common mistake is using very complex prompts, such as "Tell me what it is that you want," or several prompts together, each of which asks for a slightly different answer, such as "Do you want this block [correct answer: "Yes"]? Say that you want the block [correct answer: "Block"]." If you do this, your child may have a difficult time understanding what you want him or her to do. Therefore, pause before giving a prompt, gain your child's attention (i.e., create an opportunity for him or her to communicate), and use simple language appropriate to your child's skill level.

Prompts then *need to be related to what your child is doing.* For example, if your child is playing with blocks, prompt him or her to communicate about the blocks (e.g., "What do you want?" or "How many blocks do you have?") Don't prompt about something unrelated to the activity (e.g., "What is your name?" or "Count to 10").

It is important for your prompt to be *appropriate for your child's developmental level.* For example, if your child is pointing but not yet using single words, prompt to increase single-word approximations. If your child is not yet playing functionally with a toy, prompt functional play before pretend play.

You should typically *provide no more than three prompts* to elicit a correct response. If after one or two prompts your child is unsuccessful, move to a more supportive prompt that will ensure your child is successful in responding. If your child is unsuccessful after three prompts, he or she is not likely to be successful if you keep prompting. In addition, he or she is likely to become frustrated or lose interest in the activity. You want to make sure that your child understands that there is a way to obtain the desired item or activity from you. Thus you want to give more support to help him or her respond correctly, so that you can provide the reinforcement. One word of caution here: The exact number of times you prompt will depend a lot on your child's motivation. If your child is very motivated for the item or activity, you may be able to prompt a little more than three times. If he or she is not very motivated or is easily frustrated, you may need to help him be successful with fewer than three prompts.

Be sure to *wait after each prompt*. You want to give your child adequate time to respond before providing a more supportive prompt. Many children with ASD take a little while to process information. If you don't wait between prompts, you may move too quickly and not challenge your child enough. One rule of thumb is to wait 5 seconds before providing the next prompt.

When you are using the direct teaching techniques, *your child must respond with a more complex response* before he or she gets the desired object or activity. You must help him respond successfully by providing more support when he is unable to respond to your initial prompt.

Finally, *change prompt levels over time* to increase your child's ability to respond spontaneously. Each type of prompt differs in its degree of support. Time delay (waiting) provides the least support, since the child is not told what to do; physical guidance provides the most support, since the child is physically guided to complete the response. The goal is to reduce the amount of support you provide over time to build spontaneous communication. We will discuss specific prompts and how to move between them in more detail in the next group session.

Slide 24

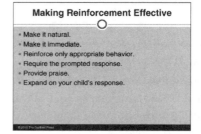

There are also several "rules" that make reinforcement most effective.

First, the natural consequence of a communication is the best reinforcement. That is, you want to make sure that the reinforcement comes *naturally* out of the situation and your child's response. For example, your child reaches for a block and you prompt, "What is this?" When he says, "Block," you want to reinforce that by giving him the block rather than some other item, such as a sticker or snack. By using *Follow Your Child's Lead* and letting him select what to play with, you can get a good idea of what will serve as strong reinforcement in the moment. For example, if your child is reaching for the bubbles and not the cars, you would know to use the bubbles as a reinforcer.

Give reinforcement immediately after your child responds correctly. This helps your child make the connection between his or her behavior and the consequence. If you wait too long, your child may not know which of his or her behaviors elicited the consequence.

Reinforcement will increase whatever behavior it directly follows. So *only reinforce behaviors you want to increase*. Reinforcing inappropriate behaviors will increase those behaviors. If your child is using an appropriate and an inappropriate behavior at the same time, such as saying, "More block" (appropriate) while hitting you (inappropriate), you should not give more blocks, because you may accidentally teach your child that the inappropriate behavior (hitting) is what got him or her the desired object.

Only provide reinforcement for good attempts at the prompted response. This "rule" works in conjunction with the prompt rule of requiring a response. Since with the direct teaching techniques you are now prompting your child to use a specific behavior, you should only provide reinforcement if your child makes a good attempt at that behavior. For example, if your child reaches for the bubbles and you prompt him or her to say, "Bubble," you should only provide the reinforcement (bubbles) when he or she attempts to respond to your prompt (says, "Bubble," or makes a good attempt, such as "Buh"). If your child does not respond to your prompt, you should provide an additional prompt or increase your support to help him or her be successful. If you give your child the reinforcement when he or she does not make a good attempt, then the child learns that he or she does not have to try harder. This holds true only when you are using the direct teaching techniques.

When you use the interactive teaching techniques, you want to continue to reinforce your child's communicative attempts, to teach the child that his or her communication carries meaning and elicits a response from you. This approach will increase spontaneous language.

After your child responds appropriately, you will want *to provide behavior-specific praise* to let him know what he did right. For example, you might say, "Good job pointing to the car." We also saw an example in the last clip, when the mom said, "Good asking, Isaac."

After your child responds appropriately, you will also want to *expand on his or her response*. We talked about this during *Modeling and Expanding Language*. You model an even more complex communication without requiring the child to respond. For example, if your child says, "Ball," after you prompt him, you would respond by saying, "Want ball" or "I want ball," while giving your child the ball. This sets the stage for what you will be prompting next!

Discuss and Assign Homework

Slide 25

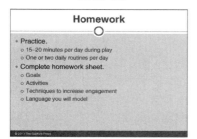

Note to Trainers: Pass out copies of Homework for Group Format: *Create Opportunities for Your Child to Engage or Communicate* (Appendix A, Form 24).

I would like each of you to think of one to two goals that you will target this week. These goals should be related to increasing your child's social engagement, such as making eye contact during play, and language, such as using a gesture or words to request. Write your goals on your homework sheet. Also, think of the type of language that you will model for your child during the week, and write it on your homework sheet.

Next, think about the techniques that we talked about today for providing an opportunity for your child to engage or communicate. These include *Playful Obstruction, Balanced Turns,* and *Communicative Temptations.* Choose one or more techniques that you will use to increase your child's engagement, and write these down on your homework sheet.

You should plan to practice these techniques for 15–20 minutes per day during play, as well as during one or two daily activities. So think about a play activity and one or two daily routines during which you can practice these techniques. Remember that you will need to add several minutes to your daily routines in order to have time to use the techniques. Once you decide on the activities, write them down on your homework sheet.

> **Note to Trainers:** If time permits, have each parent report on goals, language to model, and activities for practice. Give feedback as necessary.

I would like you to practice these techniques over the next week and to respond to the questions on your homework sheet.

You will notice that there are also questions on your homework sheet on identifying good opportunities for prompting your child to increase the complexity of his or her initiation. You are not expected to practice the direct teaching techniques this week. However, these homework questions should help you think about times when prompting will be most effective.

We will discuss your homework during your individual coaching session next week. You should come to the session with questions you have about *Playful Obstruction, Balanced Turns,* and *Communicative Temptations.*

> **Note to Trainers:** Have parents sign up for the individual session if they haven't already been scheduled.

Session 6 (Coaching)

Review of *Create Opportunities for Your Child to Engage or Communicate*

Session Goal

1. Improve the parent's ability to use techniques to increase her child's engagement and initiations.

Materials

1. Parent manual
2. Completed Goal Development Form (Appendix A, Form 4)

3. Interactive Teaching Techniques Review Sheet II (Appendix A, Form 6)
4. Group Format Coaching Form (Appendix A, Form 18)
5. Five to six highly motivating toys and activities, including items the child has trouble using alone (e.g., bubbles, tops, wind-up toys)
6. Variety of storage containers (e.g., clear containers with screw lids, Ziploc bags, large bins, shelving) that desired items can be placed in
7. Homework for Group Format: *Create Opportunities for Your Child to Engage or Communicate* (Appendix A, Form 24)

Outline of Session

- Prior to session, review coaching form and notes from previous coaching session, and arrange coaching space to support parent–child interactions.
- Review homework from preceding group session (5 minutes).
- Provide a brief review of *Playful Obstruction, Balanced Turns,* and *Communicative Temptations* (5 minutes).
- Demonstrate use of *Playful Obstruction, Balanced Turns,* and *Communicative Temptations* with the child (5 minutes).
- Have the parent practice *Playful Obstruction, Balanced Turns,* and *Communicative Temptations* while you give feedback (20 minutes).
- Discuss and assign homework (10 minutes):
    1. Give out Homework for Group Format: *Create Opportunities for Your Child to Engage or Communicate* (Appendix A, Form 24) and have the parent fill out "Goals of the Week."
    2. Instruct the parent to practice this homework over the next week and answer the questions.
    3. Have parent read *Teaching Your Child Expressive Language* and *Teaching Your Child Receptive Language* (Chapters 12 and 13 of the parent manual).

Prior to Session, Review Coaching Form and Notes from Previous Coaching Session, and Arrange Coaching Space to Support Parent–Child Interactions

During or after the previous individual coaching session (Session 4), you will have noted the parent's strengths and weaknesses for using the techniques up through *Modeling and Expanding Language.* It can be helpful to review that coaching form and your notes before this coaching session. You will want to check to see whether the parent has continued to have difficulty with an earlier technique, and may wish to provide coaching on that technique before introducing new techniques. It is important for the parent to have a good grasp of the earlier techniques before you move on.

As usual, make sure to arrange the coaching space to support parent–child interactions by having a defined physical space, limiting distractions, and selecting highly preferred toys.

Review Homework from Preceding Group Session

Begin the session by discussing the parent's answers to each of the homework questions from the copy of Appendix A, Form 24, she received in the preceding group session (Session 5). If the parent did not write down her answers, review them orally with her now. If the parent had difficulties, brainstorm solutions. Parent-reported challenges are usually related to using *Communicative Temptations* during activities at home. If this occurs, help the parent identify specific daily routines. If the parent reports that using *Communicative Temptations* during a daily routine made the routine take too long and was impractical, remind her to plan to add 5–10 minutes to the routine. If she is unable to do this (e.g., the child needs to finish breakfast quickly to catch the bus for school), help her select another routine that she can extend in which to use the techniques.

Provide a Brief Review of *Create Opportunities for Your Child to Engage or Communicate*

Briefly review the critical elements of the techniques, using the Interactive Teaching Techniques Review Sheet II (Appendix A, Form 6). These elements are also discussed in Chapters 7—9 (*Playful Obstruction, Balanced Turns,* and *Communicative Temptations*) of the parent manual. Explain that you will demonstrate these techniques and then have her practice while receiving feedback. Give the parent an opportunity to ask questions.

Demonstrate use of *Playful Obstruction, Balanced Turns,* and *Communicative Temptations with the Child*

Be sure to have the coaching environment set up with a number of containers storing toys and other desired items that can be used to demonstrate some of the *Communicative Temptations*. Also provide toys that the child will have difficulty using on his own, such as balloons, bubbles, and tops. You may also wish to provide a small snack in order to demonstrate the use of inadequate portions. Explain to the parent which technique or strategy you will use, what response you will look for, and how you will respond to the child. Then briefly demonstrate how to use the technique or strategy to increase the child's initiations. Try to demonstrate each of the techniques and strategies separately, including the seven types of *Communicative Temptations*. Identify each technique or strategy as you use it and the child's response. For example, the trainer might say to Brian's mother: "Here I was using inadequate portions and waiting to see how Brian would respond. He reached for the cracker. I waited until he looked at me before I gave him more crackers, and I provided a model of a point and the word 'Cracker.'"

Have the Parent Practice *Playful Obstruction, Balanced Turns,* and *Communicative Temptations* While You Provide Feedback

Playful Obstruction and *Balanced Turns* are most effective when the child is so engaged in an activity that he has difficulty engaging with the parent. Both of these strategies interrupt the child's activity and thus are likely to elicit a response. Thus these strategies work best during play. The *Communicative Temptations* strategies also work well during play, but have the added benefit of being easily incorporated into daily routines. Therefore, if you are providing coaching in the home, have the parent practice using the *Communicative Temptations* strategies during a specific caretaking routine, such as snack or lunch. The parent should have at least 20 minutes to practice the techniques and strategies.

Provide the parent with specific techniques or strategies to use. For example, the trainer might say to Sam's mother: "Let's use in sight and out of reach with the crackers. Remember to place the cracker box in Sam's line of sight but out of his reach, and wait for him to communicate with you."

Remind the parent to continue to respond to all types of appropriate communication by providing the desired item or activity while also modeling a more complex response. If the parent has difficulty implementing some techniques or strategies, it may be beneficial to identify one or two of them to target. Provide the parent with specific feedback related to those techniques/strategies. For example, if the child grabs the item when the parent is trying to control access, encourage the parent to stand up so the child cannot reach the item. If the child becomes distressed, acknowledge that these techniques can increase the child's frustration, and suggest ways to decrease the frustration. For example, the parent can place the desired items in containers rather than withholding access by hand. This can decrease frustration because the child perceives the containers as the barriers, rather than the parent. You may also want to help the parent to identify the child's communicative behaviors more clearly, and to respond to those behaviors immediately.

Use the Group Format Coaching Form (Appendix A, Form 18) to help you determine how to provide specific feedback on the techniques. This form can be filled out during or immediately after the coaching session. Use the "Notes" portion of the form to record information for the next coaching session, including which techniques and strategies the parent is using well, which ones should be targeted next session, and how the child is responding.

Discuss and Assign Homework

1. Give out Homework for Group Format: *Create Opportunities for Your Child to Engage or Communicate* and have the parent fill out "Goals of the Week." Give the parent a fresh copy of Appendix A, Form 24, and work with the parent to identify and fill in each goal, the techniques and strategies she will use to encourage engagement and initiations, and the new language form she will model. Have the parent choose the techniques and strategies that were most effective during the individual coaching session. In addition, have the parent select the communication form(s) she will model after the child initiates, such as gestures, signs, words, word combinations, or new vocabulary. Remember that the parent will eventually be prompting these communication forms, so make sure that they are developmentally appropriate for the specific child.

Discuss how the parent can use the different techniques and strategies practiced in this session during her daily routines with her child at home. If necessary, refer to the Daily Activity Schedule to identify specific routines. These techniques are most likely to be effective during child-led activities such as fine or gross motor play, songs, and social games, as well as at mealtimes. In particular, you should discuss ways in which the parent can place desired items in sight and out of reach in the home to increase child initiations. Remember that for children who climb, it may be more beneficial to use containers than to put items on high shelves.

Ask the parent to identify one or more activities in which she will practice using the intervention. Activities should include a play activity as well as a daily routine.

2. Instruct the parent to practice this homework over the next week and answer the questions. Remind the parent that she should be practicing for 15–20 minutes a day during play, and also during her chosen daily routines. Mention that you will be discussing the homework at the beginning of the next group session.

3. Have the Parent Read *Teaching Your Child Expressive Language* and *Teaching Your Child Receptive Language* (Chapters 12 and 13 of the parent manual). Explain to the parent that the next group session will discuss how to use direct teaching techniques involving prompting and reinforcement to teach her child both expressive language and receptive language skills. The parent should not complete the homework for these topics until they have been reviewed during the next session.

Troubleshooting Tips

Some parents are hesitant to use the more intrusive interactive teaching techniques, such as *Playful Obstruction* or *Balanced Turns*, because they do not want to upset their children. This often occurs with children who are actively avoidant of others. Without the use of these techniques, however, a parent may have difficulty getting her child to engage with her. If this occurs, remind the parent to be persistent in pursuing the interaction. Remind the parent that even protests are a type of communication. Therefore, if the child communicates protest in any form, the parent should respond. Remind the parent that communication can take the form of body movement changes, gestures, fleeting eye contact, or words. Responding to subtle aspects of the child's behavior will teach him that his behavior carries meaning and elicits a response.

A challenge that can occur when a parent is using *Communicative Temptations* is that if the child is unable to initiate at all, he may not request even his favorite items. In this case, the parent could "market" the item to the child, by handing the child the container holding the favorite item to increase the child's motivation. If the child is still not interested, the parent should follow his lead to another activity.

One caution is that sometimes children are very creative, arranging furniture to access what they want rather than requesting help. If this might be the case, encourage the parent to use clear containers that can be kept safely within the child's reach but that he cannot open without the parent's assistance. The parent may also choose to use a lock and stay near the child, so that he learns that he can open the cupboard or door with assistance.

Waiting for the child to initiate can be difficult for the parent, especially when the child is able to respond to questions or to repeat lengthy sentences. In this case, stress to the parent that while it is wonderful that she can anticipate what her child wants and prompt an elaborated response, she wants to teach her child to *initiate* language, so that he can communicate with others when the parent is not present.

Teaching Your Child Expressive and Receptive Language

Session Goals

1. Teach parents techniques to improve their children's expressive and receptive language.
2. Teach parents to use the least supportive prompt to increase their children's spontaneity.

Materials

1. DVD
2. Copies of Homework for Group Format: *Teaching Your Child Expressive and Receptive Language* (Appendix A, Form 25)
3. Whiteboard or large sheets of paper to review and introduce homework

Outline of Session

- Introduce session agenda (Slide 1).
- Review homework from preceding individual coaching session (Slide 2).
- Introduce rationale for the direct teaching techniques (Slides 3–4).
- Review the direct teaching procedure and ways to make prompting effective (Slides 5–6).
- Show video clips of *Overview of the Direct Teaching Techniques* (Slide 7).
- Discuss what language skills to prompt (Slides 8–9).
- Take break.
- Discuss prompt strategies for *Teaching Your Child Expressive Language* (Slide 10).
- Show video clips of specific expressive language prompts (at Slide 11).
- Discuss *Teaching Your Child Receptive Language* (Slides 12–13).
- Show video clip of receptive language prompts (at Slide 14).
- Discuss changing prompt levels (Slide 14).
- Discuss and assign homework (Slide 16):
  1. Pass out Homework for Group Format: *Teaching Your Child Expressive and Receptive Language* (Appendix A, Form 25) and have parents fill out "Goals of the Week."
  2. Instruct parents to practice this homework over the next week and answer the questions.
- Have parents sign up for individual coaching session.

Introduce Session Agenda

Slide 1

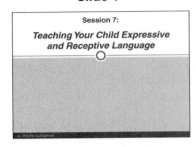

Today we will begin with a review of homework practice and another look at the direct teaching techniques in general. Then we are going to discuss specific prompting strategies you can use to increase the complexity of your child's *expressive language,* as well as your child's ability to understand language and follow directions (also known as *receptive language*).

Review Homework from Preceding Individual Coaching Session

Slide 2

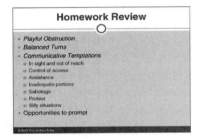

Note to Trainers: Review the homework that was given during the last individual coaching session (Appendix A, Form 24). Read through the homework questions and ask parents to respond.

Use a whiteboard to write down parents' responses. Make three columns: "Successes," "Challenges," and "Suggestions." If a parent reports successful use of a technique, write it on the whiteboard under "Successes." Ask whether any other parents had a similar success, in order to encourage group discussion.

If a parent reports difficulty using a technique, write it under "Challenges." Lead a discussion of what could be done to overcome the challenge. Based on the other parents' responses (or your own), write the best suggestions under "Suggestions" next to the specific challenge.

Point out any main themes parents report.

Introduce Rationale for the *Direct Teaching Techniques*

Slide 3

Today we will continue discussing the techniques in the top section of the pyramid. These are the direct teaching techniques. As we discussed in the second half of Session 5, these techniques all involve the use of prompting and reinforcement to teach your child specific skills. In today's session, we will briefly review our earlier discussion, and then we will discuss how to use the direct techniques of *Teaching Your Child Expressive and Receptive Language.*

You have been using the techniques in the middle section of the pyramid to encourage your child to initiate communication. So far, you have responded to any behavior that your child uses as meaningful, which means that you have reinforced all forms of communication—eye contact, gestures, facial expressions, body movements, language, and play. When you use a direct teaching technique, you still want your child to initiate communication, but now you will prompt him or her to use a specific behavior that is more complex than his or her previous communication. Only then will you give him or her reinforcement.

Often children with ASD become frustrated when you "change the rules" or begin to require them to use a specific, more complex response. For this reason, you may notice an increase in tantrums or other negative behaviors when you begin to use the direct teaching techniques. If this happens, don't worry. It is likely to drop off as your child learns that you are now requiring him or her to respond in a specific way.

The direct teaching techniques can be very effective for increasing your child's skills. However, it is important that you do not use them too often. If you require your child to use a more complex response every time he or she initiates, he or she may begin to think twice before initiating. Imagine if every time you tried to start a conversation, your partner began asking you a slew of questions. You might begin to avoid conversations with him or her, since it would become unpleasant. For this reason, you only want to use the direct teaching techniques about one-third of the time.

In addition, the interactive teaching techniques help with initiations and spontaneous language. If you constantly correct your child's communicative attempts, he or she will be less likely to use spontaneous language and may become dependent on prompts.

Slide 4

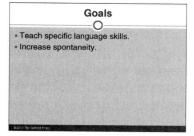

As explained in the last group session, *prompts* are cues that you use to help your child produce a specific, more complex response. When your child produces the response you are looking for, you give him or her *reinforcement*—a positive consequence.

You can teach your child language by prompting a response slightly more complex than the one the child uses on his or her own.

You can also increase your child's ability to communicate spontaneously by gradually giving a prompt at the least supportive level.

There are different types of prompts. Different prompts provide different levels of support. Some prompts are very supportive and help your child respond appropriately most of the time, while others offer less support and may be less likely to lead your child to an appropriate response, but are more likely to increase spontaneous responding. By using different types of prompts, you can help your child learn new skills and use them more spontaneously.

Review the Direct Teaching Procedure and Ways to Make Prompting Effective

Slide 5

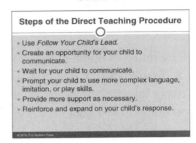

I am going to begin with a brief review of the six-step direct teaching procedure. Begin by using *Follow Your Child's Lead*. The more motivated and engaged your child is, the more likely he or she is to learn.

Next, create an opportunity for your child to initiate communication. You will want to use *Playful Obstruction, Balanced Turns,* and *Communicative Temptations* to encourage your child to initiate communication.

Once your child has initiated communication with you, you will then prompt your child to produce a more complex language, imitation, or play response. You begin with the *least supportive* prompt—that's the prompt that gives the least amount of help. This lets you see what your child can do on his or her own. You then add more support as necessary to help your child respond appropriately.

After your child produces the desired response, you provide *reinforcement*. This means you will deliver the desired item or activity and praise your child. You will also expand on your child's response.

Slide 6

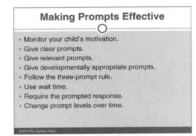

Let's also do a quick review of the prompt rules we introduced at the last group session. These rules make prompting most effective.

First, make sure that your child is motivated before you prompt him or her. Next, make sure that your prompts are clear. Your child needs to understand what you are asking him or her to do.

Make sure that the prompt is related to the activity and is appropriate for your child's developmental level.

Try to give no more than three prompts to elicit a correct response. If after one or two prompts your child is unsuccessful, move to a more supportive prompt. This will ensure that your child is successful in responding.

Be sure to wait after each prompt. One rule of thumb is to wait 5 seconds before providing the next prompt.

You should require your child to respond to your prompt. You may need to increase the amount of support you provide, to ensure that he or she can respond successfully. Over time, you will also want to decrease the amount of support you provide to encourage your child to communicate spontaneously.

Show Video Clips of *Overview of the Direct Teaching Techniques*

Slide 7

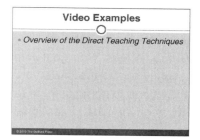

We are going to begin by reviewing the clips of the direct teaching techniques that we saw during the last group session. Then we are going to discuss specific types of prompts that can be used to teach communication skills to children at a variety of language levels.

Note to Trainers: Prepare to show video clips for Session 7: *Overview of the Direct Teaching Techniques* (three clips). Note that these are the same three clips shown in the second half of Session 5.

Before each clip, tell parents to look for how the parent uses prompting and reinforcement.

After the clip, ask parents:

"How did the parent encourage an initiation?"
"After the child initiated, what did the parent do [the prompt]?"
"How did the child respond?"
"After the child responded with a more complex response, what did the parent do [the reinforcement]?"

The important techniques to highlight and the children's responses are outlined in Session 5 (refer back to that session).

Discuss What Language Skills to Prompt

Slide 8

Now that we've reviewed how prompting and reinforcement work together, we are going to discuss different types of prompts that you can use to help your child increase his or her expressive or spoken language skills. Depending on your child's developmental level, these skills may be nonverbal, such as gestures, or verbal, such as single words, simple phrases, or complex phrases.

Slide 9

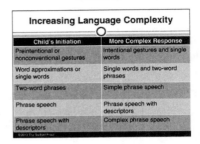

First, it is important to have a good idea about what specific language skills you want to prompt. How do you decide what to prompt?

This slide gives a very broad overview of language development. You saw this slide earlier when we first talked about *Modeling and Expanding Language.* There is also a more detailed chart of language stages in your parent manual.

As in *Modeling and Expanding Language,* your goal is to prompt language skills that are slightly above the skills your child is currently using. For example, if your child is leading you by the hand to communicate (a nonconventional gesture), you should prompt a tap or point (a more conventional, intentional gesture). If your child is vocalizing, you should prompt single words.

Wait for your child to initiate, and then prompt your child to add one level of complexity to his or her communication. For example, you might use in sight and out of reach to encourage your child to initiate for crackers. If your child then reaches, you could prompt him or her to use a point or a single word. If your child initiates by saying, "Crackers," you could prompt him or her to use a two-word phrase to request, such as "More crackers" or "Want crackers."

Alternatively, you could expand on your child's request by asking him or her to be more specific—for example, by prompting "How many?" or "What color?"

You may also start prompting the language that you have been modeling for your child, particularly what you have been modeling during focused stimulation. If you and your child's teachers have developed specific goals for your child, use those to guide what you prompt. These may include using single words, using "Yes" and "No," answering "wh" questions (such as "what," "where," and "who" questions), or retelling past events.

[Ask parents:]

How does your child usually communicate?
What language form could you prompt your child to use that is slightly more complex than how he or she usually communicates?

Take Break

Discuss Prompt Strategies for *Teaching Your Child Expressive Language*

Slide 10

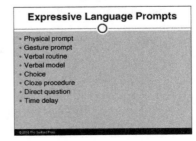

There are eight levels of prompts for *Teaching Your Child Expressive Language.* These range from giving your child a great deal of help to giving very little. This slide lists the prompts in order—with the top one, "Physical prompt," providing the most support to your child, and the bottom one, "Time delay," providing the least support.

A *physical prompt* is the most supportive type of prompt. Physical prompts involve guiding your child's body movements with your hands. This is also referred to as *hand-over-hand prompting*. This type of prompt is used for teaching your child to use nonverbal forms of communication, such as pointing, tapping, signs, or other natural gestures. Physical assistance is typically used if your child does not respond to a gesture prompt.

A *gesture prompt* is a gesture or physical action that you model for your child to imitate. In the first clip, we have seen the mother using a gesture prompt when she pats the jar lid as a sign meaning "Open." Gestures can act as a bridge to verbal communication. These gestures include a point, a tap, a sign, or other natural gesture. Your gesture should be paired with the spoken word. This is similar to the gesture cues that were discussed in *Modeling and Expanding Language*. The difference is that when you use the direct procedure, you provide a physical prompt if your child does not imitate the gesture.

Verbal routines are meaningful phrases that your child has heard many times—for example, "Ready, set, go" or "Peek-a-boo." We saw a verbal routine prompt in the clip with the dad blowing balloons: "One, two, three—fly away!" Start the verbal routine, but leave off the last portion of the phrase. This type of prompt is helpful for children who are just beginning to use verbal language, because it is repetitive and consistent.

A *verbal model* provides the target word or phrase for the child to imitate. For many children, the easiest type of language to produce is the immediate imitation of a word, phrase, or sentence—whatever you model. For children who already have some verbal language, verbal imitation is one way to build new vocabulary and to keep motivation for trying high. Pay attention to your child's current language level, and keep the model very clear and distinct. As in the verbal model that was discussed in the interactive teaching techniques, you are showing your child new language. However, this verbal model is also different: It is a prompt, which means your child is required to respond. If your child does not imitate your verbal model, add more support by providing a gesture and then, if needed, a physical prompt. If your child readily imitates your language, you want to decrease the amount of support you provide by using one of the following prompts. This helps increase the child's spontaneous language.

Giving *choices* is a prompt that helps your child begin to use language on his or her own and to become less dependent on a verbal model. Present your child with two choices. One choice should be the item your child wants, and the other choice should be an item your child does not like. Sometimes children repeat the last choice they hear because it is easier. To help your child learn to discriminate between choices, try to place the preferred item or activity (if you know it) as the first choice. If your child then repeats the second choice, give that to him or her. This strategy helps your child learn that his or her language carries meaning, and that the child has to attend to the entire language message to get a desired item rather than just repeat what you are saying.

The *cloze procedure* is a "fill-in-the-blanks" activity. The child uses clues from the environment to supply the missing word. This technique is similar to the verbal routine, in that you leave off a part of the sentence (usually the last word). It differs in that there is not always one right answer. For example, if the baby is in the bed, you might say "The baby is in the _____ [bed]." This type of prompt is particularly effective for more verbal children who may have difficulty with "word-finding" skills. It can also be used to build vocabulary. To help your child identify the missing word, you should use gestures to indicate what you are looking for. For example, in the previous example, you may point to the bed as a cue for your child to say "Bed."

Direct questions can be used to help your child communicate about many different aspects of one item or activity. For example, rather than only requesting "Tickle," your child can learn to answer questions about different aspects of this activity, such as "Where do you want tickles?" and "Who do you want to tickle you?" The type of question you ask should be directly related to your child's skill level. "What," "where," and "who" questions are easier to answer than "why," "how," and "when" questions. Avoid "yes–no" questions unless that is your specific goal for your child. These questions are less likely to build your child's vocabulary or to encourage back-and-forth interaction.

Time delay is waiting with an "expectant look" to cue your child that he or she should respond in some way. Time delay does not provide a specific cue for what you expect. Thus it is usually good to use after your child has responded correctly to a more supportive prompt on several occasions and knows what you expect. By moving from a more supportive prompt to a time delay, you will increase your child's ability to initiate and decrease his or her reliance on verbal prompts.

[Ask parents:]

Have any of you tried any of these? [If so, ask:] How does your child respond?
Let's go back to some of the activities you reported were favorites of your child's. How could you use these strategies with your child?

Show Video Clips of Specific Expressive Language Prompts

Slide 11

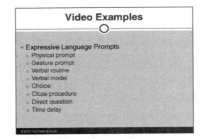

Note to Trainers: Prepare to show video clips for Session 7: Expressive Language Prompts. These clips are very short. Parents often benefit from watching each clip more than once.

Before each clip, tell parents to look for how the adult prompts the child's expressive language and gestures.

After each clip, ask parents:

"What types of prompts did the parent use to help the child respond appropriately?"
"Did you notice the parent changing the support level of prompt based on the child's response?"

The important techniques to highlight and the children's responses are outlined below.

Physical Prompt

- *Preverbal 1.* The mother uses a physical prompt to help her son sign "My turn" before giving him the ball. The child responds by using the sign "My turn" (with the physical prompt) and also imitates a word approximation ("Mmm" for "My turn").
- *Preverbal 2.* After the child requests the bubbles by using his "more" sign, his mother

physically prompts him to point to the bubbles to increase the complexity of his request (combined gestures). Her son responds by using two gestures together for "More bubbles" (with the physical prompt).

• *Emerging language.* After the child initiates with her mother to spin the top again, using a spin gesture, her mother prompts her to increase the complexity of her initiation by adding a "More" sign. Her mother initially models the gesture, but then physically prompts her daughter after she is unsuccessful at imitating. The child responds by using two signs together for "more spin" (with the physical prompt).

Gesture Prompt and Verbal Model

• *Preverbal.* The mother models the sign for "More." Her son responds by imitating an approximation of the sign for "More."

• *Emerging language.* The mother models the word "ball" and waits for her daughter to imitate it before opening the jar to allow her access to the ball. Her daughter responds by imitating the word "Ball."

• *Single words to simple phrases.* The father asks a question ("What do you want?"). To help his son respond successfully, the father models the phrase "Blow balloon." The child responds by imitating "Blow balloon." The father also uses a verbal routine ("1, 2, 3") that his son completes ("Fly").

Verbal Routine

• *Single words to simple phrases.* The father uses a verbal routine ("One, two, three— fly away!"), which is a particular verbal routine that he has used multiple times with this activity. When using the verbal routine this time, the father leaves off the end of the phrase for his son to "fill in." Giving the child the beginning of the phrase helps him retrieve the last portion. The child responds by completing the verbal routine ("Fly").

Choice

• *Preverbal.* The father presents two food items for his son to choose from and waits for the child to point to indicate a preference. The child responds with a point.

• *Complex phrase speech.* The mother uses choices to increase the complexity of her son's language by offering choices regarding the type of snack he wants and where he wants to sit to eat it. The child responds by using language to make a choice.

Cloze Procedure

• *Complex phrase speech.* The mother uses the cloze procedure to increase the complexity of her son's language by making a statement and leaving off the last word: "Dora's washing her _____ [hands]," "Doggy's in the _____ [sink]," "Doggy sees doggy in the _____ [mirror]." She also uses gestures to help cue her son for the correct response. The child responds by completing the phrase. Notice that it is not always the language that the parent may have used, but that it is an appropriate response, thus increasing the child's ability to generate language.

Direct Question

- *Single words to simple phrases.* The father asks a question and waits for his son to initiate a response. At first, the child appears to be confused between "I want" and "Can I have." His father adds more support by using the cloze procedure ("I want _____."). The child responds to the question with "I want blow."
- *Complex phrase speech.* After her son initiates, the mother prompts him to use more complex language, using a direct question, the cloze procedure, and choices. The mother adds support until her son is able to respond to the question by using appropriate vocabulary ("girl").

Time Delay

- *Preverbal.* The mother waits for the child to initiate a tickle by pulling her hands down. The child responds by pulling Mom's hands to him. The second time, she models the child's sign for "More," which he imitates. The next time, she simply says, "What do you want?" and waits for a response, at which point he uses his sign for "More" spontaneously.
- *Single words to simple phrases.* The father waits for his son to use the word "bigger" before blowing the balloon. He initially uses time delay, and then a question ("What now?"), to prompt the child to say "Fly away" before letting the balloon go. The child responds by using language without a model.
- *Complex phrase speech.* The mother waits for her son to increase the complexity of his language before pouring the toys on the table. The child responds by increasing the complexity and length of his sentence on his own.

Discuss *Teaching Your Child Receptive Language*

Slide 12

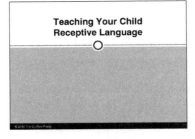

So far we have been talking about *expressive language*—how your child communicates with you. Let's talk briefly about *receptive language*—how your child understands and responds to what you say.

Many children with ASD have trouble understanding spoken language and do not respond appropriately. This can make them appear noncompliant. Teaching with prompts can improve children's understanding of language and help them follow directions at home and during daily activities. Unlike when you are using the other techniques in this program, you do not necessarily *Follow Your Child's Lead* when giving him or her directions.

Slide 13

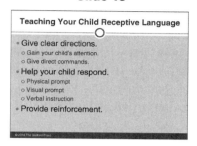

You can increase the likelihood that your child will follow your directions by making sure that they are clear and that your child knows he or she is supposed to respond.

Most people do not respond if they are not paying attention. This is also the case for children with ASD. Before giving your child a direction or asking a question, make sure you *gain your child's attention*. You may be able to do this by calling your child's name, but you may need to stop what your child is doing to get his or her attention.

Once you have your child's attention, give a *direct command* that tells your child exactly what to do (e.g., "Give the baby a drink"). *Indirect commands* are questions or statements that only imply what a child should do (e.g., "Why don't you give the baby a drink?", "Let's give the baby a drink"). Children with ASD often have a hard time inferring the meaning from an indirect message. Plus, if the demand is phrased as a question ("Are you ready to put the toys away?"), your child may respond appropriately ("No") when you did not really intend it as a choice.

It is important to tell your child explicitly what to do ("Get your shoes"), rather than to use a question ("Do you want to get your shoes?") or a direction that requires your child to infer meaning ("It is time to go"). Even when your direction is clear, your child may not respond. This may be because he or she does not understand the meaning of the words, is unable to retain the length of the message, or does not want to follow the direction. To increase the likelihood that your child will comply, prompt your child to make sure that he or she understands and follows the direction.

There are three levels of prompts for *Teaching Your Child Receptive Language*. These are listed below in order of supportiveness from the first, most supportive prompt to the last, least supportive prompt. The level of prompt you give depends on your child's communicative abilities. Remember that you want to use the *least supportive* prompt necessary to help your child respond correctly.

Use a *physical prompt* by guiding your child's body movements to help him or her follow the direction or respond to the question. This type of prompt is used when your child does not follow the verbal instruction after being given a visual prompt. For example, after you give your child the direction "Get your shoes," take your child's hand, bring your child to the shoes, and help him or her pick them up.

Use a *visual prompt* to show your child what you want him or her to do. For example, point to or hold up your child's shoes while giving the verbal direction "Get your shoes." If your child still does not get the shoes, you can model the sequence by going and getting the shoes and saying, "Get your shoes." Then put the shoes back and repeat the direction: "Get your shoes." Children with ASD usually have an easier time understanding visual prompts than verbal ones.

Once your child is able to follow a direction with visual prompts, you want to make sure he or she can follow *verbal instructions*. As always, take your child's developmental level into account. If your child has difficulty following one-step directions, do not prompt two-step directions without support. For verbal instruction alone, use words your child understands. Use physical and visual prompts with verbal instruction to promote comprehension of those words your child does not yet understand. Repetition of the instruction can help children who are having difficulty retaining the message. However, do not repeat the instruction multiple times without following through (i.e., providing a physical prompt), or your child will learn that he or she does not need to listen to your directions.

After your child follows your direction, either on his or her own or with your help, provide reinforcement. Praise your child by telling him or her what it was that he or she did right (e.g., "Good job getting your shoes"). When possible, you should also use *natural reinforcement*. For example, if your child likes to go outside, you can give the direction "Get your coat," and the reinforcement can be to go outside. If your child is thirsty, you can give the direction "Bring me your cup," and the reinforcement can be a drink of juice. However, in some cases it will not be possible to use natural reinforcement, and you may need to provide an additional reinforcer (such as a desired toy or treat) for following your direction.

Show Video Clip of Receptive Language Prompts

Slide 14

Note to Trainers: Prepare to show video clip for Session 7: Receptive Language Prompts.

Before the clip, tell parents to look for how the adult gives the child the direction and helps the child respond.

After the clip, ask parents:

"How did the parent make the direction clear?"
"How did the parent help the child respond?"

The important techniques to highlight and the child's responses are outlined below.

• *Single words to simple phrases.* The mother gains the child's attention before giving the direction by getting face to face with him and calling his name. When she gives the direction, she pairs it with a gesture (point). The child responds to this direction, but does not respond to the second step of the direction ("Come back and sit down"), so his mother uses a physical prompt to help him bring his cup to the table. The mother uses an indirect command ("Can you get your drink?") rather than a direct command ("Get your drink"), but gives a direct command the second time. The parent praises the child for following the direction.

Discuss Changing Prompt Levels

Slide 15

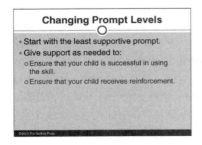

By changing prompt levels, you can increase your child's ability to respond spontaneously. Each type of prompt differs in its degree of support. Time delay (waiting) provides the least support, since the child is not told what to do. A physical prompt provides the most support, since the child is physically guided to complete the response. The goal is to reduce the amount of support provided by changing prompts over time. This will build your child's spontaneous communication. Parents often get stuck and overrely on verbal models, especially with echolalic children, because the children always respond correctly. However, if you always use a verbal model, your child will not have the opportunity to expand his or her spontaneous language.

You need to understand what skills your child does and does not have when you choose a prompt. This is because you should start with the least supportive prompt necessary to help your child respond correctly. In some cases, this may be physical assistance. For example, if your child is not yet using gestures, you would need to start with physical assistance to help your child learn how to respond. If your child is learning a new vocabulary word or phrase, start with a verbal model.

Once your child can use a skill at least some of the time, you should start using a less supportive prompt and then increase support if necessary. For example, if your child points sometimes, you might first prompt by modeling a point to help your child respond. If your child does not respond, you would then increase the support by using a physical prompt. If your child uses a word some of the time, your first prompt should be a choice, cloze procedure, or direct question (e.g., "What do you want?"). If your child cannot respond correctly, then you should increase support by modeling the correct answer.

Discuss and Assign Homework

Slide 16

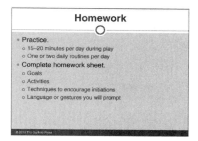

Note to Trainers: Pass out copies of Homework for Group Format: *Teaching Your Child Expressive and Receptive Language* (Appendix A, Form 25).

I would like each of you to think of at least two goals that you will target this week. At least one goal should be related to increasing your child's expressive language skills, such as using gestures, single words, simple phrases, or complex phrases to request, or answering "wh" questions. Another goal should be related to increasing your child's receptive language skills, such as following one-step directions.

You should plan to practice these techniques and strategies for 15–20 minutes per day during play, as well as during one or two daily activities. So think about a play activity and one or two daily routines during which you can practice these techniques and strategies. Remember that you will need to add several minutes to your daily routines in order to have time to use the techniques. Once you decide on the activities, write them down on your homework sheet.

Think about techniques that you have used to encourage your child to engage or initiate. Choose one or more of the techniques that are the most successful for getting your child to initiate communication, and write these down on your homework sheet.

Now think about how your child typically communicates. Chose a language form or gesture that is slightly more advanced than how your child usually communicates that you will prompt. Also decide what type of prompt you will use to help your child respond appropriately. Write this information down on your homework sheet.

> **Note to Trainers:** If time permits, have each parent report. Give feedback as necessary.

I would like you to practice these techniques and strategies over the next week and to respond to the questions on your homework sheet. We will discuss your homework during your individual coaching session next week. You should come to the session with questions you have about *Teaching Expressive Language and Receptive Language*.

> **Note to Trainers:** Have parents sign up for the individual session if they haven't already been scheduled.

Session 8 (Coaching)

Review of *Teaching Your Child Expressive and Receptive Language*

Session Goal

1. Improve the parent's ability to *teach her child expressive and receptive language*.

Materials

1. Parent manual
2. Completed Goal Development Form (Appendix A, Form 4)
3. Direct Teaching Techniques Review Sheet I (Appendix A, Form 20)
4. Group Format Coaching Form (Appendix A, Form 18)
5. Five to six highly motivating toys and activities
6. Variety of storage containers (e.g., clear plastic containers with screw lids, Ziploc bags, large bins, shelving) that desired items can be placed in
7. Homework for Group Format: *Teaching Your Child Expressive and Receptive Language* (Appendix A, Form 25)

Outline of Session

- Prior to session, review coaching form and notes from previous coaching session, and arrange coaching space to facilitate parent–child interactions.
- Review homework from preceding group session (5 minutes).
- Provide a brief review of *Teaching Your Child Expressive and Receptive Language* (5 minutes).
- Demonstrate use of *Teaching Your Child Expressive and Receptive Language* with the child (5 minutes).

- Have the parent practice *Teaching Your Child Expressive and Receptive Language* with the child while you give feedback (20 minutes).
- Discuss and assign homework (10 minutes):
  1. Give out Homework for Group Format: *Teaching Your Child Expressive and Receptive Language* (Appendix A, Form 25) and have the parent fill out "Goals of the Week."
  2. Instruct the parent to practice this homework over the next week and answer the questions.
  3. Have the parent read *Teaching Your Child Social Imitation* and *Teaching Your Child Play* (Chapters 14 and 15 of the parent manual).

Prior to Session, Review Coaching Form and Notes from Previous Coaching Session, and Arrange Coaching Space to Facilitate Parent–Child Interactions

Your entries on the coaching form from Session 6 will remind you of the parent's strengths and weaknesses, and will help guide the focus of this session. As always, make sure to arrange the coaching space to facilitate parent–child interactions by having a defined physical space, limiting distractions, and selecting highly preferred toys.

Review Homework from Preceding Group Session

Begin the session by discussing the parent's answers to each of the homework questions from the copy of Appendix A, Form 25, that she received in the preceding group session (Session 7). If the parent did not write down her answers, review them orally with her. If the parent had difficulties, brainstorm solutions.

Provide a Brief Review of *Teaching Your Child Expressive and Receptive Language*

Briefly review the critical elements of *Teaching Your Child Expressive and Receptive Language*, using the Direct Teaching Techniques Review Sheet (Appendix A, Form 20). These elements are also discussed in the parent manual. Give the parent an opportunity to ask questions before demonstrating use of the techniques.

Demonstrate Use of *Teaching Your Child Expressive and Receptive Language* with the Child

Prior to demonstrating, ask the parent to identify a language goal she would like you to address. This helps you identify the set of prompts to demonstrate and provide feedback on first. Remind the parent that you will use *Follow Your Child's Lead* and create an opportunity for him to initiate before you prompt the specific skill. This could include having toys in sight and out of reach, using toys with which the child needs assistance, or using *Playful Obstruction* or *Balanced Turns*. During the demonstration, identify the techniques and strategies you use, the child's response, and how you vary the amount of support to help the child respond. For example, the trainer might say to Sam's mother:

> "Sam was playing with the ball. I used *Playful Obstruction* by blocking the ball to create an opportunity for him to engage, and waited to see how he would respond. He said, 'Ball.' I prompted with a direct question: 'What should I do with the ball?' He responded by saying, 'Ball,' so I gave him a more supportive prompt, a choice: 'Throw ball or hide ball?' He said, 'Throw ball,' so I threw the ball to him and expanded on his response by saying, 'Throw the red ball.'"

Given the limited amount of coaching time and the importance of building communication skills, this coaching session is likely to be focused on increasing expressive language skills only. However, if the parent is already quite successful at using prompts to facilitate her child's communication, or if the child has strong language skills to begin with, you may wish to spend a portion of this session focusing on teaching the parent how to get her child to follow directions.

Have the Parent Practice *Teaching Your Child Expressive and Receptive Language* While You Give Feedback

The parent should have at least 20 minutes to practice the intervention strategies. Remind the parent of the goal she is addressing (e.g., use of gestures, single words, phrase speech, verbs, etc., or following directions), the ways to gain the child's attention, and the strategies to use to prompt the skills. Prior to having the parent implement the technique, ask her if she has any questions and provide her with specific strategies to use. For example, the trainer might say to Sam's mother: "Remember to use questions to increase Sam's use of verbs. If he doesn't respond, use a cloze procedure, and then provide him with a choice."

Provide the parent with specific and succinct feedback to improve her ability to implement the technique. If the parent has difficulty gaining her child's attention, review the interactive teaching techniques and have the parent practice that aspect before practicing prompting. Have the parent practice with a limited number of toys available, to prevent the child from leaving the activity as soon as the parent places a demand. If the child becomes frustrated, acknowledge that prompting can sometimes increase child frustration, but that the frustration usually decreases once the child understands what the parent is asking for. However, if the parent is prompting too much or the child becomes too frustrated, make sure to coach the parent to return to using the interactive techniques until the child has calmed down.

It is also important to help the parent move from one prompt level to another, to ensure that her child responds successfully (i.e., adding more support when necessary) and independent responding (i.e., decreasing support as appropriate). Thus, if the parent is struggling to get her child to respond, coach her to increase her support. Likewise, after the parent has been successful with using a prompt at one level (e.g., verbal model) several times, be sure to coach her how to use a less supportive prompt (e.g., time delay) to increase her child's independence.

If you are providing coaching in the home, you should have the parent practice using the techniques during a specific caretaking routine, such as snack or lunch. If you are coaching in a clinic or school, you may also wish to provide a snack to allow the parent to practice prompting during a daily routine.

Fill out the coaching form during or immediately after the coaching session. Use the "Notes" portion of the form to record information for the next coaching session, including which techniques and strategies the parent is using well, which ones should be targeted next session, and how the child is responding.

Discuss and Assign Homework

1. Give out Homework for Group Format: *Teaching Your Child Expressive and Receptive Language* **and have the parent fill out "Goals of the Week."** Give the parent a fresh copy of Appendix A, Form 25, and help the parent identify one to two goals she will target this week, as well as the techniques and strategies she will use to encourage her child to communicate. Then have the parent select a specific language form or gesture that she will prompt. Next, have the parent write down three prompts she will try, to ensure that her child is successful. Brainstorm with the parent how she can add more support if necessary. Have the parent decide which strategies were most effective during the individual coaching session (physical prompt, gesture prompt, verbal model, verbal routine, choice, cloze procedure, direct question, and time delay).

Discuss ways in which the parent can use the different strategies practiced during the individual coaching session during her daily routines with her child at home. To facilitate this discussion, you may wish to refer to the Daily Activity Schedule to identify specific routines. Language-prompting techniques are most likely to be effective during child-led activities, such as fine or gross motor play, songs, and social games, as well as mealtimes. In particular, you should discuss specific communication forms that the parent would like to increase and identify a number of opportunities for prompting these behaviors in the home. You may also discuss how to use prompting to improve the child's ability to follow directions, even if the parent did not get a chance to practice this technique during the coaching session. Following directions should be targeted primarily during daily routines.

2. Instruct the parent to practice this homework over the next week and answer the questions. Mention that you will be discussing the homework at the beginning of the next group session.

3. Have the parent read *Teaching Your Child Social Imitation* **and** *Teaching Your Child Play* (Chapters 14 and 15 of the parent manual). Explain to the parent that the next group session will be spent learning to use direct teaching techniques to teaching social imitation and to increase play skills. The parent should not complete the homework for these techniques until the techniques have been reviewed and practiced during the session.

Troubleshooting Tips

Parents who are beginning to use the direct teaching techniques face several common challenges. First, a parent can forget to use the interactive teaching techniques to gain her child's attention prior to prompting. When this occurs, her child is much less likely to respond appropriately. Thus it may be necessary to provide coaching on gaining the child's attention. To do this, give the parent a specific technique or strategy to use to create an opportunity for her child to communicate, and one prompt to use that you are sure will elicit a response from the child. This type of practice allows the parent to become comfortable with the steps involved in prompting before focusing on moving between prompts.

A second challenge is an increase in the child's frustration when the parent begins to prompt language. This can occur when the child does not understand the expectations, the child has difficulty waiting, or the parent is prompting too much. If the child does not understand the expectations, review the need for clear and appropriate prompts, and provide the parent with a specific prompt to use (e.g., modeling the word and pointing to the object). When the child appears frustrated because of the amount of time he has to wait before receiving the item, cue the parent to begin with a prompt to which she knows the child will be able to respond successfully. For example, if the goal is for the child to point, have the parent use a physical prompt. If the goal is for the child to use a word, have the parent provide a verbal model. Once the routine is set, have the parent decrease support every third time. This strategy often decreases the amount of frustration. If the parent is prompting too much, remind the parent to return to using the interactive teaching techniques. Suggest that she prompt her child for a more complex response after every third initiation.

A third challenge occurs when the parent has difficulty identifying when to provide reinforcement. Sometimes the parent reinforces the child for any behavior (as in the interactive teaching techniques) rather than requiring a more complex response. At other times, the parent has difficulty controlling access to the item and allows her child to grab it away before he emits a more complex response. Finally, the parent may wait too long before providing reinforcement. If the parent has difficulty identifying an appropriate response for her child, remind her of what she is looking for before she prompts, and cue her when the child has given that response. If the parent has difficulty controlling access to the item, recommend that she stand up or put the item in a place that the child cannot access when she is prompting.

Teaching Your Child Social Imitation and Play

Session Goals

1. Teach parents techniques to improve their children's social imitation and play skills.
2. Teach parents to use the least supportive prompts to increase their children's spontaneity.

Materials

1. DVD
2. Copies of Homework for Group Format: *Teaching Your Child Social Imitation and Play* (Appendix A, Form 26)
3. Whiteboard or large sheets of paper to review and introduce homework
4. Four to six toys that differ in the type of play they typically produce, to help parents brainstorm different play actions

Outline of Session

- Introduce session agenda (Slide 1).
- Review homework from preceding individual coaching session (Slides 2–3).
- Introduce rationale for *Teaching Your Child Social Imitation* (Slide 4).
- Discuss *Teaching Your Child Social Imitation* (Slides 5–7).
- Show video clips for *Teaching Your Child Social Imitation* (at Slide 8).
- Take break.
- Introduce rationale for *Teaching Your Child Play* (Slide 9).
- Discuss what play skills to teach (Slides 10–11).
- Discuss prompt strategies for *Teaching Your Child Play* (Slide 12).
- Show video clips of specific play prompts (at Slide 13).
- Conduct brainstorming of play actions (Slide 14):

    Pass each toy around the room and have parents brainstorm a way to play with it.

    Provide parents with feedback on the developmental level of their suggestions.

    Pass each toy around again and have parents brainstorm gestures that relate to the toy.

- Discuss and assign homework (Slide 15).

    1. Pass out Homework for Group Format: *Teaching Your Child Social Imitation and Play* (Appendix A, Form 26) and have parents fill out "Goals of the Week."
    2. Instruct parents to practice this homework over the next week and answer the questions.

- Have parents sign up for individual coaching session.

Introduce Session Agenda

Slide 1

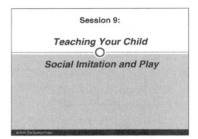

Today we will discuss specific prompting strategies you can use to increase your child's social imitation and play skills.

Review Homework from Preceding Individual Coaching Session

Slide 2

Note to Trainers: Review the homework that was given during the last individual coaching session (Appendix A, Form 25). Read through the homework questions and ask parents to respond.

Use a whiteboard to record parents' responses. Make three columns: "Successes," "Challenges," and "Suggestions." If a parent reports successful use of a technique, write it on the whiteboard under "Successes." Ask if any other parents had a similar success, in order to encourage group discussion.

If a parent reports difficulty using a technique, write it under "Challenges." Lead a discussion of what could be done to overcome the challenge. Based on the other parents' responses (or your own), write the best suggestions under "Suggestions" next to the specific challenge.

Point out any main themes parents report.

Slide 3

As in the last group session, we will be discussing techniques in the top section of the pyramid. However, today we will discuss how to use the direct teaching techniques of *Teaching Your Child Social Imitation* and *Teaching Your Child Play.*

Introduce Rationale for *Teaching Your Child Social Imitation*

Slide 4

Why?

Imitation is an important skill in early development. Children use it as a way to learn about the world and communicate interest in others. Research suggests that imitation is involved in the development of language and play skills. In fact, the modeling techniques presented in this program rely on your child's ability to imitate; thus it is important for your child to learn how to imitate others spontaneously during play and daily activities.

Discuss *Teaching Your Child Social Imitation*

Slide 5

Teaching Your Child Social Imitation
* Use *Imitate Your Child.*
* Describe your imitation.
* Model a skill for your child to imitate.
* Describe the action.
* Use wait time.
* Prompt imitation.
* Give reinforcement.

How?

The goal is to have a back-and-forth social game where you and your child take turns imitating each other. To help your child, you will use imitation, modeling, physical prompting, and reinforcement. During the interaction, you will be doing most of the imitation; your child will only be expected to imitate you once every 1–2 minutes.

Start by imitating all of your child's play with toys, gestures, body movements, and vocalizations. In other words, use the same technique that we discussed earlier as *Imitate Your Child*. Doing this lays the groundwork for teaching social imitation, because your child learns that imitation is a back-and-forth interaction. When you use *Imitate Your Child*, it helps to have two of the same or similar toys.

As you use *Imitate Your Child*, describe your imitation as you would in *Modeling and Expanding Language*. This helps to emphasize that you and your child are doing the same thing.

Model a skill for your child to imitate. Start by modeling play actions with the same toy as, or a similar toy to, the one your child is playing with. The actions should be of interest to your child and at your child's play level. Your child should be likely to want to imitate them. Remember that this is about imitation and not teaching specific play skills. If your child has a lot of difficulty imitating, start by modeling familiar actions, even if they are nonfunctional. For example, if your child only plays with cars by spinning their wheels or lining them up, model spinning the wheels when your child is lining up cars. Make sure that your child is paying attention to what you are doing when you model actions. Use *Animation*. Make sure the action is "big," so that your child notices it and knows this is something he or she should imitate.

When you model an action, you want your child to pay attention and imitate your action. Your child needs to learn to imitate you spontaneously, rather than on command. Therefore, describe the action. The verbal label should be a simple description of what you are doing, similar to self-talk as described in *Modeling and Expanding Language*. For example, if you are modeling play with a car, you could say "Vroom, vroom," or "Push car."

Give your child the opportunity to imitate your action spontaneously. *Wait* after you model and describe an action. If your child does not imitate spontaneously, model the same action again with the same verbal label up to three times.

If your child does not imitate after the third model, prompt him or her to imitate your action. You may use a verbal instruction, such as "You do it." If he or she does not respond, physically prompt your child to imitate you.

As soon as your child imitates you, praise your child and let him or her play with the toys as he or she likes for the next minute or so. It is more important for your child to match your actions in general than to perform a specific action exactly, so be sure to praise any attempt at imitation even if it is not perfect. Once your child has imitated you, return to imitating your child.

Slide 6

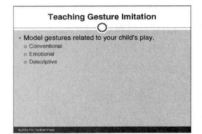

If your child has some object imitation skills, then also try to model gestures related to your child's play. For example, if your child is playing with a baby, you could model putting a finger over your lips ("Shh"). If your child is playing with toy food, you could model rubbing your tummy ("Tastes good"). Model gestures that are directly related to the toy your child is playing with. For example, if your child is playing with toy food, you can model patting your tummy to indicate that the food tastes good. As in object imitation, you should pair the modeled gesture with a related verbal label ("Yummy"). The gestures that you model can include conventional or common gestures, such as waving bye-bye, blowing a kiss, or nodding yes or no; emotional gestures, such as clapping for "happy" or putting your hands on your hips for "angry"; and gestures that describe objects or actions, such as holding your arms out for "big," blowing for "hot," pretending to hold a phone to your ear, or pretending to drive a car.

Slide 7

Some toys work better than others when you are trying to teach object and gesture imitation. For example, it is much easier to model actions for your child to imitate when you use toys that can be used in a number of different, creative ways, such as the toys on this list.

Show Video Clips for *Teaching Your Child Social Imitation*

Slide 8

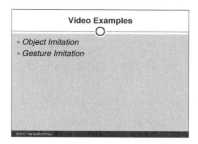

Note to Trainers: Prepare to show video clips for Session 9: Object Imitation and Gesture Imitation.

Before each clip, tell parents to look for how the adult prompts the child's imitation of play and gestures.

After each clip, ask parents:

"What types of prompts did the parent use to help the child respond appropriately?"
"Did you notice the parent changing the support level of prompt based on the child's response?"

The important techniques to highlight and the children's responses are outlined below.

Object Imitation

• *Single words to simple phrases 1.* The mother teaches object imitation to her child by alternating between imitating her child's play and modeling new ways to play. Throughout the clip, the mother imitates her child's play with the beads while using simple and repetitive language to describe her imitation. Several times during the clip, the mother models a new way to play with the beads (putting beads in a bucket, feeding a puppet, scooping beads with a net, putting beads in the net, and "washing" beads in a toy sink). When modeling the new play action, the mother describes the action by using a simple verbal label. In this clip, the child responds to all of her mother's models by imitating spontaneously. After the child imitates, the mother provides praise and returns to imitating her child's play with the beads. If the child had not imitated after the third model, the mother would have physically prompted her to complete the action.

• *Single words to simple phrases 2.* The mother teaches object imitation to her child by alternating between imitating her child's play and modeling new ways to play. The mother models new ways to blow on the harmonica and then adds a maraca. Through the play, the mother returns to imitating her child's play with the harmonica.

Gesture Imitation

• *Single words to simple phrases.* The mother teaches gesture imitation to her child by alternating between imitating her child's play and modeling gestures related to the child's play. The mother models two gestures: hands to face ("Oh, my!") in relation to the "mess," and a point to a bead ("Look!"). After her child imitates the gesture, the mother praises her and returns to imitating her play. If the child had not imitated the gesture after the third model, the mother would have physically prompted her to complete the gesture.

Take Break

Introduce a Rationale for *Teaching Your Child Play*

Slide 9

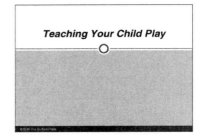

Now we are going to discuss why and how to help your child increase his or her play skills.

Why?

Children with ASD often have a hard time expanding their play skills. However, these skills are very important for language and social development. Play is an excellent place to work on problem-solving, conceptual, and imaginative skills. The more complex your child's play skills are, the better he or she is able to play with other children.

The goal is to increase both the variety and the complexity of your child's play skills. Typically, children with ASD have difficulty in both of these areas.

Discuss What Play Skills to Teach

Slide 10

How?

You can teach your child to increase the *variety* of his or her play. One way to do this is to increase the number of different actions that your child does with a favorite toy. For example, if your child likes to likes to line up blocks (combinatorial play), teach other combinatorial actions to do with the blocks, such as stacking the blocks or putting blocks in different containers. If your child likes to fill the car with gas (symbolic play), teach other symbolic actions to do with the car, such as washing the car, drying the car, repairing the car, or driving the car home and parking it.

You can also teach your child to play with new toys by incorporating new objects into play with his or her favorite activities. For example, if your child likes to play with a train, teach him or her to play with farm animals by having them ride the train or by having the train go to the farm. If your child does not play with toys, but enjoys food or gross motor activities, teach him or her to play with toys by including them in his preferred activity. For example, you can place a favorite snack in a busy box for your child to get out, or have a doll take turns with the child on the swing or trampoline.

Teach your child to expand the *complexity* of play with his or her favorite toys. One way is to increase the developmental level of your child's play actions. Observe how your child is using toys, and add one level of complexity. For example, if your child usually plays with toys by touching, banging, or dropping them (exploratory play), teach him or her to play by putting favorite toys in and out of containers (combinatorial play). If your child usually plays by pushing a car (functional play), teach him or her to wash the car before pushing it (symbolic play). If your child pretends to eat make-believe food (self-directed pretend play), teach him or her to feed the baby (other-directed pretend play), or to pretend that a block is food and pretend to eat it (symbolic play).

If your child is able to use a number of related play actions, you can increase the complexity of his or her play through teaching your child to expand the number of play sequences by linking them together. For example, if your child is pouring water into the sink, prompt him or her to pour water into another cup, before pouring it in the sink. If your child likes to feed the baby, teach him or her to expand the feeding sequence by giving the baby a bottle, burping the baby, and putting the baby to bed. Try to use sequences with which your child is familiar.

Slide 11

This slide gives a very broad overview of play development, to help you decide what play skills to prompt your child to engage in. There is also a more detailed chart of play stages in your parent manual.

Again, the goal is to prompt play behaviors that are slightly above the level of the skills your child is currently using. For example, if your child plays with toys mainly by mouthing or banging them (exploratory play), you might prompt your child to engage in more cause-and-effect play or to combine objects by placing the toys in containers. If your child is pushing a car (functional play), you might prompt putting a person in the car or giving the car gas (simple pretend).

[Ask parents:]

How does your child usually play?
In what ways could you increase your child's play skills?

Discuss Prompt Strategies for *Teaching Your Child Play*

Slide 12

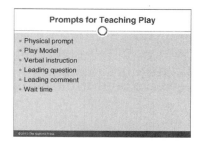

Start by using *Follow Your Child's Lead*, and use the toy your child is playing with or incorporate some part of the toy into a new activity. If your child does not engage in the new play activity independently, prompt him or her. The slide lists some levels of prompts you can use. The most supportive prompt is at the top.

When your child is playing repetitively, you can *physically prompt* him or her to play in a new way. Use this prompt if your child does not imitate your play independently after you model playing a new way.

You can *model play* in the same way you can model play during *Teaching Your Child Social Imitation*. If your child does not imitate your model, you can model again and add a verbal instruction prompt. For example, if your child is spinning the wheels of a car, you could model pushing the car. If your child does not respond, model pushing the car while at the same time saying, "You do it" or "Push the car."

You can teach your child to play more creatively by using a *verbal instruction* to indicate what else to do with the toy he or she is playing with. For example, if your child is pushing a car, you could show him or her another car and say, "Make the cars crash." However, be sure to *Follow Your Child's Lead* and give directions around his or her activity of choice.

Leading questions are appropriate for children who have good receptive language skills and are able to link several play actions together, but have difficulty expanding their play or playing more creatively. Leading questions such as "Where should the car go next?" or "What should the baby do now?" can help your child expand his or her play theme. Your child can respond to the leading question by "showing you" (e.g., moving the car to a new location) or by telling you.

Many children have difficulty responding to open-ended questions, such as "What should the baby do now?" In this case, you can give a choice: "Should the baby eat or go to sleep?" You can also make *leading comments* to prompt your child to take the next step in a play sequence. For example, if your child is feeding a baby doll repetitively, you could show your child a blanket and say, "Your baby looks sleepy." Make sure that your comment is very clear.

[Ask parents:]

Have any of you tried this? [If so, ask:] How does your child respond?
Let's go back to some of the activities you reported were favorites of your child's. How could you use this technique with your child?

Show Video Clips of Specific Play Prompts

Slide 13

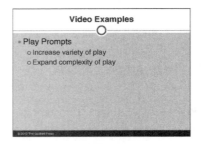

Note to Trainers: Prepare to show video clips for Session 9: Play Prompts.

Before each clip, tell parents to look for how the adult prompts the child's play.

After each clip, ask parents:

"What types of prompts did the parent use to help the child increase the complexity of play?"
"Did you notice the parent changing the support level of prompt based on the child's response?"

The important techniques to highlight and the children's responses are outlined below.

Increase Variety of Play

- *Single words to simple phrases.* The mother expands the child's play skills by increasing the variety of play schemes the child uses with a favorite toy (hot dogs). The child would prefer to play by lining up the hot dogs on a plate. The mother models several new ways to play (putting mustard on the hot dog, putting the hot dog in a bun, eating the hot dog). The child responds by imitating the mother's play, and continues to play in the new way on her own (places more mustard on the hot dog and says, "Mustard"). The mother uses simple language when describing her play, and she follows the child's lead by modeling new actions with the toy the child is playing with. Notice that while teaching play, the mother does not place language demands on the child.

Increase Complexity of Play

- *Single words to simple phrases 1.* The mother increases the complexity of the child's play by increasing the developmental level of his play actions. The child is playing with a shape sorter by placing the shapes in the corresponding openings (combinatorial play). The mother introduces a more developmentally advanced way to play by having a man figurine put the shape in the shape sorter (symbolic play). The mother uses a play model, followed by a verbal instruction, and then by a physical prompt to help the child complete the action. The mother requires the child to complete the more complex play action before she allows him to switch to a new activity. Notice that while teaching play, the mother does not place language demands on the child.

- *Single words to simple phrases 2.* The mother increases the complexity of the child's play by expanding the number of play sequences he uses. She uses a model of play to begin the sequence (going to the potty), and then uses a leading question ("What's next?"). When the child does not respond, she gives a verbal instruction and model of play ("Flush"), to which the child responds. Again she uses a leading question ("What's next?") and a model of play to help the child add a further step (washing hands). The child then spontaneously completes the sequence by drying hands. The child next initiates a new play sequence by having his doll take a bath (placing the doll in the bathtub). The mother expands his play by asking a leading question ("Is she taking a bath or a shower?"), to which the child responds both verbally ("Shower") and in play (by using the shower).

- *Single words to simple phrases 3.* The mother increases the complexity of the child's play by expanding the number of play sequences he uses. She begins by giving choices to help him use additional play sequences ("Should the man go potty or take a bath?", "Do we need to flush, or do we need to wash?"). The mother then adds an additional step by giving the choice of "Eat breakfast or play?" The child responds, "Eat," so the mother introduces food play and helps the child incorporate a new set of toys into his play, while following his interests in the Dora doll. The child initiates some pretend play on his own (giving the doll a drink, taking a drink himself). The mother then helps him "make eggs" by giving him a verbal choice and using a model of play. The child begins to lose interest in the new play themes by the end of the clip. Thus the mother should return to letting him lead the play for a while before introducing more new play ideas.

Conduct Brainstorming of Play Actions

Slide 14

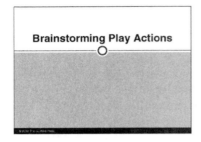

Thinking of a variety of ways to play with toys can often be difficult for adults. It can be helpful to sit with a toy your child likes when you are not interacting with him or her, and think about all of the different actions or ways to play with the toy. For example, ideas for playing with a car and a car ramp might include pushing the car up and down, taking people in and out of the car, washing and drying the car, getting gas, driving to a location such as a park, or crashing and needing repairs. Of course, the type of play you might model will depend on your child's developmental level.

We are going to do an exercise that will helps us think of different ways to play with toys and gestures that can be used during play.

> **Note to Trainers:** Bring out four to six different toys. These toys should differ in the type of play they typically produce, including some sensory toys (e.g., pom-poms, feather boas, Slinkies), some functional toys (e.g., balls, cars, blocks), and some pretend play toys (e.g., dolls, miniatures, food). Pass each toy around the room, and have each parent suggest a different way to play with the toy. For each suggestion, point out the play stage that it represents. For example, when you are passing around a doll, if a parent suggests brushing the doll's hair, point out that this type of play is other-directed pretend play.
>
> Next, pass around the toys again, one at a time, and have parents brainstorm different gestures that they could use in relation to the toy. For example, with blocks, a parent might suggest building a tower, knocking it down, and then modeling an "Oh, no" gesture by putting palms on cheeks.

Discuss and Assign Homework

Slide 15

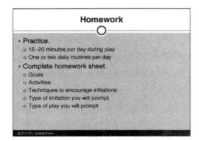

> **Note to Trainers:** Pass out copies of Homework for Group Format: *Teaching Your Child Social Imitation and Play* (Appendix A, Form 26).

I would like each of you to think of one to two goals that you will target this week. These goals should be related to increasing your child's social imitation or play skills.

You should plan to practice these techniques for 15–20 minutes per day during play. So think about several play activities during which you can practice these techniques. Once you decide on the activities, write them down on your homework sheet.

Think about how your child typically plays with toys. Choose a type of play to prompt that is slightly more advanced than how your child usually plays. This can include any of the ways to increase play that we discussed. Also, decide what type of prompt you will use to help your child respond appropriately. Write this information down on your homework sheet.

> **Note to Trainers:** If time permits, have each parent report. Give feedback as necessary.

I would like you to practice these techniques over the next week and to respond to the questions on your homework sheet. We will discuss your homework during your individual coaching session next week. You should come to the session with questions you have about *Teaching Your Child Social Imitation and Play.*

> **Note to Trainers:** Have parents sign up for the individual session if they haven't already been scheduled.

Session 10 (Coaching)

Review of *Teaching Your Child Social Imitation and Play*

Session Goal

1. Improve parent's ability to use the direct teaching strategies to teach her child social imitation and play skills.

Materials

1. Parent manual
2. Completed Goal Development Form (Appendix A, Form 4)
3. Direct Teaching Techniques Review Sheet II (Appendix A, Form 21)
4. Group Format Coaching Form (Appendix A, Form 18)
5. Number of highly preferred toys that can be used creatively, including some pairs of highly preferred toys
6. Homework for Group Format: *Teaching Your Child Social Imitation and Play* (Appendix A, Form 26)

Outline of Session

- Prior to session, review coaching form and notes from previous coaching session, and arrange coaching space to facilitate parent–child interactions.
- Review homework from preceding group session (5 minutes).
- Provide a brief review of *Teaching Your Child Social Imitation and Play* (5 minutes).

- Demonstrate use of *Teaching Your Child Social Imitation and Play* with the child (5 minutes).
- Have the parent practice *Teaching Your Child Social Imitation and Play* while you provide feedback (20 minutes).
- Discuss and assign homework (10 minutes).
  1. Give out Homework for Group Format: *Teaching Your Child Social Imitation and Play* (Appendix A, Form 26) and have the parent fill out "Goals of the Week."
  2. Instruct the parent to practice this homework over the next week and answer the questions.
  3. Have the parent read *Review of the Direct Teaching Techniques* and *Putting It All Together* (Chapters 16 and 17 of the parent manual).

Prior to Session, Review Coaching Form and Notes from Previous Coaching Session, and Arrange Coaching Space to Facilitate Parent–Child Interactions

Your entries on the parent's coaching form from Session 8 will remind you of the parent's strengths and weaknesses, and will help guide the focus of this session. As usual, make sure to arrange the coaching space to facilitate parent–child interactions by having a defined physical space, limiting distractions, and selecting highly preferred toys.

Review Homework from Preceding Group Session

Begin the session by discussing the parent's answers to each of the homework questions from the copy of Appendix A, Form 26, that she received in the preceding group session (Session 9). If the parent did not write down her answers, review them orally with her now. If the parent had difficulties, brainstorm solutions. One challenge can arise when the child does not engage well with toys. When this occurs, the parent may report difficulty knowing what to imitate or model. In this case, have the parent imitate her child's body movements and model gross motor movements, such as running across the room or spinning in a circle. Another common challenge is thinking of new ways to play with toys. To help, ask the parent to describe the child's typical play, and provide her with suggestions of actions to model and ways to expand the play. Ask questions to help her identify actions, sequences, or emotions that could be brought into the play. A further challenge can occurs when the child has a specific way in which he prefers to play (i.e., repetitive play). If this occurs, the parent could either remove the toys or provide a quick prompt to her child at a level that she knows he can successfully respond to, and then allow her child to play with the toy his way.

Provide a Brief Review of *Teaching Your Child Social Imitation and Play*

Briefly review the critical elements of the techniques, using the Direct Teaching Techniques Review Sheet II (Appendix A, Form 21). These elements are also discussed in Chapters 14 and 15 of the parent manual. Give the parent an opportunity to ask questions before demonstrating use of the techniques.

Demonstrate Use of *Teaching Your Child Social Imitation and Play* with the Child

Both *Teaching Your Child Social Imitation* and *Teaching Your Child Play* focus on increasing the child's object or gesture play; thus you may decide to only focus on either social imitation or play, for the sake of time. If you do choose only one, select the one that you think would be more effective for the child's play level. Social imitation is likely to be more effective for children with more limited play skills, who need to focus on increasing the number of play themes with a favorite toy. Teaching play is likely to be better for children with more advanced play skills, who need to focus on increasing play complexity and expanding the number of sequences they use in their play. During the demonstration, as usual, identify the techniques and strategies you use, and note the child's response. For example, the trainer might say to Sam's mother:

> "Sam was playing with the cars. I moved into his line of sight and stopped movement of his car (*Playful Obstruction*) to gain his attention. He looked at me. I asked a question, 'Where should the car go?', and let go of the car. Sam did not respond. So I stopped the car again to gain his attention and presented him with a choice: 'Should the car go to the gas station or the car wash?' Sam responded by washing the car. I reinforced him by providing praise ('Yay, you washed your car!') and letting him play with the toy for a little while before providing another prompt."

Explain to the parent how you add more support until the child is able to increase the complexity of his play. As in using expressive language prompts, it is important that the parent elicit a response from the child once she has given a play prompt. Remind the parent that if she does not have time or does not want to follow through, she should use the interactive teaching techniques (e.g., demonstrate washing the car and model language by saying, "I am washing my car"), which do not require a response from the child.

Have the Parent Practice *Teaching Your Child Social Imitation and Play* While You Provide Feedback

Have the parent practice the use of these techniques for at least 20 minutes. Prior to the practice, brainstorm with the parent the types of object play and gestures that she may teach. It can be difficult for the parent to think of how to play with the toy and gestures that relate to the toy play when she is involved in the interaction. Once you have identified a few play skills and/or gestures the parent can teach via modeling (social imitation) or with a verbal instruction, question, or comment (play prompting), provide the parent with specific techniques to use. For example, the trainer might say to Brian's mother: "Since Brian has been pushing the car for a while, why don't you model a different way to play with the car, such as putting a person in it? If he doesn't imitate you, physically prompt him to do it."

When you are teaching social imitation, provide feedback to help the parent alternate between imitating her child and asking her child to imitate her. It is also helpful to provide the parent with additional types of play to model and prompt. You may refer her to the chart of play development stages and the chart of play skills to model or prompt in the parent manual (Figures 1.3 and 8.2 there). In addition, there may be times when it is necessary to provide coaching on gaining the child's attention prior to modeling a new action or giving a verbal prompt.

Discuss and Assign Homework

1. Give out Homework for Group Format: *Teaching Your Child Social Imitation and Play* **and have the parent fill out "Goals of the Week."** Give the parent a fresh copy of Appendix A, Form 26, and help the parent identify one to two goals she will target this week as well as the strategies she will use to encourage her child to communicate. Then have the parent select a specific form of social imitation or play that she will prompt. Next, have the parent write down three prompts she will try to ensure that her child is successful. Brainstorm with the parent how she can add more support if necessary. Have the parent decide which strategies were most effective during the individual coaching session.

Discuss ways in which the parent can use the different strategies practiced during the individual coaching session during her daily routines with her child at home. To facilitate this discussion, you may wish to refer to the Daily Activity Schedule to identify specific routines. The techniques for prompting social imitation and play are most likely to be effective during child-led play activities such as fine or gross motor play, songs, and social games, as well as bathtime. In particular, you should discuss specific forms of imitation or play that the parent would like to increase and identify a number of opportunities for prompting this behavior in the home. You may also discuss how to use prompting to increase imitation and play skills at home, even if the parent did not get a chance to practice these techniques during the coaching session. Activities should include a daily routine as well as a play activity.

2. Instruct the parent to practice this homework over the next week and to answer the questions. Mention that you will be discussing the homework at the beginning of the next group session.

3. Have the parent read *Review of the Direct Teaching Techniques* **and** *Putting It All Together* (Chapters 16 and 17 of the parent manual). Explain to the parent that the next group session will be spent learning to use the interactive and direct teaching techniques together and determining the best time to use the different techniques. The parent should not complete the homework for the techniques until they have been reviewed and practiced during the session.

Troubleshooting Tips

Some children with ASD may become frustrated when their parents attempt to change their play. This is particularly true for children who have specific actions or patterns they like to complete with a toy (i.e., repetitive play). As noted earlier, there are two possible solutions to this problem. The first is to remove toys that the cause frustration from the environment. The second is to have the parent provide a quick prompt to the child at a level that she knows he can respond to, and then allow the child to play with the toy his way. For example, if the goal is for the child to use a new play action, have the parent begin with a physical prompt. Once the routine is set, have the parent decrease support every third time. This strategy often decreases the amount of frustration for the child.

Another challenge is that it can be difficult to think of new ways to play with toys. When this occurs, take time to help the parent identify actions she can complete with the toys, new toys that could be added to expand the play theme, or emotions that could be brought into play. If the child has a sibling or the parent has the occasion to be with other children, instruct her to observe how the other children play with the toys. This often leads to additional ideas on how to play with toys.

Session 11 (Group)

Putting It All Together

Session Goals

1. Teach parents to use the interactive and direct teaching techniques together to enhance their children's social-communication skills.
2. Teach parents when to use which type of technique.
3. Provide parents an opportunity to share accomplishments, challenges, and information.

Materials

1. DVD
2. Copies of homework for Group Format: *Putting It All Together* (Appendix A, Form 27)
3. Whiteboard or large sheets of paper to review and introduce homework
4. A contact sheet for parents to exchange personal information

Outline of Session

- Introduce session agenda (Slide 1).
- Review homework from preceding individual coaching session (Slide 2).

- Introduce *Putting It All Together* (Slides 3–4).
- Review similarities and differences in the interactive and direct teaching techniques (Slides 5–9).
- Discuss when to use interactive versus direct teaching techniques (Slides 10–11).
- Show video clips of *Putting It All Together* (at Slide 12).
- Discuss and assign homework (Slide 13):
    1. Pass out Homework for Group Format: *Putting It All Together* (Appendix A, Form 27) and have parents fill out "Goals of the Week."
    2. Instruct parents to practice this homework over the next week and answer the questions.
- Have parents sign up for individual coaching session.
- Take break.
- Conduct wrap-up (Slide 14).

    Encourage parents to ask any additional questions.
    Have parents share accomplishments.
    Give parents opportunity to exchange information for future contact and support.

Introduce Session Agenda

Slide 1

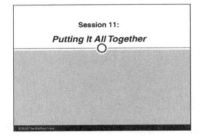

Today is our last group session. This session will be spent reviewing use of the interactive and direct teaching techniques, discussing how to use them together, answering any questions you might have, and solving problems.

Review Homework from Preceding Individual Coaching Session

Slide 2

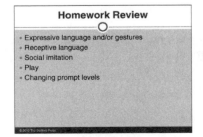

Note to Trainers: Review the homework that was given during the last individual coaching session (Appendix A, Form 26). Read through the homework questions and ask parents to respond.

Use a whiteboard to record parents' responses. Make three columns: "Successes," "Challenges," and "Suggestions." If a parent reports successful use of a technique, write it on the whiteboard under "Successes." Ask if any other parents had a similar success, in order to encourage group discussion.

If a parent reports difficulty using a technique, write it under "Challenges." Lead a discussion of what could be done to overcome the challenge. Based on the other parents' responses (or your own), write the best suggestions under the "Suggestions" next to the specific challenge.

Point out any main themes parents report.

Introduce *Putting It All Together*

Slide 3

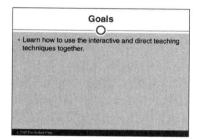

The goal of this program is for these techniques to become "second nature" to you, so that you are using them throughout your day with your child. You won't need to think about the fact that you are teaching your child. Some of you may have already experienced this at times. Some of you may still find that you have to really think about what you are doing when you are using the techniques.

Today we will focus on learning how to use the interactive and direct teaching techniques together—and, let's hope, to make the techniques feel more natural.

Slide 4

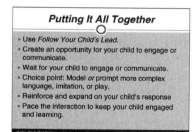

Let's look at how the interactive and direct teaching techniques work together.

You always need to start with *Follow Your Child's Lead.* Then use a technique that creates an opportunity for your child to engage or communicate with you. In essence, you set up a situation where your child wants something and must interact with you to get it.

Once your child initiates an interaction, you can choose to use an interactive teaching technique by modeling language, play, or imitation without requiring a specific response. Or you can choose to use a direct teaching technique by prompting your child to make a specific, more complex response in any of these areas. Both kinds of techniques end with reinforcing your child with the desired item or activity and expanding on his or her response.

Finally, you need to balance the use of the two types of techniques, to keep your child optimally aroused and in the interaction. In other words, pace the interaction appropriately. Make sure that you push your child so he or she gets to the next level. But do not push so hard that your child becomes overly frustrated.

You have seen the next slides before. They describe how the same goal can be targeted with interactive or direct teaching techniques. Notice how much the two types of techniques overlap.

Review Similarities and Differences in the *Interactive and Direct Teaching Techniques*

Slide 5

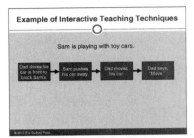

Here is an example of an interactive teaching technique. The child is playing with cars. Dad uses *Follow Your Child's Lead* by also playing with a car. Dad then uses *Playful Obstruction* to create an opportunity for the child to initiate communication. He blocks the child's car with his own car. The child communicates by pushing Dad's car away. The parent responds positively by moving his car and models a more complex response—the word "Move."

Notice that the parent immediately responds to the child's behavior as meaningful, while modeling the skill he would like his child to use. The child is not required to use the more complex skill that the parent models.

Slide 6

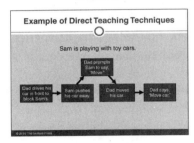

Here is an example of a direct teaching technique. It starts the same way as the last example: Dad uses *Follow Your Child's Lead* by playing with cars, and creates an opportunity for the child to initiate communication. The child pushes Dad's car away.

This is the point where the two types of technique diverge. Here Dad doesn't immediately move his car. Instead he prompts the child to use a word, "Move"—a more complex response. When the child says, "Move," or makes a close enough attempt, only then does Dad moves his car. This reinforces the child's response. Dad then expands on the response with two words: "Move car."

In the direct teaching techniques, the parent is attempting to elicit a specific response. Prompts are the way the parent helps the child respond successfully. And it's only when the child makes that response or a good attempt that the parent gives reinforcement.

Slide 7

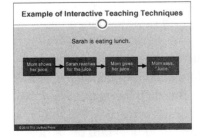

Let's look at another example of using the interactive teaching techniques.

The mother sets up an opportunity for the child to communicate. The child communicates by reaching for the juice. The mother responds to Sarah's communication by giving her the juice while modeling the word "Juice," a more complex response.

In the interactive teaching techniques, the parent responds to her child's behavior as meaningful. In this case, the child's behavior means "I want juice." By then giving Sarah the juice, Mom is reinforcing Sarah's initiation. The child is not required to use the more complex word "Juice."

Slide 8

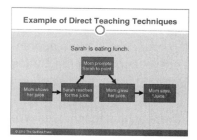

Here is the same basic situation, but with the mother using direct teaching techniques. Notice that everything is the same up to Sarah's reaching for the juice. Instead of giving Sarah the juice, Mom prompts her to point. It is only when Sarah successfully points that Mom gives her the juice, while saying the word "Juice"—a more complex response.

In the direct teaching techniques, the parent requires the child to use a more complex response (in this case, a point) before providing the child with the reinforcement.

Slide 9

Now that you are familiar with all of the techniques, you can move up and down the three levels of the pyramid throughout your interactions with your child.

When should you focus more on the techniques at the bottom, and when on the techniques at the top?. It is still a balancing act; you want to challenge your child without making him or her too frustrated.

Discuss When to Use *Interactive* versus *Direct Teaching* Techniques

Slide 10

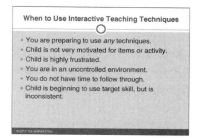

You always start with the interactive teaching techniques, and you can always use these during interactions with your child.

When your child is not highly motivated by an item or activity (e.g., getting dressed), use interactive teaching techniques. The child is not likely to respond well to prompting for a more complex response when he or she is not motivated. Instead, try modeling language around his or her focus of attention.

When your child is highly frustrated, use interactive teaching techniques to reduce your child's frustration level and help keep him or her engaged. When frustrated, your child may not respond well to direct prompting or tolerate your withholding desired items. It is not uncommon for a child to "shut down" completely, disengage altogether, or begin to have a tantrum if the child is frustrated and the parent continues to prompt more complex responses. You can always begin to use prompting again when your child is settled or at another time.

When you are in an uncontrolled environment, such as a store or other public place, it may be best to use interactive teaching techniques. You may find it harder to use the direct teaching techniques in such an environment because either you cannot withhold desired items to encourage an initiation, or doing so can lead to tantrums and you are uncomfortable allowing your child to have a tantrum in that location.

When you do not have time to follow through with a prompt or demand—for example, you are rushing to get out of the house—it is best not to begin using the direct teaching techniques. When you begin to prompt but aren't able to follow through, your child may learn that he or she does not have to respond to your prompts.

Finally, the interactive teaching techniques are great for moving your child to more spontaneous use of skills. Thus if your child is able to use a new skill, but not yet consistent (beginning to imitate single words), you should provide opportunities for him or her to use the skill during interactions without direct prompting.

Some daily routines are particularly good for using the interactive teaching techniques. We have found that bathtime, bedtime, and dressing are the most effective ones for using these techniques.

[Ask parents:] For which routines are you likely to have the most success using the interactive teaching techniques?

Slide 11

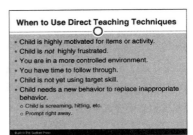

The direct teaching techniques are most effective when your child is highly motivated and not highly frustrated. Your child has to be able to tolerate your withholding of desired items or activities, while also wanting them enough to "work" for them.

Direct techniques are best when you are in an environment that you can control, and when you have time to follow through with prompting.

Direct teaching techniques are also most effective when your child is learning to use a new skill. When your child is not yet able to use a skill independently (e.g., two-word phrases), he or she will benefit from the added support that prompting provides. Once the child is able to use this skill independently on some occasions, the skill can then be targeted with the interactive teaching techniques.

Use the direct teaching techniques when your child needs to develop a new behavior to replace an inappropriate one. For example, if your child screams to get desired items, you will want to set up opportunities for your child to request and for you to prompt right away, before he or she screams, so that your child can learn a more appropriate way to get his or her needs met.

Some daily routines are better than others for using the direct teaching techniques. Activities that your child enjoys are the most effective ones for using these techniques. For many children, we have found that snacktime (provided your child enjoys eating and is not too hungry), bathtime, and transitions to favorite routines (e.g., going outside) are the most effective ones for using the direct teaching techniques.

[Ask parents:] In which routines are you likely to have the most success using the direct teaching techniques?

Show Video Clips of *Putting It All Together*

Slide 12

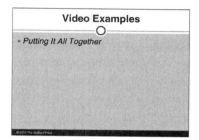

Note to Trainers: Prepare to show video clips for Session 11: *Putting It All Together.*

Before each clip, tell parents to observe how the parent prompts the child to increase the complexity of his social communication.

After each clip, ask parents:

"What interactive teaching techniques did you notice the parent using?"

"What types of prompts does the parent use to help the child respond appropriately?"

"When does the parent move from interactive to direct teaching techniques?"

"What percentage of the time is the parent using interactive versus direct teaching techniques?"

The important techniques and strategies to highlight are outlined below.

• *Preverbal 1.* The father uses the following interactive teaching techniques: *Communicative Temptations* (in sight and out of reach, control of access) and *Imitate Your Child.* He also uses the following direct teaching strategies: direct question, choices, and gestural prompt. The father uses direct teaching when he has control of the materials and his son's engagement (at the beginning with in sight and out of reach), and at the end, he controls all but one block and has his son imitate. The father uses interactive teaching to regain his son's attention/engagement by imitating banging blocks and then takes control. Interactive teaching is used more frequently than direct teaching; there are only three prompts in the clip.

• *Preverbal 2.* The mother uses the following interactive teaching techniques: *Follow Your Child's Lead* (face to face), *Communicative Temptations* (in sight and out of reach, control of access), *Modeling and Expanding Language*, and *Animation.* She also uses the following direct teaching techniques: direct question, verbal model, and gesture prompt. Direct teaching is used when the mother has control of the materials and her son's engagement (she has the bubbles; once they all pop, he comes back for more). Interactive teaching is used to model language when he is popping bubbles and to create opportunities for initiations (in sight and out of reach, toys he needs assistance with).

• *Single words to simple phrases.* The father uses the following interactive teaching techniques: *Follow Your Child's Lead*, *Modeling and Expanding Language*, and *Playful Obstruction* (turning the water off and on). He also uses the following direct teaching strategies: time delay and verbal model. The difference between *Modeling and Expanding Language* (interactive teaching) and providing a verbal model (direct teaching) is that the child is required to respond prior to receiving reinforcement when the verbal model is used. The father uses direct teaching when he has control of the materials (turning off the water), when his child is highly motivated, and after he has modeled "on and off" several times without asking for a response. This ensures that his son knows what is expected of him (clear prompt). The father uses interactive teaching to show his son how he will be expected to respond when he is prompted, and to increase his attention and motivation.

• *Complex phrase speech.* The mother uses the following interactive teaching techniques: *Follow Your Child's Lead* (face to face), and *Communicative Temptations* (assistance, silly situations). She also uses the following direct teaching strategies: time delay, direct questions, and choices. The mother uses direct teaching when her son needs her assistance to complete the task (opening the fruit leather), and when she has control of the item. She uses interactive teaching to ensure that she has his engagement and motivation.

Discuss and Assign Homework

Slide 13

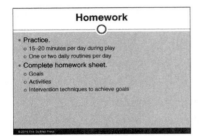

Note to Trainers: Pass out copies of Homework for Group Format: *Putting It All Together* (Appendix A, Form 27).

I would like each of you to think of two to three goals that you will target this week. These goals could include any of the social-communication goals that you have developed for your child. For each goal, identify a specific activity in which you will target the goal. Once you decide on goals and activities, write them down on your homework sheet.

Think about all of the techniques and strategies that you have learned in this program. Decide which ones you will use during the activities to achieve the goals that you have selected.

Note to Trainers: If time permits, have each parent report. Give feedback as necessary.

I would like you to practice these techniques and strategies over the next week and to respond to the questions on your homework sheet. We will discuss your homework during your last individual coaching session next week. You should come to the session with questions you have about any of the techniques and strategies or how they work together.

Note to Trainers: Have parents sign up for the individual session if they haven't already been scheduled.

Take Break

Conduct Wrap-Up

Slide 14

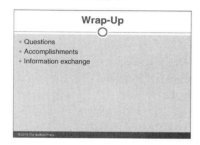

Note to Trainers: The goal of the final half of this session is to make sure that everyone has the opportunity to ask additional questions, to solve problems, and to leave the group on a high note. Furthermore, it is a great opportunity to encourage parents to maintain their relationships with other parents from the group after the program has ended.

As this is our last session as a group, I would like to give everyone the opportunity to ask any additional questions about how to apply these strategies with their child or in their daily routines.

> *Note to Trainers:* Answer parents' questions as they relate to the Project ImPACT program or to other interventions that you are familiar with. If parents ask questions about other areas that you can't answer, tell them that you will help them find the information.

Now I would like everyone to discuss something positive that came out of this program, such as an accomplishment that your child made or something that you learned.

> *Note to Trainers:* Write these accomplishments on a whiteboard to help parents appreciate their efforts. Help parents recognize how important these accomplishments are.
>
> Pass out a contact sheet for parents to exchange personal information, so that they can stay in contact with each other after the group ends.

In previous groups, parents have chosen to exchange information for future contact and support. Some families have continued to meet periodically, either as a support group or for social purposes, such as having a pool party for their children. Other parents have chosen to take turns babysitting, so that each family gets a chance to get a break from the kids or to just get together for coffee. If you would like to exchange contact information with other families, please write down your name and contact information on this sheet. I will make copies and pass these out to each of you at your last coaching session next week.

> *Note to Trainers:* If the session is close to being finished early, you may wish to allow parents to use this time to give and receive support. This can include encouraging parents to share information about other services in the community that they have found helpful, or letting parents discuss some of the difficulties that they face in parenting a child with ASD. If the session ends with the latter topic, be sure to have some type of closure to the group that leaves parents feeling positive.

Review of *Putting It All Together*

Session Goals

1. Improve the parent's ability to use the interactive and direct teaching techniques together to enhance her child's social-communication skills.
2. Increase the parent's independence in using the techniques.

Materials for the Session:

1. Parent manual
2. Completed Goal Development Form (Appendix A, Form 4)
3. *Putting It All Together* Review Sheet (Appendix A, Form 13)
4. Group Format Coaching Form (Appendix A, Form 18)
5. Five to six highly motivating toys and activities, including two sets of some toys and toys that child needs help to use
6. Variety of storage containers that desired items can be placed in (e.g., clear plastic containers with screw lids, Ziploc bags, large bins, shelving)
7. Homework for Group Format: *Putting It All Together* (Appendix A, Form 27)
8. Parent Satisfaction Survey (Appendix A, Form 15) (optional)

Outline of the Session:

- Prior to session, review coaching form and notes from previous coaching session, and arrange coaching space to facilitate parent–child interactions.
- Review homework from preceding group session (5 minutes).
- Provide a brief review of *Putting It All Together* (5 minutes).
- Have the parent practice techniques while you give feedback (25 minutes).
- Discuss and assign homework (10 minutes):
    1. Give out Homework for Group Format: *Putting It All Together* (Appendix A, Form 27) and have the parent fill out "Goals of the Week."
- Schedule follow-up session with the parent (if applicable).
- Have the parent complete the Parent Satisfaction Survey (optional).

Prior to Session, Review Coaching Form and Notes from Previous Coaching Session, and Arrange Coaching Space to Facilitate Parent–Child Interactions

Your entries on the parent's coaching form from Session 10 will remind you of the parent's strengths and weaknesses and help guide the focus of this session. As always, make sure to arrange the coaching space to facilitate parent–child interactions by having a defined physical space, limiting distractions, and selecting highly preferred toys.

Review Homework from Preceding Group Session

Begin the coaching session by discussing the parent's answers to each of the homework questions from the copy of Appendix A, Form 27, that she received in the preceding group session (Session 11). If the parent did not write down her answers, review them orally with her. If the parent had difficulties, brainstorm solutions. Challenges are usually related to knowing when to use the interactive versus direct teaching techniques and how to combine them together. Provide the parent with concrete suggestions for which techniques are best suited for specific daily activities. Activities that the child enjoys are the best ones in which to utilize the techniques.

Provide a Brief Review of *Putting It All Together*

Briefly review the critical elements of techniques using the *Putting It All Together* Review Sheet (Appendix A, Form 13 in this manual; see also Form 17.1 in the parent manual). The interactive teaching techniques are used to ensure engagement and to increase motivation and initiations. The direct teaching techniques are used to increase the complexity of the child's response. Give the parent an opportunity to ask any questions she might have about either the interactive or direct teaching techniques and how they are used together.

Have the Parent Practice the Techniques While You Give Feedback

At this point, the parent should no longer need you to model the techniques prior to practicing. However, if the parent has questions about techniques, you may demonstrate.

The parent should have at least 25 minutes to practice the intervention techniques and strategies. Use the coaching forms completed during the previous sessions to determine which specific techniques to coach. Given the limited number of coaching sessions and the large number of techniques the parent has learned in the class, it is likely that you have not provided coaching on all techniques. The final coaching session should be spent improving the parent's use of those techniques that will have the greatest positive impact on the parent–child relationship and the child's skills. Do not coach on too many techniques at one time; choose two or three on which to coach, and identify these for the parent before she begins practice. Once the parent and you have identified the goal to target and the techniques to use, have the parent practice the techniques with her child while you provide her with feedback.

Ideally, the parent will be able to use the interactive and direct teaching techniques together. However, if the parent is having difficulty balancing the use of the techniques, it may be helpful to give her a concrete rule to follow—for example, "Demonstrate a new skill three times and then prompt it. This balance will increase his engagement and decrease his frustration."

If the parent tends to rely too heavily on the interactive teaching techniques and rarely prompts her child to expand his communication, social imitation, or play, coach her to use the direct teaching techniques more often. Conversely, if the parent tends to "overprompt" or the child gets easily frustrated, coach her to focus more heavily on the interactive teaching techniques.

If you are providing coaching in the home, you should have the parent practice using the techniques during several different caretaking routines, so that the parent gets experience in using them throughout her daily interactions with her child. If you are coaching in a clinic or school, consider having the parent select a caregiving routine such as dressing or feeding, and have her practice the routine while using the intervention techniques.

Complete the coaching form during or immediately after the coaching session. The information on this form is used in planning follow-up sessions.

Discuss and Assign Homework

1. Give out Homework for Group Format: *Putting It All Together* **and have the parent fill out "Goals of the Week."** Give the parent a fresh copy of Appendix A, Form 27, and work with the parent to select several goals, the activities in which the goals will be targeted, and the intervention techniques and strategies the parent will use during each of these different activities to achieve these goals. The techniques and strategies, will vary depending on the activity. Discuss ways in which the parent can use the different strategies practiced in this session during her daily routines with her child at home. To facilitate this discussion, you may wish to refer to the Daily Activity Schedule to identify specific routines. Since this is the final session, the parent should have the opportunity to discuss any concerns or questions she has about the intervention.

Schedule Follow-Up Session with the Parent (if Applicable)

Some parents lose motivation for using the intervention techniques after the program has ended. In addition, as their children change over time, many parents need help applying the techniques to target new skills. For this reason, it is helpful to provide periodic follow-up coaching sessions with the parent and child. These sessions are likely to be most effective if they are scheduled once every 1–3 months or until the parent feels that she no longer needs support. If you will be setting up follow-up sessions, be sure to schedule them with the parent before she leaves.

Have the Parent Complete the Parent Satisfaction Survey (Optional)

If possible, take time at the end of the session to have the parent complete the Parent Satisfaction Survey (Form 15 in Appendix A). This will give you important information on ways to improve your parent training skills.

Troubleshooting Tips

The main challenge that occurs when coaching at this point is that the parent uses one type of technique more than another. When this occurs, provide the parent with prompts to move between techniques. If the parent reports difficulty with use of the techniques at home, it may be beneficial to set up a home visit. If possible, schedule the home visit during a daily activity that is particularly challenging for the parent, to help her use the techniques. During the home visit, explain the techniques you will use to improve the child's skills, demonstrate use of the techniques, and have the parent practice while you give feedback. If you are unable to make a home visit and the parent has access to a video camera, have her record the interaction and review the video with her during the follow-up session.

Follow-Up Session

Session Goals

1. Maintain the parent's ability to implement the intervention.
2. Review and update goals.
3. Teach the parent to use the techniques to address new goals.

Materials

1. Parent manual
2. Completed Goal Development Form (Appendix A, Form 4)
3. Social-Communication Checklist (Appendix A, Form 3)
4. Blank Goal Development Form (Appendix A, Form 4)
5. *Putting It All Together* Review Sheet (Appendix A, Form 13)
6. Group Format Coaching Form (Appendix A, Form 18)
7. Five to six highly motivating toys and activities, including two sets of some toys and toys that child needs help to use
8. Variety of storage containers for holding desired items (e.g., clear plastic containers with screw lids, Ziploc bags, large bins, shelving)
9. Homework: *Follow-Up Session* (Appendix A, Form 16)

Outline of Session

- Prior to session, arrange the coaching space to facilitate parent–child interactions.
- Assess the parent's needs (5 minutes).
- Review homework from the last treatment session (5–10 minutes), *or*
- Review and update the child's goals (10–15 minutes):

    Have the parent report on child's current skills.
    Observe a brief parent–child interaction and complete the Social-Communication Checklist.
    Update goals for the child with the parent.

- Provide a brief review of *Putting It All Together* (5 minutes).

- Demonstrate use of techniques to target updated goals (5 minutes).
- Have the parent practice the techniques while you provide feedback (10 minutes).
- Discuss and assign homework (5 minutes).
    1. Have parent complete Homework: *Follow-Up Session* (Appendix A, Form 16).

Prior to Session, Arrange the Coaching Space to Facilitate Parent–Child Interactions

Make sure to arrange the coaching space to facilitate parent–child interactions by having a defined physical space, limiting distractions, and selecting highly preferred toys.

Assess the Parent's Needs

Begin the session by having the parent report how things have gone at home since the last coaching session. Ask the parent to report how she has been implementing the intervention techniques and in what areas she needs additional help. For example, you might ask:

- "How are you currently using the intervention techniques at home?"
- "What techniques seem to be most successful?"
- "Are there any techniques that you continue to struggle with using or would like some additional coaching on?"

Depending on how much time has passed since the last coaching session and how quickly the child has progressed toward meeting his goals, you may choose to update the child's goals or simply to review the homework from the previous session. If little time has passed since the last treatment session (i.e., a month or less), or if the child is still working on the same goals as at the last session, you may choose instead to review the homework from the previous session. However, if a significant amount of time has passed (i.e., 2 or more months), or the child has been making substantial progress in achieving his previous goals, it is important to take time to update the child's goals with the parent. If the parent has brought a video of herself using the intervention at home, take time to view with her.

Review Homework from the Last Treatment Session (Do Not Complete If Updating Child's Goals)

Review the homework that was completed at the end of the last session. This review may take longer than it did in previous sessions, given the amount of time between sessions. If the parent did not complete the homework, ask the parent probing questions that are related to her child's goals. Here are some sample questions:

- "How has your child been indicating that he wants a toy, drink, object, or action?"
- "How do you respond to this request?"
- "What techniques do you find are effective in increasing your child's use of single words?"
- "Have any of the techniques been challenging?"

Review and Update the Child's Goals (Complete as an Alternative to Reviewing Homework)

Have the Parent Report on the Child's Current Skills

Review the child's goals from the previous session with the parent. Ask the parent to report how the child has progressed on these goals since the last coaching session. For example, you might ask:

- "You were working on increasing your child's single words. How is he communicating now?"
- "You were working on increasing your child's functional play. How is he playing now?"

Observe a Brief Parent–Child Interaction and Complete the Social-Communication Checklist

Have the parent use the intervention techniques with her child while you observe. This observation will help you determine the child's current skill level, as well as the parent's continued ability to use the intervention techniques. While she interacts with her child, use the Social-Communication Checklist (Appendix A, Form 3) to record information on the child's use of skills in each of the four core areas.

Update Goals for the Child with the Parent

Based on the parent's report and your observation of the parent–child interaction, help the parent update her child's goals. Write the updated goals on a new copy of the Goal Development Form (Appendix A, Form 4).

Provide a Brief Review of *Putting It All Together*

Briefly review the critical elements of techniques, using the *Putting It All Together* Review Sheet (Appendix A, Form 13). Give the parent an opportunity to ask any questions she might have about any of the techniques or how to use them at home to address her child's goals.

Demonstrate Use of Techniques to Target Updated Goals

Once the child's goals have been updated, demonstrate use of the intervention techniques to target any new goals the parent has identified. This demonstration should be brief, in order for the parent to have the time to practice. During the demonstration, identify the techniques you use and the child's response. It is also important to identify how both the interactive and direct teaching techniques can be used to address the child's updated goals. This explanation helps the parent balance her use of the techniques. If the parent has reported difficulty with any specific intervention strategies, be sure to demonstrate them with the child.

Have the Parent Practice the Techniques While You Provide Feedback

Have the parent practice using the intervention techniques to address the child's updated goals. Remember that feedback should not be provided on too many techniques at once. If you notice the parent is having difficulty with a particular technique, focus on that technique.

Discuss and Assign Homework

1. Have the parent complete Homework: *Follow-Up Session* (Appendix A, Form 16). Have the parent identify the goals she will target, the activities in which she will use the techniques, and the techniques she will use to address the goals. If the parent is struggling with a specific technique or behavior during certain activities, have the parent record an interaction on video and bring the video to you to review during an additional follow-up session.

Reproducible Materials for the Individual and Group Training Formats

Forms for Individual Format

---

*Form 6 should be called the Interactive Teaching Techniques Review Sheet II *only* when it is used in the group format. In the individual format, the II should be omitted.

Forms for Group Format

**Form 6 should be called the Interactive Teaching Techniques Review Sheet II *only* when it is used in the group format. In the individual format, the II should be omitted.

| FORM 1 | **Introduction Letter**
for the Individual Training Format |

Dear _____,

Thank you for contacting us regarding parent training for your child. Project ImPACT (Improving Parents As Communication Teachers) is designed to teach you techniques and strategies to improve your child's social-communication skills. These techniques and strategies are designed for parents to use during daily routines and activities. Learning how to provide intervention to your child has a number of benefits:

- The child receives many more hours of intervention.
- The child is better able to retain new learning and apply it to different situations.
- Parents become less stressed and have more time for leisure and recreation.

In this parent training program, you and your child meet with a trainer for 24 sessions lasting 60 to 90 minutes each. Ideally, the sessions are held twice a week for 12 weeks. It is strongly recommended that the same parent (or both parents) attend every session. Individual parent training sessions will be held at the following dates and times:

Day: _____   Time: _____

Day: _____   Time: _____

If you are interested in enrolling in the program or have any questions about information in this letter or the treatment program, please do not hesitate to contact _____ at _____.

Sincerely,

_____

From *Teaching Social Communication to Children with Autism: A Manual for Parents* by Brooke Ingersoll and Anna Dvortcsak. Copyright 2010 by The Guilford Press. Permission to photocopy this form is granted to purchasers of this book for personal use only (see copyright page for details).

Child History Form

Child's name: _____   **Date of birth:** _____

Parent's name: _____   **Phone:** _____

Please complete and return this form prior to your first treatment session.

---

1. What languages are spoken in the home? What is the primary language?

---

2. With whom does your child spend the most time?

---

3. Does your child have siblings? If yes, please list them and give their ages.

---

4. Please describe your main goals for your child.

---

5. Please describe goals you have for yourself.

(cont.)

From *Teaching Social Communication to Children with Autism: A Manual for Parents* by Brooke Ingersoll and Anna Dvortcsak. Copyright 2010 by The Guilford Press. Permission to photocopy this form is granted to purchasers of this book for personal use only (see copyright page for details).

6. How does your child communicate with you?

7. Why does your child communicate with you (to request something [milk, food, a toy], to play, to show you something, etc.)?

8. When was your child's communication difficulty first noticed? By whom?

9. Is your child aware of the communication difficulty? If yes, how does the child feel about it?

10. Please list some activities that your child enjoys.

11. Has your child seen any other specialists (speech–language pathologist, physician, psychologist, occupational therapist, educational specialist, etc.) for evaluations? If yes, what were the results? (Reports are helpful and can be attached in lieu of an explanation.)

(cont.)

12. Does your child have any medical concerns? Any known syndrome, diagnosis, or allergies?

13. Is your child on any medication(s)? If yes, please list the medication(s) your child is taking.

14. Has your child received intervention services, previously or currently (biomedical, speech–language intervention, early intervention, occupational therapy, etc.)? (Reports are helpful and can be attached in lieu of an explanation.)

15. If yes, what treatment methods have been used in these programs, and what has been your experience with them?

16. Please list any other information that may be helpful.

Thank you for taking the time to complete this. It will be helpful in devising your child's treatment plan. Please feel free to attach any reports in lieu of answering questions if this information has already been collected. Thank you.

FORM 3

Social-Communication Checklist

Child: _____ Date: _____ Person completing checklist: _____

Please complete this form based on what your child can do independently (without help from you). If your child used to use a behavior but no longer does (e.g., used to babble, but now uses sentences) check the *last* column.

Behavior	Usually (at least 75% of the time)	Sometimes, but not consistently	Rarely, not yet, or not observed	Not observed
Social Engagement				
Does your child prefer to play near you?				
Does your child maintain simple social games initiated by you for at least three turns (peek-a-boo, chase, pat-a-cake)?				
Does your child remain actively engaged with you during play for at least 5 minutes?				
Does your child remain actively engaged with you during play for at least 10 minutes?				
Does your child respond to your attempts to draw his attention to something or someone?				
Does your child make eye contact while interacting or communicating with you?				
Does your child initiate activities or play with you (offer you a toy or find you to come play with him)?				
Does your child take turns with you?				
Does your child point or show you objects that interest him for the purposes of sharing?				
Does your child provide greetings and farewells when people come into or leave the room?				
Expressive Language—Form				
Does your child babble or use speech-like sounds?				
Does your child use gestures that physically involve you to request items or actions (lead you to an object, place your hand on an object, give you an object)?				
Does your child use gestures that do not physically involve you to request items or actions (pointing, signing)?				

(cont.)

From *Teaching Social Communication to Children with Autism: A Practitioner's Guide to Parent Training* by Brooke Ingersoll and Anna Dvortcsak. Copyright 2010 by The Guilford Press. Permission to photocopy this form is granted to purchasers of this book for personal use only (see copyright page for details).

Behavior	Usually (at least 75% of the time)	Sometimes, but not consistently	Rarely, not yet, or not observed	Not observed
Does your child communicate a clear choice when presented with two alternatives (by reaching, using eye gaze, using sounds or words)?				
Does your child imitate your language?				
Does your child use single words spontaneously?				
Does your child combine words into simple phrases ("Go car," "Push train")?				
Does your child consistently use sentences to communicate?				
Does your child name objects?				
Does your child name actions?				
Does your child use words to describe objects ("Big red ball," "Little green ball")?				
Does your child answer simple questions ("What do you want?", "What is it", "Where is it?", etc.)? If yes, please circle the type of question your child answers.				
Does your child answer "who," "why," or "how" questions? If yes, please circle the type of questions your child answers.				
Expressive Language—Function				
Does your child use language to request desired items or activities?				
Does your child use language to protest or tell you he does not want something?				
Does your child use language to share information ("I see a plane")?				
Does your child use words to tell you how he is feeling (hurt, mad, or happy)?				
Does your child use language to gain your attention ("Mom, come here")?				
Does your child use language to tell you what to do ("Feed the baby," "Push the car," etc.)?				

(cont.)

Behavior	Usually (at least 75% of the time)	Sometimes, but not consistently	Rarely, not yet, or not observed	Not observed
Does your child tell you about events that have already occurred (at school, etc.)?				
Does your child use language to tell you a simple story?				
Does your child ask you questions for information ("What is that?", "Where is dog?", "Why?")? If yes, please indicate the type of questions your child asks.				
Understanding and Following Directions				
Does your child respond appropriately to simple directions ("Get your shoes," "Give me a hug")?				
Does your child follow directions with more than one step ("Go to your room and get your cars")?				
Social Imitation				
Does your child imitate familiar play actions (actions that your child does independently) after seeing you do them?				
Does your child imitate novel play actions (actions that your child does not do independently) after seeing you do them?				
Does your child imitate conventional gestures (wave bye-bye, blow kisses, clap hands, etc.)?				
Play				
Does your child use toys in an exploratory manner (touching, mouthing, smelling, looking)?				
Does your child combine objects together (nesting one object in another; putting objects in containers; lining, stacking, ordering toys in certain ways)?				
Does your child use cause-and-effect toys (mechanical toys, pop-up toys)?				
Does your child use toys for their intended purpose (throw a ball, push a car)?				
Does your child direct familiar pretend play actions toward himself (pretend to eat, pretend to sleep, pretend to talk on a toy phone)?				

(*cont.*)

Behavior	Usually (at least 75% of the time)	Sometimes, but not consistently	Rarely, not yet, or not observed	Not observed
Does your child direct basic pretend play toward another person or a doll or other toy (pretend to feed a parent or a baby doll, dress a doll, put a doll to bed)?				
Does your child pretend that one thing represents another (pretend a block is a car or a stack of blocks is a building), attribute characteristics to an object that it does not have (pretend that toy food is "hot" or tastes "yummy"), or animate objects (make a figurine walk or have a doll hold a cup rather than placing a cup to the doll's mouth)?				
Does your child link several pretend actions together or tell an extended story with toys (put doll in car and push car to store)?				
Does your child take on an imaginary role (pretend to be a doctor, firefighter, mommy/daddy) during play?				
Does your child tell an extended story while taking on an imaginary role with at least one other person (child is doctor, parent is patient; child is mommy, peer is baby)?				

| FORM 4 | **Goal Development Form** |

Child's name: _____

Date: _____

Global Goals	Current Skills	Measurable Goals
Social Engagement		
Language		
Social Imitation		
Play		

From *Teaching Social Communication to Children with Autism: A Practitioner's Guide to Parent Training* by Brooke Ingersoll and Anna Dvortcsak. Copyright 2010 by The Guilford Press. Permission to photocopy this form is granted to purchasers of this book for personal use only (see copyright page for details).

FORM 5

Daily Activity Schedule

Please describe the daily routines that you regularly do with your child. In the last column, please indicate if your child [E]njoys, [T]olerates, or [R]esists the routine.

	Time of day	Length of time	Brief description of routine	How does your child respond?
Wake-up time				
Mealtime				
Toileting/ diaper change				
Fine motor play (e.g., toy play, art, sensory– motor play)				
Gross motor play (e.g., rough-and- tumble play, chase, outdoor play)				

(cont.)

From *Teaching Social Communication to Children with Autism: A Practitioner's Guide to Parent Training* by Brooke Ingersoll and Anna Dvortcsak. Copyright 2010 by The Guilford Press. Permission to photocopy this form is granted to purchasers of this book for personal use only (see copyright page for details).

	Time of day	Length of time	Brief description of routine	How does your child respond?
Songs/ social games				
Stories				
Bathing				
Bedtime				
Other (e.g., computer, video, park, play with siblings/ other caretakers)				

Interactive Teaching Techniques Review Sheet (II)

---

1. Use *Follow Your Child's Lead*: *What is your child interested in?*

- Let your child choose the activity.
- Be face to face.

- Join in your child's activity.
- Comment on your child's play.

---

2. Create an opportunity for your child to engage or communicate.

- *Imitate Your Child*
- *Animation*

- *Playful Obstruction*
- *Balanced Turns*

- *Communicative Temptations*
  - In sight and out of reach
  - Control of access
  - Assistance
  - Inadequate portions
  - Protest
  - Sabotage
  - Silly situations

---

3. Wait for your child to engage or communicate: *How is your child engaging or communicating?*

---

4. Respond to your child's behavior as meaningful, comply with it, and model a more complex (developed) response.

- Give your child's actions meaning.
- Adjust your language.
  - Simplify your language.
  - Speak slowly.
  - Stress important words.
  - Be repetitive.
  - Use visual/gestural cues.

- Model language around your child's interest.
  - Model gestures.
  - Model new language forms.
  - Model new language functions.
- Expand on your child's language.
- Model new play (*Balanced Turns*).

From *Teaching Social Communication to Children with Autism: A Practitioner's Guide to Parent Training* by Brooke Ingersoll and Anna Dvortcsak. Copyright 2010 by The Guilford Press. Permission to photocopy this form is granted to purchasers of this book for personal use only (see copyright page for details).

Interactive Teaching Techniques **Video Review Form**

Child: _____ **Parent:** _____ **Date:** _____

Intervention technique	Observed: Y/N	Child's reaction to technique
❑ **Uses** ***Follow Your Child's Lead***		
Lets child choose the activity.		
Is face to face.		
Joins in child's play.		
❑ **Creates an opportunity for the child to engage or communicate.**		
Uses *Imitate Your Child.*		
Uses *Animation.*		
Uses *Playful Obstruction* (anticipatory phrase).		
Uses *Balanced Turns.*		
Uses *Communicative Temptations.*		
❑ **Waits for the child to engage or communicate.**		
Waits with anticipation.		
❑ **Responds to the child's behavior as meaningful, complies with it, and demonstrates a more complex response.**		
Gives meaning to child's actions.		
Adjusts language for child's developmental level.		
Models language around child's focus of attention.		
Models gestures.		
Models new language forms.		
Models new language functions.		
Expands on child's language.		
Models new play (*Balanced Turns*).		

From *Teaching Social Communication to Children with Autism: A Practitioner's Guide to Parent Training* by Brooke Ingersoll and Anna Dvortcsak. Copyright 2010 by The Guilford Press. Permission to photocopy this form is granted to purchasers of this book for personal use only (see copyright page for details).

Individual Format Coaching Form

Child: _____ Parent: _____ Session: _____ Date: _____

Check the box to the left of each intervention component that you will coach on this session. For each checked box, score each subcomponent based on your observation of the parent and child. After scoring each subcomponent, provide a summary score for the intervention component that best captures how the parent performed on the subcomponents. To achieve fidelity, the parent must receive a score of 4 or 5 on each of the component summary scores that are being measured.

Low fidelity 1	2	3	4	High fidelity 5
Parent does not implement throughout session.	Parent implements occasionally, but misses majority of opportunities.	Parent implements up to half of the time, but misses many opportunities.	Parent implements more than half of the time, but misses some opportunities.	Parent implements throughout the session.

Intervention technique	Fidelity					Notes
❑ **Parent uses *Follow Your Child's Lead*.** ***Summary***	1	2	3	4	5	
Lets child choose the activity.	1	2	3	4	5	
Is face to face.	1	2	3	4	5	
Joins in child's play.	1	2	3	4	5	
❑ **Parent creates an opportunity for the child to engage or communicate.** ***Summary***	1	2	3	4	5	
Uses *Imitate Your Child* (toy play, gestures, body movements, vocalizations).	1	2	3	4	5	
Uses *Animation*.	1	2	3	4	5	
Uses *Playful Obstruction*.	1	2	3	4	5	
Uses *Balanced Turns*.	1	2	3	4	5	
Uses *Communicative Temptations*.	1	2	3	4	5	
❑ **Parent waits for the child to engage or communicate.** ***Summary***	1	2	3	4	5	
Waits with anticipation.	1	2	3	4	5	
❑ **Parent responds to the child's behavior as meaningful, complies with it, and models a more complex response.** ***Summary***	1	2	3	4	5	
Gives meaning to child's actions.	1	2	3	4	5	
Adjusts language for child's developmental level.	1	2	3	4	5	

(cont.)

From *Teaching Social Communication to Children with Autism: A Practitioner's Guide to Parent Training* by Brooke Ingersoll and Anna Dvortcsak. Copyright 2010 by The Guilford Press. Permission to photocopy this form is granted to purchasers of this book for personal use only (see copyright page for details).

Individual Format Coaching Form (p. 2 of 2)

Intervention technique	Fidelity	Notes
Models language around child's focus of attention.	1 2 3 4 5	
Models gestures.	1 2 3 4 5	
Models new language forms.	1 2 3 4 5	
Models new language functions.	1 2 3 4 5	
Expands on child's language.	1 2 3 4 5	
Models new play (*Balanced Turns*).	1 2 3 4 5	
❑ **Parent prompts the child to use more complex language, imitation, or play.** *Summary*	**1 2 3 4 5**	
Waits for child's initiation before prompting.	1 2 3 4 5	
Uses clear and relevant prompts.	1 2 3 4 5	
Prompts no more than three times without increasing support.	1 2 3 4 5	
Provides sufficient opportunity for the child to respond.	1 2 3 4 5	
Requires a response.	1 2 3 4 5	
Uses developmentally appropriate language prompts.	1 2 3 4 5	
Uses developmentally appropriate imitation prompts.	1 2 3 4 5	
Uses developmentally appropriate play prompts.	1 2 3 4 5	
After several prompts, adjusts support to promote spontaneity.	1 2 3 4 5	
❑ **Parent provides more support.** *Summary*	**1 2 3 4 5**	
Adds more support to help the child respond.	1 2 3 4 5	
❑ **Parent reinforces and expands on the child's response.** *Summary*	**1 2 3 4 5**	
Provides reinforcement immediately after child responds correctly.	1 2 3 4 5	
Withholds reinforcement for inappropriate behavior.	1 2 3 4 5	
Provides praise.	1 2 3 4 5	
Expands on child's response.	1 2 3 4 5	
❑ **Parent paces interaction to keep child engaged and learning.** *Summary*	**1 2 3 4 5**	
Uses interactive teaching techniques to keep child engaged.	1 2 3 4 5	
Provides initiation opportunities when child is not interactive.	1 2 3 4 5	
Uses direct teaching techniques to increase complexity when child is motivated.	1 2 3 4 5	

Flowchart for Prompting Expressive Language

Child's goal:

Activity:

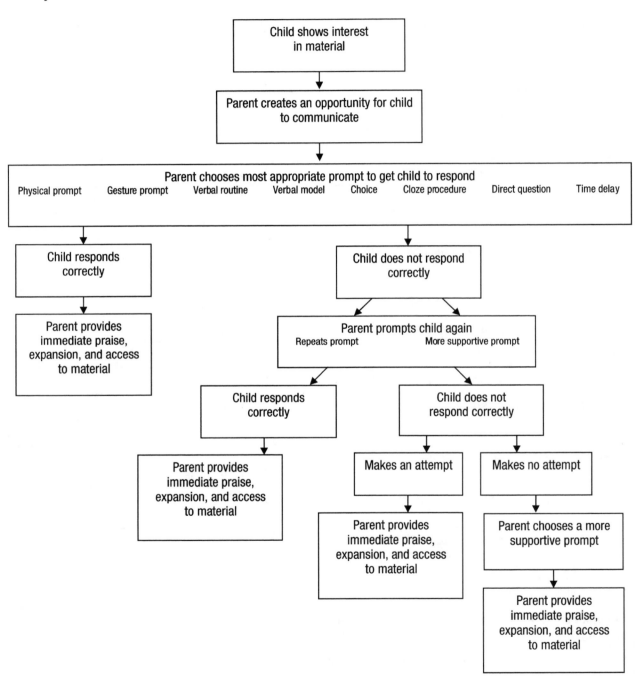

From *Teaching Social Communication to Children with Autism: A Practitioner's Guide to Parent Training* by Brooke Ingersoll and Anna Dvortcsak. Copyright 2010 by The Guilford Press. Permission to photocopy this form is granted to purchasers of this book for personal use only (see copyright page for details).

Flowchart for Prompting Play

Child's goal:

Activity:

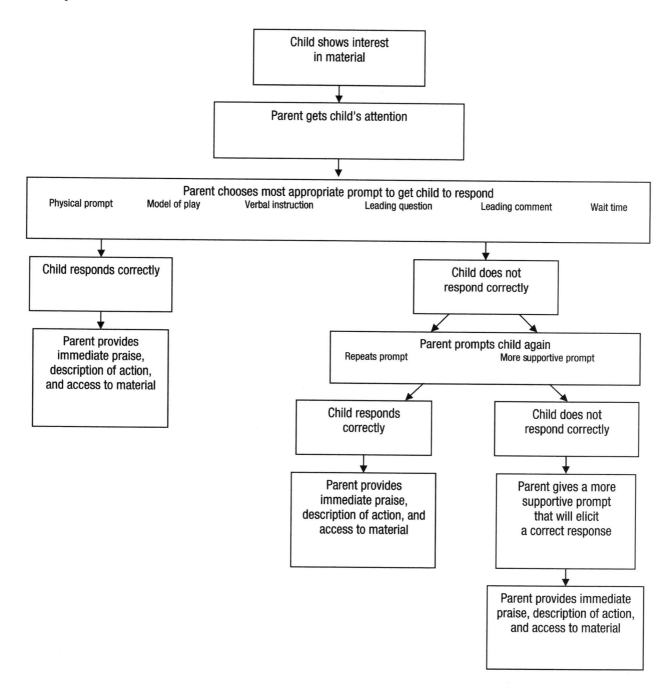

From *Teaching Social Communication to Children with Autism: A Practitioner's Guide to Parent Training* by Brooke Ingersoll and Anna Dvortcsak. Copyright 2010 by The Guilford Press. Permission to photocopy this form is granted to purchasers of this book for personal use only (see copyright page for details).

FORM 11

Direct Teaching Techniques **Review Sheet**

---

1. Use *Follow Your Child's Lead*: *What is your child interested in?*

- Let your child choose the activity.
- Be face to face.

- Join in your child's activity.
- Comment on your child's play.

---

2. Create an opportunity for your child to communicate.

- *Playful Obstruction*
- *Balanced Turns*

- *Communicative Temptations*
  - In sight and out of reach
  - Control of access
  - Assistance
  - Inadequate portions
  - Protest
  - Sabotage
  - Silly situations

---

3. Wait for your child to communicate: *How is your child communicating?*

---

4 and 5. Prompt your child to use more complex language, imitation, or play, and give a more supportive prompt as needed.

Teaching Your Child Expressive Language	*Teaching Your Child Receptive Language*	*Teaching Your Child Social Imitation*	*Teaching Your Child Play*
• Time delay	• Clear directions	• Model of play	• Wait time
• Question	• Verbal instruction	• Model of gestures	• Leading comment
• Cloze procedure	• Visual prompt	• Verbal prompt	• Leading question
• Choices	• Physical prompt	• Physical prompt	• Verbal instruction
• Verbal model or routine			• Model of play
• Gesture prompt			• Physical prompt
• Physical prompt			

---

6. Reinforce and expand the prompted response.

- Give your child the desired object or action.
- Add one more element to your child's language.

From *Teaching Social Communication to Children with Autism: A Practitioner's Guide to Parent Training* by Brooke Ingersoll and Anna Dvortcsak. Copyright 2010 by The Guilford Press. Permission to photocopy this form is granted to purchasers of this book for personal use only (see copyright page for details).

338

FORM 12	*Direct Teaching Techniques* Video Review Form

Child: _____   Parent: _____   Date: _____

Intervention technique	Observed: Y/N	Child's reaction to technique
❑ **Uses** *Follow Your Child's Lead*		
Lets child choose the activity.		
Is face to face.		
Joins in child's play.		
❑ **Creates an opportunity for the child to communicate.**		
Uses *Playful Obstruction* (anticipatory phrase).		
Uses *Balanced Turns.*		
Uses *Communicative Temptations.*		
❑ **Waits for the child to communicate.**		
Waits with anticipation.		
❑ **Prompts the child to use more complex language, imitation, or play.**		
Waits for child's initiation before prompting.		
Uses clear and appropriate prompts.		
Prompts no more than three times without increasing support.		
Provides sufficient opportunity for the child to respond.		
Requires a response.		
Uses developmentally appropriate language prompts.		
Uses developmentally appropriate imitation prompts.		
Uses developmentally appropriate play prompts.		
After several prompts, adjusts support to promote spontaneity.		
❑ **Provides more support.**		
Adds more support to help the child respond.		
❑ **Reinforces and expands on the child's response.**		
Provides reinforcement immediately after child responds correctly.		
Withholds reinforcement for inappropriate behavior.		
Expands on child's response.		
❑ **Paces interaction to keep child engaged and learning.**		
Uses interactive teaching techniques to keep child engaged.		
Provides initiation opportunities when child is not interactive.		
Uses direct teaching techniques to increase complexity when child is motivated.		

From *Teaching Social Communication to Children with Autism: A Practitioner's Guide to Parent Training* by Brooke Ingersoll and Anna Dvortcsak. Copyright 2010 by The Guilford Press. Permission to photocopy this form is granted to purchasers of this book for personal use only (see copyright page for details).

Putting It All Together **Review Sheet**

---

1. Use *Follow Your Child's Lead*: *What is your child interested in?*

- Let your child choose the activity.
- Be face to face.

- Join in your child's activity.
- Comment on your child's play.

---

2. Create an opportunity for your child to engage or communicate.

- *Imitate Your Child*
- *Animation*

- *Playful Obstruction*
- *Balanced Turns*
- *Communicative Temptations*

---

3. Wait for your child to engage or communicate: *How is your child engaging or communicating?*

---

4. Choice point: Model *or* prompt a more complex response.

- Give your child's actions meaning.
- Adjust your language.
- Model language around your child's interest.
  - Gestures
  - New language forms
  - New language functions
- Expand on your child's language.
- Model new play (Balanced Turns).

- Use clear, relevant, and developmentally appropriate prompts.
- Require a response.
- Prompt a more complex response.
  - Expressive or receptive language
  - Social imitation
  - Play
- Add support if needed

---

5. Reinforce and expand on your child's response.

- Give your child the desired object or action.
- Add one more element to your child's language.

---

6. Pace the interaction to keep your child engaged and learning.

- Use interactive teaching techniques to keep your child engaged.
- Use direct teaching techniques to teach your child a new skill.

From *Teaching Social Communication to Children with Autism: A Practitioner's Guide to Parent Training* by Brooke Ingersoll and Anna Dvortcsak. Copyright 2010 by The Guilford Press. Permission to photocopy this form is granted to purchasers of this book for personal use only (see copyright page for details).

Session Data Sheet

Trainer: _____ **Date:** _____

Child: _____ **Technique:** _____

Goal	Spontaneous	Time delay	Question	Cloze	Choice	Model	Gesture	Physical

NOTES

Activities:

Child's behavior:

Parent's implementation of technique:

Reminders for next session:

From *Teaching Social Communication to Children with Autism: A Practitioner's Guide to Parent Training* by Brooke Ingersoll and Anna Dvortcsak. Copyright 2010 by The Guilford Press. Permission to photocopy this form is granted to purchasers of this book for personal use only (see copyright page for details).

Parent Satisfaction Survey

Date: _____   **Number of sessions/week:** _____

Trainer: _____   **Number of weeks:** _____

Training format (circle one)   *Individual*   or   *Group*

	Strongly agree	Agree	Not sure	Disagree	Strongly disagree
I am satisfied with my child's goals.					
I understand how to use the different techniques to address different goals I have for my child.					
I understand how to use the techniques at home during everyday activities.					
The homework assignments were clear and manageable.					
The trainer was concerned that I learn the information.					
The trainer was available to answer my questions.					
My child showed improvement in social engagement.					
My child showed improvement in language skills.					
My child showed improvement in imitation skills.					
My child showed improvement in play skills.					
I feel that my child enjoyed the program.					
I would recommend this program to others.					

PLEASE WRITE ANY ADDITIONAL COMMENTS ON THE BACK.

Thank you for your responses! This information will allow us to keep improving our services.

From *Teaching Social Communication to Children with Autism: A Practitioner's Guide to Parent Training* by Brooke Ingersoll and Anna Dvortcsak. Copyright 2010 by The Guilford Press. Permission to photocopy this form is granted to purchasers of this book for personal use only (see copyright page for details).

Homework: *Follow-Up Session*

Rationale: Ongoing work with your child increases the complexity of your child's language, imitation, and play skills. It also decreases your child's reliance on prompts.

Key points to remember and carry out:

Use *Follow Your Child's Lead.*

Create an opportunity for your child to respond.

Wait for your child to respond.

Model *or* prompt a more complex response.

Reinforce and expand on your child's response.

Pace the interaction to keep your child engaged and learning.

Child's goal:

Activities:

Intervention techniques to achieve goal:

Child's goal:

Activities:

Intervention techniques to achieve goal:

Child's goal:

Activities:

Intervention techniques to achieve goal:

---

1. Which skills (social engagement, expressive language/gestures, receptive language, social imitation, play) do you feel that you have been most successful at teaching?

---

2. Are there any skills that you have had difficulty teaching?

(cont.)

From *Teaching Social Communication to Children with Autism: A Practitioner's Guide to Parent Training* by Brooke Ingersoll and Anna Dvortcsak. Copyright 2010 by The Guilford Press. Permission to photocopy this form is granted to purchasers of this book for personal use only (see copyright page for details).

3. Are there any daily routines during which you struggle to use the intervention? If so, what are the challenges?

4. Which techniques seem to be the most effective for increasing engagement?

5. Which techniques seem to be the most effective for teaching new skills?

6. Which techniques are you most comfortable using?

7. Which techniques do you struggle with using?

8. Please list any additional goals you would like to target.

Dear _____ ,

_____ will be holding a 12-week group parent training program. Project ImPACT (Improving Parents As Communication Teachers) is designed to teach you techniques and strategies to improve your child's social-communication skills. These techniques and strategies are designed for parents to use during daily routines and activities. Learning how to provide intervention to your child has a number of benefits:

- The child receives many more hours of intervention.
- The child is better able to retain new learning and apply it in different situations.
- Parents become less stressed and have more time for leisure and recreation.

Workshop dates: The workshop will consist of six group sessions and six individual parent coaching sessions. It is strongly recommended that the same parent (or both parents) attend every session. Group sessions will be held at _____ from _____ to _____ on the following days:

_____

_____.

Individual parent coaching sessions will be held on the following days: _____

_____

_____.

Parents and staff will set up individual 45-minute coaching session appointments on these dates.

Presenters: _____

To register: Please contact _____ at _____

Sincerely,

_____

From *Teaching Social Communication to Children with Autism: A Practitioner's Guide to Parent Training* by Brooke Ingersoll and Anna Dvortcsak. Copyright 2010 by The Guilford Press. Permission to photocopy this form is granted to purchasers of this book for personal use only (see copyright page for details).

FORM 18

Group Format Coaching Form

Child: _____ Parent: _____ Session: _____ Date: _____

Check the box to the left of each intervention component that you will coach on this session. For each checked box, score each subcomponent based on your observation of the parent and child. After scoring each subcomponent, provide a summary score for the intervention component that best captures how the parent performed on the subcomponents. To achieve fidelity, the parent must receive a score of 4 or 5 on each of the component summary scores that are being measured.

Low fidelity 1	2	3	4	High fidelity 5
Parent does not implement throughout session.	Parent implements occasionally, but misses majority of opportunities.	Parent implements up to half of the time, but misses many opportunities.	Parent implements more than half of the time, but misses some opportunities.	Parent implements throughout the session.

Intervention technique		Fidelity	Notes
❑ **Parent makes play interactive.**	*Summary*	1 2 3 4 5	
Lets child choose the activity.		1 2 3 4 5	
Is face to face.		1 2 3 4 5	
Joins in child's play or uses *Imitates Your Child*.		1 2 3 4 5	
Uses *Animation*.		1 2 3 4 5	
Waits with anticipation.		1 2 3 4 5	
❑ **Parent models and expands child's language.** *Summary*		1 2 3 4 5	
Gives meaning to child's actions.		1 2 3 4 5	
Uses simplified language.		1 2 3 4 5	
Models language around child's focus of attention.		1 2 3 4 5	
Expands on child's language.		1 2 3 4 5	
❑ **Parent creates opportunities for child to communicate.** *Summary*		1 2 3 4 5	

(cont.)

From *Teaching Social Communication to Children with Autism: A Practitioner's Guide to Parent Training* by Brooke Ingersoll and Anna Dvortcsak. Copyright 2010 by The Guilford Press. Permission to photocopy this form is granted to purchasers of this book for personal use only (see copyright page for details).

Intervention technique	Fidelity	Notes
Uses *Playful Obstruction* or *Balanced Turns* to elicit engagement.	1 2 3 4 5	
Helps child anticipate interruption.	1 2 3 4 5	
Models appropriate play.	1 2 3 4 5	
Uses *Communicative Temptations* to encourage initiations.	1 2 3 4 5	
❑ **Parent helps child increase complexity of language, imitation, or play.** *Summary*	**1 2 3 4 5**	
Prompts child for more complex response.	1 2 3 4 5	
If parent receives 3 or higher, please rate the following:		
Waits for child's initiation before prompting.	1 2 3 4 5	
Uses clear and appropriate prompts.	1 2 3 4 5	
Prompts no more than three times without increasing support.	1 2 3 4 5	
Provides sufficient opportunity for the child to respond.	1 2 3 4 5	
Provides reinforcement immediately after child responds correctly.	1 2 3 4 5	
Withholds reinforcement for inappropriate behavior.	1 2 3 4 5	
Expands on child's response.	1 2 3 4 5	
Uses developmentally appropriate prompts.	1 2 3 4 5	
After several prompts, reduces support to promote spontaneity.	1 2 3 4 5	
❑ **Parent paces interaction to keep child engaged and learning.** *Summary*	**1 2 3 4 5**	
Uses interactive teaching techniques to keep child engaged.	1 2 3 4 5	
Provides initiation opportunities when child is not interactive.	1 2 3 4 5	
Uses direct teaching techniques to increase complexity when child is motivated.	1 2 3 4 5	

FORM 19 **Interactive Teaching Techniques Review Sheet I**

---

1. Use *Follow Your Child's Lead*: *What is your child interested in?*

- Let your child choose the activity.
- Be face to face.

- Join in your child's activity
- Comment on your child's play.

---

2. Create an opportunity for your child to communicate.

- *Imitate Your Child*
- *Animation*

---

3. Wait for your child to engage: *How is your child engaging?*

---

4. Respond to your child's behavior as meaningful, comply with it, and model a more complex (developed) response.

- Give your child's actions meaning.
  - Adjust your language.
  - Simplify your language.
  - Speak slowly.
  - Stress important words.
  - Be repetitive.
  - Use visual/gestural cues.

- Model language around your child's interest.
  - Model gestures.
  - Model new language forms.
  - Model new language functions.
- Expand on your child's language.

From *Teaching Social Communication to Children with Autism: A Practitioner's Guide to Parent Training* by Brooke Ingersoll and Anna Dvortcsak. Copyright 2010 by The Guilford Press. Permission to photocopy this form is granted to purchasers of this book for personal use only (see copyright page for details).

FORM 20 **Direct Teaching Techniques Review Sheet I**

---

1. Use *Follow Your Child's Lead*: *What is your child interested in?*

- Let your child choose the activity.
- Be face to face.

- Join in your child's activity.
- Comment on your child's play.

---

2. Create an opportunity for your child to communicate.

- *Playful Obstruction*
- *Balanced Turns*
  - Control of access
  - Assistance
  - Inadequate portions
  - Protest
  - Sabotage
  - Silly situations

- *Communicative Temptations*
  - In sight and out of reach

---

3. Wait for your child to communicate: *How is your child communicating?*

---

4 and 5. Prompt your child to use more complex language, and give a more supportive prompt as needed.

Teaching Your Child Expressive Language

- Time delay
- Question
- Cloze procedure
- Choices
- Verbal model or routine
- Gesture prompt
- Physical prompt

Teaching Your Child Receptive Language

- Clear directions
- Verbal instruction
- Visual prompt
- Physical prompt

---

6. Reinforce and expand the prompted response.

- Give your child the desired object or action.

- Add one more element to your child's language.

From *Teaching Social Communication to Children with Autism: A Practitioner's Guide to Parent Training* by Brooke Ingersoll and Anna Dvortcsak. Copyright 2010 by The Guilford Press. Permission to photocopy this form is granted to purchasers of this book for personal use only (see copyright page for details).

Direct Teaching Techniques Review Sheet II

1. Use *Follow Your Child's Lead*: *What is your child interested in?*

- Let your child choose the activity.
- Be face to face.

- Join in your child's activity.
- Comment on your child's play.

2. Create an opportunity for your child to communicate.

- *Playful Obstruction*
- *Balanced Turns*

- *Communicative Temptations*
  - In sight and out of reach
  - Control of access
  - Assistance
  - Inadequate portions
  - Protest
  - Sabotage
  - Silly situations

3. Wait for your child to communicate: *How is your child communicating?*

4 and 5. Prompt your child to use more complex imitation or play, and give a more supportive prompt as needed.

Teaching Your Child Social Imitation

- Model of play
- Model of gestures
- Verbal prompt
- Physical prompt

Teaching Your Child Play

- Wait time
- Leading comment
- Leading question
- Verbal instruction
- Model of play
- Physical prompt

6. Reinforce and expand the prompted response.

- Give your child the desired object or action
- Praise your child's behavior

From *Teaching Social Communication to Children with Autism: A Practitioner's Guide to Parent Training* by Brooke Ingersoll and Anna Dvortcsak. Copyright 2010 by The Guilford Press. Permission to photocopy this form is granted to purchasers of this book for personal use only (see copyright page for details).

Homework for Group Format:
Set Up Your Home for Success

Rationale: This increases your child's engagement and attention.

Key points to remember and carry out:

> Set up a defined space.
>
> Limit distractions.
>
> Rotate toys.
>
> Schedule predictable play routines.

Goals of the Week

Daily playtime(s):

Daily routine(s):

1 Do you play with your child during your scheduled playtimes? If yes, how do you indicate to your child that it is time to play? If not, what are the challenges?

2 How much time will you need to add to your chosen daily routines to make them successful? Do you anticipate any difficulties teaching within these routines?

(*cont.*)

From *Teaching Social Communication to Children with Autism: A Practitioner's Guide to Parent Training* by Brooke Ingersoll and Anna Dvortcsak. Copyright 2010 by The Guilford Press. Permission to photocopy this form is granted to purchasers of this book for personal use only (see copyright page for details).

3 What area (room, space within a room, space outside, etc.) are you arranging to improve your child's engagement and attention? Is it difficult to find a space in which to interact? If yes, what are some of the challenges?

4 How do you reduce the number of distractions in the home? Is it difficult to reduce distractions? If yes, what are some of the challenges?

5 Are you setting up a toy rotation? If not, what is the reason?

6 How does your child respond to you when the space is defined and the number of distractions is reduced? How long are you able to interact with your child after these modifications?

7 Is it difficult to play with your child? If yes, what are some of the challenges?

Homework for Group Format:
Make Play Interactive
and *Modeling and Expanding Language*

Rationale: *Follow Your Child's Lead*, *Imitate Your Child*, and *Animation* all increase your child's engagement, motivation, and initiations. *Modeling and Expanding Language* teaches your child that his actions carry meaning and elicit a response from you, and increases your child's receptive and expressive language skills.

Key points to remember and carry out:

Follow Your Child's Lead in play.

Imitate Your Child (play, gestures, and vocalizations).

Use *Animation* to emphasize your nonverbal language.

Adjust your language to help your child understand.

Model language around your child's focus of attention.

Expand on your child's language.

Respond to all of your child's behavior as meaningful.

A specific response by your child is not required; rather, you are trying to increase his engagement. If your child moves away or ignores you, follow him to the next activity.

Goals of the Week

Child's goals:

Activities:

Techniques to increase engagement:

Language you will model:

1 | How does your child respond when you engage in his activity of choice? How long are you able to play with him?

2 | How does your child respond when you imitate his toy play or actions? Does he look at you or smile? Does he change activities to see if you will continue to imitate him?

(cont.)

From *Teaching Social Communication to Children with Autism: A Practitioner's Guide to Parent Training* by Brooke Ingersoll and Anna Dvortcsak. Copyright 2010 by The Guilford Press. Permission to photocopy this form is granted to purchasers of this book for personal use only (see copyright page for details).

3 How does your child respond when you exaggerate your gestures, facial expressions, or vocal quality? Does he look at you or imitate your nonverbal language?

4 How does your child respond when you pause during games that involve social interaction?

5 How does your child respond when you adjust your language?

6 How does your child respond when you talk about what he is doing or seeing? Does he imitate your language?

7 How does your child respond when you expand on his language?

8 Which techniques seem most successful at increasing your child's engagement and initiations?

9 Is it difficult to use any of these techniques? If yes, what are some of the challenges?

FORM 24	**Homework for Group Format:** *Create Opportunities for Your Child to Engage* *or Communicate*

Rationale: These techniques increase your child's attention and initiations, and create opportunities for language modeling and prompting.

Key points to remember and carry out:

Use *Playful Obstruction*: Playfully block your child's play or motor actions to gain his attention.

Use *Balanced Turns* with your child.

Use *Communicative Temptations* to encourage initiations:

> In sight and out of reach
> Control of access
> Assistance
> Inadequate portions
> Sabotage
> Protest
> Silly situations

A specific response by your child is not required; rather, you are trying to increase his initiations. If your child moves away or ignores a *Communicative Temptation,* follow him to the next activity.

Goals of the Week

Child's goals:

Activities:

Techniques to increase engagement:

Language you will model:

1	How does your child respond when you interrupt what he is doing with a toy or his motor activities? How does he indicate that he wants to continue?

(cont.)

From *Teaching Social Communication to Children with Autism: A Practitioner's Guide to Parent Training* by Brooke Ingersoll and Anna Dvortcsak. Copyright 2010 by The Guilford Press. Permission to photocopy this form is granted to purchasers of this book for personal use only (see copyright page for details).

2 How does your child respond when you take turns with him? Does your child allow your turn? Does your child initiate his turn? How? How many turns can your child take during a given activity?

3 How does your child respond when you model new play during your turn? Does he imitate your play?

4 What *Communicative Temptations* do you use? How do you use them? How does your child respond?

5 Which of these *Communicative Temptations* is most successful at getting your child to initiate?

6 Is it difficult to use any of these strategies? If yes, what are some of the challenges?

(cont.)

Homework: Create Opportunities for Your Child to Engage or Communicate

The following questions relate to identifying good opportunities for prompting your child to increase the complexity of his response. *You will work on prompting new skills in the following session.*

1	Which interactive teaching techniques are most effective at getting your child to initiate (*Playful Obstruction, Balanced Turns, Communicative Temptations,* etc.)?

2	How does your child currently communicate what he wants? What skill would you like him to use instead?

3	Please list opportunities that you could prompt your child to use a more complex response within your child's daily routine.

Homework for Group Format:
Teaching Your Child Expressive Language and Receptive Language

Rationale: These techniques increase your child's expressive language skills and ability to follow directions (receptive language skills).

Key points to remember and carry out:

Use *Follow Your Child's Lead.*

Create an opportunity for your child to respond.

Wait for your child to respond.

Prompt a more complex response.

Provide more support as necessary.

Reinforce and expand on your child's response.

Goals of the Week

Child's goals:

Activities:

Techniques to increase initiations:

Language or gestures you will prompt: *Type of prompt:*

1 What language or gestures do you prompt your child to use? What is your child's response? What type of prompt do you use to get this response?

2 Which expressive language prompts are most successful at getting your child to increase the complexity of his response?

(cont.)

From *Teaching Social Communication to Children with Autism: A Practitioner's Guide to Parent Training* by Brooke Ingersoll and Anna Dvortcsak. Copyright 2010 by The Guilford Press. Permission to photocopy this form is granted to purchasers of this book for personal use only (see copyright page for details).

3 Are there any language prompts that do not seem successful?

4 Are you able to decrease the amount of support you provide to encourage your child to use language spontaneously? If so, please describe. How does your child respond?

5 Is it difficult to prompt your child's expressive language? If yes, what are some of the challenges?

6 What directions do you try to get your child to follow at home? What prompts do you use? How does your child respond?

7 Is it difficult to prompt your child's receptive language? If yes, what are some of the challenges?

FORM 26

Homework for Group Format:
Teaching Your Child Social Imitation and Play

Rationale: These techniques increase the complexity of your child's imitation and play skills.

Key points to remember and carry out:

Use *Follow Your Child's Lead.*

Create an opportunity for your child to respond.

Wait for your child to respond.

Prompt a more complex response.

Provide more support as necessary.

Reinforce and expand on your child's response.

Goals of the Week

Child's goals:

Activities:

Techniques to increase initiations:

Type of imitation you will prompt: *Type of prompt:*

Type of play you will prompt: *Type of prompt:*

1 What type of object play do you model for your child to imitate? How does he respond? Do you have to physically prompt him to imitate you?

2 What type of gestures do you model for your child to imitate? How does he respond? Do you have to physically prompt him to imitate you?

(cont.)

From *Teaching Social Communication to Children with Autism: A Practitioner's Guide to Parent Training* by Brooke Ingersoll and Anna Dvortcsak. Copyright 2010 by The Guilford Press. Permission to photocopy this form is granted to purchasers of this book for personal use only (see copyright page for details).

3 How does your child respond when you imitate his toy play or actions when teaching social imitation? Is he more likely to imitate your models?

4 Are you able to expand the number of play schemes your child uses? What type of prompts do you use?

5 Are you able to increase the complexity of your child's play? What type of prompts do you use?

6 Are you able to increase the number of different toys your child plays with? What type of prompts do you use?

7 What prompts are most successful at getting your child to increase his social imitation and play skills? Are there any prompts that are not successful?

8 Is it difficult to prompt your child's social imitation and play? If yes, what are some of the challenges?

Homework for Group Format:
Putting It All Together

Rationale: This increases your child's social-communication skills and decreases his reliance on prompts.

Key points to remember and carry out:

Use *Follow Your Child's Lead.*

Create an opportunity for your child to respond.

Wait for a response.

Model or prompt a more complex response.

Reinforce and expand on your child's response.

Goals of the Week

Child's goal:

Activities:

Intervention techniques to achieve goal:

Child's goal:

Activities:

Intervention techniques to achieve goal:

Child's goal:

Activities:

Intervention techniques to achieve goal:

1	In which daily routines are you most successful at using the intervention?

(cont.)

From *Teaching Social Communication to Children with Autism: A Practitioner's Guide to Parent Training* by Brooke Ingersoll and Anna Dvortcsak. Copyright 2010 by The Guilford Press. Permission to photocopy this form is granted to purchasers of this book for personal use only (see copyright page for details).

2 Think about your daily routines. When are you most likely to use the interactive teaching techniques? How does your child respond when you use these techniques?

3 Think about your daily routines. When are you most likely to use the direct teaching techniques? How does your child respond when you use these techniques?

4 Are there any daily routines during which you struggle to use the intervention? If so, what are the challenges?

5 Which techniques seem to be the most effective for increasing engagement?

6 Which techniques seem to be the most effective for teaching new skills?

7 Which techniques are you most comfortable using?

(cont.)

8 Which techniques do you struggle with using?

9 How does your child respond to the interactive versus direct teaching techniques?

10 Which skills (social engagement, expressive language/gestures, receptive language, social imitation, play) do you feel that you have been most successful at teaching?

11 Are there any skills that you have had difficulty teaching?

12 Please list any additional goals you would like to target.

13 Please list any additional questions or comments.

FORM 28 **Fidelity of Intervention Implementation Form**

Child: _____ Trainer: _____ Observer: _____ Session: _____ Date: _____

Score each subcomponent based on your observation of the trainer and child. After scoring each subcomponent, provide a summary score for the intervention component that best captures how the trainer performed on the subcomponents. To achieve fidelity, the trainer must receive a score of 4 or 5 on each of the component summary scores that are being measured.

Low fidelity **1**	**2**	**3**	**4**	**High fidelity** **5**
Trainer does not implement throughout session.	Trainer implements occasionally, but misses majority of opportunities.	Trainer implements up to half of the time, but misses many opportunities.	Trainer implements more than half of the time, but misses some opportunities.	Trainer implements throughout the session.

Intervention technique	*Fidelity*	*Notes*
Trainer uses *Follow Your Child's Lead* *Summary*	1 2 3 4 5	
Lets child choose the activity.	1 2 3 4 5	
Is face to face.	1 2 3 4 5	
Joins child's play.	1 2 3 4 5	
Trainer creates an opportunity for the child to engage. *Summary*	1 2 3 4 5	
Uses *Imitates Your Child*.	1 2 3 4 5	
Uses *Animation*.	1 2 3 4 5	
Waits with anticipation.	1 2 3 4 5	
Trainer models and expands child's language. *Summary*	1 2 3 4 5	
Gives meaning to child's actions.	1 2 3 4 5	
Uses simplified language.	1 2 3 4 5	
Models language around child's focus of attention.	1 2 3 4 5	
Expands on child's language.	1 2 3 4 5	

(cont.)

From *Teaching Social Communication to Children with Autism: A Practitioner's Guide to Parent Training* by Brooke Ingersoll and Anna Dvortcsak. Copyright 2010 by The Guilford Press. Permission to photocopy this form is granted to purchasers of this book for personal use only (see copyright page for details).

Intervention technique	Fidelity	Notes
Trainer creates opportunities for child to communicate. *Summary*	1 2 3 4 5	
Uses *Playful Obstruction* or *Balanced Turns* to elicit engagement.	1 2 3 4 5	
Helps child anticipate interruption.	1 2 3 4 5	
Models appropriate play.	1 2 3 4 5	
Uses *Communicative Temptations* to encourage initiations.	1 2 3 4 5	
Trainer helps child increase the complexity of language, imitation, or play. *Summary*	1 2 3 4 5	
Prompts child for more complex response.	1 2 3 4 5	
If trainer receives 3 or higher, please rate the following:		
Waits for child's initiation before prompting.	1 2 3 4 5	
Uses clear and appropriate prompts.	1 2 3 4 5	
Prompts no more than three times without increasing support.	1 2 3 4 5	
Provides sufficient opportunity for the child to respond.	1 2 3 4 5	
Provides reinforcement immediately after child responds correctly.	1 2 3 4 5	
Withholds reinforcement for inappropriate behavior.	1 2 3 4 5	
Expands on child's response.	1 2 3 4 5	
Uses developmentally appropriate prompts.	1 2 3 4 5	
After several prompts, reduces support to promote spontaneity.	1 2 3 4 5	
Trainer paces interaction to keep child engaged and learning. *Summary*	1 2 3 4 5	
Uses interactive teaching techniques to keep child engaged.	1 2 3 4 5	
Provides initiation opportunities when child is not interactive.	1 2 3 4 5	
Uses direct teaching techniques to increase complexity when child is motivated.	1 2 3 4 5	

FORM 29 **Fidelity of Implementation for Group Sessions Form**

Trainer: _____ **Session:** _____ **Date:** _____ **Observer:** _____

Please observe the trainer throughout the entire coaching session. Check the appropriate box to indicate whether each procedure is or is not observed.

Procedures	Observed	Not observed	N/A
The trainer welcomes the parents.			
The trainer provides a brief explanation of the session.			
The trainer reviews the homework from the previous session.			
The trainer gives each parent the opportunity to report.			
The trainer points out common themes among the parents' comments.			
The trainer helps the parents problem-solve any issues from the previous week.			
The trainer uses the provided lecture to explain the rationale for each treatment technique.			
The trainer uses the provided lecture to explain the key points of each treatment technique.			
The trainer uses and explains the videos with the lecture.			
The trainer invites comments, questions, and concerns.			
The trainer answers the parents' questions.			
The trainer reviews the homework and helps parents select goals and activities for practice over the week.			
The trainer uses a clear presentation style.			
The trainer facilitates discussion between group members			
The trainer sets and maintains a positive tone.			
Total fidelity = Observed/Observed + Not observed × 100			

From *Teaching Social Communication to Children with Autism: A Practitioner's Guide to Parent Training* by Brooke Ingersoll and Anna Dvortcsak. Copyright 2010 by The Guilford Press. Permission to photocopy this form is granted to purchasers of this book for personal use only (see copyright page for details).

Fidelity of Implementation
for Coaching Sessions Form

Trainer: _____ Child: _____ Session: _____ Date: _____ Observer: _____

Please observe the trainer throughout the entire coaching session. Check the appropriate box to indicate whether each procedure is or is not observed.

Procedures	Observed	Not observed	N/A
The trainer arranges the coaching environment to promote parent–child interactions (e.g., distractions are limited).			
The materials for the session are available (e.g., developmentally appropriate toys, trainer manual, parent manual, homework, coaching form).			
The trainer has reviewed information from the previous session prior to the family's arrival.			
The trainer greets the family warmly.			
The trainer provides a brief explanation of the session.			
The trainer reviews the homework from the previous session.			
The trainer helps the parent problem-solve any issues from the previous week.			
The trainer explains the rationale for the technique(s).			
The trainer explains the key points of the technique(s).			
The trainer assesses the parent's understanding of the information.			
The trainer invites comments, questions, and concerns.			
The trainer provides a demonstration of the technique(s) with the child while explaining the impact on the child's behavior.			
The trainer encourages the parent to practice the technique(s) with the child.			
The trainer provides positive and corrective feedback to the parent regarding her use of the technique(s) with the child.			
The trainer helps the parent work through any obstacles in the implementation of the technique(s).			
The trainer reviews the homework with the parent and helps her select goals and activities for practice over the week.			
The trainer assigns the reading for the following session.			
The trainer uses a responsive interaction style with the parent throughout the session.			
The trainer addresses unrelated concerns that the parent raises.			
The trainer completes the coaching form and/or writes session notes.			
Total fidelity = Observed/Observed + Not Observed × 100			

From *Teaching Social Communication to Children with Autism: A Practitioner's Guide to Parent Training* by Brooke Ingersoll and Anna Dvortcsak. Copyright 2010 by The Guilford Press. Permission to photocopy this form is granted to purchasers of this book for personal use only (see copyright page for details).

DVD Guide

The DVD that accompanies this manual contains video clips of parents using the techniques in this program with their children in a clinic setting. The clips are primarily intended for use during parent group sessions, and they are organized on the disk according to the group session in which a given technique is introduced. Because children are not present when parents meet as a group, the clips allow parents to see what a technique looks like in action. They also help parents identify the different ways a child may respond to a technique. Two or more clips of a technique are often provided, in order to show its use with children at different language levels. This can help parents understand how it may be used to teach different skills and how children's responses may vary according to their abilities. The session guidelines in Part III detail when and how to use the specific clips within the group sessions. They include a description of the key elements of each video clip, along with questions that can be posed to the parents to help them analyze the clip.

You (the trainer) should view the video clips before you begin working with parents. This will increase your familiarity with the intervention techniques, regardless of whether you plan to use the individual or group training format. You may also wish to use the video clips when conducting training with individuals; however, these clips should not be used in lieu of live demonstration of techniques when the child is present.

An Overview of the Video's Organization and Contents

Figure IV.1 depicts the main menu and submenus for the video clips on the DVD, as well as cross-references to where the clips are described in Part III. There are a total of 61 video clips; however, some of these are duplicates, since interactions on the clips often illustrate more than one technique. Clips may be repeated in different sessions when they serve to illustrate different techniques.

Session 1 of the group format, *Overview of the Program* and *Set Up Your Home for Success*, introduces the Project ImPACT parent training program and overviews the two main teaching technique categories: interactive (three clips) and direct teaching (three clips). The clips within each category illustrate the same basic technique sequence, but do so with children at different language levels: preverbal, single words to simple phrases, and complex phrase speech. Here and in other sessions where there are multiple clips, it is usually best to show all the clips. This helps parents understand how a technique may be used to teach different skills to different children at different ability levels. Session 2 is a coaching session when a parent and child meet with you (the trainer) to review *Set Up Your Home for Success* and to develop goals for the child.

Session 3, *Make Play Interactive* and *Modeling and Expanding Language,* introduces parents to the first four interactive teaching techniques. These are used to increase child engagement and motivation. There is not a specific clip for the first technique, *Follow Your Child's Lead,* since this technique is illustrated in the subsequent techniques. There are several clips of each of the following three techniques: *Imitate Your Child* (four clips), *Animation* (two clips), and *Modeling and Expanding Language* (five clips). Session 4 is a coaching session when a parent and child meet with you to review the parent's progress in learning the first four interactive techniques.

Session 5, *Create Opportunities for Your Child to Engage or Communicate* and *Overview of the Direct Teaching Techniques,* first introduces parents to three additional interactive teaching techniques. As the first part of the session title indicates, these are used to induce the child to engage or communicate; they include *Playful Obstruction* (two clips), *Balanced Turns* (two clips), and *Communication Temptations* (seven clips). Session 5 also includes an *Overview of the Direct Teaching Techniques* (three clips). Session 6 is an individual coaching session.

Session 7, *Teaching Your Child Expressive Language and Receptive Language,* introduces parents to each of the seven types of expressive language prompts; it also shows how to teach following directions (receptive language). The DVD repeats the three *Overview of the Direct Teaching Techniques* clips included in Session 5, and offers a total of 15 clips illustrating the specific types of prompts that can be used to teach expressive language to children at different language levels. It also offers one clip illustrating how to teach receptive language. Session 8 is an individual coaching session.

Session 9, *Teaching Your Child Social Imitation and Play,* introduces parents to strategies for teaching object and gesture imitation (three clips) and for increasing the variety and complexity of their children's play skills (four clips). Session 10 is an individual coaching session.

Session 11, *Putting It All Together,* gives parents guidelines on prompting with more versus less support and when to use interactive versus direct teaching strategies. There are four clips in this session, all grouped under the session title, *Putting It All Together.* Session 12 is an individual coaching session.

Procedure for Using the Video Clips within Group Sessions

The same basic procedure is used whenever the video examples are shown in a group session. You (the trainer) first describe the techniques and give verbal examples with the aid of PowerPoint slides, as described in Part III. You then show the video clips for that session, one at a time. Before showing each clip, you should ask the parents to watch for specific techniques or behaviors. After each clip, you should also ask questions to determine whether the parents observed the technique and the child's response. If the parents are unable to identify the technique and the child's response, explain these and then show the video clip a second time, to provide them with an opportunity to observe the behavior.

Technical Guidelines for Using the Video Clips and PowerPoint Slides Together

What you will need:

- Computer or laptop with DVD-ROM or DVD-RW drive.
- DVD-playing application (most systems these days come with this as standard equipment).

- Microsoft® PowerPoint 2003 or higher.
- Optional: hookup to display on a screen (if using the video with a group). These systems vary widely, so check with the facilities manager where you will conduct your training session for help.

Accessing the PowerPoint slides: In order to use the PowerPoint slides, you will need to copy them from the DVD-ROM onto your computer. If you plan to use them often, you may wish to put them in their own folder or in a location where you can easily find them.

1. Insert the DVD-ROM into the DVD drive of your computer. The video will start automatically, but will stop at the Main Menu. Minimize the DVD playing application.
2. Open Windows Explorer and find the DVD-ROM, which should be labeled "Project_Impact."
3. Highlight the folder called "PowerPoint" by single clicking on it and copy it by using the copy command on the menu (Edit > Copy) or by using Ctrl+C.
4. Using Windows Explorer, navigate to the place on your system where you would like to copy the files, then use the paste command from the menu (Edit > Paste) or by using Ctrl+V.
5. Feel free to rename the folder on your system. To do so, while still in Windows Explorer, highlight it again where you have copied it by single clicking on it, then using the Rename command from the menu (File > Rename) and entering the new name.

Using the PowerPoint slides: Once you have copied the PowerPoint slides onto your system, open Microsoft PowerPoint. Open the slides for the session you would like by using the open command (File > Open, or in new versions, Office Button > Open) and find the files where you have copied them. If you have set your computer to connect to another monitor, use the "Presenter View" mode in PowerPoint. Click the Slide Show menu, then check the check box called "Presenter View." This allows your viewers to see the slides full screen and nothing else, while you have the usual "Speaker View" on your system. For more information, consult the manual that came with your version of PowerPoint or consult the Help screens.

Showing the video clips and the PowerPoint slides together: Insert the DVD-ROM into the DVD drive of your computer. The program will start up and eventually open the main menu. You can now easily toggle back and forth between the video clips and the PowerPoint slides by clicking on the appropriate button at the bottom of your screen. To see which video clips correspond to which sessions, see Figure IV.1.

When you come to a part in the session where you want to show the relevant video clip, navigate to the clip by using your mouse or by using the arrow keys, as your application allows. By running your cursor over the area of the screen where the video is being shown, a menu comes up with more options. Most applications allow you to show the video in a full-screen mode. Volume adjustments can be made in the DVD viewing application and on the computer or laptop itself. If showing on a monitor for a large group, audio may be adjusted there as well. Be sure to test this before beginning a session.

You can use the video clips on their own in one-on-one sessions with or without the PowerPoint slides by inserting the DVD-ROM into the DVD drive of your computer and playing the clips as needed.

Note to Macintosh Users: You may view the video clips through your computer's built-in DVD player application. Double-click on the disk's icon on the desktop to display the contents of the disk. Drag the PowerPoint folder from the disk to the desktop, and you can open the PowerPoint slides using Macintosh's Keynote (version 5.0.1).

Figure IV.1. DVD video clips: Main menu and submenus.

References

Aldred, C., Green, J., & Adams, C. (2004). A new social communication intervention for children with autism: Pilot randomized controlled treatment study suggesting effectiveness. *Journal of Child Psychology and Psychiatry, 45,* 1420–1430.

Alexander, J. F., Barton, C., Schiaro, R. S., & Parsons, B. V. (1976). Systems-behavioral intervention with families of delinquents: Therapist characteristics, family behavior, and outcome. *Journal of Consulting and Clinical Psychology, 44,* 656–664.

Alpert, C. L., & Kaiser, A. P. (1992). Training parents as milieu language teachers. *Journal of Early Intervention, 16,* 31–52.

American Psychiatric Association. (2000). *Diagnostic and statistical manual of mental disorders* (4th ed., text rev.). Washington, DC: Author.

Baker, B. L., Brightman, A. J., Blacher, J. B., Heifetz, L. J., Hinshaw, S. R., & Murphy, D. M. (2004). *Steps to independence: Teaching everyday skills to children with special needs* (4th ed.). Baltimore: Brookes.

Bartak, L., Rutter, M., & Cox, A. (1975). A comparative study of infantile autism and specific developmental receptive language disorder: I. The children. *British Journal of Psychiatry, 126,* 127–145.

Bates, E., Benigni, L., Bretherton, I., Camaioni, L., & Volterra, V. (1979). *The emergence of symbols: Cognition and communication in infancy.* New York: Academic Press.

Bates, E., Bretherton, I., Snyder, L., Beeghly, M., Shore, C., McNew, S., et al. (1988). *From first words to grammar: Individual differences and dissociable mechanisms.* New York: Cambridge University Press.

Berk, L. (2002). *Infants, children, and adolescents.* Boston: Allyn & Bacon.

Bitsika, V., & Sharpley, C. F. (2004). Stress, anxiety and depression among parents of children with autism spectrum disorder. *Australian Journal of Guidance and Counselling, 14,* 151–161.

Bloom, L., & Lahey, M. (1978). *Language development and language disorders.* New York: Wiley.

Bornstein, M. H., Tamis-LeMonda, C. S., & Haynes, O. M. (1999). First words in the second year: Continuity, stability, and models of concurrent and predictive correspondence in vocabulary and verbal responsiveness across age and context. *Infant Behavior and Development, 22,* 65–85.

Bouma, R., & Schweitzer, R. (1990). The impact of chronic childhood illness on family stress: A comparison between autism and cystic fibrosis. *Journal of Clinical Psychology, 46,* 722–730.

Brookman-Frazee, L. (2004). Using parent/clinician partnerships in parent education programs for children with autism. *Journal of Positive Behavior Interventions, 6,* 195–213.

Bruck, M. (1982). Language impaired children's performance in an additive bilingual education program. *Applied Psycholinguistics, 3,* 45–60.

Camarata, S. M., Nelson, K. E., & Camarata, M. N. (1994). Comparison of conversational-recasting and imitative procedures for training grammatical structures in children with specific language impairment. *Journal of Speech and Hearing Research, 37,* 1414–1423.

Carpenter, M., Nagell, K., & Tomasello, M. (1998). Social cognition, joint attention, and communicative competence from 9 to 15 months of age. *Monographs of the Society for Research in Child Development, 63*(4, Serial No. 255), 1–143.

Carpenter, M., Pennington, B. E., & Rogers, S. J. (2002). Interrelations among social-cognitive skills in young children with autism. *Journal of Autism and Developmental Disorders, 32,* 91–106.

Chadwick, O., Momcilovic, N., Rossiter, R., Stumbles, E., & Taylor, E. (2001). A randomized trial of brief individual versus group parent training for behaviour problems in children with severe learning disabilities. *Behavioural and Cognitive Psychotherapy, 29,* 151–167.

Chakrabarti, S., & Fombonne, E. (2005). Pervasive developmental disorders in preschool children: Confirmation of high prevalence. *American Journal of Psychiatry, 162,* 1133–1141.

Charlop-Christy, M. H., & Carpenter, M. H. (2000). Modified incidental teaching sessions: A procedure for parents to increase spontaneous speech in their children with autism. *Journal of Positive Behavior Interventions, 2,* 98–112.

Charman, T., & Baird, G. (2002). Practitioner review: Diagnosis of autism spectrum disorder in 2- and 3-year-old children. *Journal of Child Psychology and Psychiatry, 43,* 289–305.

Cooper, J. O., Heron, T. E., & Heward, W. L. (1987). *Applied behavior analysis.* Prentice Hall.

Curcio, F. (1978). Sensorimotor functioning and communication in mute autistic children. *Journal of Autism and Childhood Schizophrenia, 8,* 281–292.

Davis, C. A., & Fox, J. (1999). Evaluating environmental arrangement as setting events: Review and implications for measurement. *Journal of Behavioral Education, 9,* 77–96.

Dawson, G., & Adams, A. (1984). Imitation and social responsiveness in autistic children. *Journal of Abnormal Child Psychology, 12,* 209–225.

Delprato, D. J. (2001). Comparisons of discrete-trial and normalized behavioral intervention for young children with autism. *Journal of Autism and Developmental Disorders, 31,* 315–325.

DeMyer, M., & Goldberg, P. (1983). Family needs of the autistic adolescent. In E. Schopler & G. B. Mesibov (Eds.), *Autism in adolescents* (pp. 225–50). New York: Plenum Press.

Drew, A., Baird, G., Baron-Cohen, S., Cox, A., Slonims, V., Wheelwright, S., et al. (2002). A pilot randomised control trial of a parent training intervention for pre-school children with autism: Preliminary findings and methodological challenges. *European Child and Adolescent Psychiatry, 11,* 266–272.

Dumas, J. E., Wolf, L. C., Fisman, S. N., & Culligan, A. (1991). Parenting stress, child behavior problems, and dysphoria in parents of children with autism, Down syndrome, behavior disorders, and normal development. *Exceptionality, 2,* 97–110.

Egan, K. J. (1983). Stress management and child management with abusive parents. *Journal of Clinical Child Psychology, 12*(3), 292–299.

Elder, J. H., Valcante, G., Yarandi, H., White, D., & Elder, T. H. (2005). Evaluating in-home training for fathers of children with autism using single-subject experimentation and group analysis methods. *Nursing Research, 54,* 22–32.

El-Ghoroury, N. H., & Romanczyk, R. G. (1999). Play interactions of family members towards children with autism. *Journal of Autism and Developmental Disorders, 29,* 249–258.

Feldman, M. A. (1994). Parenting education for parents with intellectual disabilities: A review of outcome studies. *Research in Developmental Disabilities, 15,* 249–258.

Feldman, M. A., Ducharme, J. M., & Case, L. (1999). Using self-instructional pictorial manuals to teach child-care skills to mothers with intellectual disabilities. *Behavior Modification, 23,* 480–497.

Fenson, L., Dale, P., Reznick, J., Thal, D., Bates, E., Hartung, J., et al. (1993). *The MacArthur Communicative Development Inventories.* San Diego, CA: Singular.

Fey, M. (1986). *Language intervention with young children.* San Diego, CA: College-Hill Press.

Fiese, B. H. (1990). Playful relationships: A contextual analysis of mother–toddler interaction and symbolic play. *Child Development, 61,* 1648–1656.

Forehand, R., & Kotchick, B. A. (1996). Cultural diversity: A wake-up call for parent training. *Behavior Therapy, 27,* 187–206.

Forehand, R., & Kotchick, B. A. (2002). Behavioral parent training: Current challenges and potential solutions. *Journal of Child and Family Studies, 11,* 377–384.

Gerber, S. (2003). A developmental perspective on language assessment and intervention for children on the autistic spectrum. *Topics in Language Disorders, 23*(2), 74.

Gillett, J. N., & LeBlanc, L. A. (2007). Parent-implemented natural language paradigm to increase language and play in children with autism. *Research in Autism Spectrum Disorders, 1,* 247–255.

Greenspan, S. I., & Wieder, S. (1999). A functional developmental approach to autism spectrum disorders. *Journal of the Association for Persons with Severe Handicaps, 24*, 147–161.

Greenspan, S. I., Wieder, S., & Simons, R. (1998). *The child with special needs: Encouraging intellectual and emotional growth.* Reading, MA: Addison-Wesley.

Griest, D. L., & Forehand, R. (1982). How can I get any parent training done with all these other problems?: The role of family variables in child behavior therapy. *Child and Family Behavior Therapy, 4,* 73–80.

Harachi, T. W., Catalano, R. F., & Hawkins, J. D. (1997). Effective recruitment for parenting programs within ethnic minority communities. *Child and Adolescent Social Work Journal, 14,* 23–39.

Hart, B. M., & Risley, T. R. (1968). Establishing use of descriptive adjectives in the spontaneous speech of disadvantaged preschool children. *Journal of Applied Behavior Analysis, 1,* 109–120.

Hastings, R. P., & Beck, A. (2004). Practitioner review: Stress intervention for parents of children with intellectual disabilities. *Journal of Child Psychology and Psychiatry, 45*(8), 1338–1349.

Hoff-Ginsberg, E., & Shatz, M. (1982). Linguistic input and the child's acquisition of language. *Psychological Bulletin, 92,* 3–26.

Howlin, P., Goode, S., Hutton, J., & Rutter, M. (2004). Adult outcome for children with autism. *Journal of Child Psychology and Psychiatry, 45,* 212–229.

Hume, K., Bellini, S., & Pratt, C. (2005). The usage and perceived outcomes of early intervention and early childhood programs for young children with autism spectrum disorder. *Topics in Early Childhood Special Education, 25,* 195–207.

Ingersoll, B. (2008). The social role of imitation in autism: Implication for the treatment of imitation deficits. *Infants and Young Children, 21,* 107–119.

Ingersoll, B., & Dvortcsak, A. (2006). Including parent training in the early childhood special education curriculum for children with autism spectrum disorders. *Journal of Positive Behavior Interventions, 8,* 79–87.

Ingersoll, B., Dvortcsak, A., Whalen, C., & Sikora, D. (2005). The effects of a developmental, social-pragmatic language intervention on rate of expressive language production in young children with autistic spectrum disorders. *Focus on Autism and Other Developmental Disabilities, 20,* 213–222.

Ingersoll, B., & Gergans, S. (2007). The effect of a parent-implemented imitation intervention on spontaneous imitation skills in young children with autism. *Research in Developmental Disabilities, 28,* 163–175.

Ingersoll, B., Lewis, E., & Kroman, E. (2007). Teaching the imitation and spontaneous use of descriptive gestures in young children with autism using a naturalistic behavioral intervention. *Journal of Autism and Developmental Disorders, 37,* 1446–1456.

Ingersoll, B., & Schreibman, L. (2006). Teaching reciprocal imitation skills to young children with autism using a naturalistic behavioral approach: Effects on language, pretend play, and joint attention. *Journal of Autism and Developmental Disorders, 36,* 487–505.

Ingersoll, B., & Stahmer, A. (2002, May). Teaching peer interaction skills in toddlers with autism: Effects of contingent imitation training. In A. Stahmer (Chair), *The role of typical toddlers in the early social development of children with autism.* Symposium conducted at the annual meeting of the Association for Behavior Analysis, Toronto.

Ingersoll, B. R. (2009). Teaching social communication: A comparison of naturalistic behavioral and development, social pragmatic approaches for children with autism spectrum disorders. *Journal of Positive Behavior Interventions.* Available from *pbi.sagepub.com/cgi/rapidpdf/1098300709334797v1.*

Jarrold, C., Boucher, J., & Smith, P. (1993). Symbolic play in autism: A review. *Journal of Autism and Developmental Disorders, 23,* 281–307.

Jocelyn, L. J., Casiro, O. G., Beattie, Bow, J., & Kneisz, J. (1998). Treatment of children with autism: A randomized controlled trial to evaluate a caregiver-based intervention program in community daycare centers. *Journal of Developmental and Behavioral Pediatrics, 19,* 326–334.

Jones, C. D., & Schwartz, I. S. (2004). Siblings, peers, and adults: Differential effects of models for children with autism. *Topics in Early Childhood Special Education, 24,* 187–198.

Kaiser, A. P., & Hancock, T. B. (2003). Teaching parents new skills to support their young children's development. *Infants and Young Children, 16,* 9–21.

Kaiser, A. P., Hancock, T. B., & Nietfeld, J. P. (2000). The effects of parent-implemented enhanced milieu teaching on the social communication of children who have autism. *Early Education and Development, 11,* 423–446.

Kaiser, A. P., Hemmeter, M. L., Ostrosky, M. M., Alpert, C. L., & Hancock, T. B. (1995). The effects of group training and individual feedback on parent use of milieu teaching. *Journal of Childhood Communication Disorders, 16,* 39–48.

Kaiser, A. P., Hemmeter, M. L., Ostrosky, M. M., Fischer, R., Yoder, P., & Keefer, M. (1996). The effects of teaching parents to use responsive interaction strategies. *Topics in Early Childhood Special Education, 16,* 375–406.

Kaiser, A. P., Hester, P. P., Alpert, C. L., & Whiteman, B. C. (1995). Preparing parent trainers: An experimental analysis of effects on trainers, parents, and children. *Topics in Early Childhood Special Education, 15,* 385–414.

Kaiser, A. P., Ostrosky, M. M., & Alpert, C. L. (1993). Training teachers to use environmental arrangement and milieu teaching with nonvocal preschool children. *Journal of the Association for Persons with Severe Handicaps, 18,* 188–199.

Kaiser, A. P., Yoder, P. J., & Keetz, A. (1992). Evaluating milieu teaching. In S. F. Warren & J. E. Reichle (Eds.), *Causes and effects in communication and language intervention* (pp. 9–47). Baltimore: Brookes.

Kasari, C., Freeman, S., & Paparella, T. (2006). Joint attention and symbolic play in young children with autism: A randomized controlled intervention study. *Journal of Child Psychology and Psychiatry, 47*(6), 611–620.

Kasari, C., Paparella, T., Freeman, S., & Jahromi, L. B. (2008). Language outcome in autism: Randomized comparison of joint attention and play interventions. *Journal of Consulting and Clinical Psychology, 76*(1), 125–137.

Kazdin, A. E., & Wassell, G. (1998). Treatment completion and therapeutic change among children referred for outpatient therapy. *Professional Psychology: Research and Practice, 29,* 332–340.

Klinger, L. G., & Dawson, G. (1992). Facilitating early social and communicative development in children with autism. In S. F. Warren & J. E. Reichle (Eds.), *Causes and effects in communication and language intervention* (pp. 157–186). Baltimore: Brookes.

Koegel, R. L., Bimbela, A., & Schreibman, L. (1996). Collateral effects of parent training on family interactions. *Journal of Autism and Developmental Disorders, 26,* 347–359.

Koegel, R. L., & Koegel, L. K. (2006). *Pivotal response treatments for autism: Communication, social, and academic development.* Baltimore: Brookes.

Koegel, R. L., O'Dell, M. C., & Koegel, L. K. (1987). A natural language teaching paradigm for nonverbal autistic children. *Journal of Autism and Developmental Disorders, 17,* 187–200.

Koegel, R. L., Schreibman, L., Britten, K. R., Burke, J. C., & O'Neill, R. E. (1982). A comparison of parent to direct clinic treatment. In R. L. Koegel, A. Rincover, & A. L. Egel (Eds.), *Educating and understanding autistic children* (pp. 260–279). San Diego, CA: College Hill Press.

Koegel, R. L., Schreibman, L., Loos, L. M., Dirlich-Wilhelm, H., Dunlap, G., Robins, F. R., et al. (1992). Consistent stress profiles of mothers in children with autism. *Journal of Autism and Developmental Disorders, 22,* 205–216.

Koegel, R. L., Schreibman, L., O'Neill, R. E., & Burke, J. C. (1983). The personality and family-interaction characteristics of parents of autistic children. *Journal of Consulting and Clinical Psychology, 51,* 683–692.

Koegel, R. L., Symon, J. B., & Koegel, L. K. (2002). Parent education for families of children with autism living in geographically distant areas. *Journal of Positive Behavior Interventions, 4,* 88–103.

Kumpfer, K. L., Alvarado, R., Smith, P., & Bellamy, N. (2002). Cultural sensitivity and adaptation in family-based prevention interventions. *Prevention Science, 3,* 241–246.

Laski, K. E., Charlop, M. H., & Schreibman, L. (1988). Training parents to use the natural language paradigm to increase their autistic children's speech. *Journal of Applied Behavior Analysis, 21,* 391–400.

Lewis, V., & Boucher, J. (1988). Spontaneous, instructed and elicited play in relatively able autistic children. *British Journal of Developmental Psychology, 6,* 325–339.

Lifter, K., Sulzer-Azaroff, B., Anderson, S. R., & Cowdery, G. (1993). Teaching play activities to preschool children with disabilities: The importance of developmental considerations. *Journal of Early Intervention, 17*(2), 139–159.

Lord, C., Rutter, M., & Le Couteur, A. (1994). Autism Diagnostic Interview—Revised: A revised version of a diagnostic interview for caregivers of individuals with possible pervasive developmental disorders. *Journal of Autism and Developmental Disorders, 24*, 659–685.

Lovaas, O. I., Koegel, R., Simmons, J. Q., & Long, J. S. (1973). Some generalization and follow-up measures on autistic children in behavior therapy. *Journal of Applied Behavior Analysis, 6*, 131–166.

Loveland, K. A., & Landry, S. H. (1986). Joint attention and language in autism and developmental language delay. *Journal of Autism and Developmental Disorders, 16*, 335–349.

Mahoney, G. (1988). Maternal communication style with mentally retarded children. *American Journal on Mental Retardation, 92*, 352–359.

Mahoney, G., Finger, I., & Powell, A. (1985). Relationship of maternal behavioral style to the development of organically impaired mentally retarded infants. *American Journal of Mental Deficiency, 90*, 296–302.

Mahoney, G., Kaiser, A., Girolametto, L., MacDonald, J., Robinson, C., Safford, P., et al. (1999). Parent education in early intervention: A call for a renewed focus. *Topics in Early Childhood Special Education, 19*, 131–140.

Mahoney, G., & MacDonald, J. (2007). *Autism and developmental delays in young children: The responsive teaching curriculum for parents and professionals.* Austin, TX: PRO-ED.

Mahoney, G., & Perales, F. (2003). Using relationship-focused intervention to enhance the social-emotional functioning of young children with autism spectrum disorders. *Topics in Early Childhood Special Education, 23*, 77–89.

Mahoney, G., & Powell, A. (1988). Modifying parent–child interaction: Enhancing the development of handicapped children. *Journal of Special Education, 22*(1), 82–96.

Mandell, D. S., Novak, M. M., & Zubritsky, C. D. (2005). Factors associated with age of diagnosis among children with autism spectrum disorders. *Pediatrics, 116*, 1480–1486.

Manolsen, A. (1992). *It takes two to talk.* Toronto: Hanen Centre.

McCollum, J. A. (1999). Parent education: What we mean and what that means. *Topics in Early Childhood Special Education, 19*, 147–149.

McConachie, H., & Diggle, T. (2007). Parent implemented early intervention for young children with autism spectrum disorder: A systematic review. *Journal of Evaluation in Clinical Practice, 13*, 120–129.

McConachie, H., Randle, V., Hammal, D., & Le Couteur, A. (2005). A controlled trial of a training course for parents of children with suspected autism spectrum disorder. *Journal of Pediatrics, 147*(3), 335–340.

McGee, G. G., Almeida, M. C., Sulzer-Azaroff, B., & Feldman, R. S. (1992). Promoting reciprocal interactions via peer incidental teaching. *Journal of Applied Behavior Analysis, 25*, 117–126.

McGee, G. G., Krantz, P. J., & McClannahan, L. E. (1985). The facilitative effects of incidental teaching on preposition use by autistic children. *Journal of Applied Behavior Analysis, 18*, 17–31.

Meltzoff, A. N., & Moore, M. K. (1977). Imitation of facial and manual gestures by human neonates. *Science, 198*, 75–78.

Miranda-Linné, F., & Melin, L. (1992). Acquisition, generalization, and spontaneous use of color adjectives: A comparison of incidental teaching and traditional discrete-trial procedures for children with autism. *Research in Developmental Disabilities, 13*, 191–210.

Moes, D. (1995). Parent education and parenting stress. In R. L. Koegel & L. K. Koegel (Eds.), *Teaching children with autism* (pp. 79–93). Baltimore: Brookes.

Morgan, S. B., Cutrer, P. S., Coplin, J. W., & Rodrigue, J. R. (1989). Do autistic children differ from retarded and normal children in Piagetian sensorimotor functioning? *Journal of Child Psychology and Psychiatry, 30*(6), 857–864.

National Research Council (NRC). (2001). *Educating children with autism* (Committee on Educational Interventions for Children with Autism, C. Lord & J. P. McGee, Eds.). Washington, DC: National Academy Press.

Özçaliskan, S., & Goldin-Meadow, S. (2005). Gesture is at the cutting edge of early language development. *Cognition, 96*(3), 101–113.

Pelligrini, A. D., & Smith, P. K. (1998). Physical activity play: The nature and function of a neglected aspect of play. *Child Development, 69*, 577–598.

Piaget, J. (1962). *Play, dreams, and imitation in childhood.* New York: Norton.

Pierce, K., & Schreibman, L. (1995a). Increasing complex social behaviors in children with autism: Effects of peer-implemented pivotal response training. *Journal of Applied Behavior Analysis, 28*, 285–295.

Pierce, K., & Schreibman, L. (1995b). *Kids helping kids: Teaching typical children to enhance the play and social skills of their friends with pervasive developmental disorders.* La Jolla: University of California, San Diego.

Pierce, K., & Schreibman, L. (1997). Using peer trainers to promote social behavior in autism: Are they effective at enhancing multiple social modalities? *Focus on Autism and Other Developmental Disabilities, 12*, 207–218.

Prizant, B. M., Wetherby, A. M., Rubin, E., Laurent, A. C., & Rydell, P. J. (2006). *The SCERTS model: A comprehensive educational approach for children with autism spectrum disorders* (2 vols.). Baltimore: Brookes.

Prizant, B. M., Wetherby, A. M., & Rydell, P. J. (2000). *Communication intervention issues for children with autism spectrum disorders.* In A. M. Wetherby & B. M. Prizant (Eds.), *Autism spectrum disorders: A transactional developmental perspective* (pp. 193—224). Baltimore: Brookes.

Quill, K. A. (1995). *Teaching children with autism: Strategies to enhance communication and socialization.* Clifton Park, NY: Thomson Delmar Learning.

Renty, J., & Roeyers, H. (2006). Satisfaction with formal support and education for children with autism spectrum disorder: The voices of the parents. *Child: Care, Health and Development, 32*, 371–385.

Rocha, M. L., Schreibman, L., & Stahmer, A. C. (2007). Effectiveness of training parents to teach joint attention in children with autism. *Journal of Early Intervention, 29*, 154–172.

Rogers, S. J. (1999). An examination of the imitation deficit in autism. In J. Nadel & G. Butterworth (Eds.), *Imitation in infancy* (pp. 254–283). New York: Cambridge University Press.

Rogers, S. J. (2000). Interventions that facilitate socialization in children with autism. *Journal of Autism and Developmental Disorders, 30*(5), 399–409.

Rogers, S. J., & Bennetto, L. (2000). Intersubjectivity in autism: The roles of imitation and executive function. In A. M. Wetherby & B. M. Prizant (Eds.), *Autism spectrum disorders: A transactional developmental perspective* (pp. 79–107). Baltimore: Brookes.

Rogers, S. J., & DiLalla, D. L. (1991). A comparative study of the effects of a developmentally based instructional model on young children with autism and young children with other disorders of behavior and development. *Topics for Early Childhood Special Education, 11*(2), 29–47.

Rogers, S. J., & Lewis, H. (1989). An effective day treatment model for young children with pervasive developmental disorders. *Journal of the American Academy of Child and Adolescent Psychiatry, 28*(2), 207–214.

Rogers, S. J., & Pennington, B. F. (1991). A theoretical approach to the deficits in infantile autism. *Development and Psychopathology, 3*, 137–162.

Sainato, D. M., Goldstein, H., & Strain, P. S. (1992). Effects of self-evaluation on preschool children's use of social interaction strategies with their classmates with autism. *Journal of Applied Behavior Analysis, 25*, 127–141.

Saltz, E., Dixon, D., & Johnson, J. (1977). Training disadvantaged preschoolers on various fantasy activities: Effects on cognitive functioning and impulse control. *Child Development, 48*, 367–380.

Schreibman, L. (1988). *Autism.* Thousand Oaks, CA: Sage.

Schreibman, L., & Ingersoll, B. (2005). Behavioral interventions to promote learning in individuals with autism. In F. R. Volkmar, R. Paul, A. Klin, & D. Cohen (Eds.), *Handbook of autism and pervasive developmental disorders: Vol. 2. Assessment, interventions, and policy* (3rd ed., pp. 882–896). Hoboken, NJ: Wiley.

Schreibman, L., Kaneko, W. M., & Koegel, R. L. (1991). Positive affect of parents of autistic children: A comparison across two teaching techniques. *Behavior Therapy, 22*, 479–490.

Schreibman, L., O'Neill, R. E., & Koegel, R. L. (1983). Behavioral training for siblings of autistic children. *Journal of Applied Behavior Analysis, 16*, 129–138.

Schwartz, I. S., Anderson, S. R., & Halle, J. W. (1989). Training teachers to use naturalistic time delay: Effects on teacher behavior and on the language use of students. *Journal of the Association for Persons with Severe Handicaps, 14*, 48–57.

Shearer, M. S., & Shearer, D. (1977). Parent involvement. In J. B. Jordan, A. H. Hayden, M. B. Kaines, &

M. M. Wood (Eds.), *Early childhood education for exceptional children: A handbook of ideas and exemplary practices* (pp. 85–106). Reston, VA: Council for Exceptional Children.

Siller, M., & Sigman, M. (2002). The behaviors of parents of children with autism predict the subsequent development of their children's communication. *Journal of Autism and Developmental Disorders, 32,* 77–89.

Skinner, B. F. (1957). *Verbal behavior.* Upper Saddle River, NJ: Prentice-Hall.

Smith, C. M., Rogers, S. J., & Dawson, G. (2007). The Early Start Denver Model: A comprehensive early intervention approach for toddlers with autism. In J. S. Handleman & S. L. Harris (Eds.), *Preschool education programs for children with autism* (pp. 65–101). Austin, TX: Pro-Ed.

Smith, I. M., & Bryson, S. E. (1994). Imitation and action in autism: A critical review. *Psychological Bulletin, 116,* 259–273.

Smith, T., Buch, G. A., & Gamby, T. E. (2000). Parent-directed, intensive early intervention for children with pervasive developmental disorder. *Research in Developmental Disabilities, 21,* 297–309.

Snow, M. E., Hertzig, M. E., & Shapiro, T. (1987). Expression of emotion in young autistic children. *Journal of the American Academy of Child and Adolescent Psychiatry, 26*(6), 836–838.

Stahmer, A. C. (1995). Teaching symbolic play skills to children with autism using pivotal response training. *Journal of Autism and Developmental Disorders, 25,* 123–141.

Stahmer, A. C., & Gist, K. (2001). The effects of an accelerated parent education program on technique mastery and child outcome. *Journal of Positive Behavior Interventions, 3,* 75–82.

Stern, D. N. (1985). *The interpersonal world of the infant: A view from psychoanalysis and developmental psychology.* New York: Basic Books.

Stone, W. L., Ousley, O. Y., & Littleford, C. D. (1997). Motor imitation in young children with autism: What's the object? *Journal of Abnormal Child Psychology, 25,* 475–485.

Stone, W. L., & Yoder, P. J. (2001). Predicting spoken language level in children with autism spectrum disorders. *Autism, 5,* 341–361.

Strain, P. S., & Danko, C. D. (1995). Caregivers' encouragement of positive interaction between preschoolers with autism and their siblings. *Journal of Emotional and Behavioral Disorders, 3,* 2–12.

Sullivan, C. L. (1999). The effects of sibling-implemented training on social behaviors of autistic children (Doctoral dissertation, Western Michigan University). *Dissertation Abstracts International, 60,* 2964B.

Sussman, F. (1999). *More than words: Helping parents promote communication and social skills in children with autism spectrum disorder.* Toronto: Hanen Centre.

Sylva, K., Bruner, J. S., & Genova, P. (1976). The role of play in the problem solving of children 3–5 years old. In J. S. Bruner, A. Jolly, & K. Sylva (Eds.), *Play: Its role in development and evolution* (pp. 244–257). New York: Basic Books.

Thordardottir, E. (2006). Language intervention from a bilingual mindset. *The ASHA Leader, 11,* 6–7, 20–21.

Thorp, D. M., Stahmer, A. C., & Schreibman, L. (1995). Effects of sociodramatic play training on children with autism. *Journal of Autism and Developmental Disorders, 25,* 265–282.

Tonge, B., Brereton, A., Kiomall, M., Mackinnon, A., King, N., & Rinehart, N. (2006). Effects on parental mental health of an education and skills training program for parents of young children with autism: A randomized controlled trial. *Journal of the American Academy of Child and Adolescent Psychiatry, 45*(5), 561–569.

Tsao, L., & Odom, S. L. (2006). Sibling-mediated social interaction intervention for young children with autism. *Topics in Early Childhood Special Education, 26,* 106–123.

Turner, L. M., Stone, W. L., Pozdol, S. L., & Coonrod, E. E. (2006). Follow-up of children with autism spectrum disorders from age 2 to age 9. *Autism, 10,* 243–265.

Tymchuk, A. J., & Andron, L. (1992). Project Parenting: Child interactional training with mothers who are mentally handicapped. *Mental Handicap Research, 5,* 4–32.

Uzgiris, I. C. (1981). Two functions of imitation during infancy. *International Journal of Behavioral Development, 4,* 1–12.

Uzgiris, I. C. (1991). The social context of infant imitation. In M. Lewis & S. Feinman (Eds.), *Social influences and socialization in infancy* (pp. 215–251). New York: Plenum Press.

Vismara, L. A., Colombi, C., & Rogers, S. J. (2009). Can one hour per week of therapy lead to lasting changes in young children with autism? *Autism, 13,* 93–115.

Warren, S. F., Yoder, P. J., Gazdag, G. E., Kim, K., & Jones, H. A. (1993). Facilitating prelinguistic communication skills in young children with developmental delay. *Journal of Speech and Hearing Research, 36,* 83–97.

Wetherby, A. M., & Woods, J. J. (2006). Early Social Interaction Project for children with autism spectrum disorders beginning in the second year of life: A preliminary study. *Topics in Early Childhood Special Education, 26,* 67–82.

Whalen, C., Schreibman, L., & Ingersoll, B. (2006). The collateral effects of joint attention training on social initiations, positive affect, imitation, and spontaneous speech for young children with autism. *Journal of Autism and Developmental Disorders, 36,* 655–664.

Whitaker, P. (2002). Supporting families of preschool children with autism: What parents want and what helps. *Autism, 6,* 411–426.

Williams, J. H. G., Whiten, A., & Singh, T. (2004). A systematic review of action imitation in autistic spectrum disorder. *Journal of Autism and Developmental Disorders, 34,* 285–299.

Winter, J. M. (2006). Father involvement in parent training interventions for children with autism: Effects of tailoring treatment to meet the unique needs of fathers (Doctoral dissertation, University of California, San Diego). *Dissertation Abstracts International, 67,* 1751B.

Index